RACE & RALLY CAR SOURCE BOOK

A D.I.Y. GUIDE TO BUILDING OR MODIFYING A RACE OR RALLY CAR

ALLAN STANIFORTH

Foulis

Haynes

Other titles from the Haynes Publishing Group which will be of interest to readers of this book —

Performance Tuning in Theory and Practice — Four Strokes by A.G. Bell. (Book No. F275).
Performance Tuning in Theory and Practice — Two Strokes by A.G. Bell. (Book No. F329).
The Piper Tuning Manual, by Bob Gayler of Piper FM Ltd. (Book No. F292).
The Anatomy & Development of the Formula One Racing Car from 1975 by Sal Incandela. (Book No. F320).

These books should be available from all good bookshops but, in case of difficulty, please write to the publisher.

ISBN 0 85429 317 5

A FOULIS Motoring Book

First published 1983

Published by:
Haynes Publishing Group
Sparkford, Yeovil, Somerset BA22 7JJ, England

Distributed in North America by:
Haynes Publications Inc.
861 Lawrence Drive, Newbury Park, California 91320, USA

Editor: Rod Grainger
Page Layout: Madaleine Bolton, Peter Kay
Printed in England, by:
J.H. Haynes & Co. Ltd

Author's Preface & Acknowledgements

As few readers I have met (including myself), spend much time on an author's preface, these observations may reach only a limited circle! So, it will be more than enough to say that a major part of this book is owed to others. Their help, insult, inspiration, goading and the defeats they inflicted on me all made invaluable contributions to the raw material.

The aim of this book is to be enjoyable, informative and helpful, in no particular order, to anybody fascinated by competition and the motor car.

If it helps you to win anything – or do better than you did before – it will be a reflection of all those who helped me to help you.

Allan Staniforth

"No man is an island" said John Donne, and he never wrote a truer word. Had the help and generosity of any one of the following been refused to me, there would have been a gap somewhere in this book.

Avon Tyres (IRTS).
Andrew Andersz (Ford).
Richard Blackmore (designer/builder).
Bugatti Owner's Club (timekeepers).
Frank Bott (photographer).
Wyn Bott (researcher)
Dave Bradley (750 MC secretary).
Peter Brockes (Beaulieu Museum library).
Helen Burr (SAAB G.B.Ltd).
Brian Clayton (750 MC).
A.D.Clausager (BL Heritage historian).
Martin Eyre (750 historian).
Andrew Ferguson (Lotus).
Andrew Ferguson (Stratos owner).
Jack French (designer/builder).
A.M.Galloway (Michelin)
Derek Gardner (Tyrrell designer).
Goodyear (tyre creators).
Beverley Gale (VAG UK Ltd).
Keith Gowers (designer/builder).
David Gould (designer/builder).
Chris Hague (750 designer).

Mike Hayhurst (organiser).
Stephen Holliday (stopwatcher).
Dick Hartle (designer/builder).
Sean Gould (stopwatcher).
Denis Jenkinson (author/reporter).
Jacquie (Team Williams).
Dale Kitching (graphic artist).
Longton & Dist. M.C. (timekeepers).
London Special Builders' Group (750).
Bob Marston (designer, Royale).
Mike Massingberd (Quattro man).
Arthur Mallock (designer/U2 creator).
Dr.George McCrae (head weigher).
Gordon Murray (designer, Brabham).
Mike Mullen (honeycomb expert).
Monica (picture finder).
M&H (racing tyres).
Peter Norfolk (timekeeper/mechanic).
Doug Nye (author).
Eva Newby (cryptographer/typist).
Geoffrey Newby (assistant cryptographer).
James Ogier (Brabham).
Mike Palmer (Fiat UK).
Cyril Posthumus (author).
Mike Pilbeam (designer/builder).
Pirelli (tyres/seat webbing).
Maurice Phillipe (designer, Lotus/Tyrrell).
David Reilly (750/aerodynamics).
Daryl Reach (adviser).

David Scheldt (Stratos owner).
Brian Smith (aerodynamics).
Darell Staniforth (draughtsman/artist).
Peter Smithson (scrutineer/aerodynamics).
Patrick Stephens (publisher).
Colin Taylor (famed photographer).
Ken Tyrrell (F1 team creator).
Eric Taylor (Fothergill & Harvey plastics expert).
Ron Tauranac (designer/builder/driver/businessman).
Frank Williams (F1 team creator).
Ray Wilson (designer/builder).
Jeff Ward (driver/builder).
Tony Walton (750).
Bryan Wilkinson (mechanic/adviser).

My gratitude must also go to the builders and drivers of some fifty Terrapins of which I have a record (and others for which I do not), many of whom have been willing to share their ideas and development knowledge over the years, with quite extraordinary frankness. They include:

John Aldred.
Mike Atwell (Barbados).
Brian Alderton.
David Anastasi (Malta).

Gerry Brown (Canada).
John Buck.
Brian Brown.
Martin Baugh.
Mike Bainbridge.
Pete Butcher.
Tony Briggs.
Donald Brown.
Ian Barnes (Canada).
John Beeden.
David Carr.
Dorian Chambers.
Bryan Collins.
R. Capstick.
David Conway.
Pete Cummins.
Norman Cachia (Malta).
D. Crocker.
John Corbyn.
Mike Crockford (Australia).
David Calvert.
John Crowson.
Chris Cramer.
John Coulson.
Dr. Geoffrey Cowell.
Alan Dignan.
Jack Dillard.
R. Douglas (N. Zealand).
John Frampton.
George Frampton.
Frank Fowler.
Ted George.
Brian Gates.
Trevor Gibbs.
Bob Graham.
Fred Godley.
Roy Goodman (Australia).
Graeme Glew.
Mike Gerard.
Lennox Gonsalves (St. Vincent).
Martin Haley.

Bob Hardy.
Roderick Hall.
Paul Hawkins.
Martin Hook.
Vince Henderson (Tasmania).
Jeremy Hawke.
Mark Harbord.
Tet Shin Ho (Malaysia).
Kevin Ingram (N.Zealand).
Tom James (Mombasa).
Mike Jukes (UAE).
Geoffrey Jardim (Guyana).
Keith & Andy Johnson.
Anthony Koeller.
Peter Kirkby.
David Keer.
Mike Lawson.
Alda Laferla (Malta).
Alan Lloyd.
Dr. George McCrae.
David Milne.
W. Mason (N.Zealand).
Tom Miller (Jamaica).
Philip Mann (Australia).
Richard Machado (Jamaica).
Terry Mould.
D. McKie.
Brian McLuckie.
K. Nolan.
Stuart Nix.
Errol Norris (N.Zealand).
Stephen Neale.
Richard Owen.
Ed Praxel (Panama).
Robert Parker.
Roger Perkis.
Don Powell.
Alan Purdy.
Bill Peake (USA).
Jack Pinkerton (Canada).

Murray Rose.
David Rowe.
Dr. Geoffrey Roberts.
Graham Ashley Smith.
Fred Smith.
Dick Storey.
Stephen Sharp.
Iain Sword.
Derek Sharman.
Richard Smith.
Kostas Seputis (Australia).
Rodney Stansfield.
Alastair Smith.
Norman Sawatsky (Canada).
Breen & Darryl Seymour (N.Zealand).
Robert Stephenson (N.Zealand).
Terry Sims.
Bob Swallow.
Peter Solman.
Bill Southworth.
Irvin Spruce.
David Tebb.
Andrew Turnock.
Ian Tomlinson.
John Taylor.
Peter Ullyett (Barbados).
Tony Vella (Malta).
Eric Wharton.
Peter Wilkins.
David Woolams.
Norman Webster (Australia).
Alan Workman.
Jan Warring (N.Zealand).
John Wilkinson.
Ken Williamson.
Ralph Williams (Barbados).
Brian Wilkinson.
Alan Yorke (Australia).
Tony Yeomans.
Peter Zammit (Malta).

Contents

1 You Have To Start Somewhere ...

Man seems to be the only truly competitive animal on earth consumed with the desire to be faster, or better than his fellows at almost anything whatever the current levels of achievement. No other creature that springs to mind could even conceive the *Guinness Book of Records,* let alone keep it flourishing year in and year out, always in urgent need of an update in some part or other. Because the *GBR* is British conceived and created, and thus largely confined to the West, it does not mean that similar determination does not pulse beneath African or Chinese skins. You only have to think of the Olympic Games.

Fundamental to this sort of person – both sexes of course, although, I think, more rarely among women – is The Race, whether on a horse or bicycle, in a boat or aircraft, using their own muscles against others, or simply against the clock.

Some purists would say it is the striving against the clock (which after all is simply the measuring stick of the high jumper in a different form) with the unaided human body that really matters.

But we are concerned here with man on four wheels (or rarely six) with an internal combustion engine ahead, beside or behind him, in battle against others similarly mounted, struggling against each other as digital measuring clocks flick the hundredths of a second away quicker than an eye can blink, checking their claims to temporary fame.

Extending this into a world of computer technology and vast sums of money, it is still a somewhat mysterious and enigmatic art to persuade a car whether sports, F1 or a more modest single-seater to do superbly well exactly what you want it to do.

It is fortunate it is not yet an exact science or there would be no longer any scope for the dedicated amateur to create or modify his own vehicle with the target of upsetting the established order of things – a long-winded way of saying WINNING.

In the seventeen years since the original Terrapin first rolled off its trailer to debut at Harewood in Yorkshire, racing cars, rally cars and hillclimbers have changed out of all

recognition – that is, to the casual observer.

Surprisingly they have not changed in *principle* at all under the skin. Two things are still paramount in the design of a successful car: stiffness and through this, control of what the wheels are doing at the ends of their supporting suspension links. The fact that wheels were doing almost nothing but keeping the tyres in place in recent F1 was a curious *cul-de-sac* now being blocked as the rulemakers can get to grips with it.

I have ignored the third aspect, that of a powerful and reliable engine, because there is now ample literature and other available expertise concerning power units of almost every type. It would be pointless simply to duplicate it. The first two aspects mentioned are not nearly so well served and hopefully the pages which follow will shine a bit of light into corners hitherto dark – or even pitch black!

One of the reasons I think Terrapins (the Mini rear-engined single-seater a friend and I designed in the mid 60s), and various other relatively old competition cars, can still beat newer cars on occasion is that they were firmly based on those first two principles, and so have been able to make full use of tyre improvements as they came along. The really huge advances in this field, over which few designers except those at the very top have any control, have been in tyre construction and rubber tread compounds.

However, always consider tyre technology as secondary to the two criteria already mentioned, in that good tyres will often conceal suspension design defects but they can only further enhance a good chassis.

Aerodynamics and the downforces generated by the wing cars of the late 70s and early 80s certainly produced huge improvements in lap times – but only because chassis accepted the forces involved and suspension and tyres applied these forces successfully, and efficiently, to the road surface.

The resultant increase in effective grip within the area of the 'footprint' of each tyre raised cornering speeds so enormously that drivers began to need supports to prevent their heads trying to fall off their shoulders as a result of the sideways G-forces involved.

The situation arose that the tyre had to take over virtually every function of the 'suspension' in the conventional sense of the word, because these wing and ground-effect cars had no suspension movement at all. Doubting Thomases have only to study the numerous top quality head-on photographs of F1, taken on any corner producing high G-forces, in the contemporary magazines.

The relationship in space between the top front suspension arms and the leading edges of the front pontoon or side bodywork will show identical angles. Certainly in 1978 it was being whispered, and by 1980 openly admitted, that what movement didn't come from the tyre had to come from flex in the top link.

Much of the information that follows emerged from the development of a series of hillclimb cars – the Terrapins. Perhaps surprisingly those years have proved without doubt that an enormous number of lessons learned or design aims that make a

single seater work on the generally poor and narrow surfaces of British hillclimbs can be applied to sports, sports racing, circuit and rally cars on both tarmac and the loose. This means that, whether you are Formula Ford, 750 racing or stage rallying, referring to 'brakes', 'tyres' or 'suspension' for example in the index should produce information of direct use to you in your own field, although the flying testbed was generally one or other of the 50 plus Terrapins built and then modified and modified again from the original Mk1 by their builder/drivers.

Some things of course never change. There is still the pleasantly direct approach of purchasing the best car around, either brand new or last year's champion, carried in or behind a motorhome with air-conditioning, luxurious beds for six and colour T.V. getting aboard the racer, pointing it in the appropriate direction and pressing the right-hand pedal to the floor.

No doubt a similar approach was employed with victorious chariots after the games in ancient Rome, but even the most innocent beginner will suspect there may be more problems to this approach than raising the cash .... Motorsport in every branch is packed with examples of people who bought last year's championship winner – and then found it didn't win for them!

We have all heard how the car was sold with a duff engine, or minus the secret chassis tweaks that had made the glories of the previous twelve months possible. The much more likely, and much more painful, truth is that what is lacking is last year's driver.

You can buy the car but you, your team and mechanics or friends have got to start from the beginning to understand what you've got and what you are going to do with it. *Understanding* is the key word to which this is all dedicated, whether from the point of view of the driver, designer, enthusiast or spectator.

It should be made clear about now that, as the trendy literary reviewers have it, you can read this book on several levels. On one level it will help you build your own car from a clean sheet of paper, and get competing with the knowledge that it should perform reasonably, or at any

rate without horrible and mysterious vices. On another level it will supply a really basic approach to design and development of your own car, as there is no attempt to hide the boobs of history – or keep the secrets of what has proved successful. On a third level it could be simply an enjoyable read, shedding some light on various designs, the men who built and developed them and also on what often seems a total mystery to the outsider – why one day's loser can suddenly become tomorrow's victor.

Whatever you do, don't fall into the trap of thinking that the principles needed to win are any different in F. Ford, super saloons, stock cars or F1. Ultimately, all of them need a car that has a good power/weight ratio, low drag, strength and accessibility, adhesion to the road and, above all, good handling. 'Handling' is a bit of an omnibus term, often meaning different things to different men, but it might be defined as 'doing perfectly what the driver is capable of asking it to do'.

Engine power can be bought, teams put together, sponsors lured, bodywork exquisitely painted, mechanics trained, wives converted – but if the car won't handle you won't do any good. Witness the great Gilles Villeneuve working near miracles with the early Ferrari Turbo, but it didn't give him the world championship.

This certainly does not mean I subscribe to the view that the car is more important than the man, currently getting a new airing in F1. This is because the leading cars in any formula are highly likely to be broadly similar in potential performance at a given moment. If one is a little below that level, the magic of what a truly talented human being can extract from it over and above the next human being comes into play with all its finesse and beauty. This skill is present to a greater or lesser degree in every branch of the sport, but to the uninformed, or disinterested eye such talent may well manifest itself as a repetitive act bordering on lunacy.

Hillclimbing, the area in which I have specialised for a long time as a competitor, certainly has this air about it. Get up at 4.0am, tow 150 miles, unload to pass scrutineering, change wheels (if you have any) when it begins to rain, and queue under an umbrella for the right to forty or fifty seconds in which you risk your neck whilst racing against the clock and trying to memorise every fault in the road, car and self. Then another queue, change wheels again as it has suddenly dried out, and another forty or fifty seconds to try and analyse a quite different set of conditions and circumstances.

Next comes a 'lunch break' – a period usually devoted to rectifying the troubles that have inexplicably appeared in a perfectly prepared machine – followed, in the afternoon, by two more chances to achieve total perfection. Lengthen only the time involved in practice and the event and you could easily be talking about Formula Ford or F1. The back-up and finance are different, that's all.

To show how difficult it is to achieve a really effective performance, even for the best, some selective timing at Barbon – a fast swerving hill in Westmorland, with an ultra-sharp hairpin at the end – showed that in four different sections of the hill four different car/driver/engine combinations were individually quickest. Adding these four 'best bits' together gave a time a full second faster than that achieved by anyone on the day – champion and FTD man included. Effectively a new record was set – but the hill is still there waiting to be driven faster and better by someone in time still ahead, as are the circuits, the Forestry Commission tracks and country roads of the world's top tarmac events.

This search for the perfect run or lap or race is often a personal matter for those less talented than the world's best, having little or nothing to do with the official results. I have always recorded a private thumbnail sketch of every event, noting weather, problems, opposition and my own performance. Given such information you can better assess, with honesty, what you have actually achieved whatever the printed list of results may say.

It would be as well at this early stage to dispute the endlessly repeated argument – '... of course he's got the money. If only ...' Those who use this excuse are the eternal dwellers in fairyland. The real world is tough and often unfair but it does provide the

choice of various levels for each of which different amounts of cash are needed to do the job properly. We all have to choose our appropriate level and tailor our aims to what we can afford or raise. Money is relative; it oils the wheels but it does not buy real success.

You can have a quite magnificent model train layout in your attic for the cost of a season of 750 racing at the back of the field. Conversely a single season with a one-car budget in F1 would keep you going in Formula Ford very well equipped indeed for nearly 100 years.

Personal knowledge, experiment and logical thought can give you a genuinely better chance and are a valid substitute for very large sums of money.

No one should imagine that any top driver in a formula or class is an unthinking 'heavy welly' lad in a fast car. He isn't. The difficulty is that there are no 'ground trainers' in car racing of the sort that permit pilots and space crews to practise every aspect of the job complete with noise, G-forces, instrument readout and reacting controls so that they can finally 'crash' without harm or danger.

The racing driver on his way up is on a personal and private voyage of discovery and seeking an endlessly varying solution to a single question: 'How fast can I go and still stay on the road?'

Having the precisely correct answer at any given moment with a particular car is the only difference between you and the current leader – right up to World Champion. While there are undoubtedly natural born world champions still driving lorries, there are certainly no natural born lorry drivers operating in F1.

The selective filters on the way up are ruthless.

Being Britain's – or the world's – best with 300bhp/ton to control in no way guarantees you can cope with 650bhp/ton; a fact well proven by the careers of innumerable 'coming men' who went to secret tests for F1 teams and found they were not asked a second time.The bitter truth was that even given the right machinery they could not go fast enough.

Generally, flat out corners or

situations where the car will go no faster however hard you try are no problem. The trouble comes when there is so much power it will always go faster, always accelerate or spin the wheels anywhere anytime.

In that happy situation where do you draw the line? You draw it, if you want to stay unhurt or keep your vehicle reasonably unbent, at the point when your right foot lifts off as your brain tries to order 'keep on' but cannot.

Skill and experience, more power, better rubber, an improved chassis will all push that line further out but still only so far. The limit, I am convinced, is inborn. You have it or haven't. Forcing over your personal edge rather than skilfully balancing on it puts you into an area where you simply don't know what to do when things start going wrong. What a better driver will extricate himself from will put you in hospital or, even worse for your motor racing career, a mortuary. The whole situation needs treating with healthy respect. The danger is always there.

As one world class driver observed when asked how he could be worth his massive retainer. 'There are several golfers and tennis players who get more than I do – but you do not hear of many fatalities at Wimbledon or St Andrews'.

This book is not intended to teach you to be a Formula 1 pilot, a quite impossible task anyway. It is intended to be some sort of encouragement and source of information on which to base the building of your own car, modification and improvement of one you already own or to assist someone else sensibly. This last is deeply rewarding to many people, at least two of whom I have had good fortune to meet and be helped by with total unselfishness.

If you now ask on what sort of basis these bold claims rest, I have to point again to the Terrapin, jointly conceived and designed with friend Richard Blackmore who forsook cars for great success in the elegant world of gliding. It put a Mini engine/gearbox unit into the back of a very rigid tubular frame, using Mini driveshafts, brakes, hubs and wheels. It had – and still has – its own suspension geometry tailored to the Mini front uprights used on all four corners.

It sat originally on daringly widened 4½-inch steel rims with road tyres. Remarkably (or unbelievably depending on your point of view) current Terrapins with the same geometry are able to employ 12-inch rims, whilst keeping treads that have tripled in width on the road!

After nearly a quarter of a century the Mini engine unit is inevitably a somewhat dated and too top-heavy lump of cast iron, but a whole range of compact transverse engine/gearbox units, many largely of light alloy, have now appeared in production small cars all over the world.

Even supercharged Japanese motorcycle engines of 750cc (bearing the penalty of 1.4 x capacity ordained by regulations) have overhauled Mini power with half the weight or less.

Terrapin weight figures are still the sort of target to aim for – 7cwt with Mini unit, or as little as 5½cwt with a bike engine, while still being a 'proper sized' racer in RAC regulation terms which are framed for better or worse to exclude karts or any other attempt at a miniature machine.

Even with an ordinary gearbox a Terrapin still puts its power on the road better than a Mini saloon with LSD. It steers, stops and handles predictably and precisely as do a lot of other competition cars. But then quite a number also handle like pigs, jump about unpredictably, change from under to oversteer at awkward moments and fail to put all the available power on the road when you want it.

The faults just described sometimes seem insurmountable and, the poorer and more amateur you are, the more difficult they are to solve. Even after eighty years of motor racing there are not very many books describing methods of tackling these difficulties – it should therefore be good news that with this book we are getting onto just that.

Building your own car of course needs certain facilities and skills that will have to be arranged before you begin, acquired either personally or by a link-up with someone else.

What it needs above all is determination, and you cannot get that out of this or any other book. You also need information to back the conviction that a high speed vehicle to which you will entrust life and limb is not beyond the amateur to build and develop on his own.

It needs emphasising that you do not have to be an engineer to embark on this. It can be a help, but proper engineers tend to know how things have always been done before, while some of the very best ideas in the development of the Terrapin have come from a farmer, a furniture restorer, an electric contracts manager and a teacher. A short pause while the wittier reader observes that you only have to see one to realise this is only too true!

Anyone with misgivings about his or her talents and qualifications in the field should take heart from my own experiences since the Mark 1 first took shape in the icy garage beside my house. Much of what was learned then is still fundamental to the latest Gould/Terrapin 80.

The Balsa Model

The original quest included a ruthless search for the greatest possible stiffness in the chassis in order to provide precise location of the suspension pickup points when under load. The construction of a scale balsa wood model, including engine and gearbox, to pave the way for full size building was very helpful.

As it happened the later constructor had the extra talent of being able to do drawings from the scale model ... which told him a lot more than it did me – including the fact that a small section of the clutch linkage (not modelled) would bisect a vital chassis tube! This was corrected in good time, but it was the balsa model that confirmed a hefty step forward in chassis stiffness over earlier cars.

The balsa model approach has so much to recommend it in car construction that I would regard it an an essential tool. Without having to own or understand massive equipment, a set of strain gauges plus a degree in structural engineering, it allows a lot of low-priced high-speed research.

Without wishing to labour the obvious, the triangle is the ultimate two-dimensional rigid structure, while a pyramid is the same thing in 3-D. Whether the triangles and pyramids are in sheet or tubular frame form is immaterial. Neither the thickness of the sheet nor size of the tubes affects this fundamental law – only the load level at which they will finally fail structurally.

Clearly something made from 2-inch tube with ¼-inch wall appropriate to scaffolding a seven storey building is stronger than small diameter, thin walled light alloy archery arrow. But correctly put together in a pyramid both are similarly rigid. If you construct the pyramid from thin sheet you have a monocoque.

Where the science starts becoming an inspired art is how you employ this principle while allowing a human being and an engine to enter and leave the structure, without having to insert a tube or panel through the middle of either of them. Exactly how this was well done in the Mark 1, rather less well done later with rubber suspension in the Mark 7 and done – we believe – almost to perfection in the Gould car, is shown in detail at a later stage.

It can be argued that the modern monocoque is not necessarily the answer to every maiden's prayer for every type of car or course. So before adopting anything you have seen in the paddock or at scrutineering on someone else's car, try to decide the reason for its being there in the first place. Is it by design, accident, trendy fashion or as compensation for some other shortcoming? The other driver might quite freely tell you on enquiring – if he knows – or he may not. Some deceitful fellows might even give you a load of the old codswallop in the hope that you will make the same mistake.

Rally car rollover cages are a good example of where thought can be used to improve construction. They can be bolted in where they touch or they can be used to create a hugely valuable spaceframe within the car, absorbing and spreading loads from stress points in the shell and so making the car much stiffer, and in consequence more reliable and long lived.

Costing

For the self constructor the awful question at this early stage has got to be 'how much'? A prime advantage for the one man band is that you can usually get a foot in the door by first competing with a vehicle that will accept more power and better rubber when you can afford it.

To attempt a costing you have three headings: (1) chassis or shell and bodywork totally complete to the wheel studs; (2) engine/gearbox, including carbs/injection/exhaust and other ancillaries; (3) one, two or three sets of wheels and tyres.

Obviously (2) and (3) can easily range from £100 to £5000 each, but both can be quite basic to begin with and then improved as cash becomes available.

The biggest items in (1) are coil spring/damper units which can range from £40 to £400 a set. On the other hand spherical suspension joints have actually become cheaper in real terms since my Mark 1 Terrapin was built in 1965. The number and variety of secondhand spares available from Formula Ford, Super-Vee and F3 have vastly increased. So has the quantity of secondhand tyres.

My 1965 car cost just under £340 on the startline – but average wages were then around £20-£25 a week. After careful study of current small advertisements you should come up with a realistic cost of between £750 and £2000. If you feel spending that money on a ready-to-roll car is a better bet, remember that you will still be at the beginning. To get anywhere you will still have to measure, make notes, look at the opposition, think and finally act – with your hands, more money or both.

Consider for a moment some of the slightly wider aspects of what you hope to do. The world has too many people who spend time regarding with contempt an activity or sport they do not do themselves. Circuit racers sneer at rally drivers, while hillclimbers view stock car men less than warmly. But put one type of driver into another field and he may find a lot of unexpected difficulties: GP *versus* rally drivers on

the 'box' is an annual full colour illustration of this. Different sports make different demands on drivers and machinery.

Accidents

Circuits, hills and tracks can vary a great deal. An imprecision of complete unimportance on a circuit, such as bouncing a chicane kerb, can be a total disaster on a hill or in a forest section, taking off a wheel, demolishing the front bodywork, wrecking a set of wishbones and finishing your day – or season – there and then. Car damage can be sudden and extreme. An error of perhaps two inches in where I placed the front of my own car in an Isle of Man event is a painful example ....

The Longton Championship climb uses part of the bike course going the 'wrong' way and includes Kate's Cottage, a stone-wall-flanked blind left-hander taken at about 130 mph by bikes. This becomes a right-hander for cars, taken by me at a more modest 90: I just brushed the inside banking and the resultant spin had the car bouncing from the bank to the wall finishing a hundred and four yards further on pointing the wrong way .... Scattered over those yards were a rear wheel, wing and stays, complete exhaust system, a lot of bodywork and a stream of radiator water. There was a huge hole in the drystone wall which had cut all the timing wires and temporarily stopped the event. The ligaments of my left knee had also been stretched a lot further than nature intended.

Although by my standards this was far and away the worst accident I had ever had, it has to be put into the perspective of 28 seasons, with a rough average of some 20 events annually and four runs per event. I should add moreover that friends very charitably did not put the accident down to lack of driving talent, but to advancing old age. I *suppose* it was a sort of compliment? More to the point was that the ligaments in my knee got better through exercising and at no cost, but a new wheel, rose joints and tubing did take money to put right. The

tyre astonishingly survived unmarked and still inflated. The chassis needed a bit of work on one corner, but was not basically out of shape. I had to make two new wishbones and acquire a new Mini upright from the scrap yard. Plus doing a lot of fibre-glassing (a mucky, smelly, laborious task not at all as effortless as some of the advertisements might imply). But at least it was back competing without wrecking myself or the family finances.

The relatively undramatic result of this accident could be explained by an ultra stiff frame, progressive collapse of the wishbones, a full harness (in conjunction with a perfectly fitting seat), a crash helmet, the luck of not rolling, and hitting the wall at an angle rather than head on. You cannot control everything, but you can take sensible precautions to try and keep the cost down. There are obviously lessons to be learned from this when constructing a new car or modifying an existing one. A lesser accident which took the front corner off a friend's new and then professionally repaired car, left little change from £1000!

Looking ahead

In your forward planning there is no substitute for having a good look at the successful opposition and attempting to analyse *why* they are successful. If your immediate answer is 'Money' you have not been paying attention to what I said earlier! There is normally a trend of some sort going on in most formulae – 'tweak of the day', or month, or even season. It can be hydro-pneumatic suspension in F1, a set of Bilstein dampers where Bilsteins have not been used before, a demon new tyre from Japan, plates that alter the suspension pickups to turn a family saloon into a forest tiger.

All such developments need treating with healthy suspicion. A monocoque is not necessarily superior to a tube chassis, a side radiator to a front, a soft suspension to a rock hard one, a wide tyre to a narrower one. It all depends on so many other things that you should beware of dogmatic advice from anyone. They may well be speaking the truth but it does not necessarily apply to *you* and your car.

Is there a 'coming car' that isn't winning at the moment (and is consequently cheaper) but might win in due course if the right things are done to it? Have you any specialised knowledge through owning and maintaining an Imp, Mini, Escort or Sunbeam as a road car? Do you already have spares around, or access to a breaker's yard or a friend with a similar vehicle? Do you happen to live near where it was made? Few of us have total freedom of choice and other things may have a heavy influence.

As an example, and at the risk of being assaulted by the Mini faithful (and heaven knows I have been one for twenty odd years), *all things being equal* the rear engined RWD Imp will beat a front-engined FWD Mini. However, to start rallying or sprinting in a 1000cc Mini you will need hardly more than a rollcage, modified cylinder head, cam and carbs, negative camber on the front wheels and a set of adjustable dampers. You need every one of these mods and more on an Imp as well, but the problem is that to start with it only has 875cc. To get to one litre you need a special block and pistons, a Wills-ringed head, special cam carrier, different cam and oil pump gears, modified conrods with oversize end bolts and you will probably have to add front suspension modifications, body and crossmember plates to stop it trying to break in two, transfer the radiator to the front, fit different coil springs and a redesigned throttle cable. None of this is impossible but it needs skill, knowledge and more money than for a similar result with a Mini. And should you go to the 1000cc engine, and it's a good one, be ready for clutch trouble!

There is a vast fund of information and parts on Escorts – but do you want to struggle in a swarm of Escorts or walk a more individual path?

The world and the small advertisements are full of F.Ford cars at apparently bargain prices: so many that you will need to do a bit of reading to try and disentangle them. Are you going to buy one, put on better carburation with a race cam and hillclimb it? If so, wheels, tyres and suspension will all be wrong and you will find 235bhp BDAs sitting in the

back of much of the opposition. On the other hand, some clubs run classes for 1600cc pushrod vehicles – fine if you live near Birmingham but not so good in Newcastle or Penzance.

These are simply very basic examples of the need to try and decide what you want to do and how you are going to do it on the most cost-effective basis.

Finally, your own temperament and aims. There are rally drivers who could not be paid to do a hillclimb, and circuit drivers who view driving over the stones and suspension breaking ruts of the forests as a pointless, tiring, expensive exercise.

Are you intent on enjoying the weekends while working for a living properly the rest of the time, or are you one of that very small number with the conviction, the skill and the murderous determination necessary to go in search of the very top?

The costs in different branches of sport vary so much that your money may be better spent to be well equipped at one thing than hopelessly out of contention in something else. Nobody can make these decisions but you. And any decision will be at the mercy of regulations, and alterations to regulations, that may be made for good or, quite often, bad.

It might seem a bit obvious, but do go to a few meetings of the sort that interest you. Regard the cost of getting into the paddock as part of the total cash to be spent on the car, and acquire the *Motorsport Year Book* from the RAC and any other helpful paperwork from the clubs involved.

This thinking and preparation may not only save you a lot of money, but is going to put you in with at least a chance even to begin with, mainly because so many other people will not be taking this sort of trouble. The old saw about marriage – 'dive in in haste and repent at leisure', is probably just as valid in relation to constructing a competition car.

Wheels and tyres

As wheels and, in particular, tyres are nowadays so expensive and so important to success (affecting the

handling of even the most amateur vehicle dramatically), it is important to have a few signposts in the jungle. At the top levels of motorsport tyres can be the difference between the winner and the also ran. In the beginning – and not all that long ago in Mini sizes – there were road tyres and that was the end of it. The international field ran mainly on 15 inch 'bicycle tyres' with treads moulded in rubber that ranged from hard to bloody unbelievable. The slick was seen now and again in photographs of American dragsters alleged to be doing the standing quarter mile in times generally considered to be a load of Yankee bull.

How times have changed – not least those of the timed to 1/1000th of a second dragsters accelerating at way over 2-G when 1-G was once considered technically impossible to exceed. Shades of men with red flags walking ahead to keep everyone from death or damnation ....

While the situation with Mini-sized racers has improved a great deal even the softest rubber now obtainable is still tailored to some extent to the huge heat generation of circuit racing cars balanced delicately as always on the outer front wheel and not much else. Where there's freedom of choice under the regulations, even Mini drivers butcher the wheel arches and slide 13 inch wheels and tyres inside them. They are unlikely to be going to such trouble and expense if it is not getting them somewhere.

Moving on to the 13 inch diameter wheel around which most competition revolves, the first decision is not to take a final decision at all at this stage. Waiting and watching those small advertisements while building or modifying other parts is going on will almost certainly pay a decent dividend in due course.

As there are hundreds of wheels and thousands of tyres, all different, knocking around, the field has somehow to be narrowed and the first criterion must be wheel stud pattern, closely pursued by rim width, with a wary eye on offset. This last is generally taken to be the dimension between the edge of the inner rim and the surface inside the wheel which seats on the hub. Usually of the order of 4 inches. Try not to get less unless there are good reasons (financial more often than technical). Up to $5\frac{1}{4}$ inches should not cause trouble as the combination of alloy spacers and special long studs or tube nuts will usually deal with a bigger dimension.

Many of the one piece alloy wheels are thick and heavy to cope with abnormal road use and rally abuse. Some are barely lighter than steels of similar width particularly if the steels have the widening insert of especially thin sheet — 16g instead of the normal $\frac{1}{8}$ inch.

Widened steel wheels are now easy to obtain and so competitively priced there is no point in going into the hard labour and technique with which co-designer Richard Blackmore and myself originally produced our own. You just have to persuade your supplier to make the insert a thin one and pay your money. An interesting but irrelevant aside is that a large proportion of the latest steels are not made in the UK any more but are currently imported from Brazil.

It is vital to keep a very sharp eye on stud holes and surroundings. Although the car should be as light as possible the loadings at these points will be high. Do not over-tighten, do grease taper seatings and watch like a hawk for cracks.

The best type of alloy wheel to aim at owning is a multi-section pattern of which Mamba Solar is an excellent example. I have used them, and had accidents on them so I am unfortunately well qualified to know how they stand up to mistreatment and paddock repair. They have a cast centre which can be drilled to any pattern of stud with tube nuts passing through the holes. The inner and outer rims are quite separate, spun to the shape of bottomless saucepans and held to the centre casting with a multitude of plated screws and nuts. There are no 'O' rings between sections, a skim of silicone rubber sealer doing an effective job of keeping them airtight. This construction method means you can replace a damaged rim, build up a wider wheel, or alter inset simply by changing one section.

Class or formula rules often limit rim and tyre size. Read them before you buy even the best of apparent bargains. A very rough guide on which to start is to measure the tread width and add one or two inches to get the minimum rim widths. Two and a half inches is about the maximum differential between tyre and rim but you can go the other way fitting the tyre to a narrower rim but risking some nasty unstable lurches driving into corners.

You soon find there is a bewildering array of sizes, size markings, shapes, wall stiffness and mysterious figures in little boxes all over the walls of every tyre you see. Then just to disprove this observation one turns up with nothing but a faint stencil of the maker's name. Not to mention small holes or slots like mice have been at them. What are these you ask yourself? These slots are as vital to the secondhand buyer as to any professional team. They are the depth indicators to show how much the tread rubber on a slick has worn.

Let us not jump ahead but try and put things in some sort of order. Any serious competitor needs to start adding his own researches to this, beginning today!

The makes you are most likely to meet are Goodyear, Dunlop, M & H and Michelin, and more rarely Firestone, Pirelli, Yokohama and Bridgestone. Wall markings have varied over the years, not only from inches to millimeters as well as mixtures of the two, but also in what those markings indicate. They can mean tread width, width across the fattest part of the wall when a tyre is inflated on a particular rim, total outside diameter when inflated or a rather hypothetical distance from rim to tread face. This last has to be doubled and then added to wheel rim size to get an equally hypothetical diameter.

As far as the diameter of any tyre is concerned, there is also the distance from the ground to hub centre which is not half of the diameter because of squash where the tyre touches the road. Because of these various complications there is little point in trying to work out a circumference. If available look it up in a helpful manufacturer's chart of revs per mile, for it is vital that it be accurate for gear ratio calculations. You are highly likely to be fitting tyres with nominal diameter between 19.5 and 23 inches depending on various considerations. When the time comes you can simply roll the car across the floor fully loaded, with chalk marks on the driven and/or speedo drive roadwheel and find the actual distance it travels in one revolution.

Back again to the subject in hand. Until Michelin turned up on the scene, all racing tyres were textile crossplies with subtle variations in the angles at which the cords inside the carcase lay in relation to each other. These tyres were all considered to be 'progressive' in that they broke away relatively early, did not do it savagely and remained controllable by the driver.

Radials, it was felt, might hang on much longer but the breakaway when it came was much more sudden and consequently potentially disastrous. This was thought to be unacceptable until Michelin entered the fray, not unnaturally with a radial tyre which immediately began to become very acceptable indeed. What can be done by a really great driver after a radial has broken away was amply demonstrated by Villeneuve in his F1 Ferrari again and again, but never more impressively than in taking it right round the outside of a Renault at such an angle it looked unbelievable watching on TV. What it felt like in the car at 11/10ths defies my imagination. Yet he stayed in control ... just.

The complexities of tyre markings, compound tyres, carcases for different jobs and varying approaches to size definitions are so great that they are more properly and fully covered in an Appendix. This will permit the serious student to refer to it at leisure, without boring to death anybody just passing through.

Suffice it to say that the most basic all-weather fitting for any beginner able to afford only four wheels and tyres is either a set of boldly-patterned top quality road covers, or four medium racing slicks on stiff carcases, cut (if necessary by you) with a generous water drainage pattern, the driven pair at least, and preferably all four. in both cases mounted on rims one or two inches wider than the tread rubber width. This is the crudest of guides, but you have to start somewhere.

The road tyres will probably need over-inflating anything up to 70% over road pressures for circuit or tarmac, less for the rain. The slicks will warm up more quickly in the dry thanks to the slotting, a good thing as racing tyres are extremely temperature sensitive when it comes to giving of their best. The relative hardness will keep wear within bounds, and the stiff walls provide a firm and predictable feel.

In the wet the slotted pattern will cope with everything including standing puddles and wear will be almost negligible. This simple and very basic choice will not be ideal in either wet or dry, but it will be a workable compromise until you win the pools or get to know a seller of the right sort of secondhand covers.

In general terms, the top men and teams buy the best brand new and change it as often as proves necessary. What they consider as past its best may still be ten times better than what you are using and well worth buying at perhaps half or quarter new price.

The front tyres from F1 and F2, for instance, make admirable rears for a variety of smaller and lesser classes. Catching the right tyres as they roll down the ladder from the top contenders is what we are about to try and arrange. Even going to Dunlop or Goodyear with cheque book in hand and gratefully accepting what they suggest can still leave you in trouble. Expert as they are at an international level they may not be so interested or knowledgeable about more specialised corners of the sport.

The alternative, as ever, is that you have to learn something about tyres, try to decide what you really require and then seek it out. The subtleties of carcase construction are really out of our hands except in the sense that the stiffness varies hugely. At one extreme there are carcases that can be folded inside out, they are so flexible, and can certainly be fitted wearing carpet slippers and using a set of Halfords 9 inch levers.

At the other end of the spectrum are many of the F2 Pirelli and heavy saloon circuit tyres or thick beaded rally specials that need a six foot lever or hydraulic assistance on a tyre fitting machine and may badly damage a light alloy rim in the process.

Along with the carcases you have a huge variety of tread rubber and a selection of patterns from full wet to slick. Obviously the permutations are virtually endless. We have to get the odds down a bit.

Several years of experiments by numerous drivers will be here reduced to certain cardinal rules aimed as much at stability in handling and life, as at out-and-out grip.

(1) Remember that racing tread rubber is designed to operate at high temperatures – higher than boiling water, so you may never ever reach its optimum heat. Until this heat is reached it will not grip well, it will not be as sticky as it ought to be, but it will not wear so quickly either.

(2) Always buy a tread that is about 2 inches narrower than the wheels you possess – or wheels 2 inches wider than your treads. In bigger tyres I have fitted 8.6 rears onto 11 inch rims quite successfully. On the other hand an experimental 9.5 on 12 inch rims started to come away from the rim shoulder at speed leaving a $\frac{1}{8}$ inch slot – and then sank back to its proper place standing in the paddock! Mysteriously, stretching the bead outwards appears to stabilise treads well against the road. But ultra-flexible wet carcases allow the wheels to move within the tyre a massive amount with the resultant feeling that the back end of the car is breaking away when it is actually realigning itself while the tread is still gripping. Two examples: a side-mounted radiator one and a half inches clear of a rear wheel at standstill had paint polished off to a gleaming brass line under the distortion of cornering by the first Gould car, and Gowers' Monopin had paint taken off the wing endplates similarly, both apparently impossible when studied in the paddock.

(3) Get a medium to stiff carcase with the softest tread rubber possible.

It is difficult to describe what is a flexible and what is a stiff carcase, but a very flexible wet has the feel of a comfortable pair of light shoes while an ultra-stiff may be more like a rubber sheathed piece of steel plate.

All the foregoing refers primarily to rears. The backend is what largely governs how a car feels. At the front should be the softest tread rubber

consistent with survival at the job on a medium carcase, more able to tolerate larger wheel movements, steering load distortions, and any tendencies to understeer.

It may be handy to know when checking wear slots or tread depths that wets can be only 4mm deep brand new, slicks up to 7mm and rally tyres 9mm, or more.

Cutting your own tread pattern while illegal for road cars is still standard practice in motorsport where tyres are deliberately designed to accept it.

The device that does the job has Vee or Square-shaped blades in a thing that looks like an electric jigsaw. There is a depth control on the cut and the blade works red hot, exactly like the proverbial knife through butter, but two things make the job easier. Fit and inflate the tyre on the rim and paint or chalk your pattern on it before you begin. It really is not difficult, simply slow and laborious for the beginner.

One important thing to understand about tread compounds is that one man's demon soft can be another's Flintstone Special. It all depends on the weight of the car, the length of time of the tyre will be running under racing conditions, the abrasiveness of the track surface and the temperature of the day.

Two extremes might be Le Mans under the French midday sun, a ton of car and 220mph on the straight versus an April hillclimb meeting with flakes of snow on a Yorkshire wind, 45 seconds running time and a $7\frac{1}{2}$ cwt single-seater.

The differences are simply so enormous that the perfect tyre for one will be totally useless for the other. And quite a lot of the tyres that turn up tend to be more orientated to the Le Mans situation than frosty or club circuits, if only because hard compounds last longer, whereas owners keep softies until the most benevolent of scrutineers has to comment unkindly about their suitability for further combat.

If you have enough power to do several 'burn-outs' or controlled wheelspin blasts on the way to the line you can heat up a relatively hard compound to a bit nearer its proper operating temperature. Most drivers do it nowadays, but it is not kind to clutch or driveshafts. One burn-out on tyres that heat up more quickly or work at lower temperatures could be just as good: in fact, recent US-made Goodyear Blue Streak and Eagle soft compounds do just this. A difficulty stemming from this is a tendency towards fundamental understeer because fronts never warm up at all and attempts to heat up all four treads with some outside source may make their appearance soon. To what degree organisers may accept pit crews of the Top Ten or pole position runners applying miniature flame throwers to their charges as they come up to the line, I leave others to guess. It will surely be one to stretch RAC or FISA administrative powers to their outer limits.

Once everything is fitted on your car you can get a good idea of tyre stability by trying to push and pull the chassis sideways and checking any movement of the wheel rim within the tyre itself. If there is more than half an inch then you are probably going to feel it on the road as a fleeting impression of break-away at the back which is actually the car's attitude altering as it settles itself into the corner.

This does not apply to full wet covers, possibly because the driver is so switched-on and expecting trouble in the rain that he does not feel it in the same way and of course side loadings on corners are less.

Although general setting up of a car for wet or dry is dealt with in the suspension chapter it might be as well to clarify one point on wet weather tyres and how they work now. Studying the track of a road-going saloon ahead of you while driving down the M1 in a thunderstorm will demonstrate that tyres shift an enormous quantity of water off the road surface for a short time leaving a near dry line behind.

This can and does happen on a track and the effect is that the front tyre removes much of the water and the rear tyre is then operating in relatively much drier conditions. Its grip is better, its slip angle is smaller, contributing to wet weather understeer. Contrary to general wet settings, it may be necessary to take

off wing and stiffen the rear roll-bar to deal with it.

This phenomenon of the dry line may also enable you to hold on to a faster man by using his tracks.

So far as personal equipment goes, I ran for some time a 'half-and-half' arrangement which involved keeping a rather aged, but still soft, heavily cut stiff carcase on the fronts at all times. This was combined with rear slicks for the dry and proper wets in rain. These latter also function very well in damp, dusty and (as at Blackpool and Wallasey) sandy conditions. It meant that I only carried two spares instead of four and financial outlay was much reduced. Not perfect, but it worked very well ninety percent of the time for me and does illustrate how reality for most of us compares to those photographs of stacked F1 wheels and tyres piled six deep in pits from Monza to Long Beach.

This may have seemed to some readers altogether too much about tyres, but it is impossible to exaggerate how important they are and how they will affect a car's handling and your success or the interpretation of what is happening. They can be the ace in your hand or the joker in the pack.

Having recently changed the personal arrangement just explained to a spare set of wets (nonetheless home cut) and superb ultra soft M&H 61 front slicks with Goodyear Blue Streak on the rears, it is hard to describe the enormous extra grip immediately available. As well as difficulty in realising and exploiting it, what was formerly 'on the edge' is now so far within the capability of the car and the tyres that lifting off in sudden uncontrollable fear of having gone too far over the edge, merely slowed me down as if the car was saying 'for God's sake stop panicking – there is plenty left yet'. And I am sure there is, but it takes time to come to terms with it.

Using tyres for circuit racing so that they heat up properly to a black stickily tenacious surface is a still bigger step up in grip. U2 driver and sprint champion Nick Bridge found this when he moved to circuit racing observing 'third gear corners with a dab of brakes became flat in top with the tyres warm. The difference was

enormous'.

An even bigger eye-opener for me was to hear Maurice Phillipe, of Lotus and Tyrrell design fame, talk about the difficulties of finding exactly matched pairs of covers. Radials offer extremely accurate control of the diameter and consequently rolling circumference. Crossplies can vary so much that his team had at times needed to try up to 80 different covers, all having to be mounted on wheels, inflated and measured to isolate matched pairs.

The tolerances he was talking about were an acceptable maximum of only 0.050in on diameter, whereas they were finding up to 0.25in, an amount more than capable of causing handling troubles. As if this wasn't bad enough, once hot and run in, even matched pairs could sometimes grow or contract by different amounts, thus providing a driver with an oversize tyre on one side and an undersize one on the other in the middle of practice. Such a variation in effective diameter also affects skirt clearances and sealing, but in general we of the lower echelons do not have these particular crosses to bear.

A few further points before moving on to other things.

Slip angle: the difference between the direction in which the wheel is pointing and the way it is actually going. Once the car has started to turn, it will increase depending on a complex mix of factors that include the road surface, the type of carcase, suspension geometry, and whether it is wet or dry. Even in a straight line, the tyre will be operating at a very small slip angle if any toe-out or toe-in has been built into either front or rear suspension. The ultimate slip angle is when you have full lock on, but you are still going off the road!

Always remember that a great deal of talk about tyres is subjective – that is to say it is how you feel with a particular tyre, not how somebody else feels with it nor how they tell you it ought to feel.

Toe-in at the front or rear will sometimes prevent lurch on turn-in to a corner because it has already put a distortion into the carcase and the contact patch.

'Chunking' is when bits come

right out of the tread rubber, often as neatly as if carefully carved with a small knife.

Other people's rubber on the track may help or hinder. If it has rolled off and still lies in little balls or tendrils loose on the road surface it will wreck your grip, but on the start lines of hillclimbs and sprints it attaches itself to the tarmac, literally coating the road with rubber, and subject to a dry surface may be a help.

The 'thumbnail dent' test, is much indulged in by paddock wanderers. High hysteresis rubber is very 'dead', and will retain a nail dent for some time. Still not a bad guide to comparing the softness of various tread mixes, but the temperature once the tyre is working will have the major influence on its performance.

If you feel you have got your tyres nicely warm and up to temperature, just remember that F1 covers are capable of lasting a Grand Prix only when working properly between 210 and 240°F. 'Above or below the proper working temperature and you are in immediate trouble', says Gordon Murray of Brabham. At these levels of temperature tyres are warm enough to give you a nasty burn should you start patting them.

Now a pocket guide to some aspects of the tyres generally available:

Goodyear: Vastly experienced firm. Huge range of compounds. Generally light. Major concentration on circuits, so club and sprint tyres are often uncut wets – very soft compound on a flexible carcase with humped centre. G45, their classic wet rubber on some flatter stiffer slicks was for a time many people's secret weapon, particularly the U2 brigade. US-built tyres are starting to arrive in Britain with 'D' prefix 4-figure numbers and 'Eagle' or 'Blue Streak' markings. Stiffer, lighter with very thin tread rubber. Few around secondhand.

Goodyear made the Tyrrell 6-wheeler fronts of 16 inch outside diameter to fit a 10 inch wheel. Some 'escaped' before they went out of production, but are hardly worth considering as you have in all probability to redesign the car to use them. Also 'tall fronts' for 15 inch wheels slow the rotational speed, increase the footprint and provide more rubber to wear out.

M&H: Early with ultra-soft compounds on a stiff carcase. Pay enough attention to lesser events to send a wagon and fitters to some. Generally very flat tread profile. Exceptional as cold-running fronts and often teamed with Goodyear rears, possibly because early rears a bit more flexible than later ones and do not feel as stable to some drivers. Vast US experience in drag racing with standing start tyres to draw on.

Michelin: Radial pioneers of course. Excellent traction. Very stable and reliable in circumference. Good choice of compounds and sizes. Marginally cheaper than the opposition. Tolerate considerable camber change. Some asymmetrically moulded with a curved inner shoulder to accept the wheel going negative. Official advice if in trouble: 'increase the negative'. A bit vague on suggested pressures, but do not seem ultra sensitive to this.

Pirelli: Both stiff and heavy to begin with, but have altered a great deal. Not many secondhand, and difficult to get detailed information on construction and rubber. Using Kevlar and a lighter construction got one cover down from 35lbs to 22;bs!

Dunlop: 'The old firm'. Produce an excellent and comprehensive guide to their tyres, all colour, bright pictures and detailed advice. Over any period of years they seem to have swings from superb to mediocre compared to the opposition. Ultra-conservative attitude to rim widths, recently relaxing a little.

Avon: In racing tyres for a long long time, but often thought of until recently as primarily for bikes. Link with IRTS at the time of Goodyear's temporary withdrawal brought them into F1 in a major way, and thereafter every category you care to name including rallycross and hot rods. Their m/cycle sidecar sizes very useful on small single-seaters and sports/racers. Provide a suggested pressure list. Quite excellent, lucid and simple guide to racing tyre basics with a very full list of sizes and data. Their A9 compound became instant 'tweak of the year' when it appeared in the sprint and hillclimb world – undoubtedly a superb, grippy ultra-soft mix that works.

2 What, Why, When ... and some of the How.

As has always been the case if you are planning to build, tune or modify a competition car, possession of any worthwhile parts or knowledge may be 9/10ths of the decision on what to do. A wrecked bike available for silly money or a fully tuned and prepared power unit in a Mini suffering serious tinworm attack can both be perfectly valid reasons dictating plans for the future – with only one reservation.

It might seem a touch of the obvious, but there is no point in putting a year of midnight oil into something that at the end of it all impresses the neighbours as you roll it proudly onto the front drive, but cannot actually be used in competition.

The British motor sport scene has a bewildering variety of formulae, capacity classes, circuits, hillclimbs, grasstrack and rallycross courses. A little research into the maze, not to mention some honest thinking about what you or your bank account will realistically achieve, are surely worthwhile before spending anything.

First decide where you are going. Only then go on to how. Just for the moment we will take the view that a car is going to be built from scratch. Modification, however radical, does not give you quite the same free hand, and is dealt with elsewhere in the book.

Whether sports or single seater, a fundamental question is spaceframe, monocoque or a mixture of both?

Mixture? Well, the first Terrapin was such a device with a spaceframe of square tubing, but "D" section side panels of alloy riveted on to form stressed sections from the roll-bar bulkhead to instrument panel. Also, if you consider a current F1 car from nose to tail rather than the tub by itself, it could be argued that it is a "mixture construction".

All my own practical experience has been in tube spaceframes, so we will take these first. Tube chassis are generally built of mild steel square or rectangular tube (properly called "hollow section" to distinguish it from "tube" which is round).

This can be bought in a variety of size and thickness, with dimensions of $\frac{7}{8}$ inch x $\frac{7}{8}$ inch, $\frac{3}{4}$ x $\frac{3}{4}$ inch, $\frac{5}{8}$ x $\frac{5}{8}$ inch, or perhaps $\frac{1}{2}$ x $\frac{1}{2}$ inch in 18g or 20g doing almost anything a constructor may wish.

In general terms it is technically better to go to a bigger tube with a thinner wall if you want more rigidity with the same weight. You can see this in rear suspension links of any of the more powerful single-seaters or saloons, and in rally cars that have a fabricated four link location for the rear axle.

However, the amateur is also building for solidity that will withstand an occasional off-course, possibly one bad bang in the life of the car and five to ten seasons use, rather than sale or scrapping at the end of the first year as professional teams will generally do.

So if in doubt, go up in thickness as well as size. Very thin wall tube is anyway more difficult to obtain so most cars finish up with a mixture of 16g and 18g. You can study photographs of spaceframe chassis elsewhere in the book for an idea of how they were approached or use your own judgement.

The overwhelming consideration is never to ask a tube to accept a bending load. Stresses and strains must go into the ends. Simply putting in a thicker heavier tube to accept an improper load I consider to be the shipbuilder's approach – "if in doubt double the thickness". It *can* work; however, while putting in ¼ inch plate where 16g broke because of bad design may well cure the problem, the new plate will still flex minutely, will weigh four times as much and ... but I don't really have to go on, do I?

Nobody ever got to play tennis without a racquet or to be an Olympic ice champion without skates. You are not going to build anything without a certain minimum of equipment of which the key part has got to be flame or electric welding gear (or access to same) together with the skill to use it. If you do not have either, a partner is needed who does, and even if you are planning a monocoque or are modifying a rally or trials car, while this need will be much reduced, it will not be eliminated altogether.

Weld or braze?

The level of welding talent required for a vehicle that, if sensibly designed, will stick together for you is not ultra-high. There is no need for the sort of expertise that will force-arc North Sea gas piping against the clock, with an immediate high speed X-ray film check, or hang bits together for Concorde.

In fact, technically speaking you are not really required to be able to weld at all. The Terrapin tube chassis, wishbones and brackets, like those of very many small production or one-off units are brazed or bronze welded, although semi-automated MIG and TIG arc welders are now becoming popular with many professionals.

Without delving into the finer points, welding is when two pieces of steel and similar steel filler rod are all turned molten by the heat of the flame or arc and flow together into a seam with its characteristic and delicate herring-bone pattern.

In brazing, the two pieces of steel only become red-hot, never melt, and the brass or bronze filler rod runs in between and sticks them together in a manner akin to soldering.

Among the good reasons for the amateur to choose brazing are:

(a) The inevitable but invisible stress line on each side of a weld at the exact point where the solid metal became molten will be left every time you join two or more tubes, a potential source of future trouble. This is dealt with industrially in ways not available to the DIY man.

(b) A nickel-bronze alloy is actually stronger in tensile than the mild steel it is joining together.

(c) All things being equal, it is easier to do a good braze than a good weld. Further, a poor brazing job is virtually certain to be better, stronger and more reliable than a poor weld. It gives your perhaps mediocre talent a little more elbow room.

(d) You need less heat and cause less distortion on the job, particularly when there are multiple junctions of tube, or an appreciable difference in bulk or thickness of pieces to be joined.

One word of warning – bronze joints do not like bending loads one little bit. I had to learn this lesson in a most frightening way when, having modified (and plated) the tie bars on my son's rally car, I grossly underestimated the fearful shock-loads that suspensions on forest stages must accept. Though the joint was good, one bar was torn physically in two. The car rolled, and I was left to thank God the only thing damaged was the car.

There are one or two flame welding sets working on low pressure self-generated gases or propane, that do an admirable brazing or light gauge welding job. As you can buy one complete for less than the hard cash you will have to give on permanent interest-free loan to British Oxygen to get an account and be permitted to rent a pair of bottles, they are well worth investigating.

Beware, incidentally, of buying a bargain pair of bottles from anyone. Torch, yes. Gauges, yes. But legally you have got to be buying stolen gear in the bottles. They all stay the property, so far as I am aware, of British Oxygen, Air Products or one or two smaller firms and to get 2000psi of oxygen or 200lbs of acetylene into the pair you cannot roll them into your friendly local goodie shop. You have to go to one of the firms named, and if you turn up out of the blue unknown to them, they are more likely to be ringing the local

constabulary than changing your empties!

Small electric welders are also now appearing on the scene, many of which have brazing facilities in which you use the arc like a flame, feeding in a bronze rod filler in the same way as with gas.

Commercially the MIG and TIG welders already mentioned with an insert gas shield around the molten metal are fast, economic and of extreme high quality, but you need skill and practice and a lot of money for the equipment.

Terrapins, (like dozens of other brazed spaceframe cars) have had various accidents over the years. In every case in which I have personal knowledge, the driver has survived in good condition and the chassis has been repaired successfully. The two things which made this possible were the basic stiffness of the frame and a degree of progressive collapse. In other words, wheels fall off, wishbones fail or attachment bolts and brackets bend, decelerating and absorbing G-forces and shock-loads while still protecting the driver.

This does not mean any car, however well built, is indestructible. Happily nobody I know has had a truly appalling "stop dead in inches" type of accident. It simply means a sensibly built or modified car will cope with the sort of mistakes that club level competitors are likely to make.

The Gould Terrapin went far beyond this, and a lot of the design was related to D.G.'s having a wife and four children. It was aimed at protecting him as completely as possible at the considerably higher speeds and cornering forces of which this car was to be capable.

It looks very complicated at a quick glance but still has its roots in the original Terrapin spaceframe. Most things on it are doing two jobs, some three or even four, which should be the constant aim of the good designer.

Unlike the apparent design results of all too many road cars it is also reasonably accessible, easy to repair and incorporates an ingenious approach to get the engine and gearbox out in a hurry. All these aspects affect very much how reliable the car will be in practice and how rapidly you can be in action again in the event of mechanical or other trouble.

Why work in the dust and rain of the paddock when doing it properly in a garage with light, warmth and coffee can save you trouble? Unless that is, it is essential to compete. I have done a lot of jobs, as have hundreds of other drivers and mechanics, in horrible conditions including once stripping out a seized piston, carefully levering the rings free, filing out slots, rebuilding and running again within two hours at Silverstone's Six Hour Relay.

The monocoque car

The detailed construction of a spaceframe chassis comes a little later, so we'll move on to the monocoque which is universal in some formulae, but certainly not in all.

Keith Gowers, a Blackpool exhaust expert for one of Britain's largest firms is responsible for the information that follows. It is totally practical as well as being proven, by a car that was highly successful virtually off the drawing board – despite his never having designed or built a monocoque before.

His "apprenticeship" was to build an early tube chassis Terrapin without knowing drawings were available from which to work. He used only the outline and undimensioned sketches from my original book about the car. This resulted in his using round instead of square tube, a good deal of "guesstimation" and his own suspension geometry. His only real error was to make everything a bit heavy which meant he had a weight penalty throughout the car's life. A penalty which could only be overcome by increased power or a lighter engine unit.

He, and later another Terrapin builder, John Buck, decided to attempt the installation, in place of the Mini engine unit, of a supercharged motorcycle engine. With an effective capacity penalty of x1.4 *(ie:* an 1100 engine when blown = 1540cc) they needed a maximum of 785cc. The 750 Honda 4, DOHC, short stroke all alloy unit was, except for its cost, tailormade.

It is always easy after something has been done successfully to say how obvious it all was, and, if a failure, what a daft idea to attempt anyway.

To be early on the scene is usually a lonely time, full of misgivings because money is restricted – you would be paying someone else to do it if it wasn't – few of us are totally confident behind the facade, and there are all sorts of technical problems about which you cannot consult anyone.

Keith, a demon for punishment, decided that doing all this was not enough. He'd do the power unit first, test it in the steel tube car, and then create a tiny ultra-lightweight monocoque to carry it. The idea promised extremely well: cut power unit weight by about half, and the rest of the car's weight by at least a third and the result, if it handled, had to be good.

Keith, having by the end of the season developed a reliable and powerful alternative engine unit, lifted it out for the winter, left the faithful tube chassis in the garden and began his monocoque. After completing it he now says he would never make another steel tube chassis and, as his new car began taking as much off some British records as F1 drivers were taking off theirs in its first full season, who am I to argue against such a standpoint?

Monocoques are a series of boxes of varying shapes and sizes with the edges generally riveted and/or glued together to form the same sort of coherent whole with the same duties as a spaceframe – supporting a driver, power unit and suspension pickup points accurately and reliably in space and not flexing about when subject to complex and varying loads.

It is as well to bear in mind that when the monocoque first arrived on the scene it was not inherently better or even as good as the best tubeframe – but it was superbly suited to regulations and car knowledge of the time. What it did was to provide two big hollow boxes, one on each side of the car, into which could be inserted flexible rubber fuel tanks.

If only for this one reason, it solved a number of design problems with fuel tanks, as well as making a

substantial step forward in driver safety. Long experience in the aircraft world had shown that a flexy bag tank could not only survive considerable impact and deformation, but was extremely resistant to tearing and, if foam fillled, would only leak slowly even if it was punctured.

Compared to the horrifying disasters caused by split metal tanks full of petrol it was a gigantic step forward and it should be no surprise to students of the art that it was Lotus founder Colin Chapman who took it. The Chapman monocoque put the writing on the wall and there it has stayed, indelible, while endlessly copied and improved.

The racing monocoque began life as, effectively, two big hollow tubes joined at each end by a robust cross bulkhead. The bulkheads are needed because although the tubes or boxes in themselves are extremely stiff, they can still move easily in relation to each other unless tied together in a satisfactory manner. That is problem one, and problem two is how to feed high loads into a hollow box? You cannot drill a hole and put a bolt through. It falls out again, pulling the skin of the panel with it, very shortly after loads are applied: a more scientific approach is needed.

The solutions are 1) a bracket on a plate which is itself riveted on a wide area of metal, and *as nearly as possible in line with the plane of the sheet,* 2) internal bulkheads within the monocoque at critical positions, or 3) by not putting the loads into it directly at all.

Very many F1 cars have taken this latter course by mounting the whole of the rear suspension onto the Hewland gearbox, leaving the cylinder heads of the Cosworth DFV, together with two points at the bottom of the block, to carry all the loads via four mounting bolts into a fabricated or cast alloy bulkhead across the back of the monocoque. The magnitude of forces involved in this approach is indicated by several instances of failure where a car has, literally, come apart in the middle.

Even if the engine is specifically designed to accept all these stresses, it is in my view no more than tolerable. It creates innumerable suspension design

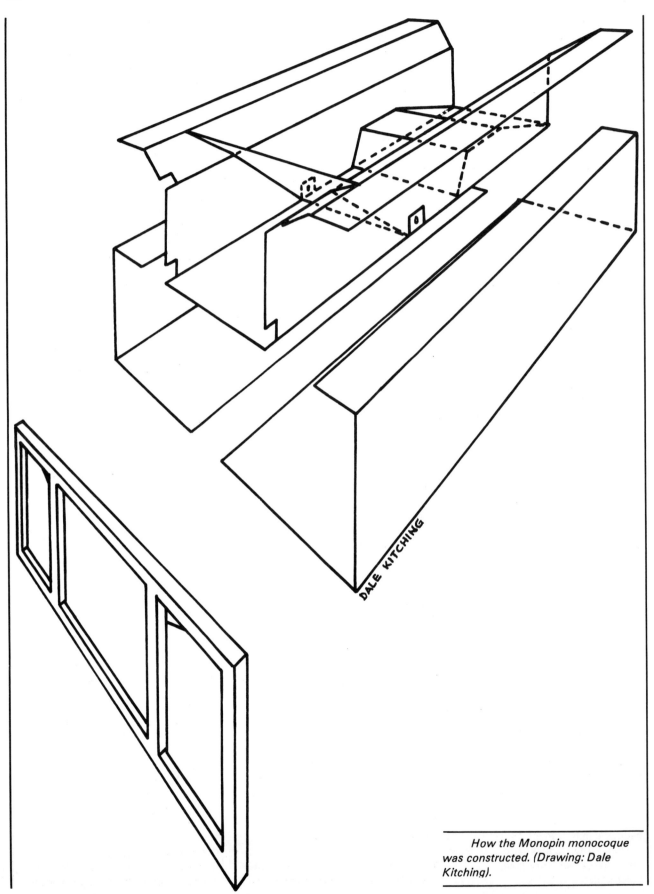

How the Monopin monocoque was constructed. (Drawing: Dale Kitching).

problems and asks an expanding and contracting engine to accept a lot of pushing and shoving, and worst of all, twisting that it could well do without.

At the front of these F1 cars there is a similar robust full width bulkhead normally carrying a baby-sized boxed chassis ahead of it, which not only bears all the front suspension loadings, but also contributes handsomely to tying the front ends of the side boxes together.

All this outlines the state of play when Keith Gowers decided his highly successful Honda engine should have a new car around it. The end result was a tiny, elegant single-seater that fitted him better than a Savile Row suit. Trying it for size myself much later when it was complete, I found I could breathe easily enough, but the steering wheel and gearlever were so close, an improper thought would have had me off the road.

When the monocoque first appeared, it had, apart from its supposed extra stiffness, a number of less obvious virtues to recommend it. When necessary it was able to meet the requirement to have a deformable structure down the side, at first by explaining it already had just that, and when this was no longer acceptable to the powers-that-be, double-skinning with a rigid foam filler poured in between.

Monocoques would also accept the discreet and centrally balanced installation of a battery, fuel pumps or oil tank. And the human being in the middle, sat, more or less happily, on the angled panels riveted down the two pontoons tying them together. When you added that totally rigid six sided box at the front, and a stressed engine to hold the rear in place, the monocoque had even more going for it.

In production terms, skilful detail design alternatives enabled one "tub", as the centre sections rapidly came to be called, to do F1, F2, F3, Atlantic, "B" – you name it – with modifications that were sometimes little more than a different gauge of sheet and one size up on the rivets.

Herewith one man's approach to monocoque building. It is his experiences which follow – the reasons, planning, building methods and snags that were behind the

creation of Keith Gowers' Monopin Honda, which, by the middle of its second season, proved capable of giving a nasty shock to the established fast men in the 1100 hillclimb class. It was, incidentally, cunningly designed to take advantage of the size of the only metal folding machine to which he had access, and also the dimensions of alloy sheet available.

As there turned out to be no stampede of would-be purchasers for his old spaceframe car, a large number of its parts gave a flying start to the new enterprise including wheels, tyres, driveshafts, steering, hubs, brakes, uprights, dry sump tank, instruments, sundry Rose joints, and the complete differential unit with its variable chain wheels and mounting bearings.

I suspect that hidden somewhere inside Keith's decision that the new car would be a monocoque, was a degree of taking up the irresistible challenge of something new. For a start no useful literature could at the time be traced in his local reference library, so it was balsa wood models, and scale pieces of cardboard folded again and again in a long series of experiments which had to provide the basis for full size construction.

In my view the masterstroke of the design was the approach of making the tub in three pieces and the sequence in which they were used. The complete inner skin could be made on a six foot commercial bender, and the finished monocoque did not actually exist until the car was complete, including fuel lines, brake piping, seat, tanks, instruments and all the suspension. Only then were the separate left and right hand panels riveted into place to create the finished structure.

The sketch which accompanies this text will make clear just how many difficulties of access, reliable riveting, installing internal strong points and so forth are made easy by this method.

The dimensions are simply guidelines for a slightly built five feet nine inch driver, well reclined, and willing to wriggle his feet underneath the high mounted rack to reach pedals mounted with their master cylinders within the alloy skinned square tube front subframe.

Said Keith later: "After I'd built

nine tenths of the car, I went round to Chevron to see how the professionals do it, and got a serious shock. Everything I'd done seemed far too heavy and strong. They put no internal bulkheads into their side sections, were obviously happy about riveting bent up edges together, and had quite a lot of panels that seemed lighter than I was using".

We have to bear in mind of course that professionals are probably thinking of only one season of totally reliable life for their cars, with complete tub replacement in the event of crinkling it a bit with an "off". The amateur is naturally hoping to get both a longer life and a higher degree of resistance to the result of any errors of judgement he or she might make.

To that end, the basic materials used by Keith were 18G NS4 alloy sheet, 1500 $\frac{5}{2}$ inch Monel rivets, and $\frac{3}{4}$ inch x 18g square steel tube for subframes. It was decided not to take on the possible extra hazards of glue but to use dichromate paste to stop any electrolytic reactions in the steel/alloy joints.

Some points for anyone following the same route, all essential to a first class result. Ignore them and not too long after completion your creation will start to fall apart, an unhappy event normally first signalled by tiny chips of paint coming off around the rivet heads. This means they are moving and you will be in the most serious and fundamental sort of trouble.

To guard against this the 1500 rivet holes were all drilled twice – undersize followed by correct size. Rivet pins (a removable device usually called "Avdels" to temporarily take the place of permanent rivets, widely used in the aircraft industry) held parts in line and position for the drilling, so everything could be dismantled for deburring before the final riveting. As there were in some cases more than two sheets at particular points this meant about 7600 holes deburred by hand!

Any folds in the sheet up to three feet long were done in a homemade angle iron bender held in a bench vice, and all the holes for access or lightening given swaged edges with a fairly simple handmade tool of two shaped metal blocks with a bolt

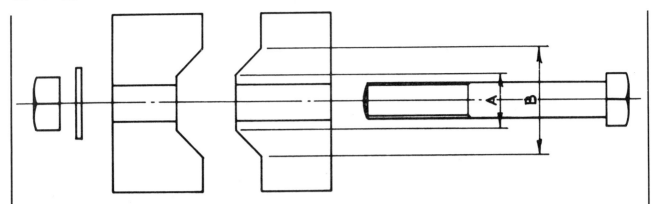

Simple swaging tool to provide a 45° stiffening lip on holes in thin alloy or steel. Can be turned from hardwood or metal. Dia 'A' = hole size. Dia 'B' = limit of swage edge.

A refined version can give a curved swage rather than an angular one by machining the two halves with a matching radius.

through the middle (see illustration).

The battery, fuel, and all ignition electrics were sealed away from the weather behind the small of the driver's back, with a removable access panel under the seat cushioning.

The construction sequence used was: 1) make subframes and hold inner sheeting to pattern; 2) rivet front and rear subframes to centre section inner skin; 3) with front and rear sections set level, put all internal panels in place (seatback, bottom, instrument bulkhead, safety harness steel mounting plates, various captive nuts); 4) the car was then completed totally, but for wings, top bodywork and nose, before the two side panels were finally riveted in place.

His highly skilled amateur's approach to really serious stress points was that of any thinking man with a wife, family and a job between weekends: generous steel plate reinforcements riveted in over a relatively big area. The trick, as will stand repeating, is never to put a load – any load – into an unsupported thin sheet. It either has to go into the edge, in line with the sheet itself, or a reinforcing sub-bulkhead or a plate has to be installed to take the load edgeways.

The most substantial things on the car were the rollover bar and subframe mountings which doubled up their duties in carrying the safety harness shoulder strap pickups as well.

Keith also had the same vague feeling he could not prove which D.G. and I had much later on the 1600 car: that stressing the engine as part of the structure was not a good idea. The magnitude of the forces involved was certainly proven in due course, when asking the engine to do a tube's job in the rear bay produced handling troubles instantly cured by a full, if complex, separate bracing of the area in every plane.

The needle nose of Keith's monocoque carried two small adjustable wings, while at the rear an ingenious approach was used in which the rear body panels became a flat deck carrying marine ply end plates for the wing mounted above it. The complete aerofoil section pivoted inside these end plates, generally running at an angle of attack of about 5 to 6 degrees.

Experiments without the wing showed an immediate loss of stability in a straight line, plus spinning off once: it was replaced never to be left off again.

The Oulton weighbridge measured the complete monocoque car ready to go at 650lbs – distributed 41 per cent front: 59 per cent rear – and 5.8cwt with some 120bhp to push it is an impressive power/weight ratio by most people's standards, even after the driver has been added.

While it turned out to be virtually an immediate winner, it also fell squarely into the category of machinery that people look at after it has been done and remark: "Obviously – with that sort of power and weight it ought to win". They overlook the courage needed to embark on the enterprise alone and full of uncertainty many months, and many pound notes, earlier.

An indication of the degree of progress made by the combination of monocoque and motorcycle engine is in the overall wet weights. Original Terrapin, blown Mini = 922lb. Same car with unblown Honda = 727lb. Monopin, unblown Honda 600lb to which was later added 50lb for the supercharger installation.

Among the snags encountered during the car's first season, and their solutions, were:

Rear tyre flex bridged a two inch gap to rub on the wing end plates – stiff carcase M&H 61s stopped it. They also had enough grip to break one Mini driveshaft and twist another. Brand new, instead of ex-breaker's yard, items then fitted.

Chassis pickup for bottom rear wishbone tore out. Needed bracing and stiffening plate.

Leaving paint on the ends of certain suspension bushes allowed everything to get loose within two meetings.

Monopin. This picture shows details of the tub design and its construction. Note Imp-pattern twin reservoir for dual circuit brakes, tricky exhaust route and high-mounted rack and pinion – just above driver's shims! (Picture: Allan Staniforth).

Monopin. 14000rpm rev-counter (!), push-pull gearlever and central stressed bulkhead. (Picture: Allan Staniforth)

Engine permitted rear bay flex when used as stressed member. Separate bolt-in strut required.

Steering arms fabricated from $\frac{1}{8}$ inch mild steel plate cracked. Original Mini forged items substituted.

Supercharger manifold fitted with intercooler, screen washer pump circulating water through it via a small oil cooler.

Design criteria

Before jumping in at the deep end for a particular design approach, there are a

Monopin. The neat and space-efficient installation of a supercharged Honda 4-cylinder motorcycle engine. (Picture: Allan Staniforth).

Monopin. Mini driveshafts, differential and bearings cunningly adapted to accept chain drive – a practical illustration of what can be achieved with a little imagination and ingenuity. (Picture: Allan Staniforth).

number of things on which the compromises must be made, (not including suspension, dealt with in its own chapter).

An educated guess will have to be made at the relative values of weight/tyre grip/acceleration and braking and the consequent weight transfer front to back. Hot on the heels of these come drag and frontal area, bhp and the torque characteristics of the engine.

The importance placed on any of these can vary with the branch of sport in which you are operating. Rear wheel grip off the start line and out of slow corners could be a total priority in hillclimbing, max bhp at peak revs the difference between win and lose on circuits, especially fast ones. A good torquey engine sacrificing bhp at the very top end of its rev range could win on short twisty circuits. Even CanAm sports racer constructors with 6-700bhp available thought it worth fitting different length inlet trumpets to move the engine peak about for different courses.

The drag of a big "banana" wing or full flap is relatively unimportant at

Monopin. The finished car, complete with aerodynamic aids, is a fine example of what can be accomplished by the home-constructor at relatively modest cost. (Picture: Mark Harbord

low speeds where it could be giving a cornering bonus. Ultra soft tyres, ideal for less than a minute on a hillclimb, will almost certainly wear appallingly, overheat, and begin to fall to pieces if asked to cope with racing.

As a useful quick reference when trying to consider a large number of possibilities, let us present them as a table of "fundamentals of performance" with some of the major pros and cons.

Frontal area: Smaller the better. What you haven't got, you don't have to push through the air at any speed.

Drag: The more "slippery" the car the better, *BUT* wings, shovel noses and aerodynamic side pods all have a drag penalty. F1 cars give away huge amounts of top speed to stick down in the corners. You may not have the power to give away.

Power: Max bhp at extreme rpm with wild cams usually extorts a penalty in the mid-range. It also makes a close-ratio box mandatory.

Torque: Can you operate as well with a good torquey middle range motor, especially if you cannot afford a CR box?

Wheel size/tyres: Mini ten inch are going to be lighter, smaller, with less inertia starting or stopping. But ninety per cent of the racing world operates on thirteen inch so that the tyre selection is vastly more varied and accessible secondhand in this size.

Weight/acceleration: No such thing as a car that is too light. Whatever you are going to be doing with it, you are always having to speed it up or slow it down. The heavier it is, the harder are both tasks and the more time they take, not to mention needing better, bigger brakes, and getting rid of the heat they generate.

Centre of Gravity: The lower the better. Rally extinguishers, mandatory and heavy, placed high on the rollcage tubes, seats that could be lowered an inch or so, batteries, fuel pumps, coils and tanks higher than they need be – all bad.

While it is frequently asked "how can half an inch in the centre of gravity or a few pounds possibly make any difference?" records, grid positions, class wins and FTDs are often won and lost by hundredths of a second. Tenths are commonplace. You cannot even stop a digital watch to a chosen tenth, let alone a hundredth, the interval is so tiny. Therefore everything counts towards the "racer's edge".

If a driver wins despite a less than demon engine, or bodywork resembling a poorly designed garden shed, he will be faster still without those handicaps. This becomes extremely relevant when you realise that several annual championships are not calculated on outright wins, but on a points system based on existing class records. Overall victory needs more than a win on the day, especially

should it be wet and slow. It needs speeds or times that equal or excel the best anyone has ever done at any time. And that has to be the ultimate opposition.

Fitting everything in

Whether you are going monocoque or tube or modifying an existing car in seating or suspension departments there are certain "critical minimums" that have to be established.

The ones that normally cannot be altered at all are the engine/gearbox unit and you (subject only to your weight mentioned in a moment).

Once you have calculated the correct pickup points for suspension these should not be moved *at all*. If it appears impossible to get one of them in the spot where it is designed to go, you have made a mistake or the original designer was on a different track. Under no circumstance move it "just a little to clear" but alter other things to accept your design points. If you wish to experience some mysterious and possibly awful feeling in the car later on that cannot be pinned down to anything in particular, moving suspension pickups about is the ideal approach.

At the very worst you have got to start again with the String Computer (see Chapter 3) or whatever other method you employ to decide the geometry and make the best you can of the position forced on you by circumstances. If it is your own design this really should not happen. The chassis is there simply to locate suspension points, keep the engine firmly in place, accept strong brackets for seats, steering, pedals, plus all minor but essential bits and pieces needed to make it complete. it is *NOT* there to dictate the position of these, but to accept them and do its job of holding them all rigidly and accurately in space.

As you are the human being who is going to be involved, your own vital dimensions must be obtained. These may not be what immediately spring to your mind, but the importance of these and the difficulties caused when one driver tries to take the place of another

are amply demonstrated in F1 team car swaps or Le Mans driver changeovers.

Pedals, steering wheel, gearlever and seatbelt are all in the wrong place for the other man. As perfection is the modest aim here, they must all fit you exactly. The dimensions required are detailed in the accompanying drawing. You get them by putting your crash helmet on, gripping a steering wheel of the correct diameter for the car and steering leverages, suitably composing yourself on the floor of garage or kitchen, while wife, girlfriend or mechanic wields a tape measure.

Most people's gearlever hand will want to be about level with the knee, and be sure that when the gearlever movement requires it, the elbow has somewhere to go. My seat in every car has been offset slightly to the right for a left-hand gearchange, but while obvious to paddock prowlers I am never aware of it once things are moving. This is much less important with a Hewland or motorcycle box, both of which have relatively tiny and light movements of the lever and can almost be operated with the little finger while the hand is still on the wheel.

The seat shape of internal monocoque panelling will probably dictate a slight knees bent position. This makes the operation of foot pedals both easier and more sensitive, while the pedals themselves should be floor mounted rather than pendant if at all possible. This is because the foot is pivoting on the heel (surprise surprise) and if the pedal is pendant it is moving on an arc that takes it away from that of the foot rather than coinciding with it. The foot then has to rise or scrape downwards across the pedal pad. As you have hopefully put a highly abrasive surface on the pad (glued on a rectangle of aluminium oxide paper) to avoid slipping off at some critical moment, your foot does not want to do this.

Having got all this right, changing your shoes may upset it. When a friend bought his first pair of "proper" racing boots at great expense, he could not understand the next time out why the car gave a convulsive leap forward every time he did a smooth change down. Trying to be smoother still only made it worse. Finally he cottoned on to the fact that the beautiful new boots

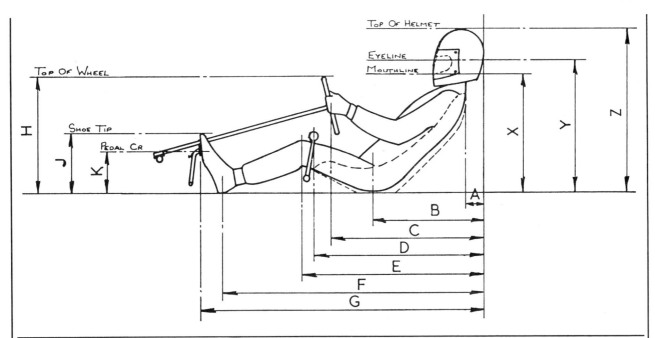

All driver-related dimensions shown in this illustration are important, but three are vital and must fit your personal physique if you are to be fast and comfortable.

They are: 1) The top of the steering wheel rim – as soon as this rises above the mouth, it will intrude into the field of vision; 2) Gearlever knob in every gear, and elbow clearance when moving backwards; 3) Height of pedal pads and their arcs of movement

Time spent now in remaking seat
or steering column brackets, heel supports and elbow space will be richly rewarded later. If you drive for a works team they would insist on this tailoring. Why behave less well to yourself?

Other decisions will include bent knees or straight, gearknob/wheel clearance 'A' might helpfully be at least doubled to permit seat movement rearwards for some taller driver.

Example dimensions for 5ft 8in driver (using datums of seat pad and rear of helmet radius):

A	–	to shoulder = 3in.
B	–	hip joint = 21in.
C	–	steering wheel centre = 29.5in.
D	–	gear/lever knob = 31in.
E	–	kneecap = 34.5in.
F	–	heel contact = 49.5in.
G	–	boot sole – 54in.
H	–	top edge of wheel – 21in.
J	–	boot toe tip = 11in
K	–	pedal pad height = 8in.
X	–	mouthline = 22in.
Y	–	eyeline = 25in.
Z	–	helmet top = 30in.

(Drawing: Darell Staniforth).

had a small heel unlike the villainous and vintage tennis pumps in which he had previously encased his feet. The new heel just caught the accelerator as he braked and gave the throttle an unwanted and unexpected blip. He cured it of course, but without revealing whether it was by bending the pedal, sawing bits off his new boots or having an operation on his leg to alter the angle of his right foot!

The slight knees bent position could mean your legs coming up to interfere with the steering wheel rim, particularly with your hands on it as you undertake some brilliant cross-hands work at a stress-filled moment. No way do you want this, so you raise the steering wheel and it then hits a body panel or worse still starts intruding into your eyeline – the most critical thing of the lot. Everything

ahead of a driver that is above the level of his mouth will most certainly intrude badly into his field of vision under one situation or another. In practice an eleven inch wheel will avoid all this for most people, and give sensitive reasonably light steering, but a glance in many monocoque cars will show they are down to a nine inch wheel, which really is small once you get on the move. It can make keeping the car straight without overcorrecting on a bumpy high speed course with perhaps a gusty cross-wind more than tricky.

Safety harness

Putting a safety harness in the first Terrapin was quite a pioneering move, and even obtaining one not easy. You
now have only to put suitable pickups for belts into the chassis and buy one of half a dozen on the market. The reason for doing so is the same as always – self protection. Buy the best you can afford, not because the cheaper ones are weaker or are going to break, but because the more expensive ones have much better and simpler locking and adjustment devices on them. It not only saves a lot of messing about threading yourself in and out, but may just be vital to getting you out in a hurry if something awful happens.

If you can find an aircraft breaker's yard, and they do exist, you can save yourself a lot of money getting a genuine RAF harness. It is unlikely to have a crutch strap, but I made mine from a saloon car diagonal strap pattern suitably chopped up.

You need to think hard about the mounting points. As a guide, I have used $\frac{1}{4}$ inch plate threaded for $\frac{7}{16}$ inch bolts or a sandwich of two $\frac{1}{8}$ inch plates with $\frac{3}{8}$ inch HT bolt through both. Most important is where and how they are brazed to chassis tubes or riveted into the monocoque. Ideally there should be "progressive collapse" in a bad impact in which brackets will tend to bend the mountings under great stress rather than rip out.

This is much easier to achieve with a tube frame than a monocoque and I have seen one bad accident involving the latter in which various mounting brackets ripped out completely. The shoulder straps stayed attached to their massive alloy plate perfectly well, but the plate itself came partly away from the rivets and screws connecting it to the tub. There is no easy or one hundred per cent assurance. You just have to go back along the line looking for the weakest link – and try to have your accident going backwards rather than forwards and least of all upside down, if you get a choice.

One of the really surprising things about a lot of chassis is that while the rules make a rollover bar mandatory as well as a suitable bracing tube to stop it collapsing backwards or forwards if the car turns over, the full utilisation of this as a fundamental part of the chassis is often ignored. Yet putting in forward braces as well as rearward ones with a suitably designed point down the side of the cockpit can radically raise the stiffness of the frame. This is covered in much greater detail in the description of how it was done on the 80/81 1600 car.

Wishbones/links

Moving on to wishbones, they need to be as rigid as possible in themselves without hoping the chassis pickup points will do part of the job. Force of circumstances and available supplies at the time meant my first car used entirely female spherical (Rose) joints, bolted to the wishbones through plain bushes rather than the more conventional male joints screwed into a threaded bush employed on the majority of cars. I now feel this can be the best approach if the design will permit it, even though a slight "dog-leg" end does not look, and theoretically *is* not, perfect.

Against this the "pros" include:

1) A change of a dozen or so "S" quality $\frac{3}{8}$ inch bolts during the winter rebuild effectively renews the major stress points in the suspension at much less cost than a dozen new joints.

2) It is much easier to throw an apparently unharmed bolt into the scrap bin than a similar spherical joint at twenty times the price when you are double checking the results after an excursion up a kerb or into a bank.

3) Size-for-size the bolt shank, in proper tension within the support of the bush, is several times stronger than a similar sized male threaded shank of a joint. Experience has shown that the bolt will bend where a joint will snap, which means it is at least still connected to the car.

Only for perfect straight line loads does it have to be a male joint.

As far as joints currently on the market are concerned an outline guide to some of the commoner types, as well as strength and quality comparisons will be found in an appendix.

Buy the best joints you can afford but not for the apparently obvious reason of outright strength. The more expensive ones resist corrosion very much better and have a longer life before going rattly. This fault can arrive with only minimal wear. Two thou between ball and housing will convince an alert scrutineer that the wheel is going to fall off shortly and it may be difficult to change his mind.

Nearly all now have an interliner between ball and housing of some sort (joints not scrutineers). While this is excellent for wear qualities it means that the ball may be physically small enough to come right out of its housing if there is enough sideways strain. As long as it is held each side by a sandwich bracket this does not matter. If this is not the case, a large diameter washer should be used on the "open" side to prevent it happening.

The wishbones are the "expendable" part of the car that hopefully will take most of the shock and damage in an accident, preventing major and expensive damage to frame or monocoque.

As they are likely to be one-offs in the sense that spares will not be on the shelf of your enthusiastic British Leyland or Datsun dealer it is as well to make a simple jig or jigs for all the suspension links when first building them. The time taken will be easily recouped in the construction of the links, the accuracy will be better, and spares can be very rapidly made in confidence that they will fit properly.

The jig I use is built on a piece of $\frac{3}{4}$ inch blockboard (an old kitchen unit door is excellent). Some thought will show that more complex angles and bush positions can be incorporated by moving the various brackets. Keep a set of requisite nuts and bolts with the jig, as they will all get red hot at some stage and you do not want them to wander back into your nut and bolt stores and thence on to the car somewhere after they have given the best of their tensile strength to the welding torch flame.

The method employed with the jig makes the very awkward job of cutting and angle recessing round tube quite easy. Make all the bushes first and remember they *MUST* be faced off square in a lathe on the ends so that when the joint is attached the joint shank, bush and bolt should be, when torqued up, virtually a solid piece of bar. This will not be achieved if the bush end is not true and flat. The bushes are then bolted to the jig brackets and pieces of round tube cut generously long to go from one to another. A little experiment will show you can cut and file a good fit so that the tube will almost keep itself in position and a small block of metal on either side will hold it put while you generously tack braze each end. Put every tube in place and complete as much as possible of each joint before moving it out of the jig and finishing all brazing on the bench.

As your life is going to hang, all too literally, on the wishbones or links you may prefer a more talented person than yourself (with a welding torch that is) to do all the final brazing. You can safely do all the tacking in position because your tacks will melt on the completion of the joints. All the bushes and joints should be at such an angle that there is a large area of braze on each one.

Even in an accident sufficiently violent to tear a wheel off, none of my attached bushes failed or pulled off, although in one case the wishbone tube itself was torn into two pieces alongside a brazed joint that stayed in one piece!

The alternative of arc welding them all will need some skill from the welder to avoid risks of distortion in the finished article. That's your problem and his, not mine.

Bulkheads

Whether a tube chassis or a monocoque is involved it will have certain bulkheads or stations in it where loads are collected and distributed in various ways. The three main types are: tube with proper triangulation and/or sheeting, a solid plate, or a casting. Both of the latter are technically completely rigid and admirably suited to footwell, front and rear of monocoque, rear of a tube chassis and firewall behind the driver. Good – but not quite as good – is a diaphragm bulkhead beloved of aircraft designers even in this day and age, the sort that has the skin perforated with biggish neat rounded edge holes. Laborious to make but strong for the weight.

Of similar strength, and faster to make, is a tube-type bulkhead triangulated all round with small tube: effectively a twin of the diaphragm pattern but generally heavier.

My original Terrapin had diaphragms behind the engine and at the driver's knees. The latter had no tubes across for the obvious reason that my legs were in the way, but at the back of the car I had a feeling that if the differential was left open and accessible it would be possible to do a rapid change of the final drive. This proved a bit of a pious hope and a later car had pure triangulated bulkheads. As this part of the car carries the very heaviest loads, the tube arrangement also permitted better dispersal of them.

Any car using the engine/gearbox as a stressed unit has everything dangling from specially cast lips. In my view this has a number of shortcomings. The loads are doing their very best to twist the power unit into any shape but its proper one, and it cannot be too good an idea to put sundry shafts, bearings and the crank out of line even if we are only speaking of a couple of thou. Secondly, cast-in lugs on the engine and gearbox dictate totally your suspension geometry for the life of the car. Any alteration will of necessity involve building little frames everywhere and praying there will be convenient studs or bolts on which to hang them.

While a stressed engine/transmission unit can mean better accessibility and a slight weight saving, it seems less than perfect, and often totally unsuitable when using a unit that was never designed to accept suspension loadings in the first place. The engine anyway will always be doing its best to tear itself out of its supports in any competition car, and suitable stays and mountings need a lot of thought.

Very many cars with Ford production iron blocks have to hang them from the centre in some sort of fabricated cradle. Study of a few will show that they are admirable while the car is standing still in the paddock but a good deal less so when the reaction of acceleration is trying to rotate the whole engine between them.

One part of the car that depends to a great extent on regulation as opposed to pure design ideals is the side pods or panelling. Some formulae require a "deformable structure" down each side to protect the driver from side impact, while others do not. Without a test schedule that would involve you in somehow sliding your pride and joy sideways into a calibrated concrete pole and measuring the resultant wreckage, some rough rules of thumb will have to be accepted.

Regulations may specify a thickness. If they do, fine. If not, a minimum of 4 inches with a practical maximum of perhaps 12 inches is one bracket in which to aim. The general approach is that you build a hollow box on the side of the car and fill it with rigid foam. Most fibre glass firms supply this material in the form of two containers of liquid. Once they are mixed they boil up into a space-monster-type creeping froth that pours into all the nooks and crannies – and out of them and all over you if you are too generous with quantities – and then sets. Hey presto! A rigid deformable structure.

It will have already occurred to keener students that all this can be very readily adapted to the construction of an aerodynamic wing section on the bottom face of the side pod.

Less convenient if you planned to put an oil tank, radiator, battery, or fire extinguisher where the foam is going and there will have to be a rethink. It may be possible to put in a suitable recess or ducting especially if the foam is very thick.

If using foam remember that while it is very light it still weighs about 2lbs a cubic foot and, consequently, will add to the final overall weight of your creation.

Nuts, bolts & Dzus

In the beginning there was only one thread, that of the first bolt and nut, but it did not take humanity long to start multiplying it in a big way. First craftsmen and then countries produced their own specifications with small variations that contributed little to strength or efficiency but made dead sure they didn't match those of the hated opposition.

The first Industrial Revolution was largely held together by Imperial threads; BSF and BSW (British Standard Fine and Coarse) plus a huge proliferation of gas, bicycle, pipe, electrical, ultra-fine and special versions. Even as late as 1959 the introduction of the Mini brought with it a mysterious thread for the flywheel centre bolt that seems to be unique, probably the result of a single tap and die of unknown parentage found under a bench during the creation of the prototype ....

Neither the New Americans nor the beastly foreigners across the Channel fancied aping the British, hence American National Fine and Coarse and Metric Fine and Coarse, American Gas, French Bicycle, etc, etc. After some 150 years of serious industrial battle, it looks as though Metric may win in the end, and if you are starting from the beginning anywhere but in the States, you would probably be well advised to build a stock and spanner kit around Metric.

All are marked in a variety of ways, but the human eye is still the best and fastest sorter once it has been familiarised with the variations. Most important is how to distinguish quality in a bolt that is going to hold your life in its threads; excellent from average or rubbish?

In general, the quality of the steel, marked in some code on the bolt head and nut side, is your guide. If you cannot find anything, then throw it away (other than ex-aircraft industry stock which you always use if they come your way. They are quite certain to be better quality, more resistant to corrosion, more accurately made and often lighter).

As a rough guide my own car is almost entirely held together with "S" quality fittings, the type of steel widely used in industry and that normally supplied in any purchase. If in need of a particularly strong nut, those fitted to engine big ends and main bearing studs are admirable. Go to "T" quality bolts (cap or socket head type) for really dramatic load situations if you are worried. (Torque setting guide in appendices will give more detail.)

A small but great timesaving point once the car is running is the way panels and bodywork are to be attached. The quickest and crudest, worst looking and most unsatisfactory after a very short time are self-tapping screws. A few moments with a correct size drill and they are in place. You can then spend the rest of the season having them vibrate loose, eat holes in your panelling, fall into the grass in the paddock and disappear at the most inconvenient times.

Small bolts and nuts are generally not a great deal better than self-tappers except in being more secure, but more awkward too as locknuts are essential.

It is really no contest against the ubiquitous and rightly famed Dzus. Their trouble is that they are a major job to fix in the first place and ideally the base plates, which carry the "S" spring into which the outer section

locks, need to be brazed permanently into the chassis while it is being built. But however long and awkward a job, they will repay you again and again and again in reliability and saved time and frustration. Recently Dzus have developed a plastic version, easier to fit and very much more tolerant of varying thicknesses in the panels being joined together.

One other type of fastener that can be extremely well adapted, particularly to the front bodywork, are "rally bonnet pins". Buyable in chrome plated kits, the pin is attached to the chassis either projecting horizontally forward or any other angle up to vertical. Of necessity it projects through the panel and the lock pin is not only visible but not too aerodynamic either. Nonetheless efficient and not unattractive aesthetically.

Getting started

We have now covered enough ground to provide a format and approach for anyone planning to go it alone either from the basic heap of tube and invaluable rusty spares lying on the garage floor, or with the recently purchased dream car that was so good in somebody else's hands.

This all assumes you will have to employ major components produced for other cars by someone in no way thinking of you or your design plans. These will almost certainly include wheels, uprights, axle, engine and gearbox. As these are going to impose certain dimensions and approaches, the planning sequence is highly likely to be as follows:

1) Uprights and Links. It can be very difficult and time consuming to try and alter the pickup points on uprights. Far better to accept what you already have or can buy reasonably, and design your suspension geometry around it (see Chapter 3). The pattern of studs on the average hub is not nearly so difficult to modify but if employing a Mini 4 inch PCD or Ford 4.25 inch 4 stud approach it will be made easier to acquire suitable wheels than if you have some exotic arrangement.

2) Wheels: Effectively dictated by

tyres. The only decision is 10 inch or 13 inch in view of the present tyre supply situation. A 10 inch wheel and tyre is better, superior in a number of ways – smaller, lighter, with a lower flywheel effect on acceleration or deceleration – BUT tyre selection is extremely limited. 13 inch will open the door to three-quarters of the racing tyres made in the last twenty years. Normally this might be the professional's first decision not second.

3) Geometry design will provide the position of the inboard wishbone pickups (see Chapter 3 on these).

4) Sketches of driver, engine and gearbox can be made and perhaps cut out of cardboard to a known scale. Using graph paper start drawing your chassis or shell with a colour code employing different ball point pens to avoid a total visual shambles. Views needed will be a side and top plus head or tail or for each bulkhead for a racer. Aim at the longest straight runs of tube or monocoque section you can get as well as the best true triangulation in the relationship between rollcage and shell surrounding it.

5) The ratio between track and wheelbase: can be calculated as WB over TR (eg 85 inches over 53 inches = 1.6:1). It usually falls within the 1.4 to 1.7 bracket but an ideal figure is like that of the ideal woman: hard to find and even harder to define. Not only is this ratio much argued at the design stage but it can even be altered in various crafty ways once a car is actually running. One method is to insert a big spacer casting between the engine and gearbox, thus pushing the rear axle line back by that amount. A more recent ploy is to replace front suspension wishbones with alternatives that point forward or backwards from the inboard pivots. This is not as difficult as it sounds and four wishbones are certainly quicker and easier to make than another car. Applicable to sports cars but a lot more difficult with saloons.

6) Build a balsa wood model (all raw material from a local model shop) to about $\frac{1}{8}$ or 1/10 scale, using $\frac{1}{16}$ inch and $\frac{1}{8}$ inch square for tubing, $\frac{1}{32}$ inch sheet for alloy panelling and $\frac{1}{8}$ inch sheet to represent honeycomb sandwich. Some balsa block will also be needed for a rough outline model of

the engine and gearbox. This will do two things particularly well for the non-engineer. It stops you building something in which it later proves impossible to insert the required engine and gearbox and it allows very realistic estimates both of stiffness and, if things are going to bend, where they will do so.

Although the theory of outboard bracing with a rigid horizontal deck beside the cockpit was most certainly known to, and employed by, various constructors in the early sixties it is rather mysterious why the 1980s F1 cars, for example, appear to have only a very slender midriff: particularly vulnerable to twisting forces from extremely stiff "anti-ground effects" suspension.

With the balsa model you can insert or cut out experimentally any of the chassis tubes or sheeting and thus do on the kitchen table a tolerable stress job that would require professionally a draughtsman, a B.Sc. (Eng) and ten grand's worth of equipment. This may sound a gross over-simplification but the Mk. 1 Terrapin was done this way, and whatever has gone wrong with Terrapins over the years, chassis failure has not been a fault, despite at least three major accidents. At the same time it is still one of the lightest chassis running in the class, while having to carry one of the heaviest engine units.

7) Mark on the model or plan unalterable points – where the wishbones will join it – and be certain there is space for the bushes, Rose joints etc, to go in, come out and rotate through a scale four or five inches of outboard movement without hitting anything. It is also essential, even at this early stage, to consider where some other major components will go including the fuel tank, battery, radiator(s) and oil tank (if dry sumped). Small alterations, or a planned lightweight subframe incorporated now may be the saving of your sanity later on!

8) Using very thin cardboard, we can now attempt some tentative body panelling, aiming in general at the low-nosed dart profile, with a gradually increasing side area as it goes rearwards towards large wing end plates, whether integral with the car or

independently hanging from the wing itself. This approach is a simple but most useful help towards a car that will in due course run true and be stable in a straight line.

The little things

Having got this far, we are perilously near having to go into the garage or workshop and begin physical toil. Before doing so write out on a piece of cardboard in large letters "I will never, never, NEVER put bending loads into the middle of a tube or panel" and hang it up where you will read it every day.

The next necessity, or perhaps logically the first, is a decent roof over one's head, and if at all possible some modest source of heat. As these sort of projects tend to be winter ones, or even two winter ones with a cool summer between, a little warmth can be the difference between working and stopping. Although I once built two successive specials in garages that had only a tiny paraffin stove directly under the bench vice, this was simple lack of cash rather than a love of the hair shirt.

Talking about a vice, a solid bench to which it will be attached is also a must.

Finally you need a selection of hand tools. There is a suggested list among the appendices at the back, but I cannot emphasise enough that you buy the best you can afford, including those acquired apparently only for one job. They will extend the range of what you do without having to give someone money to do it for you, a basic principle for the impecunious enthusiast, and they truly come into their own when a job needs doing at a time of the day or night when even money cannot persuade someone else to take any interest at all.

While not strictly a tool, a crack testing kit of the type that uses a cleaner, a dye and white powder detector like Ardrox can be most useful even if only to reassure one about a valve, conrod or crank.

Although we are now a two-electric-drill-family, plus a small vintage lathe, I built my first three

specials with only a hand drill and never having seen a lathe, remarkable as that may sound. Like the cold garage, those were aspects of too little cash, rather than a lust for hard labour.

There is one more thing before work begins – a building table or flat true platform for the chassis, shell or four wheels of your vehicle. A table is not utterly essential but is an enormous help, if only to avoid attacks of housemaid's knee as you creep and grovel about on a freezing concrete floor during the building, and will result in a much more accurately made chassis. The simplest approach if you don't know anyone with a suitable table they are keen to lend is an 8 foot x 4 foot x ¾ inch sheet of blockboard supported on a slotted angle frame with six legs. Each leg is made of two overlapping sections allowing the length to be adjustable. This means the working surface can be set perfectly horizontal with a spirit level before work begins, however mountainous your garage floor.

As the whole thing can later be converted into a set of trendy shelves, a wardrobe or a room divider, you should have no difficulty in convincing your wife, or housekeeper, of the wisdom of this purchase at least.

Apart from having an accurate flat surface to which you can screw or clamp the bottom rails of the chassis and keep a constant eye on its truth as it is assembled, it also serves as somewhere to sketch wishbones or the exact outline of that young maiden in the paddock, stand coffee cups, and rest your thumb-marked copy of this masterpiece on as you go along.

Blockboard is, incidentally, quite reluctant to burn, and should you scorch it while brazing will only emit smoke and a terrible stench. Wipe your eyes, dab the burned bit with a wet cloth and get on with it.

No doubt everyone has his own system of working, but a couple of observations on mine may be helpful. To keep some sort of order in things, I use a clipboard hanging on a garage wall nail, ruled into three vertical columns. The first identifies the job to be done, the second any dimensions, part numbers etc needed, and the third what must be bought or otherwise acquired.

JOB	PARTS (New-S/H)	BUY/MAKE
Front hubs/brakes overhaul.	Brg. nos. Lining type and number Oil seals ditto.	New shoes, stove enamel backplates.

Not the least advantage of this is the pleasure of crossing them off when completed and it allows a Gemini like me to keep moving temporarily to some other task when bored with the original without forgetting it completely.

Much of the foregoing, apart from the building table, will apply whether you are creating a single seater, modifying a sports racer, rebuilding an ageing Can-Am beast, or creating your own rally car from a shell.

Using the rollcage

The other thing common to all such projects and equally important to them all is stiffness and still more stiffness (as the Actress may have said reproachfully to the Bishop). Do not accept what other people say or have done. Devote some thinking to the project, how it is already made, how the rules may be utilised to your advantage, if there are apparent restrictions to what is permitted.

Perhaps the most brilliant example of this in recent years was the use of the rollcage in American saloon car racing. Saloons when raced or rallied are notorious for revealing weaknesses in the design of the stressed shell, betraying by a continuing series of cracks anywhere and everywhere, that they have too much to do and are crying "enough!"

The US approach was to design a spaceframe of great strength and sophistication which was then welded inside the 200mph saloons at every critical point. From the point of view of scrutineers and rule makers it was simply a rollcage as required by the safety regulations to protect the driver in the event of one of the notably impressive crashes that happen on the US Ovals. For good measure they welded up the doors "for safety" as well which did the stiffness of the shell

no harm at all.

Much of this same approach is open to British competitors, particularly since rollover bars with bracing struts have become mandatory. You are forced to carry the weight so why not use it. Cursory paddock inspection will show that a surprising number of people still do not.

Two examples should suffice:

1) Saloon regulations often give the choice of either a rollover bar, normally braced backwards to keep it steady in the event of your spending time upside down, or a full cage. The latter requires a second hoop ahead of the driver and running over the top of the screen. Tie bars connect the hoops across the tops of the doors and rear bracing stays are normally duplicated.

You can get far more than safety from this fairly heavy contraption by making sure that its feet sit in the right places, and that the tubes themselves are welded or linked to the shell with bolts and reinforced inserted captive nuts at critically chosen points.

Examine your shell carefully. Plenty of people bolt the feet of the cage straight into the floor panelling (rather thinner and barely more robust than a cigarette packet ...). Either go somewhere else, or reinforce with a welded-in plate of generous area which, if at all possible, turns at right angles somewhere into a different panel.

While awkward, it is worth all the work to put welded-in nuts on the screen pillars. Matching brackets are attached to the cage so that it can be bolted in firmly at these points.

Finally, and perhaps most important is to utilise the rear bracing legs to help prevent the rear suspension, particularly the dampers or the tops of the coil springs, punching their way into the car. Again a carefully thought-out reinforcing plate curved to the wheel arch and braced into any adjacent panel at a different angle can

work a minor miracle. I have always used the cardboard template approach. Make it all in something you can cut about and attach with masking tape before transferring to metal. If you stick to 16g you can – just about – cut it all out yourself with a small wheel cutter sold by some metal merchants. Thicker than this and you will have to find commercial size shears, and even then it is difficult to bend without heat. Attempting it cold has resulted for me in merely loosening the vice on the bench or on one memorable occasion tearing the bench right off its wall brackets!

What might be termed an "invisible" result of all this work will be that the car is highly likely to feel just that bit firmer and more precise in its handling as well as being more reliable. And the dents when you roll it, should not be as bad.

2) The second example, detailed fully in the chapter on the Gould Terrapin is using to the full the mandatory bracing bar on a single-seater or open sports racer. It took even the professionals an extraordinarily long time to bother about the freedom this gave to build a "pyramid" over the rear engine bay, and even longer still to utilise the rigidity that provided to try and do something about the necessarily open bay the driver unfortunately causes.

Forward stays might look wasteful, but they are far from it. As long, that is, as they do not end in the middle of an unsupported tube or on the surface, however beautifully plated and apparently reinforced, of the top face of the tub. It certainly needs a wide horizontal surface, whether the top of the tub, tubular outriggers or a combination of these. But it also needs vertical support, either an internal bulkhead within the tub, or a tube going down to a fully triangulated corner somewhere.

Possibly *THE* foundation of good design for stiffness is never letting anything anywhere anytime just end in thin air. Loads must always go somewhere. If not supported or carried on to a fundamental strong point, they will bend and eventually break the weak part.

They will also allow the suspension points to move in space

and all your brilliant design and creative thinking over the suspension geometry will have gone for nought.

Analysis of your "Best Buy"

What have you bought? Possibly the most difficult situation for all would-be competitors, the majority of whom are not for several hundred good reasons going to build a complete car, is knowing where or how to start improving what they have got.

The first thing is a complete inventory, as detailed as you can make it, of the car as it stands. Engine modifications as has already been said are not covered here but you need to identify as much as possible about the power unit including the camshaft, distributor, carburettor sizes, including all the minor jets, needles, etc., valve size and compression ratio.

Always bear in mind that the man who sold it to you may have thought he was telling you the truth about that demon race cam, or special chokes, or big mains. It could still be duff gen from the man before the man from whom he bought it.

You have to know. If there is more than one carburettor or choke, check them all. Take the head off, and measure compression ratio, valve sizes, and decoke and polish while you are at it. Only then will you be able to think and talk sensibly about how it may be further modified.

The minimum information on a rolling vehicle is as follows:

1) Wheels/tyres – rim width, PCD, tyre tread widths, compound/pattern or type.

2) Dampers – type, max/min length, is one or more of them worn out?

3) Springs – coil free lengths, any colour codes or other markings, rate lbs/inch (ie: how many pounds of force does it need to compress the spring exactly one inch), length and number of leaves, type of ends and axle mountings.

4) Suspension geometry. *Front:* location of pivot points in space seen from head on, both on the upright and the shell or chassis. Dimensions are usually taken outwards from centre line of the car and upwards from ground level with the car at fully loaded normal ride height. Pivot centres of track rod ends. *Rear:* axle bracket dimensions, lengths of any links and wishbones leverage ratios on the spring bottom platforms. Diameter and approximate leverage of any rollbars.

5) Steering – rack and pinion length to rack bar ball centres *(not track rod ends)*, height above ground, turns lock-to-lock. Distance travelled by rack bar for one turn of the steering wheel. This last will allow an instant check on any other "quick" or high ratio rack you might plan to buy, even if it is on a shelf rather than in a car.

6) Final drive/gearbox ratios. Chalk flywheel or engine pulley to count engine revs while pushing the car for exactly one turn of the driven wheels using marked tyres and floor. You should get a set of figures approximating to 12 engine revs in bottom, 8 in second, 5.5 in third, 4 in top. Dividing each figure by top (or final drive ratio) gives actual box ratios.

Bottom, $\frac{12}{4} = 3{:}1$;

Second, $\frac{8}{4} = 2{:}1$;

Third, $\frac{5.5}{4} = 1.375{:}1$;

Top, $\frac{4}{4} = 1{:}1$ (direct).

Given this lot carefully noted down you are in an excellent position to talk to the drivers of other cars, competition departments, breaker's yards, search parts lists and so on, with some hope of finding out what you want. Without them, you have no basis on which even to begin.

The suspension dimensions are essential to analyse what sort of roll centre levels and stability the car has and what happens when the wheels bounce about and the car rolls, and just as important, discover if it is likely to have bump steer at the front or roll steer at the back. (Refer to Chapter 3 for how).

You now have three main approaches:

1) Faithfully copy somebody else's car which puts you exactly where you were before but with a new set of problems ....

2) Use a combination of studying the opposition and your own thinking to decide what is right or acceptable about your own car, what is wrong and what must be altered.

3) Go it alone from a clean sheet of paper.

The difficulty with 1) is that unless you can utilise identical uprights, wheels, tyres, and chassis location points it is quite impossible to copy another suspension. You might as well buy that car and save yourself a lot of hard work.

Option 3) is virtually the preserve of the man designing and building from scratch – although he will almost certainly have to use some dimensions forced on him by proprietary front uprights if nothing else.

Option 2) is the route most people will have to follow and is the one on which the next chapter will hopefully throw most light, and the result of which can be most rewarding.

Never ever feel that because you have bought a car professionally built by a person or company who ought to have known what they were doing, it is perfect. Highly unlikely if only because other owners may have altered things since it left the maker.

One friend of mine was deeply depressed by the appalling handling of a quite immaculate Vixen Imp he had bought and had had set up professionally "ready to go straight off the trailer". The handling threatened to make him old before his time. When a fairly perfunctory check lifting a front wheel up and down in the paddock demonstrated appalling bump steer, he recalled that the previous owner said he had fitted a brand new special high ratio racing rack. He had, but unfortunately it was the wrong length and in the wrong place. Only laborious checking, drawing, relocation and probably having to cut or lengthen the rack bar would cure this, but unless it was done the car would always handle badly.

While on the subject of steering, a high ratio, quick rack and pinion is not necessarily an essential. These units can produce a car so sensitive to corrections that you cannot keep it going in a straight line, particularly on a poor surface. At lower speeds on really bad rally surfaces, the effort involved in moving the wheel together with kickback shocks will tire, if not actually injure a driver all too quickly. My son had his shoulder partially dislocated in exactly this situation.

F1 teams and works rally teams make arrangements to alter the ratios from course to course. A Monaco ratio to deal with two hairpins per lap would be far from ideal on an ultra high speed course like Dijon with corners demanding that the car be balanced and controlled at speeds we amateurs will probably never touch in our lives.

Remote controls

It is unlikely that your purchase will have a cockpit adjustable brake balance bar and very highly unlikely indeed that it will have similarly tuneable roll-bars.

Both can make possible in moments alterations that may otherwise take several minutes and mean removing the bodywork or grovelling on wet ground. The consequence of this slow and awkward approach is that these settings do not get altered at all, and you have given yourself a little built-in handicap against the opposition. On the day when it rains as you roll onto the grid or starting line, both will be worth their weight in gold – or at least pewter if you win.

You can buy a suitable balance bar but they are expensive. The illustration shows one that can be made from bits of plate, a section of redundant speedo cable and the knob that fell off that old radio in the workshop before it stopped working completely.

Anti-roll bars are an altogether more difficult proposition. Given "proper" anti-roll bars (ie: a length of rod or tube turning in needle roller bearings at each extremity), the lever is normally a spring steel blade which can be rotated by a cable from the cockpit. It can then be turned from flat, when it is at its most flexible, through 90 degrees to edge-on when it is virtually solid. Variations in thickness of both blades and the bar to which they are attached give endless combinations of stiffness, but ideally they need an inboard suspension or the rear bodywork of a saloon for any convenience of installation.

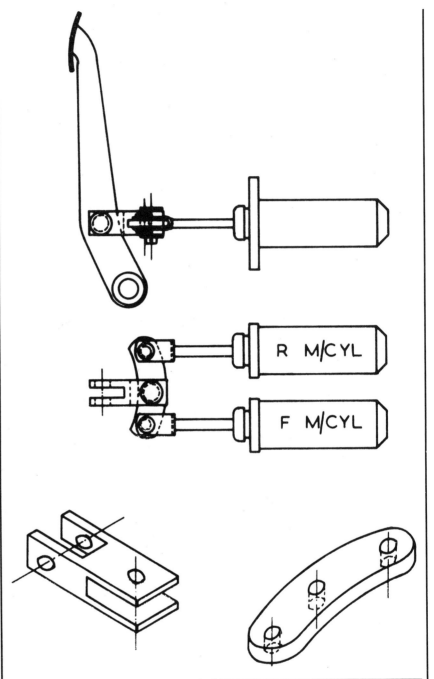

A really effective way to remotely adjust the conventional bar with its attachment link out in the air is awaiting your inventive powers.

Fuel tanks

Fuel tanks are very tightly controlled in some formulae, much less so in others. If at all possible obtain a flexi rubber bag tank. Secondhand are normally in excellent condition in either

Brake balance bar. Adjustment of this type is achieved by making up alternative bars with different offsets to alter front/rear bias. (Drawing: Darell Staniforth).

rectangular shape (for rally cars) or wedge shape to go behind the seat in the single seater.

These have then to have a liquid tight metal box made in which they can sit. The filler and breather tube must go completely outside open or saloon

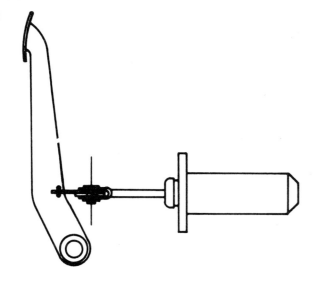

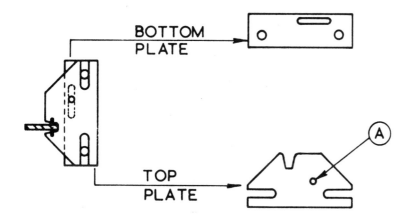

BOTTOM
PLATE

TOP
PLATE

(A)

Brake balance bar. Made up with $\frac{1}{8}$in alloy or steel plates with a locking bolt through hole 'A' when slackened it allows bottom plate to move either way carrying master cylinder pushrods to any chosen front/rear bias. Setting bolt 'A' is then tightened. (Drawing: Darell Staniforth).

bodywork and any fuel feed has to be via metal piping wherever it passes through the cockpit. Visualise a heavy impact accident ending upside down and feel confident that your work will not allow a drop of petrol to get at you. Work put into this is worth much more than any set of fireproof overalls.

Alternatively if it has to be a metal tank, skin it with a generous layer of glass fibre and beef up the mounting brackets or locate it

positively with extra tube or bracing bars.

Finally whether you make radical alterations or leave the car substantially unaltered it will need setting-up and the method and sequence is covered in Chapter 3.

Talking about glass fibre and strength leads logically to some consideration of the huge technological steps that have taken place in materials available to vehicle builders, whether in the air, on water or land.

Honeycomb, carbon fibre & the future

It might be thought that truly exotic materials and the ways in which they can be employed barely have a place

here, but this is not so if only for one excellent reason. The whole history of industrial development shows that today's ultra-expensive "magic product" is very likely, if it has true worth, to be tomorrow's cheap and popular DIY product. While this change of availability takes time to happen in any formal way, it has always been the case that offcuts, aircraft industry rejects and experimental bits and pieces find their way downmarket.

Light alloys of every type (sheet, bar, rod and plate) are an excellent example, and the man intent on modifying his vehicle will already know roughly when he needs 20g aluminium sheet, $\frac{1}{4}$ inch alloy plate, long or short pop rivets or a chunk of bar to be machined by a friend. Much of this was the province of only the technically qualified specialist relatively few years ago.

The materials of nineteen-eighties technology might be loosely described as "sandwich products" in metal, a variety of plastics and wood. In general they are employed in the form of two thin outer skins with an ultra-light filler in between. They arrived on the aircraft scene some 30 years ago, and adhesive and plastic progress accelerated the production of a bewildering variety of skin/filler combinations.

Difficulties attached to these sandwich materials are three-fold: producing them with reliability and controlled quality, knowing how to integrate them properly in any design, and fabricating the final structure successfully.

Their lure for the designer, which has never dimished, whether he be concerned with an ocean-going yacht, aircraft, dinghy or racing car is greater strength and rigidity with less weight. As simple as that, and sandwich combinations currently offer higher strength/weight and stiffness/weight ratios than any structure known.

When a simple list of skins includes light alloy, stainless steel, plywood, glass or Kevlar laminates, combined with fillers of solid foam, balsa wood, alloy foil and paper or Nomex honeycomb, you see complications ahead, becoming ever more complex particularly in the field of adhesives where the technical

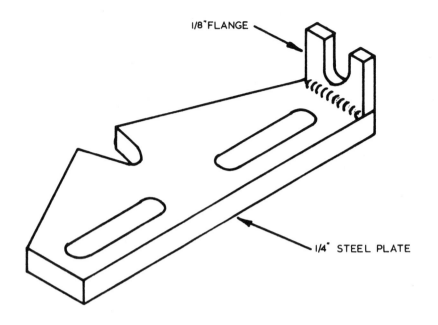

1/8"FLANGE

1/4" STEEL PLATE

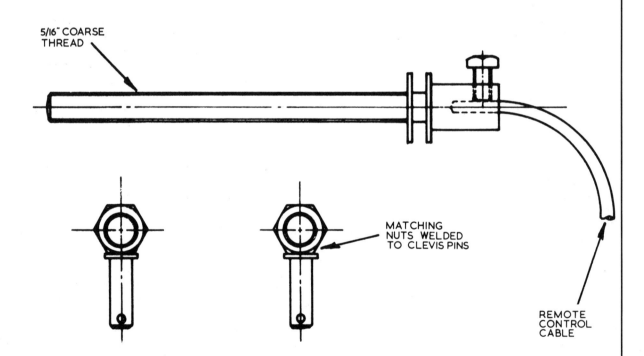

5/16" COARSE
THREAD

MATCHING
NUTS WELDED
TO CLEVIS PINS

REMOTE
CONTROL
CABLE

Brake balance bar. This has a single plate instead of the double plate shown in the previous version. Clevis pin position is altered by rotation of the threaded rod, therefore altering front/rear bias. (Drawing: Darell Staniforth).

variations are simply enormous (a file four inches thick in the case of one expert in the field).

Whatever the results the name of the game is "synergistics", loosely translated as the art of making two and two add up to at least six, and preferably ten. The makers are already

achieving this all the time, and knowing a little about their products may well permit you, for instance, to employ several hundred pounds worth of honeycomb alloy aircraft flooring — at scrap value by weight — as a stressed rear bulkhead in a saloon racer or rally car.

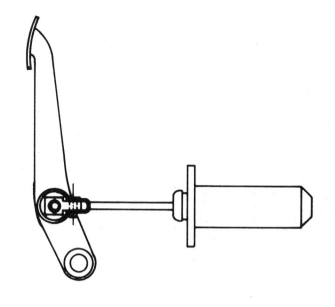

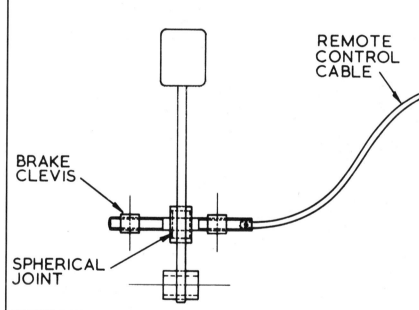

REMOTE
CONTROL
CABLE

BRAKE
CLEVIS

SPHERICAL
JOINT

stabilise one relatively thin strip of metal in relation to another with something at least equally light filling the gap, you gained rigidity out of all proportion to the sum of the basic trio, the industrial steel "H" or "I" girder being an excellent example.

Doing the same with large areas of flat thin sheet posed the question of what to use as a filler and how to persuade it to stay permanently in place between the two sheets. Wood was obvious and easy, rigid foam less so, metal foil or paper difficult indeed. As so often before, the money available for aircraft experiment and research fuelled the drive for success. It came in the form of a two-fold achievement: mass-production of a honeycomb web of ultra-thin metal foil, and heat-setting glues in thin film sheets.

In somewhat simplistic terms they were used thus: on the bottom sheet of the outer skin is placed a sheet of glue film. Onto this goes the web of honeycomb, followed by a second glue film and then the outer skin. All this is done in a chamber in which the pressure can be lowered or pressure-bags can inflate against the sheet. With either method, the outer skins are pressed into perfect contact with the honeycomb cell edges.

Heat then melts the glue film so it flows perfectly around the ends of tens of thousands of cells before setting. Beam strength and torsional rigidity is increased gigantically over that of the original parts. Just how gigantically can be appreciated by the fact that an F1 car built with such material would

Brake balance bar. This type is often used by professionals and is similar in principle to the previous type, but uses threaded rod as balance bar with clevis mounted on a threaded bush. Spherical joint in pedal allows rod to be rotated thus altering front/rear bias. (Drawing: Darell Staniforth).

It will become clear that to try and categorise such things in any simple way is very difficult because new variations are making them ever less exactly defined. However we have to start somewhere, and they will be

broken down into the following sub-divisions: 1) Metal honeycombs; 2) GRP; 3) Aramids (Kevlar); 4) Carbon-fibre; 5)Polyesters; 6) Hybrids.

1) Metal Honeycomb: Engineers have long understood that if you could

The construction of a 'Cellite' sandwich panel with its aluminium foil honeycomb giving a tensile strength of 11 tons per square inch. (Drawing: Technical Resin Bonders Ltd).

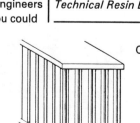

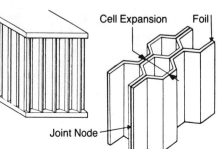

Cell Expansion   Foil

Joint Node

Gould honeycomb monocoque. Proof positive that ambitious schemes can be carried out in a private garage — even without room to swing a very small kitten! Note the wooden baseboard and formers and the use of Avdel clips to temporarily hold panels in place. (Picture: Allan Staniforth).

Roll bar mounting shows the superb quality of detail on the Gould car. (Picture: Allan Staniforth).

be using for its major panels two 20g skins attached to honeycomb $\frac{1}{2}$ inch deep formed from foil barely thicker than that protecting the average cigarettes .... Hence the reaction of one supplier when approached in the research stage of the Gould monocoque car, (the enquiry was a complete guess and for something about an inch thick with 18g skins); "What are you making — a bloody Chieftain tank?"

Later refinements allowed a choice for F1 constructors of main load-bearing panels of every sort into the regions of 22g to 30g skins weighing only about 1lb per square foot. And should it be required, as long as the two skins are correctly bent, the production of single curvature panels thickness that is required and that is that. The resin sets chemically and irrevocably. You then pull your moulding out, trim the edges and the job is complete.

The mould in which it has been shaped is normally produced by first making a full-sized model in clay, wood or metal, and then laying up resin and glass on it to form the required shape which is permanently stabilized by bonding to it a wood or metal frame.

Anyone who has tried all this, will realise I have managed one of the great over-simplifications of all time in relation to what can be a revolting and laborious task, but only comprehension of the principle is presently required.

The first really dramatic step-up in strength in every way is to abandon CSM (chopped strand matting) in favour of "woven roving" in which the glass, bunched into untwisted strands is turned into something like rough sacking. Another jump comes with the employment of properly woven cloth in a variety of finishes and thicknesses. Instead of short glass strands lying around every which way in CSM, the cloth manufacture is controlled in weave pattern, fibre diameter, and recently the introduction of several qualities of the glass itself.

In somewhat basic terms, this was about the state of the art when new materials that could be used for reinforcement in place of fibre glass arrived.

3) Kevlar. A great grandson of Nylon, and related to the famed Nomex, its full title for car use is "Kevlar 49" and all types are creations of the chemical giant Du Pont. It is an aramid fibre (no more than a sensible contraction of aromatic polyamide which itself is a great improvement over the full name of polyparaphenylene terephthalamide), it has the virtues of being better than glass in almost every way. Two results of using Kevlar are a moulding up to 30% lighter than GRP for the same strength, and a handsome bump up in cost.

In general it is woven and used in exactly the same way as glass, even looking similar but for its characteristic and rather violent yellow colour. Because of its toughness (a related version goes into bullet-proof jackets)

Projecting lugs of alloy plate let into honeycomb sandwich are front engine mountings. The covering panel is glued and riveted to honeycomb sandwich. (Picture: Allan Staniforth).

presents little more difficulty than that of flat ones.

2) Fibre glass. The colloquial and collective term we all use for what is more correctly called GRP – glass reinforced plastic. Familiar now in hundreds of ways, including boats, wheel arch flares, garage roof panels and a myriad sets of racing bodywork. In case some reader has been residing well away from popular technology for a quarter of a century, glass fibre in its cheapest and commonest form of chopped strand mat looks not unlike Shredded Wheat spread out in a flat sheet.

You utilise it in a female (or reversed shape) mould of the object you wish to make. Into this is laid resin, glass mat, more resin, more glass in successive alternating layers up to the

These three pictures show the construction of the engine compartment and rear bulkhead of the Gould car. Note how the open ends of the honeycomb sandwich were closed with thick alloy plates pre-drilled and tapped for the bulkhead fixings – the large holes are just to lighten the plates. (Pictures: Allan Staniforth).

it poses difficulties in cutting at every stage. You will have to acquire tungsten carbide blades and other tools to manage it effectively, but it does have the not unimportant advantage of not irritating the skin like glass.

4) Carbon fibre. In atom form, one of the basics of Planet Earth and life, including this book, the graphite in pencil lead and you. Improbable as the idea of woven pencil leads may be, it has been accomplished and carbon fibre cloth can be bought and used in exactly the same way as GRP or Kevlar. Why? Because it is a further step forward in rigidity for a given weight, but with some complications to do with its composition.

These led rapidly to experiments in combining it with Kevlar and glass, all of which may be mixed in the weaving stage to produce cloths tailored very specifically to deal with certain jobs. They can be particularly impact resistant, ultra-strong in one direction, strong and rigid, or strong and flexible. You will see from this that talk of their being both exotic and difficult for the designer is not entirely a smokescreen.

Casting the fibres into resin rods or discs will produce stiffening beams, golf club and tennis racket handles, and featherweight brake discs. When a 12 inch rod of anything of $\frac{1}{2}$ inch diameter can be held in a vice, bent over at 45 degrees and will then spring back straight as if nothing has happened, you know you are looking at something remarkable ...

5) Polyester. What this material lacks in rigidity it more than makes up for in a willingness to go round a double curvature and resist sharp impact damage. Highly esteemed among builders of canoes for the hairier sort of "white water" paddling, and obviously well suited as the outer layer for car body panels whether road, rallycross, racing formula where weight reduction is restricted by rules, or where contact with the opposition or the scenery is to be expected.

6) Hybrids. It naturally took no time at all for those in search of specific virtues to consider honeycomb construction using Kevlar, carbon fibre or glass reinforced plastic skins combined with each other or with metal on one side. They can also be made one-sided, curved to fit the task in hand, and then have the second skin added in situ to finish the job.

What are effectively single skin mouldings with conventional stiffening ribs are beginning to appear on rally cars for bonnets, boot lids, doors, and who knows where else.

As a honeycomb mesh formed in metal, however thin and delicate, is not too amenable to double curvature or complex shapes, and not at all to extreme ones, there is an alternative in rigid foam.

To employ this you must make an inner and outer skin of perfectly matching shapes, hold them in position with a constant gap over the whole area, the while pouring in a paint-like mixture that chemically reacts to form a solid, rigid sealed-bubble foam between them. The sealed bubbles are needed to stop it later absorbing petrol, oil, seawater, etc, should the opportunty arise, which it certainly will.

Some of the best ocean racing yachts use this technique to produce their light, strong hulls, but cars employ it primarily in front or rear wings, and occasionally in legally required 'compressible structures'' forming part of a crash-resistant plan. The foam, while lighter than metal honeycomb is not as good in crushing or crumpling situations.

Yet another unexpected hybrid, used in aircraft, is to lay up a carbon-fibre strengthening cloth skin on a metal component to enhance its reliability and performance. Expect to see this appear in F1 soon, or sooner.

Finally to multiply the permutations yet again, the normally used polyester resins can be replaced by epoxy types, much superior and much more money.

As the point strength of sandwich constructions is linked almost directly to the qualities of their thin surface skins, feeding major loads into a monocoque tub built from them is not easy. The method is common to all in principal, but difficult and varied in practice.

Exact details and dimensions of designers' solutions to these are closely guarded. Keeping a car reliable while the opposition is suffering an obscure failure on an engine mounting that could force building a new tub is the difference between winning and losing.

In general you have to have a bobbin or shaped plate that exactly fills the gap between the skins, with correct threads, holes or projection lugs in precisely the right place before the glue sets. It is not impossible to let them into the finished article by cutting into one side and carefully removing an area of honeycomb or foam. Insert the bobbin or plate, surround it with a foaming glue to fill every gap, finally glueing in place a plate to cover the hole you first cut. Even with the greatest care it has to be less than perfection, strictly for desperate emergencies only.

Perhaps THE major difference between metal sandwiches and those skinned with a plastic laminate is that of bending the final product round corners. Broadly speaking, it is practicable, if difficult, with metal, barely possible with plastic.

With metal, the skin on one side has a slot of calculated width cut in it

Table 1: Base fibres (relative to "E" glass at 100%)

	Polyester	"E"glass	"S"glass	Kevlar	Carbon fibre (hi-tensile)	Carbon fibre (hi-modular)	Steel
Tensile strength (same x-section)	29	100	118	106	91	62	291
Modulus strength (same x-section)	15	100	119	180	319	542	285
Specific tensile	54	100	117	187	132	87	112
Specific modulus	29	100	122	321	464	768	89
Relative weight (comparative densities)	54	100	98	57	69	75	307

Table 2: Lay-up laminates with ideal resin/fibre ratios (relative to "E" glass at 100%)

	Poly-woven	"E"glass (CSM)	"E"glass (Cloth)	"S"glass (Cloth)	Kevlar (Cloth)	Carbon fibre cloth (HT)	Carbon fibre cloth (HM)
Tensile strength	129	100	424	498	435	400	258
Modulus	33	100	200	233	350	633	1075
Specific tensile (identically sized bars in bending)	147	100	361	422	486	412	272
Specific modulus (bars of identical weight in bending)	38	100	169	195	388	645	1090
Relative weight* (same volumes)	76	100	120	118	91	96	96
Relative prices** (excl. resin)	–	100	300	500	700	2500	2500

* Steel = 450. ** BORON 25000. ("BORON" is much used in the US space shuttle and makes carbon fibre look as tough as boiled spaghetti).

along the line of the projected fold. This permits it to be bent until the two edges of the cut in the inner sheet butt against each other. Before it closes finally, the crushed honeycomb is injected with a foaming glue, and the lips sealed with a riveted or glued strip. There should be little or no loss of strength and a further increase in rigidity.

Trying to apply this to plastic skinned laminates invites disaster as these materials even if made with a flexible resin, are very unhappy about being forced round a sharp corner. They crack or rip away from the honeycomb and the sensible solution is that they must be moulded in the proper shape in the first place. This has given birth to such specialised problems that few firms in the world can do it well. The structure must not only be made in splittable moulds with "one-shot" lay-up techniques that permit no mistakes or second chances, but sometimes in halves or sub-sections to be later jig assembled. The shape of the current F1 tubs is such that it makes the task of moulding a racing boat look simple.

One result of this in F1 has been a development where, instead of bending up a big sheet of laminate into the "U" section of a typical tub, it is now usually made up of three flat pieces – bottom and two sides. The base has slotted edges into which the sides are glued and riveted. This is certainly a help in controlling accurate location of bushes and inserted plates in the panels, and consequent avoidance of trouble when the car is being put together.

Weights and costs can normally be worked out by simple multiplication of the skins and filler involved by volume. Glue, while costing up to £1.50 per square foot, a very appreciable part of the final cost, makes little difference in its final hardened form to the weight.

As a rough guide, F1 builds largely from L72 alloy skins of between 20g and 30g, honeycomb foil of 0.001 to 0.002 up to $\frac{1}{2}$ inch thick formed into hexagon cells from $\frac{1}{8}$ inch to $\frac{1}{4}$ inch across. Weight of a typical panel is around $1\frac{1}{4}$ lbs per square foot and the 30g versions are so delicate the pattern of the honeycomb cells faintly marks the outer skin!

At the other end of the scale, Dublin University uses at least two engineering surface plates, 8 feet x 4 feet with $\frac{3}{16}$ inch stainless steel skins on each side of a 9 inch thick honeycomb. These are not only flat, but easily capable of being used as bridges for that Chieftain tank.

In between lie British Rail carriage floors, workbenches, insulating panels and exhibition notice boards. Only in bodywork does the racing car world eschew the high technology approach. Bodywork panels stick faithfully to the cheap, simple and expendable single-skin mouldings in chopped strand mat most of the time. Direct comparisons between steel or other metals, and plastic laminates or honeycomb structures are far from easy. They are complicated by the large number of variations in materials and how they are combined, and the difficulty of obtaining utterly identical samples again and again for test purposes. Not to mention getting the production version the same as the test samples.

A very conservative five thousand years of brainwork have gone into metals; forty, or so, into GRP ....

The two preceding tables are as accurate as current data permit, but consulting the experts can still give different results for apparently similar tests.

Table 1 is the more exact in that it reflects tests under laboratory conditions. **Table 2** makes the comparison in a more realistic but less precise way, with the materials doing their job re-inforcing a resin moulding laid up by hand in conventional manner.

To illustrate just one of many difficulties that can arise, Kevlar not only needs more resin – the weakest part of the structure – than woven glass but is not keen to "wet out" thus risking a drop in quality and therefore of final strength in the finished moulding. One way of combating this is to put glass in as an alternating layer – but we have now lost a part of the original strength for which Kevlar was being used in the first place ....

To make the two tables a little more comprehensible, and get away from giga and megapascals, raw "E" glass used in the majority of industrial applications, and "E" glass Chopped Strand Mat laminate are each used as a baseline of 100. This permits all other figures to be read off as a percentage improvement or deterioration. The serious student will require vastly more than this, and one excellent source can be found in the book *Design Data* (see bibliography in appendices).

Improving YOU

Much of this chapter has dealt with vehicle efficiency, but how about the driver? Fitness and an athletic glow are not universally admired characteristics in the British. They are more likely to bring jovial contempt in direct proportion to the fatness and unfitness of the critic. As that talented and substantially built actor Robert Morley once demanded "Get fit? Get fit for what?" Well, you could argue that fitness is one tuning device that is free. You have to put down hard cash for better tyres or a few more bhp, but an improvable part of power/weight ratio is down to your waistline.

An extra edge on one's personal performance in the cockpit has got to come from making the human machine function as well as possible. I am not suggesting you become a competitive marathon runner to this end. Different people have different standards. One may need only a really good night's sleep and no hangover to function well, while another requires squash five times a week as well as monastic abstinence from the joys of the flesh to rise to the peak.

However that may be, and I have to admit I know several fat – sorry, well-built, hard-drinking drivers who are very good indeed, slim, fit successful drivers are much more numerous. As they tend to save anything up to half cwt on the laden weight of their racer, they also have an extra advantage.

Before venturing into suspension and handling it is worth examining one or two basics, particularly brakes, that will apply whatever route you follow, whether driver, mechanic or informed spectator.

Brakes

Brakes are all about heat. A foot on the middle pedal converts the velocity and momentum of a moving vehicle into considerable quantities of heat which must be absorbed somehow through brake pads or linings, into drums and discs, calipers and brake fluid, wheels and hubs, and from these dissipated into the passing airflow.

If this is kept clearly in mind, it will be apparent there are no shortcuts, no magic answers, only materials more resistant to the temperatures involved, and more efficient ways of cooling.

Once again you have to have some idea of what you are going to be doing to choose the correct equipment. Brakes start off stone cold, and surprisingly enough spend quite a lot of their life well inside the temperature of boiling water, even in some forms of competition.

While boiling water is clearly hot in terms of the human hand, it rates as 'cool' compared to full race or rally temperatures of 700°C where discs at red heat are a more normal state of affairs.

A 'league table' of the demands on a braking system and the percentage of running time spent below any serious level of heat may be very roughly summarised as:

Road use: motorway – 99% cool, town commuting – 85%, crosscountry – 60 to 75%
Sprint/hillclimb: 80% cool
Circuit racing: long – 20%, short – 15%
Rallying: 5 to 20%

These assume driving styles and equipment appropriate to the circumstances.

The heat is dealt with in three main ways: a) friction materials that will cope through different bonding resins, high metal content and being, literally, harder; b) high boiling point fluid; c) vented discs and backplates with forced or centrifugally induced airflow. This should illustrate why buying a set of competition

pads/linings to 'improve' your road car is rarely a good idea.

The penalty to be paid is that the harder versions do not work at all well when cold, even with servo assistance. Without a servo you may have a job to stop it at all for unexpected traffic lights.

On the other hand, using a simply superb set of road brakes on a Ferrari 308GT4 around seven laps of Zandvoort GP circuit boiled the fluid and faded the pads totally to the point where the car could be pushed about in the pit lane with the brake pedal on the floor! Its owner and driver Frank Bott, who deserves to be named if only because he is the one friend I have who has lent me a Ferrari to use on a circuit, was naturally reluctant to go out again even after a lengthy session of pouring cold water on the alloy wheels (NOT the discs or calipers). However he was persuaded, and went home with a trophy from a later event. Once faded to this extent the pads have given their best and must be changed. Unlike the driver they can never do it again quite as well.

Brakes are not unlike valve springs in that there is no point in having them bigger or stronger than is required for their task. Road linings are not only adequate, but work far better cold for a sprint car. The massive calipers and vented discs required for Le Mans are inappropriate to the 750 Formula racer. As an example my Terrapin single-seater of about 8½cwt (960lb) laden, is stopped superbly by Minifin alloy drums all round (7in x 1½in, twin leading shoe) with normal road linings. These are excellent cold, cope with every hill and sprint course current, and only begin to protest if any club puts on a two-lap event on a blazing hot day. Fitting competition linings uprated them to coping with 7-lap short circuit races, although getting round the first three or four corners before they warmed became a bit hairy.

If brakes are already fitted you will be governed by three parameters, all very difficult to alter:

a) Size of the drum or disc
b) Area of pads/linings
c) Brake leverage (the difference between the diameter of the tyre tread face and the diameter of the centreline of the friction material)

Should you have free choice then the decisions are:

a) Drum or disc, or mixture which is normally disc front/drum rear
b) Brake diameter and thickness of disc
c) Two or four pot (piston) calipers
d) Inboard or outboard mountings
e) Is a handbrake required by regulations? This can be very awkward both to install and to raise to legal efficiency on rear calipers

Back to heat. Rally spectators are quite familiar, on icy nights, with the sight of red hot discs glowing inside the wheels hurtling by, and Grand Prix watchers would be too if they were not normally watching in sunlight. Unless you devise and build an efficient watercooling system, air is your only ally. Fabricated or moulded tailored ducts are generally excellent, but with the risk of blockage by mud or stone damage on rally cars. Backplates can be drilled remembering that air exit is as important as entry if not more so.

Vented discs have internal radial slots between the two faces which centrifuge hot air out as they spin, often augmented by ducts that feed cold air to the hub centre area. Calipers, wheels and hubs of light alloy all absorb and radiate heat more quickly than steel equivalents, thus providing a better heatpath.

It can be taken that you will have to do something, probably radical, to the system of any road car to be used in serious competition. Fortunately big brake kits, whether tailormade from the works or hybrids from existing discs and calipers, mated through suitable spacers and mounting brackets, can generally be found if you look hard enough.

Originally the first hydraulic brake systems were operated through a single master cylinder that transferred the pressure exerted by your right foot (or even the left if you are that expert on the loose) to each wheel. This had the shortcoming that it was difficult to alter the proportion being applied to front and rear, and verging on the impossible to alter it in a hurry.

This was dealt with by using two master cylinders in parallel, one operating the front brakes and the other the rears through separate pipe systems with the refinement of an adjustable balance bar between them that would give any desired split of braking effort front or rear. There followed the super-refinement of making this adjustment possible while the vehicle was in motion through a flexible cable to a knob on the dashboard.

If you already have this, the balance you are using can always be checked visually by measuring with a ruler and noting it down in your book of such data. *The shorter the distance between the pedal and a master cylinder rod, the bigger the proportion of braking force is going on that circuit.*

There are two problems that come with twin master cylinders which it is easy to forget. You halve the actual fluid pressure for a given pedal effort in each system which may require the installation of twin servos or increasing the mechanical leverage of the pedal which in turn increases the amount the foot will move. And bleeding the brakes becomes a three man job, as a front and a rear wheel have to be done simultaneously. This is because any properly designed balance bar has another function – it will (or should) only skew so far before locking solid in its pivot to give braking on one pair of wheels should the other circuit fail. A typical leverage incidentally is in the region of 5:1.

Legislation aimed at road safety now requires split systems but don't get over-excited. Apart from often being piped so that one front and the diagonally opposite rear are interconnected, they work through two pistons within a single, non-adjustable master cylinder which is virtually useless for our requirements.

As the twin systems will need separate fluid reservoirs, an Imp-type designed for that car's brake and clutch

can be utilised, located within the driving compartment and remotely piped. Apart from easy checking, it also indicates any pad wear by a falling level, and assuming use of coloured fluid can be seen by the driver quite easily. It is fitted to a number of Terrapins, and would seem an extremely good idea for any long distance competition vehicle. Experiment could even calibrate it so you didn't have to grovel underneath or remove a wheel.

At risk of insulting those zealots who absorbed it all at school, any pressure in a sealed system is exerted equally everywhere, BUT its force will be proportionate to the area over which it is applied. A line pressure of 1000psi would exert varying forces at the wheels depending on the area of the wheel cylinders or caliper pistons (*ie*, 1500lb on a 1.5sq.in piston but only 500lb on a 0.5sq.in piston). Thus changing rear wheel cylinders for a smaller diameter version would reduce rear wheel braking and vice-versa.

Looked at from the opposite viewpoint of the master cylinder, applying a pressure of 1000psi with your foot would provide a system line pressure of 1000psi with a 1.0 sq.in cylinder, but 2000psi with a smaller 0.5sq.in one. So it is quite practical, if in search of more front braking, say, than the balance bar can provide even when screwed to its limit, to fit a slightly smaller master cylinder for the front circuit. There are several diameters from 0.6 to 0.75in quite commonly giving plenty of elbow room.

Although we are discussing the technicalities of brakes rather then their use, it might be appropriate to mention that locking up the front leaves you sliding helplessly straight on without steering, while locking the rears breaks the back-end away and will finally spin the car. Practice and mental discipline can often enable you to get out of either situation by forcing yourself to take the brakes off immediately, however desperate the situation. The tyres are then given a new chance to grip, and despite the speed may hang on well enough and long enough to get out of trouble. This is not armchair advice but personally proven.

How your brakes work and which end, if any, locks up first is affected by a number of factors including weight transfer from back to front, whether the road is wet or dry, mud or tarmac, and tyre size, pattern and tread compound. In general you will need increased front bias in the dry, on tarmac, using big rears and with disc front/drum rear installations.

In perfect conditions the front tyres may be doing anything up to 80% of the stopping, yet a rally man on a loose surface may need a similar figure on the back to get the car sideways and controllable for corners. Only actual experience with your own car will give the final settings that suit you, and it is in choosing these, as well as altering them correctly for different circumstances that a cockpit adjustable balance bar will really repay the work or money you have invested in it.

As a last thought, when you get down to piping, buy one of those little kits that produce the flared ends so you can make it all yourself, and use Kunifer tubing. Though a bit more expensive than the ordinary plated steel variety, it bends far more easily to last for ever – you will never spend better money.

Limited slip & locking differentials

Most of us are familiar with the principle of a differential even if we can't give an illustrated lecture on it. It is a device that, without destroying the drive being fed into an axle, permits one wheel to go faster than the other, round the outside of a corner for example thereby avoiding awful tyre wear, scrub and odd handling because the driven wheels are fighting each other.

Fine until we start venturing into extremes of a lot of power, a lot of roll, a lot of mud or gravel, a non-independent axle or poorly designed independent or any combination of these.

When the lesser loaded wheel finally loses grip and starts spinning, the peculiarity of the differential is that the power transfers itself to the spinning wheel, thus chucking it all away just when it is desperately needed to advance your progress or career.

Were it possible to limit or stop that spin, goody goody. And it is. With an LSD (Limited Slip Differential). There are two main types, one of which really is an LSD and the other more correctly a self-locking differential. The first has miniature clutches which lock up so that the spinning wheel is kept in check in a progressive and civilised way and power is sent to the stopped wheel again. A locking differential is either off or on, a fairly violent transition that can make life and the balance of the car difficult.

Both, when in operation, give back the lost grip at the driven wheels. When this is at the rear, potential understeer with the front wheels washing off may appear, while if a front drive, the new grip pulls the car into what feels like oversteer, so they are a mixed blessing. They can affect the steering violently and many are the dramatic tales swapped by Mini drivers of darting from verge to verge while fighting shock loads up the arms that would bring tears to the eyes of lesser men.

Low powered cars, particularly those with a low centre of gravity, well designed independent suspension or well located solid axle have very little, if any, need of an LSD. Use the money on something else.

The Terrapin will cope with 100hp at rear wheels with an ordinary Mini production differential, leaving equal tyre stripes off the start line and behaving perfectly in corners, even in the rain. Admittedly it is rear-engined with soft wide rubber to help deliver power to the road. Front-engined rear-wheel-drive saloons are those most in need, and anything at all with really massive amounts of power.

If you do invest, don't expect too many instant miracles for your money. You may well have to learn to drive it all over again as well as altering approach line, turn-in points and probably brake balance too, to get all the benefits.

The five-link axle

The energy and investment needed to fit an LSD is often better used to five-link a solid axle, and convert it to coil springs if regulations permit. The five links consist of:

1) A Panhard rod (you can tell how long ago that was devised) which runs across the car, from the strongest possible chassis pick-up to a fabricated bracket, normally electrically welded to the axle casing. It should run very slightly downhill towards the axle, be as long as possible, and use a top quality spherical joint at the axle end, and a compressed hard rubber bush at the other.

2) Two links on each side of axle, of equal length and parallel to each other and the ground, at least for the beginning. These are spherical jointed both ends, adjustable for length, as long as physically practicable, picked up by very strong boxes or brackets in the shell/chassis and by welded brackets on the axle casing.

There are many inferior variations of this system on production cars, design mostly dictated more by ease and costs of production, dodging passengers' buttocks, spare wheel spaces or exhausts than true geometry. A number cannot work at all without flex (compliance is the trendy word) in the rubber or plastic bushes at each end.

Don't try to combine this system with leaf springs, unless they float in sliding blocks at both ends. Coil spring/damper units are better, but you may be able to employ the original trailing arm at the bottom of the axle if it has a spring pan in it to carry the standard sized coils. In this case, your fabricated top link must be a twin dimensionally of the bottom one.

Locating an axle by the five-link system can be quite remarkably rewarding for a driver in handling, road grip, and steering precision. It will give mild understeer characteristics, something everyone needs at the beginning, and some never abandon. More extreme under or oversteer can be built-in at will for experiment, by

putting alternate higher and lower holes in shell/chassis for forward ends of the links. Drop them for more understeer, raise them for oversteer.

Narrowing a solid axle

While considering the solid axle, there is a small but determined group who either want a narrower axle for weight or aesthetic reasons, or the differential offset to move the propshaft driveline sideways, often to cope with a steeply inclined engine.

Half of such a job is easy. Cut the casing tubes, sleeve outside with suitable tube, and weld or braze the joints. The difficult part comes in finding shorter halfshafts. As these items are often 'waisted', thinner in the middle section than at each end, the metal with which to fashion a new tapered or splined end does not exist. Really top class welding may join two reduced halves successfully depending on the material, but there are considerable problems in keeping the shaft straight and true through such a modification. The only course may be to have new shafts made from scratch, possibly in syndicate with some like-minded souls in the Formula or Club in which you are operating.

Strengthening a solid axle

Finally, axle strengthening. Not easy. Reinforcing pressed-in axle tubes with weld may only result in still earlier failure and weld edge cracks.

Ford's solution when their World Cup Mk 1 Escorts broke a series of axles, before even leaving Europe on their way to the horrors of South American roads in 1970, is still a good one. They made up a dural plate projecting along each axle tube, which was trapped by the circle of differential housing bolts. It was then locked to the axle tubes by spacer blocks and U-bolts, and proved extremely successful. Alternatives are any stronger axle the manufacturer may produce, usually with thicker tubes, or a complete change to another make with proven reliability (ie: Mk 2 Jaguar with LSD as standard into a Group 4 Sunbeam, the early axles of which were notably fragile with a decent engine).

Gear ratios

The problem of having the right gear available at right time in the right place is just as common at the bottom of motor sport as it is at the top, but those at the top usually have better means technically to try and achieve perfection. This could be to have no gearbox at all, instead infinitely variable ratios changing themselves all the time – but it would take a lot of the fun away.

All the gearbox does is to multiply the torque (leverage) an engine can apply to the rear wheels through a series of cogs which allow the engine to turn faster and nearer to its peak power for a given road speed. In due course the engine runs out of revs and you must select higher gear, until you are in top and finally flat out. Anybody beyond L-plates will appreciate all this. The subleties and complications arrive when you wish to be in a particular gear at a particular spot, be it a corner, incline, fast swerve or slow turn into a straight.

You will know instantly when something is wrong and the narrower the power band of your super-tuned engine, the more likely it is to happen. Normally manifested as too many revs. in one gear and too little urge when you change up. The answer is that the gears need to be closer together – close ratios in fact.

Solutions may vary from none, if alternative gears are not available, through a specially manufactured CR box with some other person's choice (generally good) in it, to the ultimate – a full set of 40 or so pairs of gears for one of Hewland's range of racing boxes. A glance at the Hewland graph will show the range of choice, and you should work out and then insert the figures for what you already possess.

A change in final drive or driven wheel tyres will move the ratios all up or down, but will not affect – or improve – the gaps between them. Smaller wheels/tyres or a numerically higher FD (ie: 4.7:1 instead of 3.7:1 –

divide the number of teeth on large wheel by that on the drive pinion to obtain this number) will, in theory, give better acceleration, but a reduced top speed, or vice versa. As it happens, this is not strictly correct as top speed may stay the same. This apparent anomaly can occur because many cars are overgeared in the original design, for reasons to do with wafting down the motorway more or less economically and silently.

Dropping the final drive alters the point at which the power available (bhp) curve intersects the power required (total drag). The engine is then able to rev a little higher and give the best power and you will have the double pleasure of losing none of the top speed while getting to it more quickly as well.

At least a full season will probably be needed to learn what is going to do the job. It is a field in which you don't spend a penny on anything until you know from experience what you want. Don't be depressed during this period because you appear to require to gear for a maximum of 95mph when all the opposition say they are pulling 115. They aren't. Do your own thing and you'll be astonished that your times equal or improve on all those fast men.

So vital and hard earned can some of this information be that at least one Formula Ford driver thought it worth printing his personal list of choices for every circuit in Britain and Europe. He then successfully marketed it at several pounds per copy, a brilliant bit of self-sponsorship!

The most comprehensible way to plot your gearing is in units of mph/1000 revs (see formulae in Appendix 2). This combines tyre size, final drive and the ratio inside the box into a manageable figure, and drawn in table form will tell you immediately the rev alteration on any gearchange. It may throw sudden light on how much, if at all, it is worth over-revving for an emergency or a split second. You may be risking a blown engine for nothing.

The number of downward changes you have to make rarely influence performance as they get combined with braking and generally slowing the car. But for every downward there must be an upward,

and these are the time-wasters. However briefly, the power is disconnected and in that situation you are not getting any nearer to victory, so don't get over-enthralled with a narrow rev-band screamer and CR box. A more civilised cam with lower bhp at the top end may well be quicker in the final analysis.

Electrics

Electrics start off looking simple. After all it only dashes from the plus (red) terminal to the minus (black) one, or possibily the other way, making various stops (switches) and doing various jobs (ignition, pumps, lights) on the way.

This all manages to become so unbelievably complicated on a full saloon or rally car as to be impractical to deal with here. You will need a good book, quite a bit of gear, soldering iron, meter and two weeks holiday (one to study the book and the other to attempt the loom).

Fortunately a single-seater or small sports-racer presents far fewer difficulties and is quite a practical proposition. The first step is to acquire as complex a loom as possible from the wrecker's yard, not forgetting as many of its switches and terminals as possible, together with some starter cables, battery terminals and the starter solenoid. This will save a quite enormous sum of money and provide more than enough variety of colour-coded wire and a quiet evening or two picking it all to pieces and sorting the result.

The second is to identify, and sketch in simple fashion, what is going to be operating, and where. You can avoid even the mental strain of this by consulting the illustration which has worked admirably for me. It supplies two fuel pumps and shows three auxiliary or bulkhead mounted switches (behind my head in my case). These permit either the pump or the ignition to be separately checked. Useful in the paddock or garage where you can set the ignition timing, or disconnect and check a fuel pipe without everything else getting in on the act to flood or overheat.

The earth lead is required to be

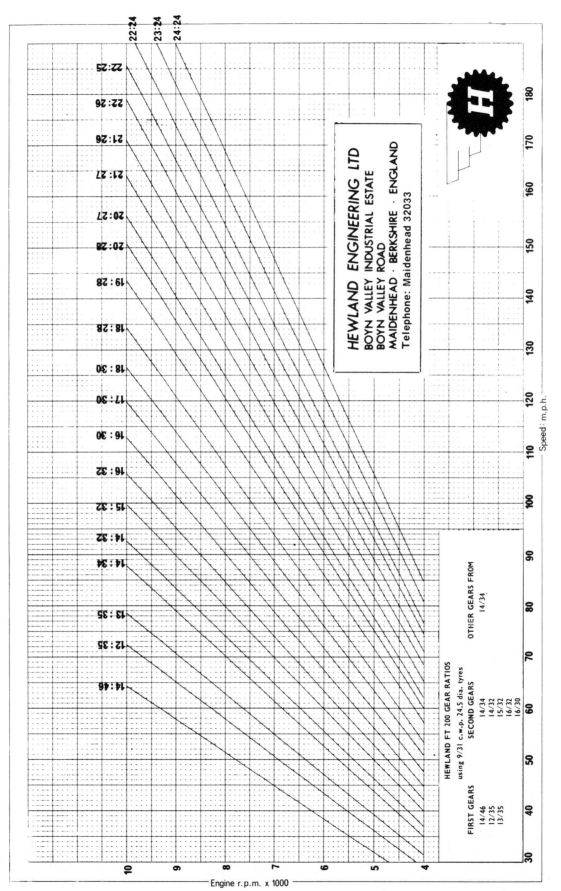

HEWLAND ENGINEERING LTD
BOYN VALLEY INDUSTRIAL ESTATE
BOYN VALLEY ROAD
MAIDENHEAD · BERKSHIRE · ENGLAND
Telephone: Maidenhead 32033

HEWLAND FT 200 GEAR RATIOS
using 9/31 c.w.p. 24.5 dia. tyres

FIRST GEARS	SECOND GEARS	OTHER GEARS FROM
14/46	14/34	14/34
12/35	14/32	
13/35	15/32	
	16/32	
	16/30	

Speed : m.p.h.

Engine r.p.m. x 1000

48

Just one example of the superb range of information charts that Hewland Engineering supply for their multi-ratio racing gearboxes.

They cover different final drives, combined with various driven tyre sizes. Paddock changes of ratio are a matter of minutes for an expert. Deciding precisely which ratio is needed is often far more difficult than the practical spannerwork. As a rough guide, the FT200 is Hewland's "middle" box (F2, Atlantic, etc) with the Mk 8/9 for lower power cars (F. Ford, etc) while many Formula 1 designers employ the FG400, often with their own tweaks both internal and external. (Courtesy Hewland Engineering).

Basic wiring diagram for a competition car. Note that tachometers and electronic ignition systems are supplied with their own wiring diagrams which will be compatible with this diagram. Usual colours are N – Brown, W – White, WB – White/Black and WR – White/Red. (Drawing: Darell Staniforth).

yellow, and the master switch must be inserted in it somewhere in such a manner as to be accessible to a marshal outside should you be upside down or otherwise incapacitated, and also to you directly or by wire pull while fully belted in the driving seat.

The dashboard master switch or ignition key wipes out everything else with one movement.

Study the relevant regulations for your Formula carefully so as to identify both what is needed technically (*ie:* red rear light for circuit racers in bad visibility) and what will keep the scrutineers happy and contented.

Other points in brief:

Battery: Usually the ubiquitous non-spill and expensive aircraft type Varley, but the supermarket lead-acid car or bike type is usually quite acceptable if in a liquid-tight box, or isolated from the driver/crew.

External isolation switch: Must be let into earth lead. If your car has an alternator you will need a special, more expensive, version to avoid blasting your diodes, so be certain to get the right one.

Electronic ignition: Has the great virtues of extremely accurate spark distribution, maintaining perfect tune, and good spark at low starting revs or

if the battery is low. But coil and points work well for me even to 9000rpm on a 4-cyl engine.

Rev counters (or tachometers): Essential, but almost all cheaper ones highly dubious on accuracy at the top end, just where you need it. Cable driven used to be the best, but very expensive electronic probably now as good.

Rev limiters: Normally supplied preset to a particular figure, though some are beginning to arrive both adjustable and built into an electronic ignition box. Lucas do a large range of pre-sets. They introduce a tiny misfire that prevents the engine turning any faster. If you are a real leadfoot, a limiter may be the cheapest present you can buy yourself before a conrod emerges into the fresh air.

Relays: Small boxes let into any circuit carrying heavy current (spotlights, etc) to do the switching. They work with very small current loads from the ordinary switches which are thereby protected from possible heat failure. Essential part of rallycar reliability.

Terminals: Use correct sizes and solder them all.

Wiring: Keep it neat, keep a note of the colours you have used, and wrap it tidily into a loom wherever possible.

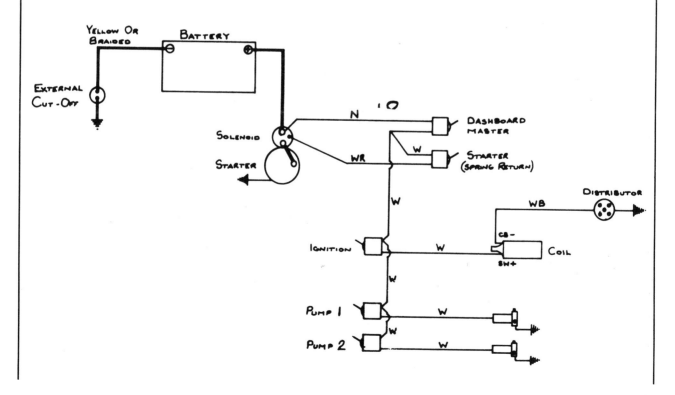

Bulbs: Almost universally quartz halogen which are brighter than tungsten. Supposedly illegal 100 watt bulbs easily available, not long lived, but excellent while they last. Delicate enquiries with The Law can show no trace that using them is an offence.

Coils: High voltage versions always a good investment. Keep top insulation scrupulously clean and protected from water.

Plugs: Use the hardest grade the engine will tolerate without oiling up or giving low speed pickup problems. Using too soft, apart from complete failure if they melt, can also give false readings of apparently weak mixture when it is not

Oil warning light: Fit a big orange or red one right in front of you, connected to a special high pressure warning switch. These light below about 30psi instead of the normal road car version at about 2-5psi when the damage is often done. Don't imagine you will be checking the gauge. You won't.

Instrument lighting: Well worth the extra work of controlling it with a dimmer switch to assist your night vision in difficult circumstances.

The future? Looking more difficult for the amateur as switches, wiring connectors and multi-plugs that cannot be dismantled without damage, make life easier for the manufacturer and assembler, but more awkward for us.

③ Suspension and Steering ~ the heart of the matter?

The fact that ninety eight percent of this chapter will be irrelevant to anyone currently involved in F1, still leaves ninety eight percent of readers to whom it will be a lot of use. Guided, or forced by wriggling around the regulations and small print, F1 designs effectively abandoned all "suspension" as it is generally understood during the venturi car era.

To be more exact they limited it to the tyre carcase and flexing of the top front link until pullrod linkages eliminated even that. Coil spring rates of 3-6000lbs/inch (an increase of ten times within three years) combined with roll-bar stiffness of simply astronomical figures to virtually prevent any movement of wheel hubs relative to the car itself.

For designers this created a whole lot of new mysteries to unravel, while being forced to rely to a high degree on tyre factory technicians, who are not part of their team, for very basic information. Worse, tyre men are generally contracted to other teams as well.

This non-suspension approach gives instantaneous vertical G-loads (read "jolts") of perhaps 20G,

combined with a steady 3G or more under braking and in corners which drivers have to survive. What this will do to their internal organs in the long term nobody knows. A change in legislation such as the FISA "flat-bottom" rule alters everything overnight, but regardless of F1, for most competitors in other branches of motorsport real suspension is not just relevant, but vital.

Its design, development and tuning look like staying an art rather than an exact science well into the visible future.

You might at first think that computers and mathematical models would provide the perfection being sought. They do not. Proof of this is the endless changes of fortune, sometimes within a week or so among F1 teams. At the peak of the sport, with huge financial and technical resources, and many excellent brains, they still find their cars apparently altering from day-to-day, even from hour-to-hour.

Almost certainly the reason is that the number of interrelated variables applying to suspension is so large that, when multiplied together, they become astronomic. You might

reasonably doubt that so many factors could emerge from what is in Concorde or Apollo rocket terms a simple device – the racing car. However, consider the sudden introduction, in mid-season, of a "taller" front tyre (ie: one of larger rolling diameter).

"Let's get it on and see if it corners and stops better" says the team manager. Ah, but hang on. Once bolted on the front hubs, the car is nose high, the centre of gravity has risen, the centroid line of the car is a different shape, and its aerodynamic balance has changed.

Lower the car of course by screwing down the spring collars a bit. Centre of gravity and centroid line back to normal, roll centre seriously altered, the small amount of travel to the bumpstops further reduced, front geometry gone into a new part of its arc of movement, too much negative camber and aerodynamic downforce is going to make the last two factors worse at speed. For good measure a roll-bar link has suddenly run out of space needed to keep it clear of the edge of the tub.

Reset camber, modify the roll-bar link, and get out to practise. Half a precious hour has gone already. Three laps and the car is back with the driver complaining bitterly that the demon new tyres are useless, "understeer into the tight bits, sudden oversteer in the fast ones and they jump about on the straight".

Consult the tyre man. A needle probe checks tread rubber temperatures. Two extra psi. Alter toe-in. Reset front dampers on rebound. Other team driver suggests different tweak for the roll-bar in one corner. None of it pure guesswork, but based on ten or a hundred similar situations.

The designer or chief mechanic is consulting his priceless little book of notes, or his memory. Practice time is trickling remorselessly away. Out again. Two laps. "Better, but I'm having to screw on a load more front brake". Another tyre temperature check and pressure change. Last chance for a decent slot on the grid.

Out again. The driver is this time all too visibly earning his money, walking that thin line between fast and disaster. Chequered flag out. The watches click.

"Fourteenth on the grid, Jesus! Last week we were on the second row. Those bloody tyres. Sling 'em, use the smaller ones. At least we know where we are with them". Just to cap it the race is a disaster. First a collision and finally an engine blow-up.

This may sound extreme but is far from it. There has been no mention at all of adjustments to the back of the car, to wing angle, roll-bar, different coils, dampers that can be altered in both bounce and rebound, tyre pressures, tyres with different carcase construction, tread compound and rolling diameter.

The rear? What has that got to do with problems at the front? A very great deal. For one thing it is very firmly attached to the opposite end of the car by what should be an extremely rigid chassis or monocoque. Anything done at one end of the car affects to some degree the other, and the cure to a problem often lies in adjustments at the other end.

Sadly, our hypothetical team manager was not even able to begin work at the rear of his difficult charge that weekend. Time ran out.

But two weeks later is a different story. Mystified rivals who had observed the earlier troubles with a certain grim satisfaction see that the tall tyres and bigger wheels are unexpectedly back on again. A new tub with different suspension pick-ups permits everything to go back to its proper place, even with the bigger wheels fitted. Roll-bar relocated, new coils to suit the different leverage, a new ration of practice time without hold-ups, plus two private test sessions during the previous week.

First time out it just misses pole and takes a meritorious third place in the race. Seemingly inexplicable to the casual observer for it may be impossible to tell just by looking what has gone on. The car looks the same and nobody in the team is likely to be explaining to you or anyone else the details of what the team has been up to in two frenzied weeks.

One of the obvious partial solutions is to get rid of as many of the variables as possible and F1 did exactly this by effectively eliminating suspension in conventionally understood terms, leaving the cars to ride solid, glued down by the giant hand of atmospheric pressure.

Solid "suspension"

Anyone with a decent memory, or much better, a video recording can verify the truth of this by studying John Watson in a McLaren MP4 circulating Silverstone before the 1981 British Grand Prix with an excellently mounted camera recording it all.

While the track swervingly unwinds itself at a pace beyond belief for most of us, Watson calmly steers with one hand, delicately fiddling at the remote roll-bar adjuster with the other for various corners.

The staggering thing is that when driving a 138mph average lap the one part that does not move perceptibly *at all* is the front suspension. The top links might as well be painted on the picture for all they alter their positions, apart from an almost invisible amount of bend when the car rides the kerbs a touch here and there

But without access to the latest tyre developments — or barred by other regulations on tyre/rim sizes from employing them anyway — a vast body of competitors whether in club racing, rallying, hot rods, hillclimbing, four-litre historic, or saloons, are going to be using moving suspension of some sort or other for a long time to come.

Getting the very best out of it is the object of the exercise. The very best *might* be defined as utilising each of the four tyre contact patches to a maximum, and improving those patches as well while you are about it. Consequently the decision, delayed until now, about wheel size, tyre diameter and width must now be made. It will be taken in conjunction with hub dimensions on the upright you have either planned for the design or already own, together with the method and dimensions of the wheel fixings.

This upright also normally dictates the outboard location of the ends of the wishbones or suspension links. Do not believe that you have to have a particular upright for the positions of the outboard points. You can acquire virtually any upright and hub assembly, front or rear, for reasons of lightness, low price or availability and with care and patience achieve most objectives.

The key question about those aims is "what do you want?" Ignoring the wits who answer "a tax rebate in black suspenders" pause for study of the roll-centres illustration so that we are all talking about the same things. It is essential to understand the dimensions, points in space, and how they are arrived at, in this drawing.

The variables we shall be trying to reconcile and so reach perfection are — wheel angle in roll, wheel angle in bounce and droop, and a fixed roll centre: all without any weight transfer to the outer wheel. Even given a free choice of the outboard points as well, total reconciliation is currently impossible, although a beam axle can get very near; hence, perhaps, all those rumours of a beam-axled F1 Lotus not so long ago.

The difficulty, in effect, is like standing in the centre of a triangle, free to move any way you wish, but always at the cost of going away from one point as you move towards any other. You are unable to stand on all three apexes at once. (Strictly speaking, for certain approaches, you have to add scrub, or track variation, thus making it a square rather than a triangle, and the choice of solutions even worse.)

It will be evident from the roll-centres illustration that once you have measured your wheel, upright and, if available, the inboard points as well, you can draw out your own suspension quite easily on a suitable large sheet of paper. With further work, and more paper, you can move the wheel up and down on successive drawings to see what angles it assumes.

A lot more work will allow you to rotate the inboard pickups round the roll centre to see how the wheel leans in a corner, not forgetting that the roll centre appears to keep altering its position and the consequent arcs of movement.

Using one degree and half inch increments we are now up to twenty four drawings, without any inter-relationship between roll and bump or droop, and you have not made a single experiment in moving one point up, down, in or out, or started on the opposite wheel.

String – and other – computers

Enter the "String Computer".
I felt during the design period of the original Terrapin that there had to be a better (or faster) way to analyse or forecast what a particular layout would do in action, and so the String Computer was born.

The dictionary would call it an analogue computer, or working model, as opposed to the mathematical model necessary to ask a computer to apply its idiot, but tireless, brain to supplying the answers. Students of the glossy adverts for wrist watches will have noticed that the old fashioned faces with hands have recently become the new fashioned "analogue" faces – with hands instead of digital readouts.

Neither the computer facility nor the mathematical knowledge was then available to me, but to quite a degree it is now.

What a computer can tell you

within seconds are the results that will be given by a particular set of dimensions, or a series of sets. What it will not do is tell you what you actually need. That decision is yours and you must sort through endless columns of figures poured out by the idiot, seeking the direction they appear to be taking, correcting it, analysing the results and so on.

In professional team terms it may be perfectly practical and indeed the only way, but it has its shortcomings. Derek Gardner, designer of the six-wheel Tyrrell, once told a university audience about one of them. Faced with rear end grip problems he fed a number of requirements into his computer. It rapidly gave him eighteen ways of achieving them some of which involved putting rose joints in the middle of a piston or gear cluster. Eliminating these left some that required a new chassis. The rest needed building into the car to evaluate the success, failure, or effect on the front of the car.

There have been many attempts to monitor and quantify what is happening to a racing car at high speed but they fail at the point essential to all scientific analysis of anything – a reliable and fixed baseline. During successive corners let alone laps the surface temperature or dust skim may have altered, the car will not be on an identical bit of track, the tyres have worn a little, the driver thinks the car feels slightly different and has changed his method of controlling it by fractions.

Instruments can measure roll, G-forces, downthrust, stresses and strains of many types but they then have to be related to the same baseline every time or they are not comparable. And if they cannot be compared you can draw no conclusion and they are useless.

The trouble, of course, is the human being; especially the driver approaching genius in his field. He can adapt so quickly and so brilliantly to extraordinary situations that would be insurmountable to lesser men, that while doing identical lap times he can be constructing each lap in a hundred subtly different ways.

This is anathema to the scientist, the mathematician, the statistician –

anyone with the responsibility of needing to know precisely what has happened so he can arrange for it to be improved. This excursion from the precise subject in hand should make the cheering point that the amateur is by no means at a total disadvantage compared to the professional. If he has a tool at hand, however apparently crude, with which he can do some of the work of a drawing office or university mathematician, all on the kitchen table in a few long evenings, he is levelling the odds still more.

So back to the String Computer. It should be clear how to make one from the data sheet illustration and photographs. Plywood or hardboard are admirable, full scale is ideal but my own half scale saves having to employ someone to hold the string at the far end of the room for experiments on long swing axle lengths.

Make and mark the Computer as accurately as you can, because all errors are harder to measure in a half scale version. Lest you feel it's all just too simple to work, the figures for my current car, when mathematically checked, years later, agreed within a tenth of a degree/inch. The critical thing is achieving required objectives in the suspension within reasonable limits rather than getting wrong ones with total accuracy.

Targets

Objectives:
1) Roll centre. In my view this is the fundamental and vital point that must not move about in roll. Others may well disagree. But if a roll centre apparently moves up and down, plotting the opposite wheel will show that it is actually moving sideways and nearly always the wrong way towards the inner wheel. This movement which can quite easily reach ten, twelve or eighteen inches and many feet under certain circumstances, makes plotting of what is happening to wheels in a corner even more difficult. It also, I believe, makes the feel of the car alter, during and out of corners, giving the driver a series of messages that

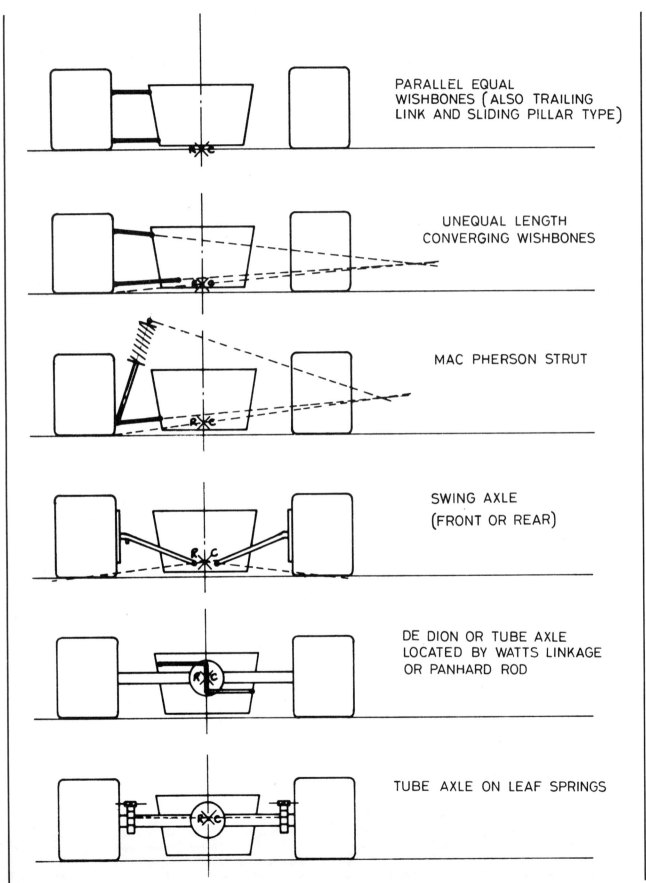

PARALLEL EQUAL
WISHBONES (ALSO TRAILING
LINK AND SLIDING PILLAR TYPE)

UNEQUAL LENGTH
CONVERGING WISHBONES

MAC PHERSON STRUT

SWING AXLE
(FRONT OR REAR)

DE DION OR TUBE AXLE
LOCATED BY WATTS LINKAGE
OR PANHARD ROD

TUBE AXLE ON LEAF SPRINGS

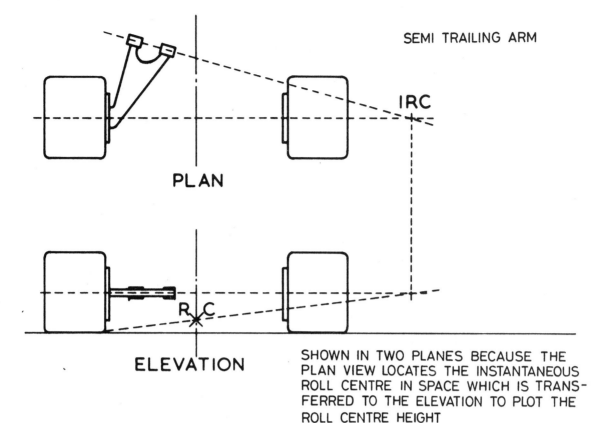

SEMI TRAILING ARM

IRC

PLAN

R C

ELEVATION

SHOWN IN TWO PLANES BECAUSE THE PLAN VIEW LOCATES THE INSTANTANEOUS ROLL CENTRE IN SPACE WHICH IS TRANSFERRED TO THE ELEVATION TO PLOT THE ROLL CENTRE HEIGHT

ARTHUR MALLOCK "WOBLINK"
LOW ROLL CENTRE LOCATION FOR SOLID AXLE (NAME FROM JAMES WATT, MAURICE OLLEY, DONALD BASTOW)

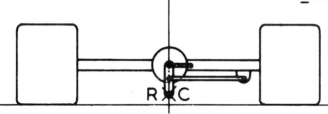

R C

FORMULA : $\dfrac{B}{A+B} = \dfrac{C}{D}$

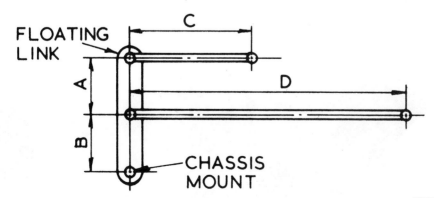

FLOATING LINK

C

A

D

B

CHASSIS MOUNT

Locating the static roll centre.
(Drawings: Darell Staniforth).

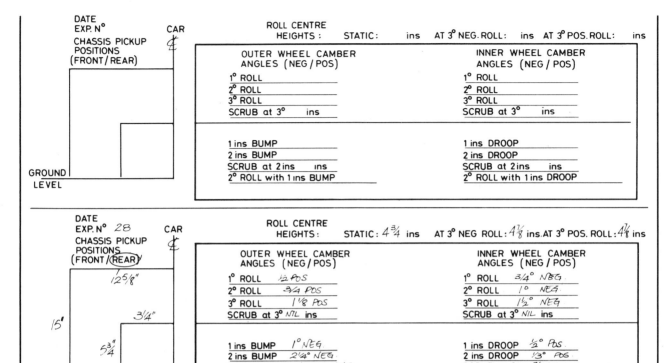

Blank version:

DATE
EXP. N°
CHASSIS PICKUP POSITIONS (FRONT / REAR)

CAR ₵

GROUND LEVEL

ROLL CENTRE HEIGHTS: STATIC: ins AT 3° NEG. ROLL: ins AT 3° POS. ROLL: ins

OUTER WHEEL CAMBER ANGLES (NEG / POS)	INNER WHEEL CAMBER ANGLES (NEG / POS)
1° ROLL	1° ROLL
2° ROLL	2° ROLL
3° ROLL	3° ROLL
SCRUB at 3° ins	SCRUB at 3° ins
1 ins BUMP	1 ins DROOP
2 ins BUMP	2 ins DROOP
SCRUB at 2 ins ins	SCRUB at 2 ins ins
2° ROLL with 1 ins BUMP	2° ROLL with 1 ins DROOP

Completed version:

DATE
EXP. N° 28
CHASSIS PICKUP POSITIONS (FRONT / REAR)

CAR ₵

12 5/8"
3 1/4"
15'
5 3/4"

GROUND LEVEL

ROLL CENTRE HEIGHTS: STATIC: 4 3/4 ins AT 3° NEG ROLL: 4 7/8 ins. AT 3° POS. ROLL: 4 7/8 ins

OUTER WHEEL CAMBER ANGLES (NEG / POS)	INNER WHEEL CAMBER ANGLES (NEG / POS)
1° ROLL 1/2 POS	1° ROLL 3/4° NEG
2° ROLL 3/4 POS	2° ROLL 1° NEG
3° ROLL 1 1/8 POS	3° ROLL 1 1/2° NEG
SCRUB at 3° NIL ins	SCRUB at 3° NIL ins
1 ins BUMP 1° NEG	1 ins DROOP 1/2° POS
2 ins BUMP 2 1/4° NEG	2 ins DROOP 1/3° POS
SCRUB at 2 ins 1/4 OUT ins	SCRUB at 2 ins 7/16 ins
2° ROLL with 1 ins BUMP 1/4° NEG	2° ROLL with 1 ins DROOP 1/2° NEG

String computer data sheet showing blank and completed versions.

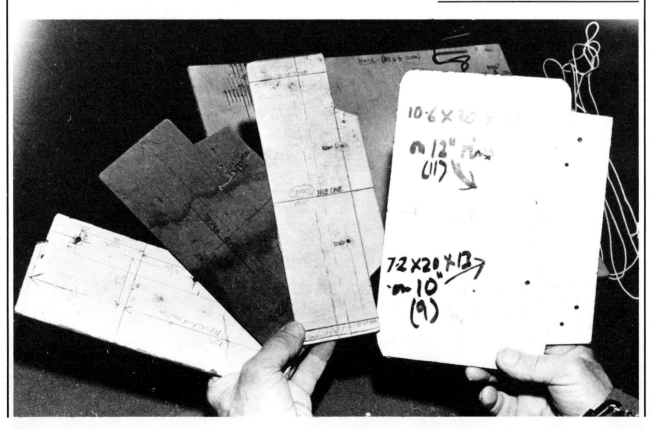

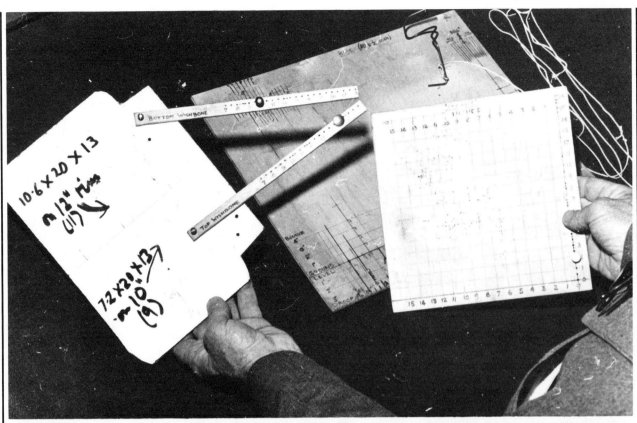

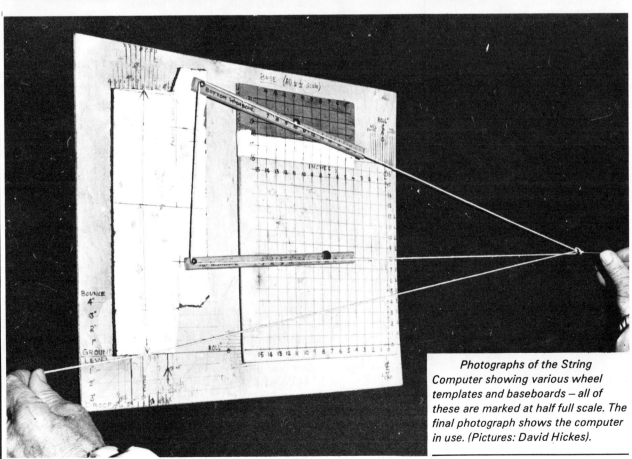

Photographs of the String Computer showing various wheel templates and baseboards – all of these are marked at half full scale. The final photograph shows the computer in use. (Pictures: David Hickes).

contradict each other and making his job even more tricky.

A useful way to demonstrate to yourself the result of extreme variations in the front and rear roll centres (an unexpectedly hard thing to visualise) is to pierce a rectangular cardboard box end to end with a long rod such as a knitting needle. The rod passes through one end near the top of the box (high RC) and through the other end near the bottom (low RC).

You then rotate the box around the needle which represents the roll axis. It will show immediately the sort of attitude your car will try to take up in cornering, and makes clearer than words why a Mini kicks up a back wheel, and many racing saloons have a front one hanging in thin air.

2) Outer wheel vertical in roll. This wheel is always doing more work than the inner up to the ultimate point where the inner is airborne. Very slight positive camber is often cancelled out by bump movement inherent in a car with some "skewed roll", ie: the roll angle is combined with some nose diving into a corner or squat out of it.

3) Wheel angle in bump/droop. Very difficult to reconcile with (2), and tends to give a lot of negative on front brake dive or acceleration squat. Pirelli produced special front covers, with radiused inner shoulders, to deal with this for both Ferrari and Toleman.

4) Track variation (scrub): Important mainly for stability on high speed straights, probably irrelevant in cornering or roll, but may also be responsible for momentary under/oversteer lurch on entering corner.

As a tentative guide to your own decisions, the original Terrapin sacrificed everything (including having too much negative camber in squat/nose dive) to fixed roll centres at 4 inch rear 1½ inch front and vertical outer wheels in cornering. Although it was based on only 4½ inch and 6 inch wide rims with 3⅞ inch tread on road, the same geometry is currently coping with 13 inch rims and up to 11 inch tread with road contact the full width across but tyre construction clearly contributes a good deal to this.

Current views are that roll centres should be much lower: sometimes below ground at the front of F1 cars.

The 1980 decision in the D.G. car went more for upright wheels in squat and nose dive, with consequent sacrifices in roll attitude of wheels reduced by stopping it rolling so much – stiffer coils and anti-roll-bars. Although we did not know it then, this appears to be paying a dividend with current trends in tyre design where "upright is everything".

Any formula with relatively narrow tyres/wheels will obviously tolerate more extreme wheel angles, but reducing these angles still gives a tyre more chance to do its job – hanging on to the road with minimum distortion and wear.

You do not have to be any sort of expert to realise that tilting an ultra-wide tyre into negative or positive camber very soon lifts most of the tread off the road. *But,* if you can keep it in the right place, the road adhesion is huge especially with fully hot and ultra-soft tread compounds.

As a guide to the use of the String Computer from scratch, the following points may be helpful.

Shade in impossible areas on the "chassis" board where there is a gearbox, driver's feet, ribs, etc, and make as accurate a model of your wheels, tyre/upright/pickup positions as possible.

Start with a bottom link as long as is physically convenient, angled slightly uphill towards the chassis (approximately ten degrees).

Use a top link ⅔ the length of the bottom one, angled downwards towards the chassis rather more sharply (20-25 degrees).

Choose a front and rear roll centre (between zero and six inches, with lower dimensions at the lower, lighter end of the car, and vice-versa). Note that some suspensions, such as a solid axle may dictate a particular roll centre at one end of the car, whether you like it or not.

Begin experiments using degree roll increments on both inner and outer wheel, plus bump and droop in one inch steps. Note the result of every experiment on paper (a suggested form that I have used will be found on page 56). This will permit speedy visual comparisons especially if marked in colours to identify good, bad and impossible.

Guidelines:

1) **Very short swing axle lengths (20-40 inches).**
a) Roll centre generally high.
b) Roll centre location very good.
c) Roll centre movement sideways for given variations in height very small.
d) Wheel angle alteration in roll very good.
e) Wheel angle alteration in bounce/droop very bad (virtually linear with some layouts).
f) Bad performance in scrub.

2) **Long swing axle lengths (70-180 inches).**
a) Roll centres low.
b) Roll centre location reasonable subject to (c).
c) Roll centre movement sideways can be large due to shallow angles involved.
d) Wheel angle in roll mediocre (worst on inner wheel).
e) Wheel angle in bounce and droop very good.
f) Good performance in scrub.

3) **Medium swing axle lengths (40-70 inches).**
As you might expect, results lie roughly between short and long.

4) **Ultra-long near parallel link swing axle lengths.**
a) Roll centres very low or below ground level.
b) Roll centre location good *in vertical terms.*
c) Roll centre movement sideways can be very great even with very small vertical increments because of the ultra shallow angles involved. May also not be solely in one direction during roll to one side or another.
d) Wheel angle in roll poor (may be near equivalency with body roll angle).
e) Wheel angle in bounce/droop excellent.
f) Scrub – good.

Further guidelines:

1) Altering wishbone lengths does not have major effects.
2) Lengthening both at once, inconclusive but often poorer.
3) Vertical movements of inboard pickups have major effects.
4) Generally, scrub in roll is not a problem.

5) Scrub in bounce/droop (ie: heavy braking and acceleration) can be a major problem.

6) A car in "skewed roll" may have two degrees of roll combined with one inch of bounce; these combination results are often excellent in terms of wheel angle.

7) Roll centre height variations become more and more important the lower the RC, because the sideways movements increase.

Although this may all sound somewhat complex and time consuming you will rapidly find a visible trend emerging. The trouble is in deciding how far you will compromise one particular aim in favour of improving another.

Nothing I have read, seen or done to do with suspension moves me away from the feeling that the control of the roll centre, knowing what it is doing, and being as certain as possible that if it does move, it does so in a similar way at each end of the car, is a major part of making a competition car handle well and predictably.

The other thing I consider important is that the "roll couple" (leverage resulting from the distance between the RC and centroid line, combined with the weights involved) at each end of the car should be as nearly similar as possible. If this is not so, the "strongest" end of the car is always trying to take charge, producing the "skewed roll" already mentioned in which the car takes up an odd angle to the road, producing combined roll/droop and roll/bounce effects at diagonally opposite corners, with consequent oddities of wheel angle, grip and driver feel.

Summing up the virtues and handicaps of the String Computer in one sentence, it works well and accurately on short or medium swing angle lengths but steadily less well as these get longer and longer. The reason is that as wishbones become nearer and nearer to parallel, the distance to their intersection becomes extremely long and very small errors are magnified accordingly. Even the thickness of the string makes proper measurements difficult.

Our first thoughts long ago that the roll centre moves about were only half right. It does, but not just

vertically. It also moves sideways if given the chance. This can be easily proved if you accept the fact that it cannot be in two places at once. If, for example it is three inches above ground level static, but falls to two inches for the outer wheel while rising to four inches for the inner wheel when in two degrees of roll, all measured on the centreline of the chassis, the only common point at which it can really be is at the intersection of the two roll centre lines, somewhere off the centre line. In general, although not inevitably, it moves towards the inner wheel.

Finding out what it does with swing axle lengths of between 50 and 100 feet (well within current F1 parameters) becomes impossible with the String Computer. However, as the virtues of such long swing axle lengths are primarily related to extremely hard suspensions with almost no movement they are not of such importance to the average competitor using less specialised tyres, who wishes to achieve the best roadholding and behaviour possible without risking impact fractures of his spinal column.

Only access to a proper computer with a particularly dogged mathematical friend revealed some of the odd secrets of ultra-long swing axle length geometries. Fellow Terrapin driver and designer David Gould worked out one way to investigate at least the basics (and even this needed a 420 line programme).

What it made clear was that the roll centre could move great distances, well outside the wheel track if necessary, to either side of the car, and could also move from side-to-side with differing degrees of roll. This provided mind boggling numbers of variations and brought us once more up against the snags of using a computer.

Firstly, it will only give you answers while the true problem is "what question, or questions, do you want to ask it?" Secondly, it disgorges so many answers that the human mind is then required to try and establish a pattern or tendency to see if investigations are going the right way or the wrong.

The single principle from the earliest experiments to the last to which we have clung is that you need similar behaviour by the roll centre at

each end of the car, whatever that behaviour might be.

If it is different, the various forces, leverages, and potential movements of the car, suspension and tyres cannot fail to alter in unpredictable and variable ways.

And computer forecasts with long swing axle lengths show some quite extraordinary movements of the roll centres. It can be persuaded to go twenty or thirty feet to the inside of a corner, but jump back thirty feet to the outside, and then return to hover near the centre line of the car, both above and below ground, all dependent on roll angle and ride height.

It raises the possibilities of a car capable of having its handling radically altered in a chosen way simply by an adjustment in ride height in the paddock.

Further, if the roll centre is thirty feet away on the inside of a corner geometrically the car will have virtually no roll, but will be forced down on the ground instead. Could such an approach be used to take the place of roll-bars? Or produce extra no-drag ground effect in corners?

Once you are working with long swing axles, very small alterations in pickup positions make very large alterations in the behaviour of the roll centre. And still you need a human brain to filter and interpret the torrent of information, which results even from a 420 line programme that is asking no questions as yet about camber or scrub.

Clearly F1 minimised this with the somewhat simplistic approach of stopping anything moving at all, but they have the advantage of being able to control tyre design to a large degree so that the rubberware takes over a number of the functions of a conventional, or moving suspension.

Bump-steer

Mixed up with the front suspension will be the steering, and a surprising number of experienced competitors are not always too clear about what bump-steer is, or if they do know, exactly how it is caused and what to do about it.

To start at the beginning it simply

Method 1

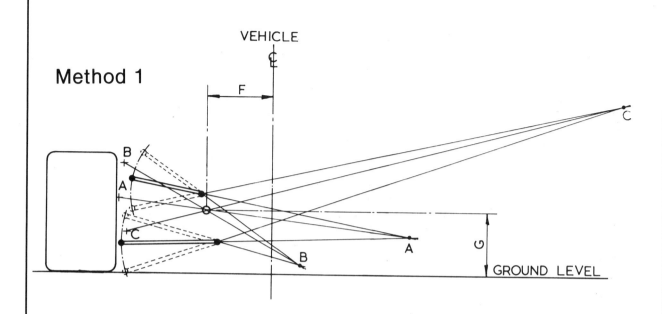

Correct R & P Length = F × 2

Correct R & P Height = G

Method 3

R & P ball ends coincide exactly with top link inboard pickups with track rods lying parallel to top link.

Method 2

A:B = C:D

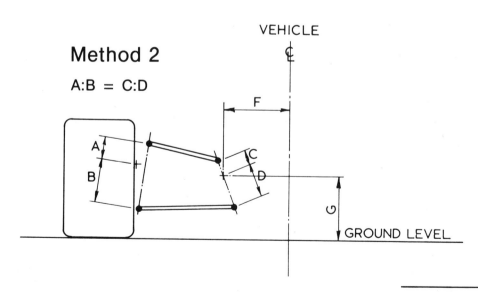

Methods of determining the best position for the rack and pinion. (Drawing: Darell Staniforth).

means that any rise or fall of one of the front wheels causes it to alter the way it is pointing without your turning the steering wheel. It is caused by the rack and pinion being in the wrong place or the wrong length or both.

The effects can range from a slight uncertainty in feel, or difficulties in placing the car accurately into corners, through to instability at speed that will make you want to give the car away to the first person you see back in the paddock!

And never think that because your pride and joy was professionally manufactured, whether saloon or single-seater it can't be happening. It can. I came across one mass production saloon where alterations in the suspension pickups had been made to accommodate a different exhaust system. In a situation where a vertical movement of the rack of a couple of millimetres can cause (or cure) serious bump steer that modification could not really have been a good idea.

There are two approaches. The simplest geometrically, but sometimes the most difficult practically is to make the rack coincide precisely with the chassis pickups for the top or bottom front wishbones. It can lie ahead of or behind the axle line, and this practice is becoming almost universal in single-seaters.

In any other type of car it is more often located at some intermediate point between top and bottom links. There are various ways of deciding what is the correct place both mathematical and graphic, but the rack and pinion positioning illustration shows three ways that I have used myself and they all work. Although they give slightly different results for the same suspension geometry, and I am well aware this is impossible, they have worked on my own vehicle – just one of those small mysteries like UFOs. You may need to make small vertical adjustments, so ALWAYS allow for this by vertically slotting the holes for clamp bolts or allowing space to shim up or down if it should be necessary.

If you are checking a car that is already built, you must measure every part of the front (and rear) suspension with the greatest accuracy open to you. Sometimes workshop manuals have excellent drawings but without any

sizes. Not to worry. Get the most accurate measurement possible off one or two of the components on the car itself and use these to scale and dimension the drawing. It is very unlikely indeed that the manual has a distorted drawing in it, so you will finish up with correct relative data on all the other parts.

Add the rack and pinion and track-rod end ball centres to your drawing and you will soon know if you are in trouble or not. (See illustration for methods of locating the steering rack or checking that its current position is the correct one). If things ARE wrong, you will have to either shorten (or lengthen) the complete rack casing and bar, put it in another place where the existing length is appropriate, and then, in all probability, radically alter the position of the steering arms.

All of these solutions are physically and technically daunting, but unless you do it, you will always have some degree of built-in handicap as a result. For most of us one more handicap is something we do not need.

To give an idea of the big effect of small movements, dropping the steering rack by $\frac{3}{16}$ inch, on a rally-modified Sunbeam, cut $\frac{7}{8}$ inch of bump steer to $\frac{1}{16}$ inch over 4 inches of suspension travel.

Steering alterations

Apart from persuading the rack and pinion to do its job properly, there arises the question of how well it does it. The most casual reader of "Bits for Sale" columns will have noticed at some time or another – "Quick rack ... Comps. R&P ... 7:1 rack for F. Ford ... high ratio rack for Escort" all aimed at selling you something to make your car hopefully more sensitive or easier to control.

What do they all mean? It is imperative to have a simple method of comparison between one and another, preferably one that can be done without dismantling and ideally even over the telephone. Tooth count, turns lock-to-lock, mathematical ratios are all virtually meaningless if only for one

simple reason – the varying lengths of steering arms.

On any given steering installation left otherwise untouched, lengthening the steering arms means the front wheels must turn through a smaller angle for the same movement of the steering wheel. The steering has slowed, become less sensitive, almost certainly lighter and needs more steering wheel rotation to go round the same corner.

Shorten the arms and the steering is quicker, more sensitive, heavier and needs less steering wheel rotation for the same corner.

How to know whether the one you are proposing to buy is right, wrong or possibly the same as that you already own? The answer is in one simple measurement: rack bar movement for one complete turn of the pinion or steering column.

First you obviously check your own, a one minute job on the bench and possibly a 20 minute one if it is still mounted in the car. This is your baseline and there is little point doing more with this dimension than noting it down somewhere until you have actually driven the car.

Once you are going quickly, you will very soon know if it is suitable, ultra-sensitive and twitchy, or requires more wheel twirling than you have arm length available. Happily you know that the one you already have moves, say, 1.75 inches for a turn of the wheel. An extra $\frac{1}{4}$ inch either way is an appreciable alteration, $\frac{1}{2}$ inch a major change, $\frac{3}{4}$ inch enormous. But it is a dimension you can get on the phone, by letter or on the counter of your local agent or breaker's yard. You know where you are.

Other dimensions – length of rack bar, spacing of brackets and so on – are almost totally unimportant as they can be chopped, welded, re-machined to suit what is required for your front suspension geometry. The vital thing is the correct gearing.

The approach of simply altering the lengths of the steering arms can be employed if the front uprights have been designed for this from the beginning. They will have a cast-in massive lug, or lugs, onto which are bolted a pair of alloy sandwich plates between which the track-rod end (normally a Rose-type joint) bolts in place, often with spacers to adjust its height.

Using such a design, either a forward or rear mounted rack can be used, and the steering ratio altered very rapidly – far more quickly than having to remove and replace a complete R&P assembly with different gearing.

Fine if you have such a pattern of upright, though problems can arise with wheelrims or calipers fouling a longer arm. Beware if the arms are the forged steel pattern almost universal on production cars. Cutting and welding these can be both difficult and dangerous, though they can be bent if generously heated and allowed the slowest cool you can manage. The stresses on them are very great and I have seen a fabricated set used on Mini uprights crack within a very short working life.

To clarify the phrase "forward or rearward rack" just used, it is all too easy to build or modify a car in such a way it will turn right when you expect it to turn left. Don't laugh. Think about it, for it has certainly been done in real life. A rapid check is that the pinion must be on top of the rack for rearward facing steering arms, and underneath for forward ones.

Should you appear to have some incompatible parts or an "insoluble" situation, there may still be ways out. Steering arms or complete front hubs can often be changed from side to side to reverse them. Alternatively the rack itself can be turned upside down. This will produce an awkward angle of take-off from the pinion that will make essential a pair of universal joints in the steering column. This could be a worthwhile, or even a required safety feature in future: a useful thing to keep in mind.

As a basis of comparison on which to apply the "distance per rev" method, the Triumph Herald rack has probably equipped more competition cars than Heralds. Well, almost. It is used in Terrapins, combined with Mini steering arms, both standard and "S" pattern, as well as in early F1, sports cars and dozens of F. Fords: all with a variety of steering arm patterns and lengths.

Herewith a basic table which will save a little time seeking out and measuring different models, and to which you can add your own data.

Vehicle	Rack bar movement per turn of pinion (inch)	Forward or rearward	"Ratio" (with identical steering arm lengths)	
Ford Escort	1.5	Both	1.5	"Slow"
Morris Minor 1000	1.51	R	1.51	
Mini	1.55	R	1.55	
Triumph TR6	1.6	F	1.6	
MGB	1.81	F	1.81	
Sprite/Midget	1.83	F	1.83	
Triumph Herald	1.87	F	1.87	
Escort (Rally Hi-ratio)	2.1	Both	2.1	
Sunbeam (Rally Hi-ratio)	2.23	R	2.23	
Chinell Racing	2.5 (or special order)	Both	2.5	
Jack Knight Racing	2.5	Both	2.5	"Quick"

This might be an appropriate point at which to apologise to everyone who has either grown up with the Metric system, or has successfully persuaded a brain trained in Imperial dimensions to change over to kg/m² and kilonewtons. I have always found maths hard going, even in Imperial , so I have been forced to stay with it. It is for fellow strugglers that various formulae, graphs and explanations are not only in Imperial, but also in a form that may attract a snigger or two from those for whom numbers leap living, vibrant and comprehensible from the page.

That said, and apropos of nothing more than re-emphasising the need to check a purchase carefully, a friend once asked me to drive his recently acquired single-seater in hope that my talents would identify a very odd feeling in the handling and how it might be cured.

There was something diabolic about the front, but I could not be more specific. Only later was it traced to half a gallon of water inside one front tyre! How it could ever have got there remained one of life's mysteries, but emptying it out made a major improvement in the handling.

Once you have decided on the geometry you are going to use, the chassis or shell has to be made to accept the resulting component positions accurately and strongly. It will have become obvious from your own series of experiments that some very small alterations on the string computer can make large differences in what the wheel will do and in what situation it will do it.

Allowing flex anywhere is simply not acceptable. It will not only nullify all your labours but introduce all sorts of erratic and mysterious handling unpleasantness once the car gets used in anger.

Coil spring selection

Having now located exactly where in your chassis or shell the pickups will be, the size and rates of the coil springs (if applicable) to be employed must be decided. Many people have trodden the path before so that there are plenty of examples or guidelines to use as starting points, but it is not impossible to ignore these in favour of a personal approach.

Being a touch elementary for a moment, a surprising number of people are still under the impression that screwing up the threaded collar at the

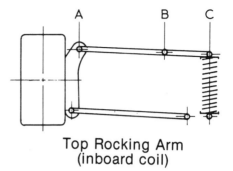

**Top Rocking Arm
(inboard coil)**

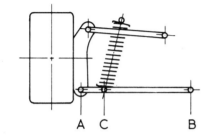

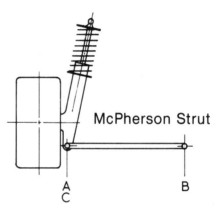

McPherson Strut

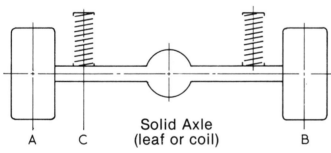

**Solid Axle
(leaf or coil)**

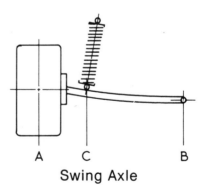

Swing Axle

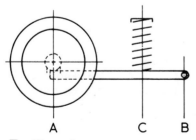

**Trailing Arm
(normally rear)**

Suspension leverage $= \dfrac{AB}{CB}$
in all cases.

bottom of a coil spring increases the rate of the spring. Careful inspection, thought or measurement will soon show that all it actually does is raise the car. The rate of the coil, a built in function of the wire diameter, number of coils and free length, is quite unaltered.

But there are three rates to do with a spring in most designs rather than one.

First is the Coil Rate, which is a measurement of how much it shortens under a given load, normally quoted in lb/inch, the figure you will find etched on the flattened end of many professionally produced springs.

Second is the Wheel Rate: how hard or soft the coil appears to be to the wheel bouncing up and down at the end of its link or wishbone.

Third is the Effective (or squash) Rate: how strong it appears to be to the car resting on it when fitted and standing at normal ride height.

Given, for the purposes of illustration, identical springs, high leverages (spring mounted a long way away from the wheel, or very near to the chassis pivot on an inboard suspension) result in lower wheel rates, larger squash rates, softer ride and more suspension movement for any given magnitude of jolt or force at the wheel. Low leverages (MacPherson struts and certain inboard suspensions approach nil) mean that wheel rates are virtually the same as the coil rate itself, and result in a harder ride and smaller suspension movements – see leverages illustration.

It should be clear from these many variables that attempting to compare a car fitted with 200lb/inch springs with one on 850lb/inch is meaningless unless you are either referring to two identical cars (eg: Escorts with the same linkage) or you know the actual leverages involved and can work out the wheel rate, frequency and so on. If one of the cars was an 8-litre CanAm monster and the other a Formula Ford car, they might still be identical in essence.

If we are to calculate anything, and if you were once the sort of student more intent on fellow students of the opposite sex than on the "Theory of Levers" you will have to pay attention this time:

Removing the jammed lid from a tin of paint with a long screwdriver is a reasonable dramatic example of the use of a lever. You convert a modest effort over a long movement to a very great force over a short distance. There is a simple mathematical relationship between the two which does admittedly become a little more complicated where a coil spring is concerned, but even this difference should shortly become clear.

Before anything else in the design or modification of a sprung suspension, you have to have some common denominator, something to which any set of coils, wishbones, leaf springs and an axle can be related so that one can be compared with another. Happily there is one – the Natural frequency at the wheel. The disbelieving or mathematically skilled will go on to check the following figures. Suffice it to say here they are based on the fundamentals of physics, metal structures and natural laws which are likely to remain unaltered well into the foreseeable future.

Accepting this we can say that: Natural Frequency (in cycles per minute) = $187.8 \sqrt{\dfrac{\text{wheel rate (lb/inch)}}{\text{sprung weight (lb)}}}$.

You may sometimes find it quoted in Hz (cycles per second) in which case you divide the previous formula by 60 which gives: Natural Frequency (in Hz) = $3.13 \sqrt{\dfrac{\text{wheel rate (lb/inch)}}{\text{sprung weight (lb)}}}$

Sticking with CPM, experience on vast numbers of road cars, a lot of competition cars, and the comfort or tolerance of human beings when riding in a wheeled vehicle have combined to reduce the practical frequencies to quite a narrow band.

It lies generally in the 60-80 bracket for comfortable road cars, 80-100 for firmer and more sporting machinery, 100-125 for non-ground-effect racers, and is creeping towards 175 in certain applications.

Below 50, suspension movement becomes so great that the vehicle risks bottoming or assuming ghastly wheel angles, while at 150 your false teeth are likely to be rattling somewhat. As current F1 would appear to be operating at 200-500 CPM the spine

jarring ride is not too difficult to imagine ....

To avoid pitch, a phenomenon sometimes devastingly demonstrated by rally cars on forest sections suddenly beginning a nose-up/tail-up sequence of oscillations that ends in a complete somersault, the standard approach is a front frequency 10 or 20 CPM lower than the rear.

Strictly this difference, and the exact frequencies chosen only work to perfection at certain speeds and on surfaces with a particular frequency of bumps, but dampers intervene to take care of all but the most extreme sets of circumstances. (There are a range of examples in the accompanying table).

The really awful difficulties of choice face the saloon car designers who, with a frequency that alters inevitably with load, have to try to get a compromise between handling with just the driver aboard, and the same vehicle bearing five people and all their holiday luggage.

In the competition world things are far easier though, as can be imagined, aerodynamic wing loads in F1 are now posing problems not dissimilar to those of passenger cars. For the average competition car we can say that everything is secondary to grip. The driver or crew will put up with a hardness of ride unacceptable in daily transport, and there will be little need to allow for huge variations in load.

A suggested starting point, whether designing from scratch, or altering an existing possession is 100 CPM, plus or minus 15 (85-115).

If the car is expected to develop any downforce either from venturi pods or front/rear wings, you should be thinking at least 125/130, and planning ahead to be able to put even higher rate coils in the space available to raise the static frequency still further.

As an alternative to measuring and calculating wheel rates, frequencies, etc, Arthur Mallock, famed creator of the U2 sports racers has a superbly simple composite figure he applies to any vehicle as an indication of its ride characteristics – "static deflection". This is the difference between the ground clearance of a vehicle jacked up with all load *just* off the springs, and its normal running

Suspension frequency examples and calculation method.

Data	1 Wheel frequency (CPM) F	2 Sprung weight (net corner wt. in lbs) SW	3 Susp. leverage SL	4 Susp. leverage squared SL²	5 Effective Coil Rate lbs/ins	6 Coil crush (inches Static)	7 Wheel Rate (lbs/ins) WR	8 Static Deflection (inches) SD	9 Coil Rate (lbs/in) CR	Remarks CR is actual spring fitted to vehicle
How obtained	Designer's choice or $187.8\sqrt{\dfrac{WR}{SW}}$	Gross corner wt. less unsprung wt.	Designer's choice or Measure		Calc. $\dfrac{CR}{SL}$	Calc. $\dfrac{SWXSL}{CR}$	Calc. SW or ECR $\dfrac{CR}{SL^2}$	Calc. $\dfrac{SW}{WR}$	Designer's choice or WRXSL² or ECRX SL	
Gould Terrapin 1600 cc (1980 to 1983)	Front: 102	138	2.0:1	4.0:1	80	1.31	40	3.45	160	First experiment
	Front: 107.3	138	2.0:1	4.0:1	90	1.17	45	3.1	180	Better
	Front: 113	138	2.0:1	4.0:1	100	1.05	50	2.76	200	Better
	Front: 120	138	2.0:1	4.0:1	112.5	0.93	56.5	2.44	225	Less improvement
	Front: 126.5	138	2.0:1	4.0:1	125	0.84	62.5	2.21	250	"Over the edge" but retained
	Front: 132.7	138	2.0:1	4.0:1	137.5	0.76	68.75	2.00	275	Too hard
	Front: 96.3	238	2.0:1	4.0:1	125	1.64	62.5	3.81	250	Ground effect of 0.55G (400 lb split equally to each wheel)
	Rear: 113.5	280	1.565:1	2.45:1	159.7	1.59	102	2.74	250	First experiment
	Rear: 120	280	1.565:1	2.45:1	178.9	1.42	114	2.46	280	Better
	Rear: 124.3	280	1.565:1	2.45:1	191.7	1.33	122.5	2.28	300	Better
	Rear: 129.4	280	1.565:1	2.45:1	207.7	1.23	133	2.10	325	Final choice
	Rear: 111.2	380	1.565:1	2.45:1	207.7	1.58	133	2.86	11	Ground effect of 0.550 (400 lb split equally to each wheel)
	Rear: 134.3	280	1.565:1	2.45:1	236.6	2.14	143	1.96	350	Future plan
LT25: F5000 (Len Terry design)	Front: 118	230	1.87:1	3.49:1	167.9	1.37	89	2.58	314	From "Racing Car Design and Development"
	Rear: 125	440	1.36:1	1.85:1	269.8	1.63	195	2.26	367	
March 763 (1976 F3)	Front: 104	190	1.75:1	3.06:1	102.8	1.85	58.8	1.85	180	Pre-ground effect circuit car
	Rear: 124.6	310	1.27:1	1.61:1	173.2	1.79	136.6	1.79	202	
Typical F1 ground effect car showing results of varying downforce (pre-'83)	Front: 410	315 Static: very low speed	2.0:1	4.0:1	3000	0.1	1500	0.21	6000	Note on weight calcs: Formula Minimum 580 kg 1276 lb; Driver 164 lb; ½ fuel 160 lb / 1600 lb; 45%F 720 lb; 55R 880 lb
	Front: 290	630 2G Medium speed	2.0:1	4.0:1	3000	0.2	1500	0.42	6000	
	Front: 237	945 3G High speed	2.0:1	4.0:1	3000	0.31	1500	0.63	6000	Est U/sprung wt. per corner: F: 315 lbs R: 385 lbs
	Rear: 504	385 Static	1.2:1	1.44:1	3,333	0.16	2.777	0.14	4000	
	Rear: 357	770 2G	1.2:1	1.44:1	3,333	0.23	2.777	0.28	4000	
	Rear: 291	1155 3G	1.2:1	1.44:1	3,333	0.35	2.777	0.42	4000	
Rally Sunbeam 1600 (5 link rear axle and MacPherson Strut front)	Front: 78	495	1:1	1:1	85	5.8	85	5.8	85	Standard
	Rear: 95	310	1.24:1	1.54:1	97	3.2	80	3.875	120	Standard
	Front: 102	495	1:1	1:1	145	3.4	145	3.4	145	First experiment loose
	Rear: 133	310	1.24:1	1.54:1	194	1.6	156	1.98	240	
	Front: 118	495	1:1	1:1	195	2.54	195	2.54	195	Final choice for loose
	Rear: 120	310	1.24:1	1.54:1	157	1.97	127	2.44	195	
	Front: 128	495	1:1	1:1	230	2.15	230	2.15	2.30	Final choice for tarmac
	Rear: 133	310	1.24:1	1.54:1	194	1.60	156	1.98	240	
	Front: 118	495	1:1	1:1	195	2.54	195	2.54	195	Tarmac experiment skewed roll onto front with bad U/steer
	Rear: 133	310	1.24:1	1.54:1	194	1.60	156	1.98	240	
	Front: 146	495	1:1	1:1	300	1.65	300	1.65	300	Future tarmac "possible" for even less roll
	Rear: 161	310	1.24:1	1.54:1	282	1.75	227	1.36	350	

ground clearance.

This craftily combines the spring rate, sprung weight at each corner and any leverages within the suspension into one simple figure without a spring balance or a geometrical calculation in sight. It is directly related to wheel and frequency figures and, as he engagingly observes, it allows you to readily compare a U2 with a London bus, should this be important!

This method can have two disadvantages – preload on the springs will complicate comparison, and access to considerable numbers of vehicles while having two hydraulic jacks handy (one for front and one for back) is needed to build up any decent amount of data. Arthur gets over the first by an additional calculation of his own (often briskly removing the relevant coil for separate measurement) and the second by keeping a list of everything he has been able to measure for the past thirty years.

In my view the method also falls a little short by being unable to readily accommodate rising rate (where a vehicle will ride harder than the figure indicates) or ground effect (where it will be softer) – but every man to his own.

Sticking with the competition car which normally ignores comfort in search of grip and stability, it is still relatively recently that even works rally teams recognised it was worthwhile to have different spring settings for road and forest. The ideal coils for tarmac and slicks were more than hard enough to break things if left on for the brutally rough surfaces of forestry commission tracks or farm land.

The more mathematical will already have realised that if a coil spring is being operated at any angle other than vertical (usually on an inclined shock absorber), its rate will be slightly reduced. For practical purposes at this stage, as long as the inclination is not ridiculous this can be ignored.

A very good guide to unsprung weight should you have neglectfully forgotten to weigh everything while you had it in bits, is that an average corner will be between 45-55 lb. This comprises an alloy wheel, racing tyre, upright, brakes (disc/caliper or drums/shoes) half a coil spring/damper

unit and a quarter of a bottom wishbone. Rally tyres, steel wheels and solid axles may push this up as high as 100-150 lb per corner.

It was once considered utterly vital that unsprung weight be cut to a minimum even if only by ounces, and it is still a good objective.

You will normally be starting with either a chosen wheel frequency you wish to obtain, or a coil already fitted to an existing car.

In the first case you work through, using the information in the ''How Obtained'' line in the table to discover what rate coilspring is required. This also applies if you plan a change.

A similar approach, but simply in a different sequence, is used in the second case to find the frequencies of the car's existing suspension.

If comprehension of this is still denied you, don't worry. Just insert your own dimensions into the equations at the top of the table and all will be well – honest! You will note that, in column 4, the leverage has to be squared.

Why? Well, a coil spring exerting its force anywhere but directly through the centre of the tyre contact patch will have its strength apparently reduced at all other points nearer the inboard pivot for any given movement of the wheel. The wheel has a mechanical leverage it uses against the spring.

When the wheel moves one inch, the coil will not be compressed one inch, but normally by some smaller dimension. Because the distance a spring is compressed is directly linked to the force it can exert it will have become weaker so far as the wheel and chassis are concerned.

How much weaker can be found from the equations already given. It may be clearer to explain this graphically. The example uses an inboard coil mainly because it is more easily understood, but the same rules apply to outboard coils. You just have to calculate the leverage correctly and the sketch should make sure of this. Keeping to the same figures and leverages, it will be apparent that for a wheel movement of one inch, the damper/coil unit will move half as much.

If we know that a 400lb/inch coil

will give us the wheel frequency we need, the chassis in this example will always look at it as a 200lb/inch coil. Therefore with, say, a sprung weight of 200lb we know the spring must be compressed one inch from its free length *although it is a 400lb/inch spring,* to achieve equilibrium and keep the chassis at a static chosen ride height.

Choosing coil/damper sizes

If we plan for a total wheel movement in bounce and droop of six inches and staying with our example leverage of 2:1 it will only require a three inch movement of the coil damper ie: wheel movement divided by leverage.

We need a coil damper unit that will fit in the chassis space available capable of *at least* three inches of movement, plus space for a bump stop (and, preferably, a spare inch to deal with uncertainties in life and design). Is there such a unit in the manufacturer's list? If not you are going to be forced to alter the chassis in some way, before it is too late. Consulting the damper/coil illustration will make sense of the following text. Dimension T3-B3 will be not only the one that fits into the chassis design, but also controls the fitted length (a) of the spring. As we know it will compress one inch, we need a coil with a free length of A + 1. This is the dimension about which you consult the spring maker.

We will divide the available movement as, very roughly, 2/3 for bump and 1/3 for droop. Taking away the bump stop of 1 inch from 5 inch stroke leaves 4 inches. We decide to split this into 2.5 inches for bounce (wheel coming up) and 1.5 inches droop. This will give us the dimension T3-B3. which needs to fit the space available in the design between wishbone and chassis, or axle and bodyshell.

If there is no suitable coil/damper you will have to take a longer one and use only 5 inches of the stroke available, *or* increase the space available for it by moving the brackets top or bottom.

This applies just as much to a car you have bought as to one you are building. Because the original creator

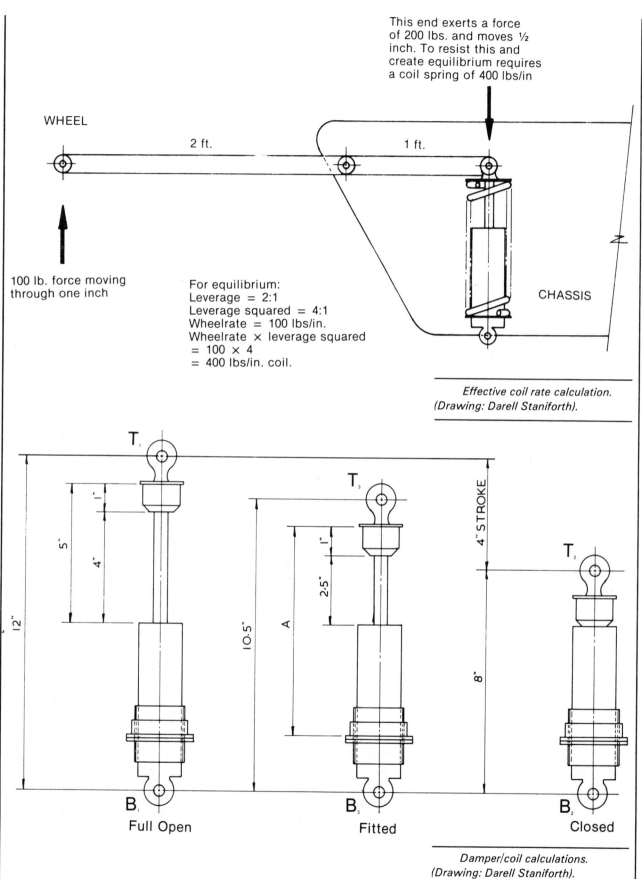

This end exerts a force of 200 lbs. and moves ½ inch. To resist this and create equilibrium requires a coil spring of 400 lbs/in

WHEEL

2 ft.

1 ft.

CHASSIS

100 lb. force moving through one inch

For equilibrium:
Leverage = 2:1
Leverage squared = 4:1
Wheelrate = 100 lbs/in.
Wheelrate × leverage squared
= 100 × 4
= 400 lbs/in. coil.

Effective coil rate calculation.
(Drawing: Darell Staniforth).

T_1

T_3

4" STROKE

T_2

1"

5"

4"

1"

2·5"

A

12"

10·5"

8"

B_1
Full Open

B_3
Fitted

B_2
Closed

Damper/coil calculations.
(Drawing: Darell Staniforth).

got it wrong does not mean you must not put it right. Failure to do so will store up insoluble trouble for later on, *particularly if there is insufficient bump movement,* essential to protect the damper from going solid in roll or bump.

Having decided on T3-B3 you will have a fitted length for the coil. Add to this the squash that the car's weight will cause and you have the free length of the coil needed.

There are two diameters of coil in common use – $1\frac{7}{8}$ inch and $2\frac{1}{4}$ inch. Like tyres one is much commoner than the other in the secondhand market. It is the larger of the two, and may require special collars on some dampers and can foul the top front wishbone where smaller ones do not.

Spring makers (and secondhand buyers too) need to know a third dimension, not usually too important; the coilbound length. If you cannot squash one up, measure the wire diameter and multiply by the number of coils – not precise but good enough.

It is essential the spring can never close up completely as, if it does, it will be instant trouble at some extreme movement of the suspension when everything goes solid and your carefully calculated wheel frequency rockets up to infinity. When this happens you normally go straight off the road either backwards or forwards and spend successive months either recovering your health, rebuilding the wreck, or both ...

There is a lesser version of this when the coil/damper goes down onto the bumpstop. Depending whether this is a slice off a redundant kitchen doorstop. or a properly scientific and expensive Silasto shaped to be progressive, the wheel rate and frequency will rise gently, or precipitately, with immediate alterations for the worse in handling and tyre grip.

Knowing a little of what we certainly do not want we can now get down to a practical plan and approach for either designing the dynamic parts that are going to be so important to the car's handling or analysis of what you have bought in order that future actions will not be blundering in the dark.

Planning falls into three sections:

data required, essential calculations to choose the correct parts, and a practical building sequence.

Data required

Note that all weights are laden, including driver (and navigator) half normal fuel load, coolant, full oil system and any spare tools or wheels correctly mounted.

1) Gross weight: distribution front/rear, and from this four corner weights.
2) Unsprung corner weights.
3) Sprung corner weights (1-2).
4) Axle/wishbone/link leverages front and rear.
5) Actual coil rate.
6) Effective (squash) coil rate.
7) Wheel rate.
8) Space available for coil at static height.
9) Crush on coil at static height (3 ÷ 6).
10) Free coil length (8 + 9).
11) Wheel frequency $187.8 \times \sqrt{\frac{7}{3}}$

Essential calculations

1) Draw the critical points and general outline onto a sheet of graph paper (easier and quicker than doing it on a drawing board).
2) Try to mount the damper/coil spring unit as near to the wheel, and as vertical as possible.
3) Calculate resulting leverages.
4) Choose suspension frequencies front and rear.
5) Calculate effective coil rate.
6) Calculate actual coil rate required.
7) Calculate static squash on coil.
8) Choose dampers that will give total required travel (normally between 3.5 and 8 inches).
9) With damper closed by 1/3 of its travel measure total overall length eye-to-eye, and also space available for fitted length of coil.
10) Calculate free lengths of coil required (fitted length plus crush).

At this point it would be wise to consult a spring maker or his catalogue to ensure that it is technically possible

to produce a coil to the length and rate you require, or better still that he has one available off the shelf.

Should there be serious difficulties in this you stick as near as possible to the chosen frequency and alter the coil/damper length and mountings to suit. You have some elbow room in all this, either adjustment on the screwed support collar, or using a spacer to effectively lengthen a spring or both.

If however the spring threatens to be too long, you are faced with cutting off a coil, inevitably increasing the rate and frequency whether you want it or not, and forcing a matching alteration at the other end of the car.

If you have got all this right, the day that everything, either new or modified, is mounted in position, the car will sit at the correct ride height and attitude ready to go. At the worst it should only need modest adjustment, its behaviour will be tolerable and you will know which way to go and how to go there should you decide things need to be altered.

There is a reasonable case for relating sprung/unsprung weight ratio to frequency in some way but there have not been enough hours in my life as yet to do the practical work essential to turn this into anything more than a suggested but theoretical wraith.

The foregoing at least explains to some extent the essence of why a successful design still has art and experience lurking among the science. If it was an equation and perfection was 100, one man might choose to add 50, 40, 6 and 4, while another utilised 29, 31, 25 and 15 to achieve the same result. The oddity is that someone else who may have only managed a total of 77 or 86 may be doing the actual winning, for the correct answer is itself a variable dependent, ultimately, on driver, circuit, weather, and ... who knows?

Choice of damper unit and its dimensions

The probable practical minimum stroke on a light car will be 3.5 inches *plus bumpstop* but a forest stage vehicle or large road car may have, and use, up to ten inches. Using five inches for the purpose of our example; we deduct a one inch bumpstop, and split the remaining movement into 2.5 inches for bump and 1.5 for droop.

For ease of assembly avoiding preload on the spring is a good idea. The ideal arrangement is a coil that just fits onto the damper fully extended without special tools. If the spring is a touch short it does not matter as you can lockwire the coil, top collar and damper together to stop separation when airborne, or jacked-up with the wheels hanging free. It also gives the bonus that the damper acts as a droop stop or strap.

A freely chosen unit will enable you to at least attempt this, otherwise circumstances will be dictating to you to work out a suitable length of coil. Remember that either the damper or the fitted length of the coil can probably be varied at the design stage, or by altering mountings on an existing car.

One simplified table of figures just to give, as they say, the flavour of things:

Nonetheless, even if it is not perfect first time out, you will know at least two things denied to much of that opposition – what you have already done and how, in theory, any alterations are likely to affect the handling. Testing, either by yourself, or with a driver who can communicate back a reasonable idea of the car's "feel", will then give a link between what has been done and the result at speed.

The tenacity and time needed to build up any solid basis of knowledge and experience in a field of such imprecision, and the near genius required to make head or tail of it in limited time, is the reason why top designers are thin on the ground.

Obviously all the foregoing can be reversed to analyse a suspension system already in existence whether sports car, production saloon or single-seater. You can check the rate of any coil by compressing it exactly one inch while it stands on your bathroom scales, and reading off the weight

of quality will be found light alloy units with adjustable everything and Rose jointed mounts at both ends. One may cost twenty times the price of the other.

Normally dampers are softest in bounce (when being compressed) and four or five times stiffer on rebound. These are ideal and long proven characteristics for road cars and give a civilised ride for passengers while killing any attempt by the vehicle to begin bouncing rhythmically.

While these characteristics cope with a lot of competition car suspensions too, particularly any that operate on bumpy variable camber, twisty or just plain diabolical surfaces, they are a lot less suitable the better the road gets.

One very big advantage of a damper that can be stiffened separately on bump is that it can be used as an anti-dive and anti-squat device. This is because for a very short interval of time after loads are fed into the suspension the car views a hard shocker as almost solid suspension. As the period of most violent acceleration from standing start will last barely half a second and braking into a corner little more, the car is very briefly restrained from what it wants to do until G-forces, though strongly controlled, start altering its attitude.

Surprisingly this bump stiffness may not prove a handicap anywhere else, but it is the type of high level experiment that many people may never be involved in: even those who are, have been known to sort out settings they like and stay with them through thick and thin. Being without such refinements removes another set of potential variables and so may not be any handicap at all.

Most adjustable dampers simply increase stiffness, proportionately, on both actions at once.

Fitted length possibilities in the design	Crush (160lb/inch coil, 240lb sprung weight)	Free length of coil (minimum required space on damper fully extended)
6 in	1.5 in	7.5 in
7.5 in	1.5 in	9 in
8 in	1.5 in	9.5 in

When you realise that a damper with a screwed bottom collar may have $1\frac{1}{2}$ inches of adjustment in the thread, the enormous advantage they give will be seen (and the value of buying this pattern if you can possible afford it) not just for fine adjustment for your chosen coil, but for fitting differently rated coils at a later stage of development without getting into insoluble ride height difficulties together with corner weight equalisation.

This just about completes an outline of arranging for the wheel at each corner to behave as you would wish it. Unfortunately the four variables in geometry described earlier in this chapter have now become more like 40, or even 400, and the only sure test of whether you have got it right will be on the track, against opposition.

indicated, or by putting a known load on it and measuring how much it compresses. This latter approach is usually a human being precariously balanced on a bit of quivering board across the top of the coil: not really recommended for accuracy, or your safety, but far better than staying in ignorance.

Before leaving suspension units it should be said that the type and quality of dampers that you fit is likely to be dictated solely by the money available. In few areas of the racing car do you so clearly get only what you pay for.

At the bottom of the scale come non-adjustable units with welded platform collars for coils, bump/rebound valving that may or may not be perfect and split rubber bushes at the top and bottom. At the pinnacle

Anti-roll (sway) bars

While there is no current way you can do without dampers, a simpler, less expensive and in many ways a far more powerful device in its effect on the car, that just about everyone will have to deal with, is the anti-roll bar,

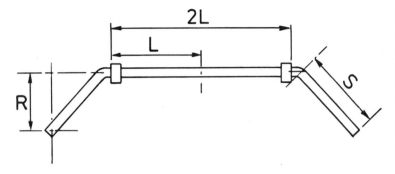

T = TRACK (INS)

K = FRACTIONAL LEVER ARM RATIO

$$\left(\frac{\text{MOVEMENT AT ANTI ROLLBAR PICKUP}}{\text{MOVEMENT AT WHEEL}}\right)$$

d = BAR DIAMETER (INS)

R = EFFECTIVE ARM LENGTH

L = HALF LENGTH OF BAR

S = LENGTH OF LEVER ARM

Q = STIFFNESS IN LB/INS PER DEGREE

$$Q = \frac{10^4 \times T^2 \times K^2 \times d^4}{R^2 \times L}$$

Calculating anti-roll bar stiffness.
(Courtesy Mike Pilbeam).

---

normally, if incorrectly, shortened to "rollbar". This is, effectively, a solid steel rod or length of tube mounted across the chassis in bearings of some sort with an arm on each end. These arms are linked to each wheel giving the result that if the car goes into roll the bar has to be twisted before one wheel can rise and the other fall. The bar has no effect whatever if both wheels are rising or falling together.

It is often not realised what a powerful instrument the anti-roll bar is, well capable of exerting three or four times the resistance offered by normal coil springs to roll on a corner. For the mathematical, Mike Pilbeam is one designer who has a method of working out the stiffness of a bar on a calculator and his formula is given in the accompanying illustration.

As with so much else there is

plenty of "guess precedent" to indicate bars from $\frac{3}{8}$ inch diameter on single-seaters, to $1\frac{1}{8}$ inch on big saloons but, as with coils, the leverage, mounting blocks and links can alter the effect of even identical bars so much that comparisons once more verge on the meaningless.

There *are* a few cardinal rules that make things easier. Get rid of any rubber in the system right away. Mount the bar in nylon or alloy block bearings with grease nipples or, better still, in needle rollers. Allow, at the design stage, for bigger or smaller diameter bars to go in the same bearings, or replacements on the same bolts lest some future development should otherwise prove to be impossible. Rose joint the links to the wishbones and get these latter attachments as near to the wheel as possible.

Check the linkage movements from full bounce to droop to make sure they cannot foul the steering, driveshafts or tyres under ANY circumstances.

Having done all this, the mountings you have made to accept different diameters of bar are likely to be more valuable than a calculator. Even Mr Pilbeam admits that there are likely to be so many small, and possibly unavoidable, variables in an anti-roll bar installation, in itself dependent on the chassis stiffness to work as predicted, that experiment with the car in action will dictate final form.

For those hooked beyond recall on the pleasures of a labyrinthine trek through a series of equations, there are at least two other lengthy and detailed expositions on bars and their interrelationship with springs. One is by Adrian Reynard and the other by Arthur Mallock. The first appears in the *750 Club Bulletin* of May 1982, and the second in the February 1979 issue of the same journal. Obtain a back number and save me the agony of trying to reproduce either with any coherence or comprehension.

Inboard suspension scores heavily in terms of the simplicity of fitting readily adjustable anti-roll bars of great efficiency – although there is the penalty of massive increases in the bending loads in the top rocking arms that have to transfer the effects of the bar to the wheel. Such anti-roll bars are usually a short piece of steel – solid, tubular or laminated in strips – free to rotate in proper bearings on the tub or chassis with a blade at each end linked to the inboard ends of the top wishbone. A big range of adjustment is available by rotating one or both blades from on edge, to flat when they are quite flexible. They are rotated by the driver via a long cable, and can even be used to alter the car in mid-race, a useful virtue with reducing fuel load, varying tyre characteristics or some change in the weather. The bar itself can also be exchanged if necessary for a thicker or thinner example.

One thing that the driver/builder is likely to need is some way of working out a tubular equivalent to a solid bar that is already working well, simply to save weight. A second is a method of estimating the alteration in stiffness of any increase/decrease in diameter of solid or tubular bars.

These can both be achieved with a sheet of graph paper and the D[4] formula, not a new rust preventer but

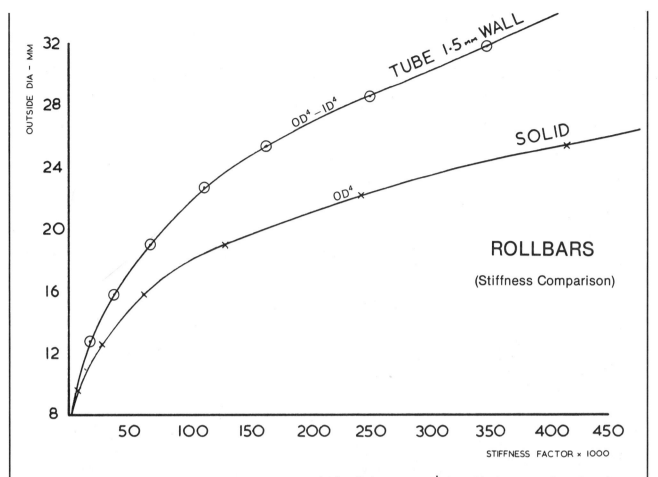

ROLLBARS

(Stiffness Comparison)

Anti-roll bar stiffness comparisons. (Drawing: Darell Staniforth).

the diameter multiplied to 4th power. This does not normally allow for differing materials. Bamboo or spaghetti clearly do not have the same "Modulus of Elasticity" as titanium.

Once again most of us will be working with steel of generally similar properties, and the information given in the accompanying graph gives an excellent, and instant, comparison between diameters.

As space will probably force any alternative bar to be of a similar shape to its predecessor, you only need a comparison. Obviously a total change in leverages and mountings will mean starting again, but even in such a case the Pilbeam formula gives an excellent starting point.

A big reaction to small adjustments of a bar means the car is already near to its best. Big movements producing little variation, mean something else is having a massive and probably unwanted effect on the suspension.

Rising rate suspension

What roll bars do not have is "rising rate", an aspect of suspension that keeps having periods of popularity before being shunted off in temporary disgrace until the next time. Rising rate simply means that the suspension of the car stiffens its resistance to loads going into it as they increase, whether these loads are forty gallons of petrol, cornering roll, nose dive under braking or aerodynamic downthrust.

There have been many different approaches to achieving rising rate suspension systems for competition use, but I will only mention three as a rough guide.

McLaren came up with a very sophisticated system in which the complete front suspension linkage altered its leverages throughout its arcs of movement and those principles are having a rebirth in F1 pushrod and pullrod designs.

The other two approaches relate to specially made springs. The hardest to produce are those springs in which the gaps between each coil gradually alter from small at one end to wide apart at the other. As the load increases the closer coils touch, and effectively shorten the spring which increases its rate and hardens it. This approach was used during the Battle of the Skirts before everyone in F1 agreeed that a 6cm ground clearance at all times when the scrutineers were looking – but which just happened to disappear at speed – was OK and legal. Less difficult to make and consequently cheaper, are coils in which, say, one third are close together and two thirds wide apart. Strictly speaking, these are dual rate springs for, at some point, which must of necessity occur abruptly, the closest coils go solid and the rate increases instantaneously to a higher figure. This approach was used

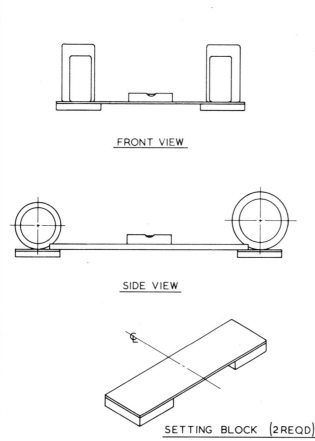

FRONT VIEW

SIDE VIEW

SETTING BLOCK (2 REQD)

Setting up (see text for details).
(Drawing: Darell Staniforth).

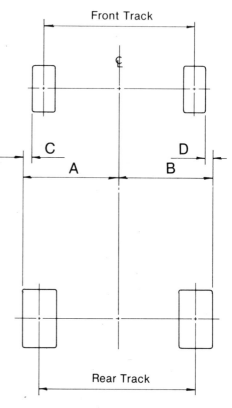

by both F5000 and F1 during the Battle of the Skirts (or Battle of Balestre if you prefer), but for uses other than with ground effect can often bring bigger problems than it solves. Nonetheless rising rate seems to have an awful fascination for many designers and, if you are interested, I leave you to go it alone.

With all the aforementioned as a basis, it should now be at least possible to look at the "enemy" and make an educated paddock guess or a carefully measured check on what is happening to their wheels, tyres, roll centres and so on when on the move.

Reverting for a moment to hurdles facing the road-going mass-production saloon designer, he not only has to plan for violently differing loads and ride quality between tolerable and excellent on a wide variety of road surfaces but, for reasons of production

practicality, vehicle shape, engine/gearbox location, or simply cost, he may not be free to do what he wants to do anyway. Some, or all, of these compromises may lie behind the apparent uselessness of a promising road car when it first gets into competition. And they are what give you a chance to do something about it yourself to the detriment of the opposition.

Curiously enough, aerodynamic downforce recently producing loads of 3G, or more, in F1 effectively mirrors the results of luggage piled into a road car. Of course the F1 loads are higher, particularly dynamic ones, varying with speed and car angle to the road and even moving backwards and forwards within the wheelbase.

Which brings us logically to Staniforth's First Law — "Treat with the greatest reserve anyone in the paddock who says he has the complete answer to your handling troubles". When the "expert" goes away, notice if he is walking on top of the paddock puddles without getting his feet wet ... it will usually be one of his other talents!

Setting-up a car

All this laborious toil, both mathematically and to earn the money to buy the equipment that is going into the suspension, will not be rewarded to the full without a method of setting it all up at the correct angles and pointing in the right directions.

Various professionals point out, quite rightly, that a car needs to be correctly set up, but do tend to give the impression it is another of the dark esoteric arts you would be well advised to leave to them, not to mention paying for this skilled service. The serious amateur will have no truck with this, not necessarily for financial reasons, but because it will inject a number of unknowns into his preparation.

Fortunately setting up requires only rather slow and meticulous work, a friend, and simple low-priced equipment. We should all be admirably equipped for these needs.

The setting up illustration gives the various dimensions, parts and markings that will be needed. The sequence of events is as follows:

1) Choose the four wheel contact points on your garage floor.

2) Mark these with painted rectangles together with a centre line.

3) Make two transverse boards, without any end supports but appropriately marked "front", "rear", etc.

4) Place them correctly on your floor marks.

5) Adjust these boards to level by building up each end support with layers of hardboard or thin ply, contact-glued in place.

6) Make up four wooden spacer blocks to the required ground clearance PLUS the total height of the base boards above the floor. It may be easier and safer to use carefully adjusted axle stands for a saloon or heavy sports car.

7) Roll car into position on the levelling boards.

8) Remove springs, but leave all wheels and locating parts in place and rest chassis/shell on the blocks or stands.

9) Set caster angle. (Lies anywhere between half a degree and nine degrees. Use recommended figure or start at four degrees to begin testing). Small caster angles give light steering with low self-centre and possibly too much sensitivity in a straight line. Vice-versa with large angles. Outside the range mentioned will probably give unacceptable problems from no feel or self-centre to heaviness with extreme kickback from road shocks.

10) Set all camber angles. If uncertain use vertical as a start. Many saloons may be better at half a degree negative. Tyre temperatures and/or wear, together with handling will point the way for later alterations. Aim at even temperature across the thread. Too much negative gives hotter inner edge and vice-versa.

11) Check steering rack is either in its right place, OR parallel to the ground and at right angles to centre line of car. Measure its

vertical height. Disconnect track rod ends from steering arms, and centralise rack exactly.

12) Set toe-in on wheels, then adjust each track rod if need be to keep wheels in position and rack centralised. Finally reset steering wheel spoke positions on column spline.

13) Check that each rear wheel has the same toe-in from the centre line of the car. Run a long piece of string, or wood from each wheel to the front. "A" must equal "B". This will also show up any skew in front wheel settings. In the case of a solid axle car it will also indicate that linkages or mountings are at fault if the axle is not square to the centre line. Unless you want it to crab down the road, this must be attended to, however major.

14) In case of IRS set rear toe-in. Usually lies between $\frac{1}{8}$ inch out (twitchy with oversteer and very good turn-in) and $\frac{1}{2}$ inch in (very stable, understeer, possible front wash-off in corners).

15) Recheck all wheel cambers are correct and that "A" still equals "B".

16) Check that springs are of similar free lengths, or similar leaf numbers and thicknesses. (Softer for rain, rough surfaces, increased roll, more grip on outer wheel and vice-versa).

17) Check dampers. Very difficult unless one is leaking or obviously useless. If adjustable, check that click adjusters work. They normally go from softish to solid. Count the number of clicks and try to estimate by feel how many clicks do what and make a note of it, otherwise you will most certainly forget. For the average single seater or small car you should be able to squeeze them shut with two hands but be barely able to pull them out on rebound. The exceptions to this are gas filled types, such as Bilsteins which gently expand themselves without help.

18) Refit all the springs and dampers and remove support blocks.

19) Set ride-height with driver or crew, half fuel and water, by

raising/lowering spring platforms. If not adjustable, raise with spacers under the coil, lower with a shorter coil. At the most desperate you can cut a loop off a coil spring but it will harden it, put up the rate and increase the suspension frequency. This may still be a far better bet than running the car at the wrong height or tilted. Remember that any downforce at speed may have to be allowed for, after experiment, by statically setting the car high, most probably at the front.

20) The ultimate refinement at this point is to check the unsprung corner weights. Surprising as it might sound, all this meticulous work may still leave different tyres bearing unequal shares of the total weight of the car. There is, so far as I am aware, absolutely no real alternative to buying, borrowing or making a corner weight gauge. These hook just inside the wheel rim and measure precisely the load on that wheel. To have any hope of accuracy (and accuracy here means a maximum discrepancy between left and right wheels, on either axle line, of 10lb and, preferably, nil) preload or stiction of any sort needs to be eliminated. Any bolts through rubber or nylon bushes should be loosened, and dampers set full soft or if at all possible disconnected completely. Our earlier mentioned pundit, Arthur Mallock, does front wheels on a pair of bathroom scales, but even he admits to problems with any wheel bearing more than $2\frac{1}{2}$ cwt (the 20 stone, 288lb or 127.2 kilo fat man limit of the average domestic weighing machine). To reduce the load on a wheel, lower the spring support collar and vice versa. Needless to say, doing this on other than our perfectly level surface is a total waste of time, and there are those who say that as the car never, ever runs on a perfect level surface anyway, how vital is such a setting? Good question, but we are presently seeking

perfection, so get on with it and don't argue.

Once a vehicle is really finely balanced increasing the load on any particular wheel will not only affect its performance, slip angle, etc, but will cause the car to pivot about a line joining that wheel and its diagonally opposite partner. We are now entering a field of induced skewed roll and unequal weight transfer known in American racing as "corner jacking", which, when combined with the dozens of other variables transforms the situation from a purely scientific one to an advanced art form. Determined artists will have to pursue their personal researches in this.

21) Try to do initial testing without any wings, spoilers etc. If not, set them at zero angle of attack and disconnect rollbars. Progress through rollbars on full soft one end at a time, small increases in wing angle, fitting spoilers. If you get any downforce at all, however modest, you may get bottoming at speed and have to set the car high statically. Bottoming on rough surfaces or after yumps requires a high static setting as well, or even an all round increase in coil rates.

After setting-up, your personal development plan may be helped by these pointers.

Bump steer

Bump steer has already been covered. You may find you have it although it never felt any embarrassment. Do not let that stop you getting rid of it, as any handicap, however small and apparently invisible, is something you can do without.

Understeer

Understeer can be reduced by increased front wing angle, wider/softer front tyres, slicks instead of cut tread, softer front coils (unless the cause is the damper going solid onto the bump stops), perfect Ackerman angle (bend steering arms when red hot with slow cool or make new ones), stiffen or fit a rear anti-roll bar, raise front or lower rear tyre pressures, increase nose-down attitude, negative camber on front wheels, toe-out on rear wheels.

Another possibility is to take a long hard look at your driving technique and decide whether you should be going much deeper into corners and turning in late so that the car is beginning to go sideways and will accept power with a smaller front wheel slip angle. Hoping to just turn the steering wheel and then boot the throttle is a guaranteed way of making most cars with rear weight bias, or extremely good rear grip, start attacking the scenery.

Oversteer

The reverse of just about everything previously mentioned for understeer, except Ackerman angle.

Straight line instability

Increase rear toe-in, but *always* suspect play, wear or flexing in the rear suspension. Check this with all spring and weight loads removed, bolting or clamping a three foot bar across the hub or disc to exert toe-in/out leverage. You may be astonished to see what starts bending and by how much! Stiffer sidewall tyres fitted to rims at least one inch and preferably two inches wider than tread width.

Wheel locking

Always strip the *opposite* side brake first, looking for any shortcoming in the *non*-locking caliper or wheel cylinders.

Wet weather preparation

Reduce front braking on the balance bar. Increase front and rear wing. Soften everything with the single exception that should the car then tend to understeer it may be because the rears are getting extra grip running on a line partly dried and cleared by the front tyres, in which case you will have to stiffen the rear, take off rear wing (or put on more front).

Beware of tightening adjustable dampers too far with soft coils. As rebound resistance is up to four times greater than bounce, the coil does not have time or strength to push the damper back out and the car "reverse jacks" itself downwards onto the bump stops, and the suspension goes solid.

The last phenomenon may be difficult to spot, as it will normally have time to reset itself to some degree on the gentler return down the pit lane or out of a stage to your service crew.

There are not many chances to compare the feel of a racer at full speed with its behaviour in normal traffic conditions, but when it occurs it is a big shock. One opportunity for this rare experience is the Longton and District Club's Isle of Man Hillclimb each autumn. The event involves driving in convoy from the ferry in Douglas some five miles to the paddock part way round the TT course. While this is in convoy the police escort usually manages to make it an interesting trip, but other traffic sometimes slows it and there are tram lines, pedestrian crossings and white lines on the way. The general impression is often that one's pride and joy rides like a plank, bumping and jolting with all sorts of awful knocks and clunks becoming threateningly audible, while darting about unpredictably with any variation in road surface.

Yet the same car becomes smooth, precise and comfortable once on the course at racing speeds. I think this is partly psychological on the part of the driver, but also because instantaneous loads are many times higher at speed and the chosen high frequency for the wheels is appropriate to these forces. They are fed in more violently, in a shorter time, to dampers and coils which naturally have to accept them where they are partially rejected at much lower speeds.

Clearly you go on progressing with this theory up and up the scale to a point at which an F1 car is riding solid up to 140mph and a 110mph corner approach under braking is so bad that the car can be clearly seen jolting and leaping about on the TV screen. Heaven knows what it feels like in the cockpit. However, as it happens, we do not have to make any celestial enquiries. Pironi told *Autosport* what it is like: "It can be so bad, I think I'm going to turn over ..."

Little really scientific research has been carried out into the loads and strains exerted on a Grand Prix driver by his job, but some of the limited data available has revealed quite staggering heart stress and G-forces. FIA medical men studying driver fatigue noted "total exhaustion of some drivers after races was recorded medically". There is only one other word in common use for "total medical exhaustion" which can be left to you men of the world to guess, but the visual corroboration is winners falling clean off the victory podium because they can no longer stand unaided.

The FIA report went further. It referred to problems caused by lateral forces in the spine, and vertical forces from extremely hard suspensions against which driver-protection is virtually non-existent. They reported 60% of drivers with neck trouble and a startling 90% with lumbar or lower back effects, with future arthritis as a possible result.

It should be a chastening thought (to some at the top of the sport perhaps), that Chapman's banned and disputed 88 might have provided amongst other things a far less brutal ride for his drivers. I suspect one of the subtleties of his approach was that as vibration is a well known inducer of fatigue in vehicles and aircraft any conductor of a Team Lotus 88 would have been highly likely to end any Grand Prix fitter and faster than the opposition.

Rubber suspension

Which leads us more or less logically to Pirelli seat webbing. It does? Well at any rate to rubber and its many variations as a suspension medium on racing and road cars. The reference to seat webbing will shortly clarify itself.

It appeared on my technical horizon when considering designs of a further version of my original coil spring Terrapin single-seater. Primarily I was seeking a simple way of building anti-squat and anti-dive into the car as these are vitally important in the hillclimbs and sprint world with its bad surfaces, standing starts and violent braking into sharp corners.

If there was any way of making the car amenable to rapid alteration, — that is a cheaper way than a garage full of coil springs — it would be worth investigating. Anti-squat/dive can be achieved either through the geometric layout of the wishbones, as seen from the side of the car, through variable leverage linkages in the wishbones, as seen from head-on, or through the coils or other suspension medium.

There have been many versions of all three, that for various reasons were not all good or valid for me. Therefore I decided it would have to be the rubber suspension medium which came in for attention.

Rubber can easily offer a true and progressive rising rate, but only combined with a deal of awkwardness in practical design terms. For instance a simple block of rubber needs very large leverages to magnify the small movement range in the block from unloaded to effectively solid.

Mini doughnuts and Aeon internally and externally shaped bump stops are much more sophisticated refinements of the simple block. But even the Mini has to build in wishbone ratios of five to one to get tolerable results and the moment the car is lightened it effectively hardens up violently.

Rubber in torsion has excellent possibilities, but needs the right size and type of bush, so I decided, finally, on rubber in tension — rubber bands if you like.

I was not breaking any pioneer ground. Mini designer Alec Issigonis had used rubber bands on a special thirty five years earlier, the Kieft 500 employed luggage rack bungey cords and various 750 MC Formula cars, including those of Jim White and Bill Cowley, had also used it.

Several 750 contestants were more than generous with information on how they had used slices off lorry and bus inner tubes to provide the necessary bands for suspension linkages to stretch. The snag appeared to be finding something that could be more of a known quantity than inner tube, especially as the natural rubber common a few years earlier was being superseded rapidly by a synthetic type lacking "life" or much stretch.

My wife, helpful as ever, was emphatic that I needed a material that would have some technical information available on its characteristics — "like those strips under the cushions of our chairs". I inspected the strips, found inch wide bands that clearly had a textile interweave of some sort — and was on the telephone to Pirelli first thing next morning. It was the beginning of a beautiful and successful friendship, although Pirelli have steadfastly refused either to take any interest in publicising it or to accept any payment for the material on which the Mk7 car has run since the first day.

The only literature turned out to be brochure graphics of the stretch characteristics of three grades of the material, Standard, Super 70 and Extraflex — capable of stretching safely to 45%, 65%, or 95% of their respective lengths.

From this modest base the calculations began. They took the form of borrowing a coil spring approach — estimated load on each corner, static deflection, possible three or four G in bump.

The graphs gave the stretch in inches per lb of weight applied to the webbing in various widths, but because it has genuine and controlled rising rate the amount of stretch obviously gets less and less the higher the load until it snaps.

The actual construction of the strip is complex but is in effect layers of rubber with textile inter-layers between at angles — not unlike a tyre carcase. The result is that when the strip stretches it is actually twisting the layers of which it is built, against each other.

My helpful contact at the factory said there was no information about the material as a wheel suspension medium — I would have to work it out for myself, then say what I thought I needed.

To cut a long story short I devised rocking top arms that combined pick-up pivots for both shock absorbers and rubber bands (shown diagrammatically in the accompanying illustration), decided on the number and length of the bands made from the least stretchy version and the factory sewed them up and put them in the post within a few days.

My alarm at finding they were joined by sewing machine was hardly allayed by the man at the factory assuring me "They'll break any where

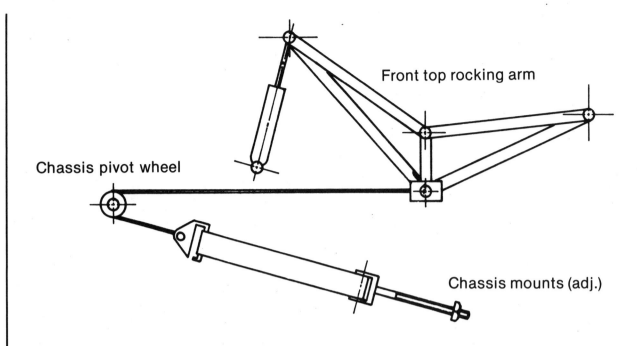

Front top rocking arm

Chassis pivot wheel

Chassis mounts (adj.)

Number of rubber
bands variable

Chassis mount (fixed)

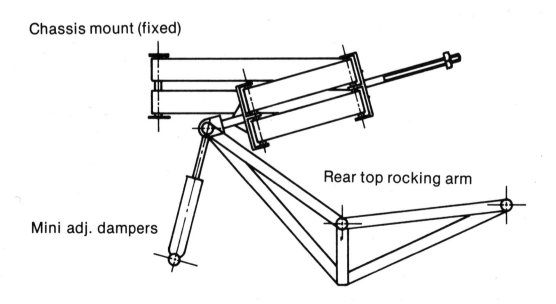

Rear top rocking arm

Mini adj. dampers

but the stitching". He was certainly right there.

First time out was a disaster. At my home hillclimb at Harewood in Yorkshire I did not even cover 1000 yards before every single band had snapped on one side and several on the other – the car collapsed ignominiously, with horrific grinding noises, onto the road surface and stopped! After the sweating and jovially Anglo-Saxon marshals had manhandled my creation into a position where the meeting could continue I took it home and had another think.

It seemed possible that although the stresses were well inside the theoretical "stretch" capabilities of the material, there might be instantaneous loads from road bumps that went way over the maximum permissible load point with immediate failure.

Would the "stretchiest" version, theoretically far too soft with more length increase than the suspension would tolerate, be the answer? Again, shortening a great deal of experiments on numbers, lengths and leverages of bands, the soft ones *were* the answer. The carriers were modified to take a higher number of bands.

After six years successful use, a new chassis is really needed to take full advantage of what could be done to produce a totally and easily tuneable suspension.

As I have recently lost a little bit of the old enthusiasm for 3.30am in the garage, in midwinter, this is how I think it should be done, not how I am going to do it.

The rubber bands would be mounted longitudinally beside the driver's body or legs in side pods and joined to the wishbones as my current fronts are, by 3mm rustproof yacht rigging wire running round light alloy pulleys on needle roller bearings. The wire and pulley method is not only low in friction but means complete freedom for the designer to put his suspension medium wherever he wishes in the car,

with refined and rapid adjustment methods for ride height, change of rate, leverage, ratios, etc, all built into the mountings.

The bands would be away from dirt, oil, heat and light, all enemies of rubber, and for good measure they are cheap and a totally sprung part of the weight of the car. It astounds me that a professional or two has not already employed material with such virtues in its favour ....

The system's only handicap was me. I found that thinking out the complications of differing lengths and widths of material as well as a varying number of loops finally had so many permutations that I ground to a halt mentally.

For instance, increase the number of bands on the linkage and because there are more sharing the same load they all stretch a little less. This puts them all into a softer or more resilient part of the elongation curve, thus lowering the wheel frequency. It may be what you are after, or you may need to alter the wishbone leverage to get more stretch for the original rate. It can go on, and on, as long as your tenacity continues. The trick is to utilise only the portion of the curve you need. Luckily I got mine near enough to satisfy me early on, and I have stayed with it unaltered.

What it certainly does is iron out bad surfaces and dips where other cars bottom, roll in corners (no anti-roll bars fitted) and the majority of squat and nose dive.

Retracing our steps for a moment, the "Flying Vicar" (Reverend Barry Whitehead) creator and conductor of one of the fastest, and perhaps the ugliest, 1100cc hillclimb cars of recent years, instigated a lot of work on persuading a computer to design a suspension for him. Apart from our amicably differing views on whether there is some ultimate Racing Paddock in the Sky awaiting us in due course, he is also a "long swing axle man" whereas I have always tended to be "short".

If nothing else his approach meant he had to get his family to support his String Computer cords at the far end of a long room. Tapping it out on a keyboard had consequent appeal, but it proved difficult and complex to analyse what a wishbone-link suspension does in mathematical terms, and even harder to explain (ie programme) it to provide the required answers.

One of the very many oddities for instance was that if one of the objectives was a fixed roll centre the computer would reject any solutions in which it had moved even a thousandth of an inch! It had to be explained that certain tolerances *WERE* acceptable and in what steps. The machine accepted its instruction with enthusiasm — and increased its output twenty fold!

This meant the human brain (Barry's in this case) was still required to deal with possibly twenty feet of paper closely covered in a mass of figures, all needing interpretation and tabulation in the light of the objectives of the suspension design.

The most recent development has been the appearance of firms and individuals willing to sell you a suitable program, or compute and supply all the answers — for a suitable fee. As every sort of cost in the world of computers has fallen dramatically in recent years, these specialists may well be within reach of your pockets.

Clearly more people, more time, and more programming expertise can improve the situation enormously. But when you are not exactly sure what you want, and need something different, but compatible, front and back, the torrent of computer suggestions may make things worse rather than better.

To avoid ending this chapter on too depressing a note, it should be recorded that the Reverend Whitehead's work on his car back at the Vicarage changed it from being so unstable it once spun simply because he was changing from second to third on the straight, into a class winner. An amateur's mega-leap by any standards

4 Aerodynamics.

Aerodynamics, whether concerned with streamlining, co-efficients of drag, front and rear wings, or venturi sidepods has to be, outside the wind tunnel, the true empirical art – full of mysteries, half-truths, whole lies, quacks and bull.

Seventy years of experience and expensive research has been directed into it, but 99% on behalf of aeroplanes, and, as might be expected, everything seems different once you want to apply such principles to a diabolically-shaped, four-wheeled vehicle rolling along the ground. Practically every aerodynamic rule then seems to either alter in some major way, or become strangely invalid.

Aircraft operate generally while enveloped in 'clean' or undisturbed air steadily flowing above and below them several thousands of feet up in the sky. The surfaces of wings and bodies are smooth and uncluttered (unless the plane has been adapted to fly off a ship, when the Navy has always had the reputation of hanging on more extraneous projections than a scrap metal man's lorry). Planes also have movable control surfaces that permit alteration in flight of the effective shape, lift and drag characteristics of the wings.

A racing car has none of these, save the extraneous projections. Those potential advantages nature has not fixed, international regulations have. We must do the best we can with the resulting wreckage, and in F1 at any rate, that best developed into a staggering degree of success that could easily double or treble the effective weight of a car at high speed and its consequent tyre grip on the road.

All this has been achieved by simply turning an aircraft wing upside down, thus converting the lift that first carried the Wright brothers, and later a hundred million holidaymakers, into the skies, to a downforce.

Once again it is as well to ensure we will all be talking the same language and reference to the wing sections illustration should clarify the terminology.

Lift – hereinafter in our application referred to as downforce – is a very delicate phenomenon dependent on air flowing very slightly faster over one surface of an aerofoil than the other. The result is that air pressure on the faster side is lowered a little – but enough when multiplied by the square footage of a wing to lift many tons into the air.

Apart from tentative ventures into "streamlining", aircraft had been around some sixty years before any serious attempts were made to borrow their attributes for racing cars. They were needed because one quality of the rubber tyre is that its grip goes up the harder it is forced against the ground. As usual nothing is quite as true or as simple as it appears, but this arbitrary statement will suffice for the moment. A new way of pushing up the road adhesion of an ultra light racer had immense appeal if it could be harnessed.

Almost from the beginning of motoring it had been understood that the teardrop, somewhat elongated, was the sort of shape air enjoyed travelling past with the least disturbance or drag.

Given the panel bashing limitations – and lack of fibreglass – at that period, early attempts were

WING SECTIONS

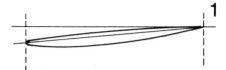

1

Thin high speed low
drag section

2

Thick medium speed/drag
section

Normal Range of
Centre of Pressure
movement.

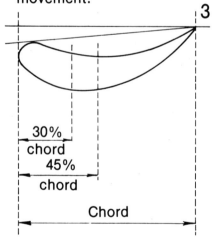

3

30%
chord
45%
chord

Chord

Cambered low speed high
drag section

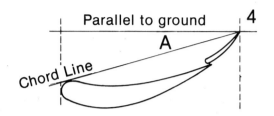

Parallel to ground

4

A

Chord Line

Heavy flap high drag
A = Angle of Attack

5

AILERON Flap

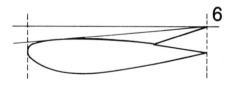

6

SPLIT Flap

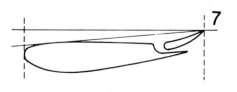

7

SLOTTED Flap

angular and fairly ugly but developed in due course into the poetically beautiful all-enveloping streamliners of Cobb, Railton, Campbell, M.G. and the Golden Rod. These produced phenomenal speeds with relatively modest power, but they did not have to go round corners.

Designers and drivers had long since found that on racing circuits it was how fast you went round the curved bits that largely dictated who won, not who went down the straights most quickly.

By the late 1970s top speeds had been standing virtually still, or even falling, in F1 for over twenty years at around 175 mph while lap records still went down and down.

The answer was cornering grip steadily rising through the invisible 1-G barrier, then through 2-G into an unbelievable – and for drivers, almost unendurable – 3-G.

Yet a bare fifteen years or so earlier horrified scrutineers surveyed the appearance of an upside down wing on struts on the Porsche Spyder sports car of two young unknowns and went into instant conference. Driver Michael May took the opportunity to at least get out to practise on the formidable Nurburgring, but long before the start the scrutineers had given him the hard word.

He had another try at Monza, but he was a man so far ahead of his time he did not get a run there either and, effectively, drove off that part of history's stage there and then.

It was ten more years before first Jim Hall with the Chaparral sports cars, and then Dan Gurney with a Ford, made America the place that began another revolution. Formula One, after some European suspicion and hesitation, could not get on the same bandwagon fast enough.

In no time at all there were wings sprouting everywhere, balanced precariously on all too fragile stilts bolted to the suspension uprights so that they might operate high above the "dirty" or turbulent air buffeting its way around the car below. That they certainly worked was shown all too

A selection of wing sections. (Drawing: Darell Staniforth).

clearly when they fell off. Graham Hill for one had a monumental accident from which he emerged for a lengthy period of gritty convalescence when one leg of his car's wing collapsed.

The revolution forged ahead despite a succession of new rules that forced different mountings, reduced heights, forbade adjustability, imposed maximum size limits and restricted positioning relative to axle lines.

My co-designer in the Terrapin project, Richard Blackmore, who could fly a fullsized plane as well as a succession of models constructed over the years, soon built a wing for his own car. While its effect on actual tyre grip was uncertain, what it did do was help steady the car very much during braking and turn-in on corners.

He followed this up with a cunning automatic adjuster which used the compression of a small spring to reduce both the attack angle and drag at straight line high speeds when it was not needed, and put it back on when the car slowed.

Almost simultaneously the administrators were banning anything adjustable at the gallop, so Richard's secret weapon never did battle – and he left the sport anyway to ride the summer winds in gliders. Something like seventeen years later this pioneering experiment developed into the sophisticated split wing shown in the photographs of the Monopin.

Lacking the freedom to adjust more than a static flap in the pits, teams very rapidly began to use a series of bolt-on varied aerofoil shapes – slim and almost flat for the ultra high speed circuits, thick and deeply curved or "cambered" for somewhere like Monaco.

Bodies flattened, joining carefully concealed engines in desperate attempts to clean up and channel the air flowing over the cars onto the wing hopefully awaiting its arrival at the back. Wind tunnel time suddenly began to appear in the bills to be paid by the team sponsors from F1 and the day of the true "Wing Car" was fast approaching.

Both rear and front wings fall for the amateur into a category not unlike that of suspension geometry. If you are in search of something to fit on your own car do you buy, copy, modify

someone else's or build it yourself?

To begin with you need to understand some minimum fundamentals, on which aerodynamicists base their enquiries and research, but don't be frightened off. What works on a plane, works less well, or not at all, on a car. Your pioneering, and mine, has at least as good a chance of working as most experiments and once again you will know more or less what you are doing rather than groping in the dark.

How to begin?

Bear in mind that the same terms "roll", "pitch" and "yaw" used for aircraft are applied to cars too. Roll is precisely that and easy to understand. Pitch is nose-up or down under acceleration and braking, while yaw (tail out) is effectively straight line instability in vehicle situations. You should also know that the characteristic teardrop shape of a wing is referred to as a "section".

Almost every word that follows could be applied to side pods as well as wings, and in certain instances they become much more important but as they have now become history in Formula 1 that area has become partly academic.

Movements of the centre of pressure can, and do, affect the attitude of the whole vehicle, setting up all sorts of undesirable happenings connected with pitch and porpoising.

The actual area of the section rather than its aspect ratio is also vital. The early Lotus 78 ended its side wing pods just where the engine began. Within a season they were stretching back and back until every car had them flowing in smooth fibreglass valleys to behind the rear suspension, nearly doubling the effective area.

Yet again it is obvious that on the majority of current circuits faster round the corners is more important than the drag incurred on the straights (except for the problems of overtaking, but that is another story). As that jovially ruthless Australian driver Frank Gardner once observed: "The important thing about being first into the first corner is that everyone can then have their accident behind you". He could have added, "and their problem then is overtaking you rather than vice-versa".

What wing to choose?

The choice of a particular shape of side pod and its angle of attack once fitted to the car has always been a much bigger task to alter, even without the pressures of time, than a wing. You desperately need to try and be right the first time. While this has to be optimism of the highest order, there follows a lucky 13 point guide, which should at least reduce the odds against disaster.

1) Angle of attack: the angle between the chord of a wing and the line of the air flowing towards it (taken as parallel to the ground with cars).

2) Speed: very thin flat wings for high speeds, thick curvy "banana" ones generally for low. Distance from the leading to the trailing edge is *chord* and the maximum thickness of the wing is expressed as a percentage of this *(ie: a twenty inch chord wing that is two inches thick is said to be "10% thick".)* Somewhere between 12-20% is suitable for car speeds and this dimension is used as the final two figures of NACA four digit profiles.

3) Flaps: use of adjustable trailing edge flaps (often a miniature version of the full wing) virtually essential, if only because it permits rapid and wide variation in downforce without requiring the main wing mountings to be adjustable. Theoretically about 20% of chord, but Williams, for one, use over 30% on some wings.

4) Centre of Pressure: the point of balance at which a wing is actually exerting its downforce at a given moment. Wanders about all over the place depending on speed. Wanders worst on banana wings. Moves approximately between 30% and 45% rearwards of the leading edge, but travels forward the higher the speed and downforce. While this is of vital importance to aircraft designers for

The sophisticated split wing of the Monopin shows how even the d.i.y. constructor can exploit technical advances in the science of aerodynamics. (Pictures: Allan Staniforth).

stability reasons it was, until the advent of the full side pod, largely irrelevant to the car man. For my car I chose a single mounting point on each side plate 33% back from the leading edge and have never had any breakage. Two schools of thought on mountings: 1) central pillar with 2 inch diameter alloy tube (TV aerial fitters always have it in stock) set into a special rear plate on the Hewland gearbox; 2) end plates reaching down to cross a tube or frame (Renault, March, Monopin).

Either method should aim at leaving the underside, the really vital bit of the wing, as smooth and undisturbed as possible, with a teardrop fairing round any centre pillar and most emphatically free of those revolting brackets and stays so often seen which are invisibly wrecking the precious airflow following (we all hope) the polished rivet-free surface.

5) Aspect ratio: Long narrow wings have a high aspect ratio (gliders, U2s, Formula 750) while short wide ones (jet fighters, F1) have a low AR.

Normally defined as length over width or span over chord, AR can vary from 1:1 to 50:1. The best lift/drag ratios, the conventional aircraft world's measure of efficiency, are found in long narrow high aspect wings, and this clearly governed early car experiments when they stood high in the air on stork-like legs, with the disastrous results already mentioned. Legislation currently limits span to 110cm and height above the ground to 90cm although these dimensions can obviously be altered by the rules at any time.

But aircraft concepts of efficiency based on staying economically in the air are not those of the car designer down on the ground. Happily for him downforce is also directly related to the area of the wing. Span is controlled by the rules while chord (except in F.750 for one) is generally free.

Doubling the chord of a wing massively increases its downforce, and, while drag, the ultimate enemy for airmen certainly increases, it will not be the disaster for a car it might at first seem.

6) Drag: The ogre which appears to be the big bogey, especially on fast courses and with limited power. However, cheer up. I am satisfied in my

own mind that *as long as you do not stall the wing* drag is not a serious problem up to about 120mph. Above this you are likely to have the brute power of 400-500 horses, which will successfully pull a vehicle with the drag co-efficient of secondhand housebrick up to 180mph before giving up.

My reason for saying that drag is not a serious problem for most of us is as follows:

The majority of drivers and tuners are all too familiar with the fact that many more bhp are needed to accelerate from 110 to 120mph, than from 50 to 60mph. Now consider this situation from the opposite standpoint. You can afford quite a drop in top end power (or increase in drag) before there is serious effect on top speed. As long as you stick to sensible angles of attack on your wing or flap the drag figures for a wing of six square feet (mine) are not large.

A friend was able to feed into a computer lift/drag figures for the section I was then using (NACA 4418) for a range of speeds, angles of attack and flap degrees. When the high speed idiot (the computer, not my friend) coughed it all back it was immediately apparent that as long as angle of attack stayed below about seven degrees at higher speeds and up to twelve degrees at lower, the drag computed as bhp stayed well inside single figures.

For example: $2\frac{1}{2}$ degrees of wing, giving drag of five bhp at 120mph resulted in a speed loss of only 2mph, *BUT* was giving theoretical downthrust of 134lb to aid the rear tyres in a corner.

Conversely, removing the flap completely from my own car's rear wing on a blazing hot day on a flat road course, put my terminal speed up from 107mph to 115mph. The car felt no different in cornering, BUT I recorded a slightly slower time!

7) Reynolds Number: One thing a deep, (big chord) wing does give is a higher Reynolds Number which is A Good Thing. A Reynolds Number is usually called a "dimensionless quantity" something I found extraordinarily hard to comprehend. Reference to it in less dedicated company may draw a witticism that it has something to do with your driving abilities, but ignore such unkindness.

What it is, is something that allows designers, text books and students of the art to compare the same wing section in different sizes and when operating at different speeds. This is essential because of a curious attribute of the aerofoil section – its performance alters both with physical size and the speed at which it is travelling. A twelve inch model version of a fullsize hundred foot span aircraft simply does not work as well at the same speed.

The Reynolds Number for any wing is derived from the formula: 6370 x speed (in fps) x wing chord (in feet).

For the same cynics who viewed my maths with suspicion earlier in the book, the source of 6370 happens to be Air Density over Air Viscosity at sea level. This is of course a variable if you are designing an aircraft, but can be taken as constant (except at Kyalami) for the car man. It also avoids confusing things like "10^{-6} slugs per cu.ft."

It should be immediately apparent even to anyone who has trouble making two and two add up to five that the higher the speed or the bigger the chord, the higher the Reynolds Number, whatever the shape of the section. And the higher the Reynolds Number the greater the wing's efficiency or lift/drag ratio. Aircraft figures are normally in the 3-9 million bracket.

Much research and data including all NACA sections is based on three million. Probable limits for a car will be inside two million, and well below one million most of the time.

Based on (5) and (7) my personal choice was to utilise an aspect ratio of 2:1 (21.5 chord with 43.3 span or 110cm less end plates). Mathematically 2.5:1 is a better lift/drag compromise, but it sacrifices area and downforce particularly at the lower speeds common in the hillclimb world and some cars are clearly using wings down to 1.5:1 ratio.

8) Stalling: This is when the airflow breaks away completely from the wing surface and its lift or downforce properties promptly vanish. Obviously of great importance to pilots, while not so apparently vital to drivers.

Nonetheless a stalled wing on a car is doing little more than acting as a built-in airbrake with some slight downforce from the "snow plough effect" of the car's slipstream blowing on it.

The most casual paddock inspection will show many wings running stalled. Any technical data on wings gives stall angles, usually in the 12 to 16 degree bracket, though flaps can increase this. Heavily flapped banana wings in the late seventies produced so much drag according to March Hesketh and Ferrari designer, Harvey Postlethwaite, that top speeds fell slightly even though Cosworth was persuading more and more power out of the immortal DFV engine. Yet lap speeds still rose because of the higher cornering speeds that became possible. It is well to bear in mind that a wing at zero or even a negative angle of attack (tail down on a car) is normally still giving some downforce at high speeds.

9) Setting up: Whatever size or shape of wing you build or buy, take the trouble to inscribe suitable markings that will permit setting chosen angles of attack in the paddock. One method is to put the car on a perfectly horizontal surface. Having made endplates with straight top edges, the wing should be mounted between them so that those edges are exactly parallel with the chord line. You then use a combined spirit level/protractor to set the wing at 5, 10 and 15 degrees and mark these at the adjustment point. It is more awkward with a flap, and you may have to draw it to scale, because each movement of the flap effectively alters the chord line and the consequent angle of attack of the whole wing. But 20 degrees of flap is certainly not a 20 degree angle of attack on the wing. What it will depend on is the size and shape of the flap, whether it pivots or moves in a controlled arc in pre-cut slots, and precisely where it goes in relation to the wing, when adjusted.

Without these markings you can have no idea what you are playing at in the pit or paddock. The importance and sensitivity of such settings were emphasised by a tantalisingly brief conversation during a superb BBC Horizon programme on F1 in which Frank Williams was ordering a further

half degree of rear wing with only moments to go to the green light.

10) Airflow: All the foregoing is based on something the car constructor/driver does not happen to have – perfect airflow over the various surfaces, although front wings do run in almost "clean" air until they start catching another car.

Mostly the airflow threatens to be, or is, a mess and any efforts to cowl engines, and smooth flow round and over the body have got to be worthwhile and likely to double or treble the practical value of a rear wing.

11) Endplates: (or spillplates). Opinions differ fairly violently. Jets usually have none but recently have started growing winglets, vertical sections on wing tips which act as endplates but without their drag. Car endplates have got steadily bigger. I plumped for very large (2ft x 2ft) from the beginning feeling that large endplates must at least contribute anti-yaw or a weathercock effect to straight line stability, particularly in crosswinds on a rear engined single seater. The technically advised minimum is to have at least the maximum wing thickness projecting all round with more generous overlap front and back. It also seems that a really good driver may be able to "lean on them" in corners.

12) Sections: (outline of a wing shape). Really the 64 dollar question. The Abbott & Doenhoff book (see bibliography) lists a large number of NACA shapes in great detail. There are also RAF designs from WWI (not as ridiculous as it sounds remembering their airspeeds) Eiffel, Gottingen, Eppler and Wortmann FX. Like suspensions you could spend a lifetime exploring the permutations. It's all yours.

13) Construction: Generally the model aircraft approach with formers as accurately made as possible in wood or alloy and threaded onto stringers running end to end, with the major one running along the chosen centre of pressure mounting line. The leading edge of each former is cut off to make a flat on which to mount a "D" section of solid wood to permit the shaping by hand of a perfect leading edge. Rivet or glue the covering skin of 22, 24 or even 26 gauge alloy sheet. It can be filled with rigid foam (but do not forget to put generous holes in all the formers for it to rush through when expanding). A fellow builder once neglected this and saw his creation bulge and crease horribly under the pressures built up, wrecking two weeks work in a couple of minutes.

The coming of the "Wing Car"

At about the time external wings were reaching the point where increases in downforce had to be paid for too dearly in drag, the Lotus 78 gave warning of what was to come while the refined 79 burst on the scene like a bomb. Chapman, as on earlier occasions, had taken things a massive step forward.

He exploited the standpoint that however inefficient a narrow slice of wing might be from an aircraft designer's point of view, if it was big enough it would still exert a hefty downforce. By running such a slice down each side of the car the potential was impressive. A little arithmetic shows what he aimed at harnessing.

Normal atmospheric pressure is 14.7 psi. The body area of an F1 car, between the wheels, is very conservatively 6ft x 5ft or 30 square feet or 4,320 square inches. Achieving the very modest pressure differential of 0.25psi, or two per cent, increased the effective weight of the car by 1080lb, almost half a ton, or by 67% on a fully loaded car.

The most intensive development had more than tripled this within three years, partly by increases in the side pod area, partly by better aerofoil choice, skirt sealing and clean exit routes for the air. The effect on tyre grip was reflected immediately in quite staggering reductions in lap times. Where a one second improvement had been enough to set people talking, drivers began to carve five and six seconds at a time off the previous year's record or pole time.

Inboard front suspension provided a reasonable flow of air between the body and wheels.

The result in 1978 was more than mystifying to the rest of the racing world – it shattered them. Andretti and Peterson were men of more than enough calibre to utilise this new tool to the full and proceeded to trample the opposition into the ground.

Grand Prix after Grand Prix fell to them. Within another season came the World Championship and eight pole positions for Andretti, second place to Peterson, and Constructors Championship to Lotus with Ferrari, Brabham, Tyrrell, trailing. It was in my view perhaps the greatest technical coup in the whole history of automobile racing and it fundamentally altered every vehicle that followed in the next four years not to mention the war of fearful attrition between the administrators and the teams.

Of course the secret had to leak, and other brains and hands set about improving the idea still further with a rapidity remarkable even in Formula One. Extraordinarily Lotus found themselves suddenly fighting for a place on the grid let alone pole position, and the bitter legislative struggles over skirts and control of racing were already in sight.

The history of that saga has no place here so let us get back to air and how useful, as well as capricious, it can be.

D.I.Y. flow checks

One way the amateur can analyse airflow, without having to find and rent a wind tunnel, still needs an old airfield runway for a single-seater, though research is possible with a sports or saloon using a bit of the M1 with extreme discretion!

To do it you first Sellotape two inch tufts of a contrasting colour of wool all over the area in which you are interested, particularly air intakes or outlets.

You then drive the car at various speeds while two colleagues drive alongside, one keeping pace and the other taking photographs of your tufted vehicle. Later examination of the pictures will provide an immense amount of information, not all of it good or welcome.

One thing about air is that it is rebuffed by the slightest rise in pressure anywhere. So for radiators the exit route is often more important than the inlet. Ample witness to this was the mounting at first of side radiators square on to the direction of travel, but then gradually at angles approaching parallel to the centre line of the car in many single seaters. The airflow into the front of these radiators can hardly be ideal, but what is behind them is a low pressure area in and around the engine bay.

Air, only too anxious to flow into a low pressure area, happily finds its own way through the cooling matrix.

The high pressure air nozzle fitted to the average garage compressor when held at the front of the car pointing backwards can be very useful setting up an airflow over the bodywork, while simple experiments with wool tufts or bits of tissue paper indicate what is happening and where. Do not decry this as too crude and simple to work. Personally dubious of some ducting on a Terrapin I once owned powered by the transverse air cooled unit from an NSU car, I used the airline technique. It proved that a positive gale dived into a NACA style duct let into a side panel, thence round a long feeder tube and across heads and barrels in a most satisfactory manner.

Airblast windscreens work well in deflecting rain and general draught off a driver's visor or goggles and are fairly easy to make by shaping a piece of Perspex or even metal to the body and mounting it some half an inch clear so that air is collected at the bottom and forced out of the top. A variation on this is that with no screen at all, a small lip on the front edge of the cockpit surround curved to point forward can eliminate serious air buffeting around the driver's head entirely. This was something demonstrated in practice by a modification to the cockpit of the 1600 Gould Terrapin.

The NACA duct

This might be a suitable moment to more formally introduce the NACA duct – often pronounced "Knacker", but "Nasser" seems to me more graceful, especially if the conversation happens to be with a lady aerodynamicist.

The excellent shapes of aircraft as they developed and the consequent smooth flow of air over them posed the double problem of persuading that flow to dive into a hole which it preferred to ignore, or conversely exit from a hole with the least possible disturbance. There proved to be a single, though far from simple answer – the NACA duct. This is the curiously tapering triangular opening, for the complex calculation of which we should be suitably grateful to American tax payers. They footed all the bills for research that produced the duct, and the methods and formulae for calculating the sizes, shapes and angles that make it work.

The NACA duct is becoming reasonably familiar on single-seaters, is used a great deal on totally enveloped CanAm and Le Mans type cars, and is discreetly and asymmetrically set into the bonnet of the production Porsche Turbo.

On the established principle that anything however small that can improve performance or reduce drag has got to be worthwhile, a guide to their design is as follows.

Knowledge on these ducts I found hard to come by and I am heavily indebted to 750 Clubman David Reilly and scrutineer Peter Smithson for the basis of much that follows.

The two things vital to any successful intake are that the momentum of the passing air should not be lost and it should not contribute extra drag to the vehicle. Easy to say, but difficult to achieve.

There are three phrases used in describing what is going on in any air intake and how good or bad it is.

1) Mass Flow Ratio: or what actually gets into it. Expressed as a fraction of 1.0 through the calculation –

What actually gets in
Free flow through an identical area

Achieving 0.5 is good going. Can be worse, worse to the point where little or nothing enters at all.

2) Pressure Recovery Ratio: or the loss of pressure caused to the air going in. Expressed as –

Pressure entering the duct
Free flow pressure along mounting panel

Can be very efficient and the NACA duct achieves around 90 percent, meaning that what does go in is at nearly the same pressure as the passing gale caused by the speed of the vehicle.

3) Boundary layer: the air closest to any moving body. Is actually standing still in contact with the body, because of friction but, speaking in thousandths of an inch, the further away from the panel the more it speeds up until it reaches the speed of passing airflow. This is laminar flow. When it has either broken away or been stirred into a thicker layer of erratically moving air, it has become turbulent flow.

Nose inlets (for radiators, jet engines etc.) have good pressure recovery, but are obviously vulnerable to swallowing debris as well as drag from poor exit routes.

Projecting scoops also have good pressure recovery, but only if they stick out far enough to be clear of the boundary layer. They usually suffer high drag, and further losses once air starts going round any corners in the duct or its connecting piping.

It will be apparent that the submerged duct, if correctly designed gets over virtually every one of these difficulties. As might be imagined, the angles, shapes and lengths of its two walls and floor ramp are vital, as is the shape of the top lip at the entrance itself (see illustration).

Firstly a little explanation of why a NACA duct looks like it does, and we will then explore a sequence with examples in designing one.

The boundary layer's "dead" air is what is going to try and fill the duct causing poor or non-existent functioning, unless it is dealt with in some way. How that is achieved is the secret of why and how a correctly designed duct works.

A thick boundary layer reduces the effectiveness of an inlet because its low velocity has little momentum and will block off part of the inlet area. One of the virtues of the scoop intake is that it projects above, and well clear of, the boundary layer.

There are in fact two boundary layers in the submerged duct – that on the ramp floor and that on two vertical walls. While the wall layers are not, for various reasons, particularly important, that on the ramp floor most certainly is. It starts off as thick and dead as that on the body panel and the need is to thin it out and get it moving.

Fortunately a natural phenomenon called the vortex is around to help. This is created below any edge across which air moves at an angle, and it will be seen from the airflow illustration that its effect in the duct is to start pulling at the boundary layer in the bottom. Because of the duct's shape the boundary layer is widening out, and therefore getting thinner as it flows down the ramp floor; vortices help this process vitally. Vortices also agitate the layer and add momentum to it. All this results in the boundary layer being thinned right out by the time it gets to the main opening of the duct.

This is probably more than enough about the reasons why – how do we design one for a particular task? It needs to be sited where passing air is at least going to get to it. The nearer the front of the car the better. If it is in a stagnant area, without the suction, for instance, of the engine induction, it is not going to work in some magical and mysterious way.

And you also have to make a calculation or an educated guess as to the quantity of air you want to pass through it. The graph shows engine air demand in cubic feet per minute (cfm). Use capacity, maximum revs and double the figure because the best flow ratio achieved is likely to be only about 50%.

For brakes, oil cooler and fuel pumps use the largest duct that can be physically inserted. You can always reduce the flow, but you cannot increase it.

Radiators are a difficult and ambitious flow calculation, but you can get at least an idea of the amount of air involved by inspecting a road car. This will show that few radiators are bigger than about 1.5 square feet, that flow

NACA duct top lip and airflow details. (Drawing: Darell Staniforth).

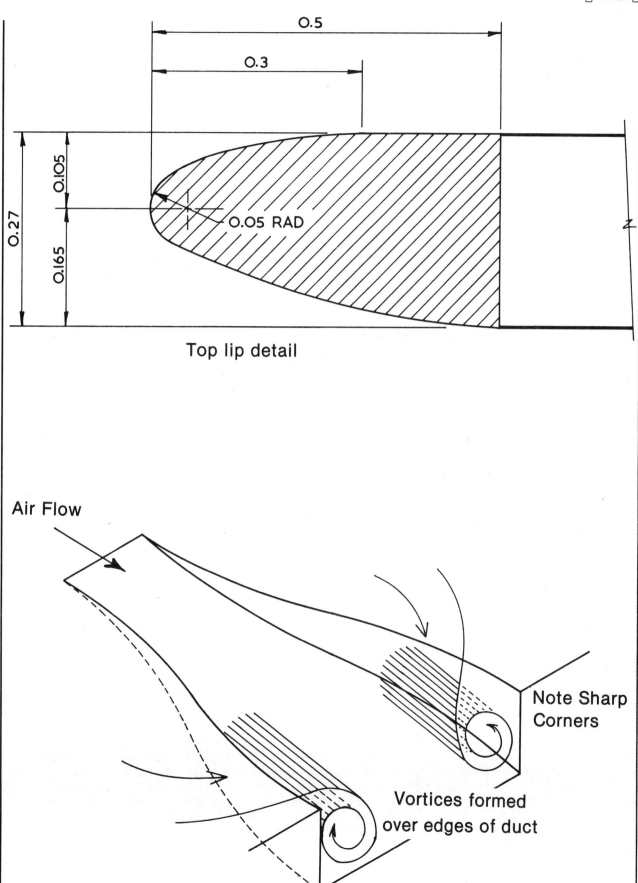

O.5

O.3

O.105

O.27

O.165

0.05 RAD

Top lip detail

Air Flow

Note Sharp
Corners

Vortices formed
over edges of duct

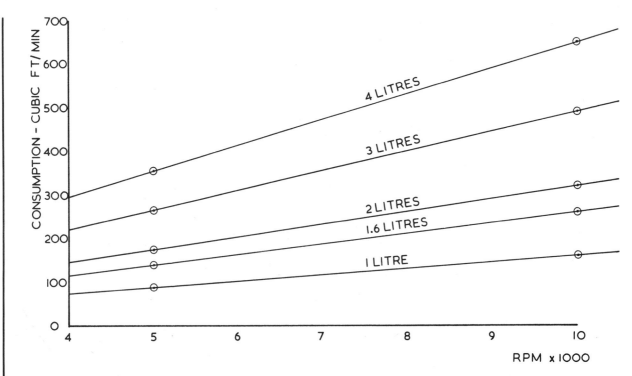

routes into them are usually poor, exits simply diabolical, and they are still over cooled for 90 percent of conditions.

From the second graph we see that an area of 1.5 square feet will pass about 10,500cfm of free air at 90mph, but assuming an efficiency of flow of 25 per cent we are actually talking about a need for 2,600cfm for an absolutely perfectly ducted radiator — and with a massive reduction in drag as a bonus.

All this has been no more than the roughest of rough guides to provide a basis on which at least to get started, but remember even Brabham's Gordon Murray knew nothing whatever about fans and airflow within them when he embarked on that famous Fan Car. It did not stop his finding out.

Before exploring how it is all actually done, previous experiment and experience point in certain directions that will save a lot of time. You can accept them as read or begin your own research project — nobody will be offended.

1)   The entry slot needs to have an aspect ratio (width over depth) of from 3.5 to 5.5. The example uses 4:1 but physical space may dictate differently for you.

2)   The point along the walls at which the ''S'' curve reverses itself has a complex relationship with both the total length of the duct and the width of the entry slot. The following table gives a series of co-ordinates to be used to plot the wall shape.

3)   Ramp angle has everything to do with both boundary layer behaviour and the ability of incoming air to stick to the ramp floor. It lies in a 6 deg. to 9 deg. bracket, and 7.5 degs. is used in our example. The steeper the angle, the shorter the total length of the duct, and the more likely that entry air will break away from its surface.

4)   The shape in plan of the duct, or how quickly and in what manner it widens out; an ultra short duct will obviously have a steep floor angle, both bad ideas.

5)   Top lip shape. Air diving into the duct has finally to split above and below the top edge of the duct entrance. This is given a wing-type leading edge with dimensions again related closely to the width of the opening, thus ensuring the least possible disturbance in the flow we have taken so much trouble to capture.

Its thickest point should be half of the intake opening depth.

Duct calculations

Finally the table of standard co-ordinates used in our example, is widely employed for the basic design of such inlets. To use it, divide the duct length into ten equal parts, or stations Multiply half the width of the maximum duct opening by the figure on the bottom line for each station. Plot this dimension out from the duct centre line. Join up your resulting ten dots.

The first set of co-ordinates are those of the Royal Aeronautical Society, the second set by American Carroll Smith in his excellent *Tune to Win.*

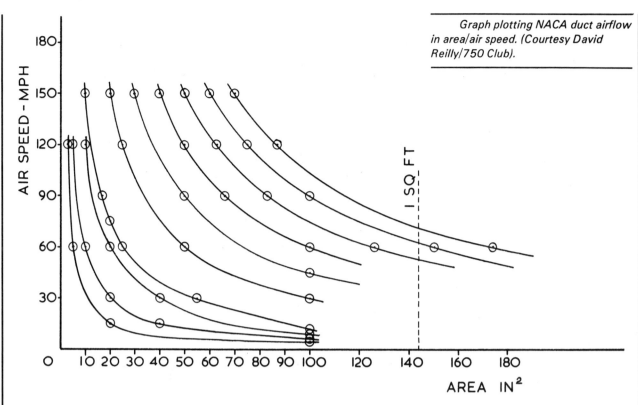

Station	Ramp 1.0	0.9	0.8	0.7	0.6	0.5	0.4	0.3	0.2	0.1	Inlet opening 0
Co-ordinate (RAS)	0.083	0.158	0.236	0.312	0.388	0.466	0.614	0.766	0.916	0.996	1.0
Co-ordinate (C. Smith)	0.084	0.140	0.204	0.276	0.356	0.454	0.590	0.754	0.920	0.992	1.0

The design sequence and example that follows is based on an intake required to feed a full-race 1600cc engine running up to 10,000rpm and geared for 130mph top speed:

1) Required flow in CFM: *260 CFM.*
2) Area of duct opening required to pass this quantity of air at max. speed of 130mph: *4.5sq.in (x 2 for est. 50% efficiency) = 9 sq in.*
3) Shape of duct with Aspect Ratio of 4:1: *6in x 1.5in = 9 sq.in.*
4) Thickness of top lip: $\frac{1.5}{2} = 0.75in.$
5) Gross maximum depth of duct (lip plus inlet): *1.5in + 0.75in = 2.25in.*
6) Using ramp incline of 7.5 degs. calculate total length of duct: *2.25in x Cotan 7.5in =17.09in.*
7) Use co-ordinate table and duct width to calculate size of ramp entrance: *0.083in x 3 x 2 = 0.5in.*
8) Use co-ordinate table to calculate

and then plot width of duct at each station: *eg (for Station 4) 0.614in x 3 x 2 = 3.684in.*
9) Draw in the shape of the duct walls (fullsize on graph paper is probably the easiest and most accurate way).

Note that it is a deceptively subtle shape (see NACA duct plan view), despite being almost a straight line for the first 30% or so. Given your fullscale drawing make an experimental cardboard pattern or two before fabricating the finished duct (all single curvature, happily) from alloy sheet which is then attached beneath a suitably sized and shaped hole cut into the panel.

Alternatively make a wooden model from which it can be moulded in fibreglass. In both cases the leading edge of the top lip is better shaped

from wood with as high a degree of accuracy and finish as you can achieve, and then fitted to the panel edge and faired-in internally. Curiously this lip has almost no thickness on, for instance, a Vulcan bomber, and many designers appear to ignore the theoretically required thickness, but until you find a good and convincing reason to the contrary keep it thick.

The final and essential refinement is that the air so carefully collected is delivered where it is needed via the fewest possible gentle corners within the body panelling – if changes of direction can be totally avoided, so much the better.

The side view illustrated (see section "AA") also shows a surprising similarity to the air intakes for radiators within the venturi side pods on single-seaters. While the entrance ramp angle has become irrelevant where the air

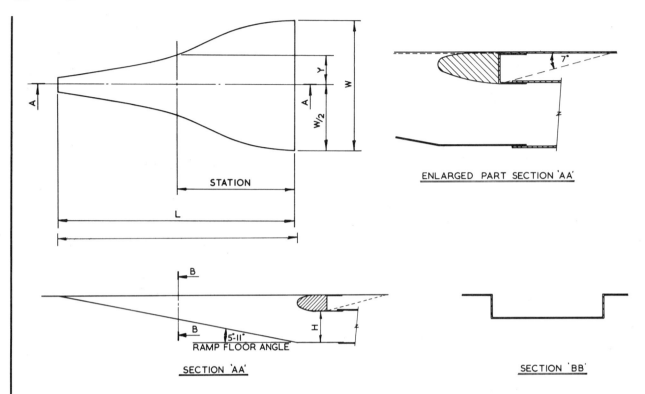

ENLARGED PART SECTION 'AA'

STATION

W

W/2

A

Y

L

B

B

5°-11°
RAMP FLOOR ANGLE

H

SECTION 'AA'

SECTION 'BB'

*NACA duct plan and section views.
(Courtesy David Reilly/750 Club).*

has free access or even semi-forced
delivery to the entrance, the duct floor
and roof built within the pod are clearly
visible. An ever-widening exit duct
permitting the heated and re-energised
air to rejoin the flow on top of the body
should always be employed for a duct
feeding a radiator. Back pressure can
stop any flow stone dead, and you find
you have cooling problems of the most
fundamental and frustrating kind.

The foregoing calculation which
was given as an example referred to a
particular engine and particular
maximum speed. You may well feel
that maximum mass flow should be
taken for a maximum speed of 50mph
which would need a much larger
opening area if full power is primarily
required at that sort of speed in your
chosen branch of the sport.

Before leaving the NACA duct, a
few other guidelines:

1)   There are less likely to be
problems with a design taking in too
much air than one for too little.
2)   Efficiency is directly linked to

boundary layer thickness – thinner the
better.
t3)   The downstream exit for a
radiator is just as important, if not more
so than the dimensions of the inlet.
Use at least double the inlet area.
4)   Twin ducts into the same intake
may save a lot of space below the
panel, but are not a good idea at all.
They give immediate trouble with
noise, vibration and instability of flow
as adjacent vortices attack and disrupt
each other.
5)   Don't put deflector or "lead in"
plates on the duct to try and steer the
air. They won't, and you may stop the
duct working at all.

Wings, pods & undersides

Air as we have just seen is very
reluctant to go anywhere offering it any
restriction or resistance. The emptier
and cleaner walled the area into which
it will flow towards the rear of a car the
better, so, getting down to the nitty-
gritty of venturi side pods or tunnels,
we see the reason for inboard
suspensions, ultra-high top links,

panelled engine bays, up-and-over
exhausts, vanishing flat-12s and so on.

If you are contemplating side
venturis for ground effect the first step
is to choose an airfoil section with, for
most people using relatively low
speeds, the maximum camber that can
be fitted into the space available *at a
suitable angle of attack.*

What angle? Yet another 64-
dollar question! Not easily answered
but it will follow a similar approach to
that used to design an external wing.
The higher the proposed speeds, the
flatter the camber and the smaller the
angle of attack. Choose one well inside
the stall angle, possibly between 8
degrees and 10 degrees as a
maximum.

The physical depth of the car may
limit both the camber usable and the
angle at which it can be installed. A
side view sketch of your car scaled
onto graph paper (as usual) will permit
experiment with cardboard cutouts of
various airfoil sections, and what is
possible and what is not will become
rapidly apparent.

Before the new regulations
affecting ground effect cars, F1
development had travelled towards a
very subtle combination of pure venturi

and the first part of a shallow camber wing section running, effectively, parallel to the ground before beginning its upward swing towards the back of the car.

The sections used were very flat, high speed ones in which centre of pressure movements are at their smallest. The leading edge becomes almost a mini-wing in itself to divide the oncoming air in orderly and non-turbulent fashion, much in the manner of the NACA duct lip, into the part that will go to the radiator and that which will be accelerated below the car itself.

The area of the curved surface each side had become so important that cars have been totally redesigned and rebuilt to acquire a narrow extra strip of an inch or less by a careful narrowing of the very bottom of the driver's seat region.

Without windtunnel information, it is difficult to guess how far you might go away from the flattened venturi throat towards a more cambered, lower speed shape, but it should be clear that any slavish copy of an ultra-high speed approach may not be a good idea at all.

The exact methods used in the Gould Terrapin/80 are covered in some detail in the relevant chapter, but as with external front or rear wings there are a number of early considerations.

The first is to assess the maximum length in which a decently uninterrupted curved surface can be accommodated along the side of the car or, in the case of a saloon, beneath it. It will begin soon after the front wheel, but a few inches aft of the driver things become tricky, complicated by piping, exhausts, rear suspension links and rods, driveshafts and the coil/damper units.

Not the least thing to be borne in mind is the movement of the Centre of Pressure once the wing begins to function. While this stays within reasonable bounds, and largely amidships where you want it on a single-seater, U2 designer Arthur Mallock hit a lot of snags when he began to turn the whole underside of his Mk.23 into a wing starting under the nose cone and running right to the tail.

The centre of pressure movements effectively made the car alternate between heavier or lighter at each end. Any increase in speed moves the centre of pressure forward, down goes the nose and up goes the tail. This immediately increases the angle of attack, producing more downforce still, and a further move forward of the centre of pressure, beginning a vicious circle .... Front wheel angles alter undesirably for braking and suddenly it is all reversed on slowing for an approaching corner.

This alternating of attitudes showed itself in the unpleasant and unsettling porpoising that had caused so much trouble in F1, and it took the Mallock team many months of work to get it under some sort of control.

It involved among other things having to use much increased spring rates to resist the downforces, body lips and alterations to the skirts and under-panelling. However, to get the full benefit of Major Mallock's long and expensive endeavours, you will either have to buy a current U2, or ask him yourself.

The next decision is the size of the gap between the thickest (or lowest) point of your chosen section and the ground. When the 'ground effect' first came on the scene they were often called 'venturi cars' and that is still a far more accurate description.

Air flowing under a car is being forced into a narrowing slot, one wall of which is the underside of the car or side pod, and the other the road. Its tendency is to keep going, just the way we want it to go — into the ever narrowing space and accelerating all the way with Mr Bernoulli's equation working overtime. He was the gentleman who first demonstrated that if you speed up a fluid, in this case air, through a narrow neck its pressure falls and if you slow it down through a widening one it rises. Hence carburettors and ducted radiators.

As the pressure falls, other air at ambient pressure naturally becomes keen to dash under the car from each side to join it — demanding determined efforts with solid skirts to form a wall sealed to the road to keep it out. Luckily because of the speed with which the low pressure area is being created, partial removal of the skirt does not give enough time for surrounding air to rush in and re-establish atmospheric pressure.

So we are still just in business. would hate to put a firm dimension on the precise distance between the road surface and point of maximum camber that should be used, but it should be as small as practicable.

Another thing that will to some extent control this dimension is the combination of chosen shape and angle of attack to give a certain angle of divergence between the wing and the road the further back we go.

Gas flow experts in the field of jets will tell you that a divergent angle of 7 degrees should not be exceeded if you want to be certain of keeping the slowing gas in contact with the surface along which it is flowing.

Proving or disproving this or any other aspect of aerodynamics and the racing car needs not only the wind tunnel but the co-operative loan of several different teams' cars. Even if you arranged this miracle, it might not be conclusive. The Williams team, with both money and talent of the highest order, did at least one experiment in their moving floor wind tunnel in which they removed the driveshafts to improve exit flow from the side pods. Result? It was worse not better! The driveshafts, contrary to all apparent theories, was making a useful contribution to the exit flow from the side pods *in that particular car under those particular conditions*. In scientific terms this example neither proves, nor disproves, anything. It only emphasises that art and luck are still in the game, even at that level.

Possibly because of the venturi effect already mentioned, the leading edge and top surface of the side pod shape do not appear to have the same significance as when in free air. Many designers have used a continuous lower surface that only begins at the centre of the leading edge radius leaving the front wide open for air to get to the radiators. They then do the best they can along the top bodywork with inevitable interruptions for radiator exits, carburettor collector boxes and sometimes exhausts and anti-roll bar stays.

Underneath great efforts are made to achieve a perfect surface, accurate curvature and smooth sidewalls contoured gently around any projections that prove totally unavoidable.

The term 'totally unavoidable' does not of course appeal to top teams as Williams demonstrated when the bulge on the side of all Hewland boxes carrying the gearchange rod intruded by perhaps three quarters of an inch into the venturi exit area.

To get rid of it, they redesigned and had made new gearbox cases with the change rod at the top and out of the way. This in turn forced radical alterations inside the box followed by the need for a reversing gearbox halfway along the change rod if the gate pattern was to remain unaltered.

What it did achieve was perfection in the glassfibre moulding shielding the engine from the exiting air. More and more cars adopted a complete moulding from end to end which was attached to subframes or a series of supports that would cope with the huge stresses involved.

The amount of work involved in constructing a simple mould (used so that the end result will have its smooth surface to the airflow) complete with gentle radii everywhere and an accurate curvature, may be a little greater, but will give an infinitely better end result than riveting panel beaten sheets to a series of formers.

Somebody like Strand Glass not only sell you the materials but hold free-of-charge evening seminars to show you how to do it. While nothing alters the fact that laying up fibreglass is a mucky, smelly, irritating and far from easy task, the results can be excellent.

Having said that, a full moulding may be too major a job to change in mid-season, whereas freedom to alter simply the venturi/aerofoil shape becomes an important consideration.

Retracing our steps for a moment, the Lotus 78 was using a relatively short and cambered section in the side pods, and while this would give a large movement of the centre of pressure, it would be over a physically shorter distance in relation to the wheelbase.

To combat this, Chapman had two men of incomparable, yet quite different types of ability.

Andretti, vastly experienced on American cars where remote control anti-roll bars, offset and variable diagonal loading on suspension springs, and other exotic approaches were well known, embraced a varying and adjustable car with enthusiasm. He was skilled and knowledgeable enough to adjust everything available to him, not just once but again and again throughout a race as fuel load, tyre condition, and even the weather altered.

Peterson, on the other hand, having once allegedly entangled his fireproof gauntlet in the roll bar adjuster, decided he would not keep fiddling about but would simply drive the car and adjust himself instead.

Both approaches put Lotus well out in front — but Andretti was the man who took the Championship ....

The rapid adoption of longer and longer sections, and ever increasing downforce, soon faced F1 designers and drivers with an even worse version of the passenger car designer's constant burden: having to allow for four more people and all their luggage as an uncertain variable in the load range. At the absolute worst this only represents a load change of 35 to 40 per cent of vehicle kerb weight and, once in the car, both the passengers and their suitcases can be expected to stay where they have been put.

In F1, even very early on, wing downforce was well on its way to one hundred per cent of static weight or 2g, soon to pass this *en route* to two hundred per cent. Worse, the load was not being applied at a fixed point, but wherever the centre of pressure happened to be. To cap it all, this extra weight was not even constant but was related to speed and the car's attitude.

For the drivers it gave the effect of variable increases in the car's effective weight, sometimes nearer the front and sometimes the rear, continually altering the natural frequency of the suspension, the car's angle in relation to the road and consequently its angle of attack, downforce and ... round in a full circle to where we came in.

Every one of these problems was compounded, generally for the worse, by skirts losing contact with the road, leaking depression away, getting it back, and finally wearing the edges off or jamming halfway through a race.

Small wonder that harder and harder springs began to make a rapid appearance. The less suspension movement the better, leaving the job as far as possible to the tyres, and making the skirts slide to deal with what little movement would be left. The dreaded porpoising was reduced, but really the problem needed a more fundamental solution.

This came in the form of alteration of the side pod shapes. Bit by bit they moved away from the fully cambered wing section towards the venturi throat running virtually parallel to the ground for an appreciable distance before flaring gently upwards and outwards. Intensive effort went into keeping the flow attached to the widening pod walls, as breakaway brings instant loss of downforce, extra drag, and an alteration in the balance of the car.

Cars which had been narrowed to reduce frontal area suddenly took advantage of every legal centimetre to expand back again to a width of seven feet. Only by taking the rear wheels outwards as far as possible could every fraction of the gap between a narrowed gearbox and inner tyre wall, brakes buried inside the wheel, be utilised.

The result was a three way split of the airflow approaching the car, The bottom slice was accelerated under the car, the middle was slowed into a large plenum chamber ahead of a steeply inclined radiator, before being heated and accelerated out of a top exit, while the third portion went above, passing over ever smoother and more carefully radiused top bodywork and engine covers on its way to the rear wing.

While the centre of pressure movements now came under increasing control, the total downforce being exerted on the car was — and is — still critically linked to the size of the venturi beneath the car, or its actual ground clearance.

While the '6cm gap' uproar is now history, (a mandatory space required between the bottom edges of any bodywork and the ground) it will now be seen how it created instant fury and horror among teams who were only just getting to grips with a whole new technical world.

The approach of Brabham's Gordon Murray was, like his notorious

Fan Car, not only technically brilliant, but picked its way with infinite delicacy between the lines of the rules. If the car was to be pressed down by atmosphere once it got going, he reasoned, a function already well used with legal double rate coils – soft to start with but iron hard after being squashed a pre-ordained amount – why not physically alter a dimension in the suspension to drop the car once it got onto the track?

As he was at the time unique in having a pull-rod link between wheel and damper/coil unit, he inserted a small driver-controlled hydraulic cylinder in this by means of which its length, and consequently the height of the car could be instantly altered.

Once out of the pits it sat down, skirt edges firmly on the road and ran away from everyone. For the opposition lacking a pull-rod to adjust, the system posed plenty of snags in the copying but, while the international rule makers hummed and hawed and finally said "get on with it, but don't be lower than 6cm on the scrutineer's laser beam measuring pad", every other team set about building its own version, and lap speeds went where everyone agreed they should not be going – up. This was all abandoned within twelve months in favour of fixed skirts "just brushing" the ground, whatever that might mean. This was by no means a bad thing from the teams' point of view as tyre technology was steadily improving in its ability to take over more and more of the suspension of the car from its coil springs.

The final result as we all know of the wrangling, bitter argument and quite unprecedented cornering speeds brought about by the venturi cars was a sudden clamp down in the design parameters of F1 cars by the FISA on safety grounds. This was the one basis on which it had the power to bring in a new rule with immediate effect rather than giving the required two or three years notice agreed with the constructors.

The order came from on high in the sepulchral tones of M. Balestre – unspeakable Gallic dictator, or saviour of the sport's future, depending on your point of view – "Flat bottoms, and skirts off, lads, right away if not sooner. Without the new shape you don't even start". With surprisingly little moaning or groaning, and even more surprisingly alacrity, the major teams were out testing flat-bottomed cars within weeks.

Among the large number of things altered by this edict, was that, overnight, parts of this book became a touch academic, though not entirely so for F2 and F3, saloons and some sports/racing cars will be using ground effect into at least the immediate future. Much of the book dealing with suspension, however, takes on a new validity and interest. Suspension looks like being back in fashion!

Although downforce induced by the F1 car's underbody shape is now theoretically outlawed, one approach that seems to me well within the new rules would be to set the car statically with its flat bottom tilted nose-down at a chosen angle. Should scrutineers insist that it be parallel to the ground when checked, it could be arranged for the car's attitude to alter once it got out on the track.

The area ahead of the mandatory flat-bottom section, would be angled or curved upwards towards the nose of the car. This curve would in its turn permit downward flanges to create a collection area for air flowing towards and under the car. Well, well! We now have a complete, if rather crude, venturi created quite legally by the underside of the car. No skirts, and not massively efficient, but working.

Given a continuation of iron hard suspension to control the car's final angle of attack, just as in the recently departed era, it could not only be accurately set but adhered to for a major part of any race.

Remember that not only does air accelerate and reduce its pressure when put through a narrowing opening, but also a wing section normally generates lift (or in this application, downforce) without any angle of attack at all and its chord line parallel to the ground.

If we add to this, freedom of shape in the underbody aft of the rear wheels, together with front and rear wings, we are really starting to get back in business. Committing oneself in this way with observations and theories before the ink on the new rules is dry risks falling on one's face

very publicly in the biggest possible way.

Whatever happens, it has to be totally fascinating to see how the battle between designers and rulemakers will now develop. There can be no truce, now or ever. The endless ingenuity of clever man will see to that, for the ferocious determination to win is not confined to the cockpit. It flourishes equally in the drawing offices and windtunnels and workshops of any top, or would-be-top, team anywhere.

Even we of the lower echelons cannot escape rules that sometimes became even more obscure because they have been passed down in an indefinite way from a different level and branch of the sport.

Consequently your own vehicle and formula, whatever it is, will be affected, or even totally governed by the rule book and, in part, by the speed range and practicalities of your chosen sport. However valuable a low clearance front apron may be on a modified saloon, if the roads of the Forestry Commision tear it off within the first mile, it is clearly a pointless exercise. If a regular 300 extra revs on the straight in a single-seater are going to make you a champion in a small capacity formula, what point is there in a high drag banana wing for a modest improvement in cornering?

More D.I.Y research

Less easy to comprehend, or even accept, is that the full width 'pig' nose with adjustable horizontal splitter, seems to give little if any drag penalty, much improved grip and low speed turn-in and even allows some flow into venturi side pods.

A season during which several cars, including my own, were all using identical front bodywork – full width noses – enabled a good check on what downforce if any was being generated.

The technique was to use field glasses to inspect the cars at the same point and consequently at reasonably similar speeds in the modest 50-70mph bracket. The downforce was so great that all the cars had to be set with extra static height. All were being forced down at least two inches even with admittedly low wheel rates – a downforce of some 160lbs.

Further, if the splitter was not statically parallel to the ground and of robust construction with a flanged reinforced edge, there was violent vibration in the centre unsupported section. This altered the downforce for the worse, so much so that one affected car was going noticeably light at speed. A little metal strut cured it on the day, the splitter level being reset with great care and varying fragments of wood, alloy and cigarette packet as spacers. The improvement was instant.

The small rear boot lid lip, now such a fashionable part of styling of the more sporting saloon, began life giving rear downforce at Le Mans, on the Mulsanne straight, holding cars on the road as speeds came up to and then passed 200mph.

It is self evident that for such a lip to work, air must be flowing over the rear bodywork. Now despite my earlier observation about a need for a maximum 7 degree divergence angle to stop breakaway I run a road car with a rear window at 27 degrees to the horizontal. It stays perfectly clear of mud on the filthiest winter run down the M1, so much so that I abandoned the planned work and investment of installing a rear wipe/wash.

Even better than this if one is to believe the dramatic advertising pictures of a wool-tufted Metro, air is flowing along the roof and then equally smoothly down the back without a hint of breakaway. As the Metro rear window happens to be at about 60 degrees to horizontal, that is the angle round which the roof airflow has had to instantly steer itself. But a little traffic driving study will soon show that a rear wiper is most valuable on a Metro to clear the muck, a situation that prevailed with the original Mini from 1959 on.

Along with quoted drag co-efficient (Cd) for three box cooking saloons of 0.3 plus which are starting to crop up with growing frequency, it seems to defy both the natural laws and mathematics of extensively tested drag research in aircraft wind tunnels.

Drag, speed & power

These apparent anomalies, together with plenty of others, mainly connected with paddock figures (bhp not blonde lady mechanics), inspired me to try and work out a graph which would make the relationships between power, size and shape of vehicle, co-efficient of drag and top speed a little clearer. It proved impossible without three graphs so the dedicated will have to hop back and forth between them, but it is not nearly as difficult as it sounds.

From these it is possible to get a very fair idea of how you compare with the opposition and, better still, how you may improve on them, discover who is bulling you rotten and generally take off the blinkers of self deception.

None of us is immune to this pleasant activity of mildly kidding oneself. It is a lot more enjoyable to feel your talents and skilful choice of parts and modifications have provided the extra bhp out of the your engine, the higher top speed or the more slippery shape with a demon wing profile. But, as has been said more times than I care to count "when the flag drops the bull stops". If things do not turn out as well as you hope the more information that can be ferreted out on the reasons why, the better your chance next time.

The three graphs are based on an ancient and fundamental law of fluid dynamics expressed in pounds and feet per second and it is:

$$Drag\ (lbs) = Cd \times \frac{Air\ Density \times Wing\ Area\ (Sq.\ ft.) \times Speed^2\ (f.p.s.)}{2}$$

To save everyone a lot of trouble, this can be converted to the bhp required for a given speed and vehicle. This modified version is:

$$Power\ required\ (in\ bhp) = \frac{Cd \times Frontal\ Area\ (sq\ ft) \times Speed^3\ (mph)}{146,750}$$

Study will show that Cd and Frontal Area are of equal importance in the equation, and improvement in one, may be far easier than in the other. Because the speed is cubed, even doubling your power, were that possible, falls drastically short of doubling your speed. In fact it puts it up by some 25%. You have to have ever increasing lumps of bhp for ever decreasing improvements in speed.

It is air resistance that finally prevents a road vehicle or any other device not below the sea, or *en route* to Venus, from going beyond a certain maximum velocity. At that point where the power required finally rises to coincide with the power available all acceleration ceases. You are flat out, full stop, whether in a Mini or a Brabham F1.

Only three things can improve this situation: more power, bodywork with a lower co-efficient of drag, or a smaller frontal area. All these avenues may not be open to you, but let us attempt an analysis of what is doing what.

Power is generally quoted as that generated at the flywheel. The figure may or may not include some, all or none of the ancillaries that will later have to be driven, and it is sometimes a figure of such robustness it has got to be aimed mainly at psyching the opposition whether Alfa Romeo or Alfie Smith.

Even supposing this figure is accurate in the first place you will have to deduct an appreciable percentage for power lost in a variety of ways *en route* to the driven wheels, including gears, universal or rubber joints, driveshaft couplings, oil seals, wheel bearings, the rolling resistance of the tyres, and the conditions in which the induction system is breathing beneath a bonnet.

The surviving horses will be the only ones available to accelerate the car and take it to its maximum speed. Existing bodywork you may or may not be stuck with. All shapes have a co-efficient of drag (Cd) generally taken to range from 1.25 for a flat plate through 0.73 for a sphere, 0.12 for a perfectly smooth, orifice-free tear drop four or five times as long as its widest point, to 0.006 for wing sections. Falling as we do somewhere in the area between these several extremes, the question is where? And is it possible to do anything about it?

Frontal area can be taken in practical terms as the total width of the vehicle multiplied by its maximum height from the ground. Forget the gap underneath, or spaces alongside your shoulders in a single-seater. The air in such a space has almost certainly to meet a wing, exhaust system, carburettor box or radiator exit air all turbulent with drag – and if it does not, the error, if error it is, will be common to your calculations on the opposition. This means that narrowing the track of a single seater or lowering a saloon, reduces the size of the object to be forced through the air.

The relationship between co-efficient of drag and the frontal area as we have seen is a simple and direct one. Halve the size of your car and you halve its drag. This will halve the power needed for its former top speed – but what it will *not* do is double the top speed. The cube law intrudes to prevent such a generous reward, but you do still get improvement, generally much more handsome in the 0-60 or 0-100mph acceleration figures than in top speed.

How to use the graphs? First measure your car's height and width very carefully (quarter inch maximum error) and calculate gross frontal area in square feet. Ignore big mirrors, aerials or any lean-in on the side window.

Then you need as accurate a top speed as possible. It has a huge effect on the resultant figures, and a two-way road test mean is mandatory for any production car. Otherwise a circuit speed trap, or careful measurement of rear rolling tyre diameter combined with a really high quality rev-counter reading. (Remember rev-counters can be much more inaccurate than speedometers as they are subject to no legislation. I have had new instruments 1000rpm optimistic, so try not to kid yourself too much).

Thirdly a power output must be found, either from the manufacturer, engine builder or a rolling road. Least likely to be on hand is an actual Cd figure, although these are beginning to be mentioned here and there.

Published ones have their hazards as Ford found with their figures for the new Escort range, which were very publicly challenged by a German magazine which paid for a selection of popular saloons to be tested for drag by an independent wind tunnel team. The unkind comparison between their figures and those of the Ford factory caused instant public uproar and a lot of bitter shouting.

Should you lack a rolling road figure for power at the driven wheels then flywheel bhp, generally given by tuners, racing engine builders and the major manufacturers should be adjusted as follows:

Type of car	Deduct from flywheel bhp	Examples
Rear engined s/seaters with cold or narrow tyres.	9%	Small hillclimb, F/Ford.
Rear engined s/seaters with wide and cool tyres.	11%	Big hillclimb.
Circuit s/seaters with hot wide tyres.	12½%	F1, 2, 3.
Full race saloon/sports with engine over driven wheels.	15%	Le Mans, 'Silhouette' Saloons, Imp, Mini.
Road-going saloon/sports with engine over driven wheels. Full race competition cars with FE/RWD.	18%	X19, Mini, Fiesta, U2, Clubmans.
Road-going saloons/sports with FE/RWD.	21%	Chevette, MGB, Rover. Jaguar XK.
Road-going saloons/sports with 4WD.	25%	Quattro, Range Rover.

Deduct a further 10% for any SAE quoted bhp.

This may seem an extraordinarily arbitrary way to attack such a highly technical matter, but do not be too contemptuous immediately. It is an attempt to deal with a number of variables that include drive trains, alternator loads, fans, modified exhausts and carburation, sticky tyres, plus road engines (and some racing ones too) that would be very hard put indeed to equal on the road the optimised factory figures taken on the brake.

Given our two figures (speed and power) we can now obtain from aerodynamics graph one or two a 'Curve Code Number' for our car. Using this number together with the frontal area of the car, we move to graph three to obtain its co-efficient of drag. This may be a shock, a pleasant surprise or several miles away from what you had read or been told.

Not unnaturally I did some cross checks before daring to suggest it as a practical or worthwhile activity for the person who does not have a wind tunnel, or any idea of what might be preventing his achieving the performance he was expecting.

Clearly an accurate Cd and Frontal Area can be employed first on graph three to obtain the 'Curve Code Number'. When transferred to graph one this should permit a forecast of top speed given the power available, or a figure for power at the wheels (and from that, at the flywheel) given a known top speed.

To save too much suspicion or any waste of the reader's energies there is a table in the appendices covering quite a wide spread of vehicles from F1 and some exotica to Golf/Rabbit and Escort ranges which use the same shells for engines ranging from mundane to diesel to high performance and fuel-injection.

The figures in each case are as accurate as I have been able to compile in an imperfect world and some 90 per cent match the graphs surprisingly closely.

Graph three, incidentally, not only allows you to work quite easily to three places of decimals, but also makes it very clear how enormous an improvement is a minute sounding increment like 0.1 in the Cd. It may not sound much, but it will have an appreciable effect not only on top speed, which it is often academic, but far more importantly on fuel consumption and 'natural' cruising speed.

It would have sounded a lot better, at least in advertising copy, if the whole thing had been based on 100 instead of one, saving a lot of fiddling about with decimals.

"Curve Code Number" graph from 0 to 200bhp – see text for details. (Drawing: Darell Staniforth).

"Curve Code Number" graph from 0 to 900bhp – see text for details. (Drawing: Darell Staniforth).

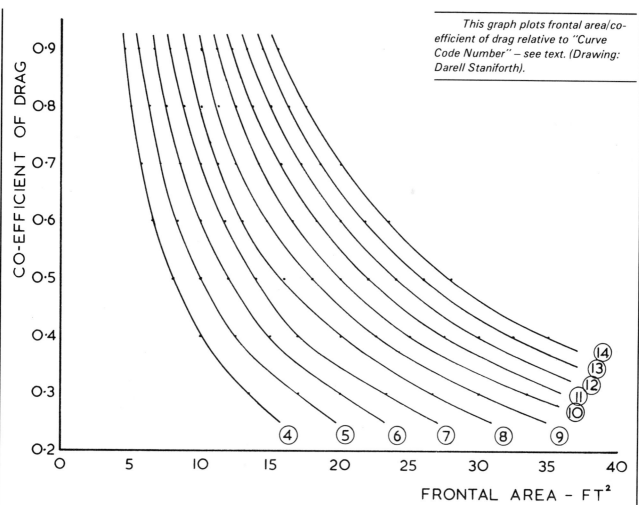

This graph plots frontal area/co-efficient of drag relative to "Curve Code Number" – see text. (Drawing: Darell Staniforth).

Comparative drag co-efficients

Model	Co-efficient of drag (from graph)	Top speed (mph)	Power (bhp) Gross/at wheels	Frontal area (width x height in sq-ft)	Curve Code Number	Remarks	
Audi Quattro (2.2 litre, fwd, turbo)	{ 0.35 { 0.365	136 158	200/150 330/247	67.8 x 53 = 24.95	8.8 9.2	Ex-showroom Rally version	Difference may be big rear spoiler with built -in oil cooler.
Citroen ID19 (1994 cc, 4wd)	0.43	86	68/53	70.5 x 60 = 29.4	12.7	One of very earliest low drag saloons of the early sixties	
Ferrari 308 GTB (3-litre)	0.37	155	255/209	71 x 46.5 = 22.9	8.3	Virtually square-cut 'KAMM' tail	
Ford Cortina 2.3 GL	0.415	109	114/90	67 x 57 = 24.66	10.2		
Ford Escort 1100E (rwd)	0.43	80	43.5/34.4	62.3 x 53.3 = 23.0	9.9		
Ford Escort 1100 std (rwd)	.455	83	52/41	23.0	10.6		
Ford Escort 1300 std (rwd)	.41 } 0.415	91	61/48.2	23.0	9.4 } 9.6	Conventional '3-box' saloons	
Ford Escort 1300 Sport (rwd)	.38	97	75/59.25	23.0	8.8		
Ford Escort 1600 (rwd)	.405 }	103	87/68.7	23.0	9.3		
Ford Escort RS2000 (rwd)	0.4	108	103/81.4	61.6 x 55 = 23.5	9.5	Droop snoot, air dam, low profile tyres spoiler	
Ford Fiesta 1100 (fwd)	.385	90	53/43.5	61.7 x 51.7 = 22.15	8.8	–	
Ford Fiesta 1300 (fwd)	.375	98	.66/54	22.15	8.3		
Ford Fiesta XR2 1600 (fwd)	.425	105	84/69	22.15	9.5	Rear spoiler, wider wheels	
Ford Escort XR3 1600 (fwd)	0.365	111	96/78.7	64 x 53 = 23.5	8.6	Rear spoiler, low profile tyres & Works Cd of .395	
Jaguar XK 150S 3.8 litre	0.42	136	265 SAE/183	64.5 x 54 = 24.2	10.9	Classic beauty – would it have been better and faster with cleaner underside?	
Lotus Elite 1220	.345	108	75/59.6	58 x 46 = 18.5	6.4	My personal 'most beautiful' ever. Totally clean below	

Model		Co-efficient of drag (from graph)	Top speed (mph)	Power (bhp) Gross/at wheels	Frontal area (width x height) in sq-ft	Curve Code Number	Remarks
Lotus Eleven SIR	(a)	0.35	120	85/70	57 x 43 = 17.0 (Outline 14.4)	6.0	One of most successful s/racers of all time (a) = Rectangle FA (b) = Outline FA
	(b)	0.41					
Mini 848cc std		.535	72	34/28	55.5 x 53 = 20.4	11.0	Ex-showroom MIRA test figure 0.46
Mini Cooper 997cc		.53	85	55/45	20.4	10.9	Ex-showroom, road test
Mini Cooper 1071'S'		.51	93	70/57.4	20.4	10.5	Ex-showroom, road test
Downton Mini 1088cc		.515	102	88/72	Lowered 2" 19.7	10.0	One of earliest expert Mini tuners
Mini 1275 'S'		.49	96	75/61.5	20.4	10.1	Ex-showroom, road test
Fullrace Mini 1293cc		.525	109	112/91.8	Lowered 2" 19.7	10.4	–
BL Metro 998 City /L/std		.455	82	45/37	60.9 x 52.3 = 22.1	10.1	Just buying the MG moulding should give you 86 mph!
BL Metro HLS 1.3		.365/.41	94/90	60/49	22.1	8.7/9.9	Massive improvement on Mini 'Two top speeds from two BL Main agents'
BL Metro M.G. 1.3		.39	101	72/59	22.1	8.6	Factory Cd 0.39 'Improved by tailgate moulding'
Porsche 928 (4.7 litre)		0.37	155	300/237	69.75 x 51.5 = 24.93	9.3	Works figures 0.38
Porsche Turbo 911 (3.3 litre)		.355	160	300/246	25	8.9	
Porsche 75 Super		.33	107	75/61.5	65.25 x 51.5 = 23.3	7.6	Staggeringly good – suspect top speed?
Rochdale Olympic (1.5-litre)		.34	102	68/53.7	62 x 50 = 21.5	7.4	Totally clean underside. F/glass moulded G.T. Saloon. Far ahead of its time in late fifties
VW Golf 1100L		.365	87	50/41	63.4 x 55.5 = 24.4	8.6	145 tyres on 4½" rim
VW Golf 1300LS		.37	93	60/49	24.4	8.8	155 tyres on 5" rim
VW Golf diesel 1.6		.395	88	54/44/3	24.4	9.5	155 tyres on 5" rim
VW Golf Turbo diesel		.390	96	70/57.4	24.4	9.4	
VW Golf GTi 1600		.390	112	110/90	64.2 x 54.9 – 24.5	9.4	Lowered flares, front spoiler, 175 tyres on 5½ rims
VW Scirocco 1300		.355	96	60/49	64 x 51.5 = 22.9	8.1	All far below factory claimed figures of .42 early 0.38 late models, but extremely consistent figure for widely differing power outputs
VW Scirocco 1457cc		.355	101	70/57.4	22.9	8.1	
VW Scirocco GLS 1588cc		.36	107	85/69.7	22.9	8.3	
VW Scirocco GTi 1588cc		.355	117	110/90	22.9	8.1	
Gould-Terrapin 1600		.575	140 Est.	224/197	75 x 35.5 = 18.5	10.6	0-130 in 12 secs. True top speed probably higher
F750	(a)	0.62	75 Est.	35/29	48 x 48 = 16	10.0	(a) Early A7 SV (b) Later lowered Reliant OHV version
	(b)	0.52	90 Est.	44/36	50 x 40 = 13.9	7.2	
F. Ford 1600	(a)	.525	117	103/94	63 x 38 = 16.6 (Outline = 12.0)	8.7	No rear wings permitted. Interesting comparison to F1
	(b)	.71	117				
F1 (Average figures from Kyalami speed trap	(a)	.545	175	525/407	83.5 x 35.5 = 20.6 (Outline 14.6)	11.3	Non-turbo (Cosworth 'screamer' version). In both cases (a) = Gross rectangle FA (b) = net outline FA Turbo engines (Ferrari, Renault)
	(b)	.765	175	525/407	(Outline 14.6)	11.3	
	(a)	.545	189	590/516	83.5 x 35.5 = 20.6	11.2	
	(b)	.765	189	590/516	(Outline 14.6)	11	
Aston Martin Nimrod (Le Mans car, 5.3-litre, V8)		.3	221 (graph)	575/472	78.4 x 39.4 = 21.5	6.5	No ground effects for ultra-low drag and Le Mans straightline speed. '550-600 BHP' Design aim – 'under 0.3 cd'

One form of check that is a big help towards a reliable base line in all this is a requirement of the German Government (which has a much tougher line on vehicle leglislation than some and remember, they banned the big rear spoiler on Porsche 911s as being 'too aggressive') which demands very closely controlled DIN power output figures for production engines before the manufacturer can get Type Approval. Without Type Approval he cannot sell his cars anyway, so it is reasonable to assume that bhp figures for the VW Golf/Rabbit range, for instance, are about as reliable as you are ever likely to get out of a brochure.

Certainly they all tie in with each other in the sense that several cars using a virtually identical shell, but wide range of engines and equally widely differing top speeds come out from the graph with similar Cd figures. What is mysterious is that these Cd figures were not only better than the factory claims, but fantastically good for a saloon. The mystery deepens when, using exactly the same criteria, country and legislation requirements, the Porsche despite its appearance emerges with an apparently identical Cd to the much more angular Scirocco.

The final part of the conundrum comes with the recently rebodied Scirocco which was unleashed on the market with much ado about ' a 10 per cent improvement in drag figures'. This inferred (earlier literature quoting 0.42) that it had come down to about 0.38 or as near as no matter to the Porsche.

Road tests following the unveiling gave power unchanged at 85 and 110bhp for the standard and injected Scirocco models, as were top speeds at 107 and 116 mph.

Now there appears no way you can have the same power, substantially improve the drag factor, and not go faster, but gearing on road cars can have upsetting effects on the calculations. These are rarely aimed at the same target as a competition car – a perfect interception between the power curve, maximum speed and power required. A five speed box with effectively an overdrive top, silent motorway cruising and the best possible consumption in the 'urban cycle' test are uneasy bedfellows with motor sport.

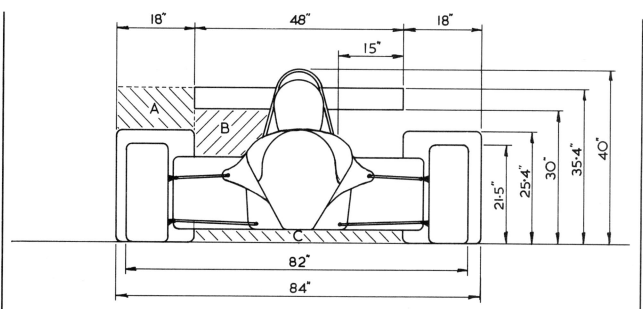

Calculating frontal area, and therefore drag figure, of a single-seater racing car.

Whatever the answer, the Scirocco still comes out first with one of the best Cd figures of anything on the road.

Leaving road cars to return to F1, the graphs may be used to compare figures quoted in the Cosworth v Turbo battle. At Kyalami, 6000 feet up in South Africa, the thinned out atmosphere was taking a slice of power off all the normally aspirated cars, but little or none from the turbos. The following table shows time trap maximums at the end of the long straight in 1982. Apart from an average disparity of a staggering fourteen miles per hour between turbocharged and normally aspirated types of car, the other remarkable thing is how close to each other are the cars in their respective groups. Decimals of an mph indicate graphically how a thousand different design approaches in detail within the framework of the F1 regulations come together to produce identically performing vehicles.

To make any comparison however tentative, we will assume everyone was taking a broadly similar approach to downforce, on the day, and were on low-drag settings.

You can now work from two different standpoints. A gross frontal area (width times height as a rectangle) gives 20.6 square feet for all current F1 cars, and a drag figure of approximately 0.55 for 175mph at sea level on Cosworth power.

But if you deduct the open area over the rear wheels and visible bits under the wing, and beneath the car between the wheels, you can get frontal area down to about 14.6 square feet. A much smaller car implies a much worse drag figure, in fact about 0.76 or very near the 0.8 much mentioned in talking or listening to designers in F1. The inference is that they work always in exact frontal areas (see frontal area drawing).

In terms of either my relatively crude approach or simple comparison, the air above all the wheels will be in an aerodynamic turmoil of lift, drag, and trying to turn back on itself, thus tending to make gross frontal area valid.

But a precise outline, to a square inch, has got to be essential if you are working in a wind tunnel with a properly scientific and technical approach towards the tiniest improvement.

Let us glance at the table of maximum speeds and the quickest individual laps, all from the Kyalami race:

Maximum speeds from Kyalami

Pironi	Ferrari turbo	190.84mph	Average 189.64
Prost	Renault turbo	190.27mph	
Arnoux	Renault turbo	190.14mph	
Villeneuve	Ferrari turbo	189.30mph	
Patrese	Brabham turbo	187.63mph	
			Average 175.42
Reuteman	Williams Cosworth	176.92mph	
de Angelis	Lotus Cosworth	175.91mph	
Rosberg	Williams Cosworth	175.91mph	
de Cesaris	Alfa Romeo	174.80mph	Average 173.58
Lauda	McLaren Cosworth	173.58mph	

'The Rest'

Yet fastest race laps were a different story:

Prost – 1m 8.7s

Arnoux – 1m 9.76s

de Cesaris – 1m 10.16s

Pironi – 1m 10.24s

Reuteman – 1m 10.52s

Villeneuve – 1m 10.55s

Lauda – 1m 10.57s

The maxima recorded are not reflected in this list of fastest laps, because a complex set of factors such as driver 'tiger', traffic, race pressures and so on, alter them more than somewhat. While Prost stands right out on his own, three turbos and three Cosworths all lie within 0.75 second of each other. Curiouser and curiouser ....

Applying the straight line speeds to our graph we get:

	Reported Gross BHP	Deduct	BHP At rear wheels	Cd with "Gross FA"	Cd with "Outline FA"
Turbos	590	12.5%	516	0.54	0.76
Non-turbos	525 (new 'screamer')	12.5% plus 10% for altitude	407	0.545	0.765

Considering the speed and power differences, these drag figures are quite remarkably similar, and the discrepancy in what is a singularly rudimentary approach is probably not really relevant. What is something of a shock is to see that a power superiority of 109bhp was apparently needed for that 14mph speed advantage. If however the turbo teams had taken a decision to run less downforce with consequently reduced drag, and an improved Cd figure, they would have been achieving that 14mph with less power than everybody imagines or guesses they have.

An intriguing thought, but forever unanswerable?

Any application of the 0.76 Cd figure into the equation without altering the method of measurement of frontal area (using gross at 20.6 not 14.6) gives an impossible flywheel bhp requirement at those sorts of speeds, in the region of 700bhp unblown and 930bhp from a turbo, clearly ridiculous. This must be a further confirmation that F1 figures are based on a meticulously measured net frontal outline.

The foregoing F1 data was much less an attempt to prove anything, than an illustration that the curves can be trusted quite a long way to do what they are intended to do – give a start in breaking down your own car's performance or lack of it into sections, or serving as a pleasant substitute for a crossword puzzle after finishing the race reports every Thursday or Friday.

Using your own data, something apparently impossible may emerge. If so, something has to be wrong somewhere, whether it is Cd, frontal area, bhp or top speed. The power figure is most likely to be the culprit, closely followed by an imaginative top speed. Some horses somehow always seem more robust than others. The poor Cd figure for the Mini comes almost certainly from an optimistic power figure on early cars. Harry Ratcliffe, that famed tuner and driver of fast Minis once muttered to me, round the stem of his well chewed pipe, that he had 'never seen 22 at the wheels of a standard Mini'. This power figure happened to fit quite well with a MIRA Cd test figure acquired some ten years later of 0.46.

Power can and does alter in the same engines over the years. Turbos which I feel must be the next generation for all cars, are very amenable to alteration for differing circumstances, whether in the pits, in the cockpit, or under the instructions of a box full of micro chips and circuits.

The Zakspeed turbo Escorts have certainly had a driver-operated control for use during races let alone in practice.

Further, at very high speeds power required, going up as a cube law, is increased or decreased very considerably by fine adjustments in wing shape, angles of attack, flap settings, and replacement of the side pods themselves. Delicate adjustment to the front wing or fins may alter the angle of attack all the way down a long straight. It would be almost invisible to the naked eye, but highly visible on a stop watch. These sorts of things can easily explain 190mph speeds at very quick circuits while the same Cosworth engines can only stagger up to a modest 170mph somewhere else.

Three points to consider when playing with the graphs:

1) Very small errors in top speed affect the theoretical Cd violently.
2) Exaggerated bhp figures or 'outline' front areas make Cd look worse.
3) Conservative bhp figures and exaggerated top speeds make Cd look better.

If you have series of reliable performance data for different versions of the same car (eg: Mini, Escort, Golf/Rabbit) it is possible to crosscheck an averaged Cd figure and then use it as a base line to monitor your own activities. The apparent discrepancies serve once more to emphasise that rules worked out in the technical environment of wind tunnels or the restful studies of Academies, often seem full of flaws and variations in sweaty, oilstained real life.

You may by now be reasonably thinking "For God's sake, what is he trying to say about aerodynamics? He doesn't seem to have a proper answer to anything".

Quite right. But I do hope to have supplied some reliable pointers and enough knowledge to keep you afloat in the early stages.

As Mr. Chapman retorted tartly when asked what had gone wrong with his once demoralisingly superior GP cars; 'If I knew, I would have cured it'.

In the event, it took even a man and team of his calibre three full years to get most, though by no means all, of the answers.

You can look at this situation in two ways: "Even the experts do not know it all – what chance have I got?" or "Even the experts do not know it all – I have got a chance".

It would be sad to think that anyone who has got this far would give the first version houseroom.

Single section timing

Moving from the rarified atmosphere of F1 at Kyalami, to the type of event in which many readers may be directly involved there are numerous ways in which you may check personal, or team performances. Ideally a split reading digital stopwatch should be available but an ordinary wristwatch with a stop facility will do a great deal.

watch (preferably a digital type reading to two places of decimals).

Getting a full set of figures usually demands more of the tenacity and dedication of a stopwatch operator than huge dexterity or later arithmetic. But an assistant to make notes can be very helpful when timing at an event where multi-channel clocks are being operated, and there may be four cars at once on the course.

In this case the timed section ('A' to 'B') uses two slight lines — one at the point where cars emerge from behind farm buildings and the second where they cross the timekeeper's eyeline to a suitable electric pylon.

The section covers from the middle of a very heavy braking area, through a 170 degree climbing corner, with no help from the camber, past a paddock exit road, almost always slippery from muck carried down on everybody's wheels, and the beginning of the final straight. Although less than 20% of the total hill, this section's effect on success is considerable, as speed out of it virtually governs performance on the whole of the rest of the hill.

It demonstrates once again (all of those listed were either class winners or in the first three) that quick men overall are always quick in the difficult bits as well — they don't get it all from blasting up the straight with sheer power ....

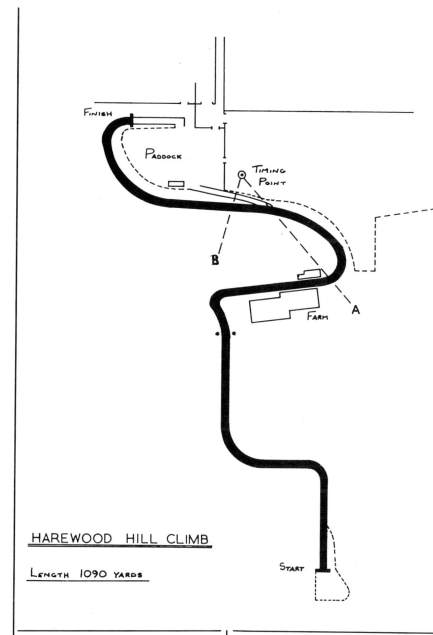

HAREWOOD HILL CLIMB

Length 1090 yards

Single section timing using the Harewood hillclimb course as an example (see text).

Whether you are a competitor, mechanic or spectator, such analysis can only add interest at the very least to an event.

Graphs can always be constructed from results sheets, given only a timetrap speed, or a set of single corner or section times, to cross-reference.

The accompanying illustration shows how to time a single section: quite practicable for one man and one

Section timings taken at Harewood

Driver	Car	Engine	Official Course Time	Corner Time
James Thompson	Pilbeam MP40	2.5 Hart	39.52	7.74
Roy Lane	March 812	2.5 Hart	40.01	8.07
Peter Kaye	Pilbeam MP22	3.0 DFV	40.13	8.14
David Garnett	Pilbeam MP43	2.2 Hart	42.11	8.06
Simon Curtiss	Mallock U2	1.7 Nelson	42.29	8.36
David Gould	Gould/Terrapin	1.6 BDA	42.88	8.46
Ray Harper	Harper Sports	2.1 BDX	42.98	8.50
Mervyn Bartram	Mallock U2	1.7 Bar	43.61	8.71
John Corbyn	Terrapin LG	1.1 BDJ	44.32	8.86
Tom Hughes	March 742	1.6 FVA	44.52	9.11
Keith Gowers	Monopin	0.75 Honda	44.92	8.69
Peter Varley	Ensign	1.6 BDA	44.93	8.81
Joe Ward	Ward WD6	1.7 Holbay	45.16	8.83
Author	Terrapin 7c	1.0 Imp	46.17	9.31
Tony Bridge	Davrian	1.0 Imp	46.80	9.38
George Swinbourne	Escort RS	1.6 Ford	47.85	9.94
Paul Eaton	Sunbeam	1.6 Lotus	49.10	9.72
Bobby Fryers	Mini	1.0 BL	50.93	10.70

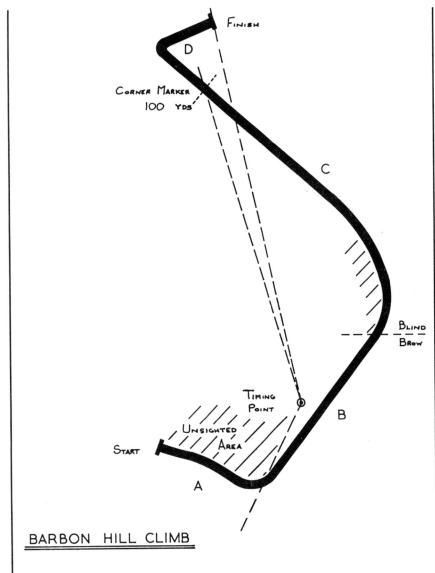

BARBON HILL CLIMB

<u>Length 890 yards</u>

Multi section timing using the Barbon hillclimb course as an example (see text).

Multi section timing

Multiple section timing to break down a complete course or lap into a number of known sections is dependent on geography, suitable eyelines and may require some arithmetic. You need to be able to see either the start or finish line, and two people will be required — one to run the watch and another to write the data quickly and accurately. A pre-prepared ruled sheet (see the example illustrated) helps. The figures in the table were obtained as follows (using round figures):

On the watch: Section 'B', 6 secs; Section 'B'+'C', 11 secs; Section 'B'+'C'+'D', 18 secs.
Official time for run: 25 secs.
Section 'A' = 25 - 18 = 7 secs.
Section 'B' = 6 secs.
Section 'C' = ('B'+'C') - 'B' = 11 - 6 = 5 secs.
Section 'D' = ('B'+'C'+'D') - ('B'+'C') = 18 - 11 = 7 secs.

Interestingly what the table illustrated shows (apart from the author's deplorable slowness; it was a bad day

for me), is that adding up the best times by any driver for each section gives a theoretical FTD of 21.77 secs.

Nobody in fact got near it, the best for these sampled runs being Chris Cramer's 22.61, later improved for FTD by Martyn Griffiths to 22.34. You can also see a number of instances of remarkably consistent driving, as well as how drivers pull back a poor showing in one part by a superlative one somewhere else.

Performance graphs

You can always utilise time trap figures, terminal speeds or your own stopwatch observations at a particular point on any circuit to plot a graph against total lap or course times. Given a wide variety of cars — or all of those in your own class — you prepare a graph similar to this. Only the choice and range of measurement units will differ.

This one happens to be of a unique event, one held on the public road of Britain at Wallasey across the river from Liverpool. Not too romantic, but an enlightened local council holds and uses the power to close part of the promenade roads for car racing.

The course is difficult as well as fast, including the unprotected ordinary road kerbs, manholes and bollards together with several roundabouts, and a final flat-out blind beside the sea in which the speed trap is set.

Having marked all the available data on the graph, you have to produce an "average performance" line, which may well offend erstwile drinking friends if they fall below it, and you come out above. Such are the penalties of disinterested research, but one interesting point at least is that there are almost never truly bad or superlative drivers in such researches (presumably they have all either just given up in disgust or been offered a

---

Multi section timing record sheet as compiled during a hillclimb at Barbon. This sort of data is invaluable when interpreted correctly. (See text).

BARBON HILLCLIMB
Westmoreland

Selective Timing by: Peter Norfolk. Shaun Gould.

DRIVER	CAR	ENG CCS	A	B	C	D	OFFICIAL TIME	REMARKS	
K. GOWERS	MONOPIN	S/C 732	6.16	5.08	6.98	7.83	26.05	New record (shared)	1100 cc Racing
A. STANIFORTH	TERRAPIN 7B	IMP 1039	6.58	5.36	8.04	8.13	28.11		OLD RECORD 26.70
C. MYLES	MARCH 745	BDA 1098	6.45	4.97	6.77	7.86	26.05	New record (shared)	
J. CORBYN	TERRAPIN 16	BDA 1098	5.98	5.05	7.14	7.98	26.15	Transverse BDA on Mini gearbox. Quickest off-line	
T. HUGHES	MARCH 722	1600 FVA	6.16	4.80	6.31	8.28	25.52		1600 cc Racing
M. BOLSOVER	MARCH 77(8)/2	1600 BDA	6.05	4.56	6.85	8.56	26.00	"JAMMED THROTTLE" Later did 24.15 for new record	OLD RECORD 24.72
A. NEWTON	HURON	1600 FVC	5.74	4.93	6.52	8.02	25.21	Quickest off line	
T. HART	MARCH 733	1600 BDA	6.23	4.49	6.22	7.68	24.62	Shortlived new record.	
D. GOULD	GOULD TERRAPIN	1560 BDA	5.82	4.53	6.75	7.99	25.08		
R. SMITH	MARCH 722	TURBO 1142	5.83	4.63	6.60	7.90	24.96		
D. HARRIS	PILBEAM MP42	2.2 HART	5.73	4.32	6.39	7.03	23.47		Unlimited racing
A. PAYNE	MARCH 712	3.5 V8	5.93 / 5.89	4.74 / 4.50	6.85 / 6.54	7.58 / 7.98	25.10 / 24.91	Big Buick F5000.	OLD RECORD 22.80
J. JACK	MARCH 722	2.0 BMW	6.12 / 5.80	4.69 / 4.34	6.08 / 6.21	7.75 / 7.54	24.64 / 23.89		
N. GAILBRAITH	MARCH 782	2.0 BMW	5.70 / 5.68	4.12 / 4.32	6.23 / 6.15	7.47 / 7.36	23.52 / 23.51	Incredible consistency	
A. RICHARDS	MARCH	2.0 BMW	5.53 / 5.53	4.31 / 4.21	6.15 / 6.00	8.03 / 7.68	24.02 / 23.42		
G. CROMPTON	MARCH 79 B	2.2 HART	5.67	4.21	6.29	7.48	23.65		
M. ALLEN	McLAREN	5.0 V8	6.09	4.69	6.62	8.75	26.15		
P. WILLIAMS	MARCH	2.1 HART	5.86	4.57	6.57	8.37	25.37		
J. CAMPBELL	MODUS	2.2 HART	5.78	4.37	6.51	7.30	23.96		
R. TURNBULL	PILBEAM MP41	2.2 HART	6.09	4.08	5.54	8.17	23.88		
M. DUNGWORTH	PILBEAM MP22	3.3 DFV	5.85 / 5.65	4.39 / 4.36	5.80 / 5.96	7.61 / 7.64	23.65 / 23.61	More remarkable consistency	
R. LANE	MARCH 792	3.0 DFV	5.61	4.12	5.89	7.30	22.92		
A. D. Osborne	PILBEAM MP31	3.0 DFV	5.50 / 5.70	3.97 / 3.96	5.74 / 5.86	7.67 / 7.55	22.88 / 23.07	Quickest off line for very temporary new record!	
C. CRAMER	MARCH 782	2.2 HART	5.62	3.96	5.74	7.29	22.61	Shortlived new record.	
M. GRIFFITHS	PILBEAM MP40	2.5 HART	5.60 / 5.54	3.70 / 3.92	6.17 / 5.97	7.41 / 7.20	22.88 / 22.63		
"X" Driving the combined "perfect" run of day.			BEST A DO. Cos. 3.0 PILB. 5.50	BEST GRIFFITHS. Hart 2.2 PILB. 3.70	BEST TURNBULL Hart 2.2 PILB. 5.54	BEST. HARRIS. Hart 2.2 PILB. 7.03	"PERFECT FTD" 21.77	Reigning Champion Griffiths did 22.34 in Top Ten Runoff for FTD & New Record.	

works drive somewhere). We general drivers all tend to fall into a narrow band of about 2.5%.

Clearly this is not a measure of driver ability alone, but a mix of a number of factors, sometimes not within the competitor's control. Some of them are detailed on the graph and should be carefully considered if you are intent on moving yourself somewhere better.

G-forces at Prescott

The (semi) secret sources of the most intriguing selective timings of all are a couple of large stiff-backed notebooks that turn up in the timekeeping box at most, though not all, Prescott hillclimbs.

For the serious student really interested in which cars win, and why, column after column of figures have been slowly building up in those books compiled largely by timekeeper Tony Fletcher and his helpers.

Not everyone is aware that this classically beautiful and difficult hill in Gloucestershire has had, since 1978, a spare light and timing channel set 64 ft after the startline, and very slightly uphill.

If that figure of 64 has not instantly alerted you, be reminded that Sir Isaac Newton gave it immortality as one of the multiples of 32; and 32ft/per sec/per sec is the acceleration rate of a body in free fall until it reaches a terminal velocity beyond which it will go no faster. So anything covering 64 ft in two seconds is equalling the force of gravity: 1G. To cover that distance in one second would be 2G.

The importance of acceleration off the line cannot be exaggerated whatever branch of the sport you may be engaged in. Once done successfully, you have that initial advantage over the opposition whether you build on it or squander it. In standing start events, not forgetting rally special stages, its value is obvious and absolute. In circuit or oval racing it may govern whether you get into the first corner in the lead or struggling in the middle of the pack.

It is a subtle amalgam of technique, bhp, tyres and the vehicle's ability to put its power on the road. The selection of cars covered in the accompanying table concentrates on the quickest in each class, and is thus less a full picture than it might be.

For those as fascinated as I am by the many lessons to be learned from later paddock study or your own photographs, a complete set of the best times ever recorded, as far as research reveals, is in the table on the opposite page. These are from the September 1981 meeting for two very good reasons. Firstly, the following year was not timed in its entirety and those times that were taken did not show improvements, meaning the 1981 figures are effectively up-to-date. Secondly, the weather plays a vital part in record times. A blazing hot, dry day with heavy rain in previous weeks to wash the track seems essential. Sunday, September 6th, 1981, was just such a day.

No doubt these figures have some way to go compared to the pure dragsters but they do not have to go round corners, stop or handle, and are permitted the flame and chemical burnouts that turn tread rubber into shortlived glue.

Perhaps the most interesting point to emerge is that one particular car, owned and driven by a series of drivers, has always been fast or fastest. It was quickest in 1978, when the trap was first set up, in the hands of the man who became British Champion, Martyn Griffiths.

When it was taken over by Rob Turnbull, it was still fastest in 1980, and a year later, new owner Ted Williams set the all-time best figure of 1.76 seconds, or 1.14G. Further, his friend Richard Fry co-drove the now rather venerable Pilbeam MP40 to the second best ever time. These two are currently members of an extremely

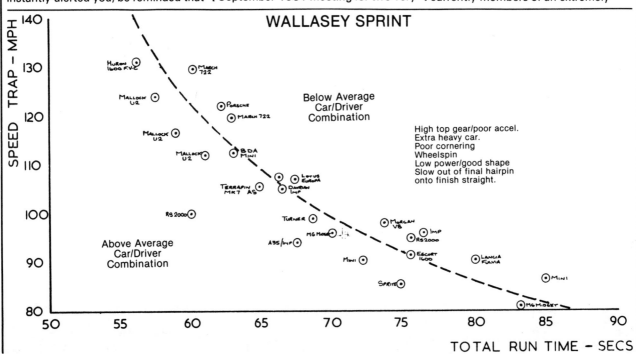

exclusive club of two – the only sub-1.8 second runners on record.

And in third place at 1.81 is the Gould-Terrapin with only 1600cc, ahead of everything in the Top Ten including the then current Champion, Chris Cramer (Toleman TG280), and the man who was to take his crown within a month, James Thompson in another MP40, both with some 360bhp available.

These figures have never been part of the club's official results, or even posted up informally at a meeting. Surely such a labour of love deserves a better fate in the future?

Table of selective timings over the first 64 feet at Prescott

Driver	Car	Engine	Time	Comments
Special Saloons up to 1300cc				
John Meredith	Maguire Imp	Hartwell 1200 Imp	1.89	Only man to break 2 secs. in his class
Special Saloons over 1300cc				
Barrogill Angus	Davrian	BMW 2000	1.89	One of two inside 2 secs.
Nic Mann	Morris Minor	Rover V8 3.5	2.08	Fastest front eng./RWD "saloon"
Wilfred Powell	Mini Cooper S	1400 BL	2.54	Fastest Mini
GT and Mod. Sports up to 1300cc				
David Watson	Davrian	1238cc	2.06	Yet another r/eng. car.
GT and Mod. Sports over 1300cc				
Roland Jones	Porsche Carrera	3000cc	1.95	Barely holding off two other Porsches on 1.96.
David Way	Turner MkII	1585cc	2.13	Fastest front eng. RWD sports car.
Sports Racing/Clubmans up to 1600cc (pushrod engines)				
Neil Crump	Mallock U2	1599 Ford	1.98	Only man under 2 secs in the class
Sports Racing/Clubmans up to 1600cc (o'head cam engines)				
Simon Dominey	Martin BM18	1594 Ford	1.94	Beating a gaggle of U2s
Jim Robinson	Mallock U2/21	1594 Ford	1.96	Fastest U2 any engine.
Ferrari Handicap				
Dudley Mason Styrron	Ferrari Dino	206 (s/c)	2.21	Fastest Ferrari of the day.
Bugatti Handicap				
Ronnie Symondson	Bugatti T57	3.3 litre	2.86	
Classic Cars (exceeding 500cc)				
Up to 1930				
Ron Footitt	AC/GN Cognac Special (1925)	1991cc.	2.54	By one of the oldest car/driver combinations still competing.
1931-1945				
Guy Smith	Frazer Nash s/sports (1934)	3500cc	2.59	–
1946-1964				
John McCartney	Cooper T79 (1964)	2.5 Climax	2.12	On contemporary narrow tyres
1965-1968				
Peter Cook	Ginetta G16 (1966)	3500cc	2.17	–
Sports Racing/Clubmans over 1600cc				
Joy Rainey	Murrain Mk3	1790cc	2.00	And the lady beat several bigger engines on the way.
Racing Cars up tp 500cc				
T.E. Hulks	Cooper Mk5	500 JAP	2.39	Using contemporary "bicycle tyre" wheels!

Driver	Car	Engine	Time	Comments

Racing Cars up to 1100cc

Eryl Davies	Anson SA1	1098BDA	1.98	Only man to break 2 secs. in the class.

Racing Cars up to 1600cc

David Gould	Gould.Terrapin 80/3	1570BDA	1.81	Third quickest time ever recorded.

Racing Cars over 1600cc

Ted Williams	Pilbeam MP40	2500 Hart	1.76	Fastest ever recorded.
Richard Fry	(same car and engine)		1.78	Only other man under 1.80

Best time that day for each of Top Ten Championship numbered cars (4 & 9 not running)

	Driver	Car	Engine	Time
1	Chris Cramer	Toleman TG280	2460 Hart	1.87
2	Martyn Griffiths	Pilbeam MP46	2.5 Hart	1.88
3	Roy Lane	March 812	2.5 Hart	1.92
5	Dave Harris	Pilbeam MP50	2.5 Hart	1.84
6	A. Douglas-Osborn	Pilbeam MP43	3.0 DFV	1.84
7	David Franklin	March 782	2.3 BMW	1.90
9	Godfrey Crompton	March 802	2.5 Hart	1.94
10	Norrie Gailbraith	Chevron 848	2.3 Hart	1.93

Also running in the "Top Ten" that day were Williams and Fry together with:

Martin Bolsover	Pilbeam MP51	1600BDA	1.83
James Thompson	Pilbeam MP40	2.5 Hart	1.82

5 Trailblazers.

Introduction

No designer ever has a free hand. The "clean sheet of paper" is a myth. All are hemmed in by a huge variety of restrictions imposed by regulations, money, time, the forces of nature, and what is technically possible with the materials of the moment.

With true genius in short supply in any field, most of the world's developments are down to a larger body of ingenious, inventive and pioneering brains bringing individual and erratic flashes of brilliance to the scene.

Whether it is to see something obvious for the first time, try out an idea that has frightened off all others, or make a part do four jobs where two had been the previous best, a new standard is set.

Bit by bit things edge forward, get faster, become better.

The portraits of cars and their designers, builders or developers that follow are a personal choice of the significant, the daring, many brilliantly successful, others equally brilliant failures. Some concepts vitally influenced every car that followed, others sadly died for a variety of reasons despite initial success – but they all shared one thing in common:

Within the framework of the times that encircled them, in widely different formulae and situations during the past quarter of a century, they all stopped the thinking aficionado in his tracks.

One or two inspired that most unattractive of human reactions – "It's going to win – let's get it banned" with instant resort to the relevant small print rather than to the drawing board to compete.

But in every case the designer had to overcome specialised hurdles peculiar to a particular category of motor sport.

The 750 Club and Formula take their name (for the benefit of younger readers) from the swept volume of the original Austin Seven engine, *circa* 1927. (To forestall the more pedantic of historians, actually 747cc).

The neat little metal box of a body sat high on two converging, top hat-shaped rails leading to a cast nose-piece, supporting on the way an alloy crankcase with a bolt-on iron block. Fragile, spoked 19 inch wheels sat at each end of a single front leaf spring, while quarter-elliptic leaves, slotted into the ends of the chassis rails, curved gracefully downwards to a rear axle located by a torque tube hooked to a knob on a pressed tin crossmember.

The curve on the rear springs ensured that in roll the cars had certain and gross oversteer, the brakes were pulled on by wires, and the engine produced a possible 13 or 14bhp on a good day.

The car was already history, a quarter of a century old when the 750 Club, created of it and for it, chose the Seven as the improbable basis for a full-blooded, two-seater, low cost, sports/racing formula.

Since then, only sheer lack of any further original parts has influenced those who guide the formula into permitting alterations in the original concept.

Year after year, discussions with drivers and constructors, a careful watch on the spirit as well as the letter of the regulations and a continual survey of costs has done the impossible – maintained Britain's cheapest form of circuit racing with full grids and ever falling lap times. It is a model lesson, set by amateurs, that the professionals in other sectors of the sport would do well to study.

World Rally Championship cars could hardly be more different. The money involved in their development, maintenance, and continual replacement has involved tens of millions, whether you wish to count in dollars or pounds sterling.

They are the flagships of commercial empires, and as such have to win, but for all that, most start off with shortcomings not dissimilar to the original Austin Seven concept.

They are not strong enough, not powerful enough, not reliable enough, not light enough. They sometimes will not handle, or develop horrific shortcomings when put into the hands of the best and hardest drivers in the world.

Competitions Departments, tiny and sometimes ill-nourished corners of the empires they serve, have to find the answers, with jobs and futures on the line if they fail. The empires then feed that success and technical improvement back into their daily bread products – or they do if the empire gaffers have the skill and sense so to do: by no means universal attributes at the top of the motor industry.

Formula Ford has got to be the most successful-ever feedback and flag waving effort of one of those empires. Firmly policed, measured to a thou, limited by an apparently impossibly tight set of restraints on chassis dimensions and methods of construction, wheels, tyres, brakes, camshafts, carburation – every avenue of the conventional tuner apparently blocked – it has got faster and faster and more and more popular. It even has its own "historic" section now restricted to "ancient" pre-1974 cars.

Men have made reputations, built careers and businesses on it, begun to climb to fame, year after year. The design ingenuity needed has been of a very specialised type, often as much concerned with economic and simple production, or easy crash repair as with a dozen minute alterations to get a

barely measurable advantage.

The awful dilemma always facing any new formula – which comes first, the formula or the cars to run in it – was neatly sidestepped by Ford themselves skillfully backing both at the same time. Since then they have had to do little more than sit back and watch it rocket into apparently permanent orbit, selling the while a significant number of 1600cc engines and enjoying the non-stop deluge of mentions of the Ford name from one end of the world to the other.

Finally we come to the top of the mountain, financially, technically, and in talent of every sort: Formula One.

Yet even on the pinnacle we do not find freedom. There is a capacity limit, and a much smaller one for forced induction engines, a width limit, a height limit, a weight minimum, mandatory compressible structures within the car, fire extinguishers that can be triggered with a fifteen foot pole, and of course ground clearance.

Theoretically all these have to be most meticulously observed but it can depend on which bit you are looking at. Cars running a wing half an inch too high or with a fraction too much on the rear track can be in trouble. No, not "can be". Certainly have been.

But there was a period when you could run with side bodywork skirts touching the track as long as they were the correct six cm clear in the paddock. Well, to be exact not just anywhere in the paddock, but just in the bit where the scrutineers were measuring it. A few yards away it did not matter.

If this sounds odd to a first-time student of F1, you are right, it is odd. So is the approach to a minimum weight requirement which builds the car illegally light, but gets it up to weight by putting on board a vast weekend caravan style plastic water bottle of several gallons capacity.

It is a permitted "essential fluid" because it is there to cool the brakes through tubing leading to the vicinity of each hub. As all fluids are topped up for the end-of-race weight checks, the fact that the water bottle happened to be empty, and perhaps fifty or more pounds lighter during the race is not relevant. Or it was not until cars started getting disqualified and a new still more violent dispute erupted.

These oddities come about because of the ingenuity of man. Along with its other "bests", F1 enjoys the skills of the best interpreters of regulations and the best protest arguers, up to and including bilingual lawyers and interpreters. It is sad that when a protest is generally a polite way of claiming the opposition is cheating, protests are often thick on the ground in F1.

These can be of such ferocity that they go, on occasion, to proper lawyers and into the courts.

The real sufferer in the end is progress, the true aim for any designer. One of the lunacies just mentioned was solved by agreeing that the edges of the bodywork *could* touch the ground after all, even in front of the scrutineers.

It enabled everybody to dismantle and throw away a complex and weighty set of hydro-pneumatic levellers, piping, air bottles, valves and controls that had previously been needed to keep the cars on tip-toe while being measured.

All these vaudeville activities should not obscure the simply gigantic strides made in the past twenty-five years despite the arguments, rows and bitterness.

A litre of engine capacity has more than doubled its power output, tyres are three times as wide and ten times as soft and grippy, the engines and gearboxes have moved from front to back, the driver has gone several feet forward, and the giant hand of atmosphere has been harnessed to treble the effective weight of the car at high speed.

In amongst all these advances lurk titanium springs, stainless exhausts, safety harnesses, self-sealing fuel tanks and pipe connections, cockpit adjustable anti-roll bars, brakes and fuel loads and small microchip brains recording all that goes on for later laboratory analysis.

Coming, I suspect, are more advanced "brains" of the type interposed between a pilot's hands and the control surfaces of jet fighter aircraft built to be fundamentally unstable. Any operation of the controls then means that the response of the vehicle is immensely speeded up to become virtually instantaneous but still held in instant check by the "brain", constantly balancing things just on the right side of the controllability.

Without doubt there will be irritated and complaining letters about automatic projectiles bombarding the magazine correspondence columns of 2002 – "not like the old days of 1983 when cars were cars and men were men and mechanics got their hands dirty".

The choice of significant vehicles which is contained in the following sections is of course a totally personal one. There are so many I have not written about, a dozen superb and truly pioneering 750 cars, Ferrari and Fiat 131, another dozen Formula Fords, McLaren, BRM, Connaught, Renault, both turbo and rally Alpine. The list goes on ... Nothing for it but to crouch down and hope most of the indignant brickbats will miss!

Rally: SAAB 96 (1960-62)

The most modest and amateurish club rallyman is likely to fall about at the suggestion that he should set out in search of fame and a works drive in a rather "sit up and beg" saloon, nearly as tall as wide, heavy, with a little demon two stroke 850 motor under the bonnet driving the narrow 15 inch front wheels, and a straining 38bhp under his right foot. To be fair, that 38 might be raised to 63bhp with a great deal of work, rather poorer than the power now available to the average representative in a firm's 1300 Escort hurtling down the M1.

So have things altered since the SAAB 96, itself a successor to the even older smaller engined and lesser powered Models 92 and 93, was able to pulverise the international rally scene including three British RAC wins on the trot.

Even allowing that they were so often driven by the great Erik Carlsson whose stature was no great help to the power to weight ratio of his steed in full rally trim, the SAAB behaviour and achievements were more than remarkable.

Ford's attack lay eight years in the future, and one of its chief architects, Stuart Turner, served part of his apprenticeship beside Carlsson on the 1960 RAC.

Although its power was so low (although not that low by the standards of many engines of the day) it was far ahead in plenty of other ways. A tough shell that had seen the inside of a wind tunnel, and coming from a firm that built successful jet fighters was one thing. Front wheel drive, only just peeping its nose in under the first Mini in England, was another. Front wishbones and coils, plus rack and pinion steering and a dead axle on coil springs at the back were a third.

Catalogues for the road car at the time mention underseal, screen washers, adjustable backrests, radiator blind, heat/demist/cold air, selfparking wipers, fuel warning light, and sometimes a laminated screen. Not to

---

SAAB Monte Carlo 850. This model superseded the SAAB Sport – the victor of countless rallies throughout the world. The '96' models were all powered by an unusual three-cylinder two-stroke engine. (Picture: SAAB GB).

mention a freewheel device, whereby the engine automatically disengaged on the overrun, its use controlled by a knob on the dashboard.

When you further consider that the standard screen pillars were said to be able to stand up to "a light roll", the cars that won almost every international rally open to them still bore a quite considerable resemblance to the production line version. Which is more than can be said of a number of other successful rally cars that spring to mind.

The oddity was to find among such quality and forward thinking a two-stroke engine, irrevocably associated with motorcycles in many minds, needing some very specialised know-how to persuade it to give those extra horses. In standard form it compared reasonably with the claimed 34 or 37bhp of the 850 Mini, but the car itself was heavier with a massive extra 25 percent frontal area to push through the air. This was at least in part compensated for by an excellent drag figure of around 0.4Cd that many manufacturers took twenty years to equal.

The fundamental qualities, both aerodynamic and structural of the shell meant that it stayed unaltered in any serious way – differently shaped lights, grille or screen hardly count – from 1949 to the early seventies.

Nobody could accuse SAAB of being slow to get into competition. The seventh and eighth cars they ever built were their entries in the 1950 Monte Carlo with two formidable Scandinavian ladies, Greta Molander and Margaretha von Essen crewing one of them. But their organisation and staff were miniscule by comparison with the giants of Ford, Fiat, Audi and even BMC that were to follow. No separate competition department at all for the first thirteen years. Ten mechanics. Four men in the engine development department, including the chief.

While engine tuning knowledge can generally be bought, strengthening shells is a different matter. Most driver/builders have to employ a technique of plating, strengthening brackets, and transferring loads by research under other vehicles and the installation of a range of self-cut and

bent bits of 16g or $\frac{1}{8}$ inch plate and thick washers.

SAAB publicly accepted their excellent shell might be made better – and produced official kits of plate, channel and angle iron with appropriate installation sketches and part numbers. These, plus a rollcage, enabled almost anybody to fall off the side of a mountain and survive.

They added various alternative coil springs for both ends of the car, and a daring road wheel with a $4\frac{1}{2}$ inch rim against the standard four inch, but the geometry of the suspension was such that big increases in rim width were not a rewarding path to follow.

Left foot braking may well have been around before the SAAB but it was certainly to reach its apotheosis in it – and later the Mini.

In passing, it is quite the most difficult thing I have ever tried to do, and emphatically needs somewhere safe and preferably private to be explored. In case there are readers to whom its precise nature is still a mystery, it is employed to get a front wheel drive car into angles that would be otherwise impossible while still keeping control and persuading it to go round the corner rather than off the road. The technique is to ignore the clutch, put the left foot onto the brake while keeping the right foot more or less hard down on the accelerator. The result is continued power and adhesion for the front wheels, locking and sliding

of the rears, and a formidable wear rate on the front pads. The feeling through one's left leg is indescribably odd, with huge problems to braking with any sensitivity, and messages to your brain that something has gone seriously wrong somewhere.

These difficulties have never prevented the inspired use of the method by many, although not all, the torrent of skilled Scandinavians that poured into Europe, as well as plenty less practised or talented. As the only alternative on loose or snow may be using the handbrake, itself an insensitive instrument on most cars, you need to try it and see.

Extras on the works cars were relatively few and mundane. Security wires on the radiator and petrol caps, sump guard, stiffer springs and Bilstein dampers, leather safety strap on the bonnet, LSD ("makes the steering a bit sticky" observes the factory literature), oil cooler, rev-counter, map lamp and navigator's grab handle. Fire extinguisher, tool and first aid kits just about completed the list. Seat, wheel and pedals to crew's personal tastes.

The engine was a different matter. Compression ratio up from 7.3 to 9.3, a crank with special full circle webs to "stuff' the crankcase and boost its compression, inlet, exhaust and transfer ports ground to new shapes and timings, twin-choke carburettor and a new four-speed box with choices of final drive to

Specification: SAAB 96 "Monte Carlo" (Showroom model)

Engine:	Three cylinder 2 stroke, 841cc, 70mm bore x 72.9 stroke, 60bhp @ 5000rpm (42 SAE*). Solex triple choke carb. (Zenith*)
Gearbox:	4-speed - (3.55, 2.1, 1.29, 0.84) 3-speed - (3.16, 1.57, 0.96*) Freewheel by dashboard control for driver.
Back axle/FD:	Integral with gearbox (front wheel drive): 5.43:1 and 4.88:1.
Chassis/shell:	Steel 2-door saloon wind tunnel developed.
Fuel tank:	Rear mounted steel, $8\frac{1}{2}$ imp. gals.
Wheels/tyres:	4x15 steel bolt on, 5.50x15 "Sports" tyres (5.20x15*)
Brakes:	Front disc, rear self-adjusting drum. (Front drum*).
Suspension:	Front: unequal length wishbones with coils. Rear: live "U" beam axle on location links with coils.
Weight:	1960lb. (1780lb*).
Bhp/ton (laden):	58. (44.4*).
Performance:	Top speed 95mph/25mpg (75mph/34mpg*)

Figures/specification for standard saloon.

complement the power unit.

Above all it did what all vehicles with the engine sitting over the driven wheels do so well – put every horse it did have onto the road with the minimum waste and maximum efficiency, particularly in snow or mud.

Most of the first arrivals in that wave of Scandinavian drivers, so practised on the snows of home winters, were able to use that combination of virtues to the full.

Any car with a long list of firsts and top threes in the RAC, Acropolis, Thousand Lakes, Midnight Sun, Safari, Monte-Carlo, Polish German, Canadian, Norwegian, Tulip and Spa-Sofia-Liege has made its own piece of history.

But an 850cc three-cylinder two-stroke in a large saloon?

As the London gentleman who had never heard of tobacco is supposed to have said to Sir Walter Raleigh concerning his purchase in the New World of a shipful of leaves to burn: "No, don't tell me Walt. Just let me guess what the hell anybody can do with that".

Rally: Mini (1963)

What can anyone possibly say about the Mini-Minor (its original formal name) that has not already been said, or written down for posterity in a score of books and ten thousand articles of every degree of competence and detail?

That it made Alec Issigonis a household name. That it set totally new standards of handling, appearance and technical pioneering to be followed willy-nilly by the rest of the world, which is also did. Or that the sills and front wings rot away deplorably, as do the rear subframes and vital curves in the handbrake cables, while brake adjusters seize irrevocably in the back plates and the transmission drop gears rattle happily on their way – which they all do.

What we cannot do is ignore it as a true competition car, as opposed to simply a car used in competition.

With all its faults it made history, mechanically, socially, aesthetically and in competition. And I don't know of any other vehicle that has had quite so much put into its development by outsiders to the factory, and certainly unpaid.

There are dozens of successful businesses still going strong today founded on the Mini, its faults, tuning and development. The things that have come from the factory over the years seem more to have been endless detail refinement – or just alterations – mostly in the gearbox and drive train, but which along the years have stolen those famous and enormous door boxes, extended the front wings and bonnet, provided a heater as a standard fitting, less crippling seats and one of the best racing camshafts ever designed for a particular engine.

A cutaway photograph of the original Mini showing the unusual packaging of the mechanical components to give maximum passenger space. (Picture: B.L. Heritage).

And I speak as owner, business driver, racer and rust fighter with a long succession of the little grotboxes.

Those fortunate enough to not only be living, but in a car buying position, at the end of 1959 when it burst upon a startled world have a special small advantage where the Mini is concerned.

We can actually recall how odd it looked, a neat tiny box with its midget wheels which gave rise to dozens of mostly deplorable jokes about the risk to passengers of dogs lifting a hind leg near the windows, and the dangers of a new generation of midget children conceived in its confines. (Although the shape and awkwardness of the original Austin Seven did not appear to have given rise to such genetic effects). Within four months the jokers, especially those who owned supposedly quick saloons or sports cars of the period were starting to look very sick indeed.

While the factory then seemed to regard the Mini as just a very new car with an uncertain future for the time being, private enterprise tuners and modifiers could not get at it fast enough. A markedly gutless 850 engine (inspired apparently by the formidable performance of the 1000cc prototypes) offered rich rewards.

But the really astonishing thing was that its grip on the road was so good, the roadholding proved far more difficult to improve than the power unit. In no time at all, club racing drivers discovered the cornering forces it could generate ripped the 12 gauge front wheels clean over the nuts. A friend, then working in Longbridge's development department, relayed the information to higher levels and was politely disbelieved. He managed to arrange the loan of one of the works hacks, and took less than an hour on a large concrete patch to pull a wheel off in front of a private audience.

After one or two more fell off in more public view, during the 750 MC Six Hour relay at Silverstone, everyone got called into the pits for scrutineers to find various cracks in the centres of wheels on other cars and the Mini teams had to withdraw. Whilst infuriating at the time, it had the right result. We all got a free set of new thick wheels from the works shortly afterwards, but more importantly, all Mini wheels got thicker in due course.

They, the exhaust pipe gallantly acting as an engine brace as well as carbon monoxide conveyor, and body water leaks, were almost the only weaknesses in the whole design, and hardly fundamental ones. Beefing up material thicknesses and reversing a panel overlap cured all three. The amount that Issigonis got right first time is quite staggering.

He chose a slightly angled axis of roll, with front roll centre at about $2\frac{1}{4}$ inches, together with an extremely long swing axle length of around eleven feet, the rear roll centre on the ground with trailing arms, basic understeer and featherlight sensitive steering. Centre of gravity was very low by conventional saloon standards of the time, and the novel Moulton rubber mushrooms that were the springs amounted to a stiffened full race rising rate suspension from the word go. So much so that later ultra light versions had, at first, experimental holes drilled in the rubbers in search of something softer or changed to coils to obtain some control over what they were altering.

Almost the only thing that factory outsiders found they could do to good effect was introduce static negative camber at both ends in varying degrees to try and get vertical outer wheels in roll on corners. Trailing arms and that ultra long swing axle length at the front, meant that roll angle and wheel angles were almost synonymous. Some also fitted rear anti-roll bars to try and persuade the rear to break away and combat the understeer when really trying, but due to the Mini's famous stance with one rear wheel high in the air and the other hardly working itself to death, these were of arguable value.

Widening the $3\frac{1}{2}$ inch rim wheels to five or even more inches helped stop the tyres wearing the maker's name off the sidewalls, and that was about the state of the art when the factory finally got the message. At long last came a really serious alternative to the 850 with its breaking cranks, long stroke, little valves, oil soaked clutch and snapping timing chains – the 70bhp, 1071cc "S". (The 997 and 998cc versions were little more than a factory enlarged 848, but including most of its shortcomings.)

Within the limitations of being made of cast iron, and on the same factory machinery as the earlier engines, the only criticisms one might have offered of the "S" were against the traditional siamesed ports and very little metal indeed between the bores. These apart it had everything to make it a tough, high-revving, efficiently breathing engine with still more tuning left in it.

The consequence of all this was that when the works decided to take on the best and the rest of the world – the actual car that achieved a classic and world-influencing victory, still preserved at the Beaulieu Motor Museum, was surprisingly standard in all sorts of ways.

Admittedly it was running Group 1 with some limitations on modifications, which did not prevent it winning outright the 33rd Monte Carlo Rally under the rather complex regulations operating that year. Remarkable as it may now sound, it was then an event with the sort of stature that ensured massive radio, newspaper and magazine coverage, before, during and afterwards.

Yet the Issigonis concept was so superior to virtually every other car in production, the opposition could not stay with it, whether larger, more powerful, or specifically developed for competition.

What did this giant killer with driver Paddy Hopkirk and navigator Henry Liddon have about it? Largely creature comforts to allow its crew to stay fit and efficient while using its built-in virtues to the full.

The specification makes it clear; engine to Group 1, ie blueprinted, but same carbs, cam, manifolds, valves, bore/stroke etc, as out of the showroom. But the driver had a decent bucket seat (reclining) and the same for the navigator. There was a lengthened throttle pedal for heel/toe changes, lowered column (every goodie shop had a bracket to do the job for about 25p), rev-counter, extra lamps, two speed wipers with large capacity washers, brake servo tucked over the navigator's feet, big heater, heated screen, navigator's button for the horn, inside fuses, twin spares and fuel tanks, sump guard, oil cooler, water

The Hopkirk/Liddon Mini Cooper 1071 'S' in the 1963 Tour de France. This car was to win the 1964 Monte Carlo rally. (Picture: B.L. Heritage).

deflector plate for the distributor and wide rear track brake drums.

Shell, engine and gearbox, steering ratio, even suspension links and geometry, and pressed tin production wheels, were all as the average aunty could purchase. It took the world more than a further decade to catch up and surpass. In the meantime, the Mini in every imaginable guise and form of motor sport built up a list of victories beyond counting and possibly the largest and most varied of any motor vehicle produced since the day the internal combustion engine first stuttered into explosive life.

Specification - Mini "S" (Monte Carlo)

Engine:	1071cc, 70.6 x 68.26, 75bhp @ 5900rpm, CR 9.0:1, 2 valve pushrod, 5 port head, twin SUs (trumpets in place of filters), oil cooler, iron block/head.
Gearbox:	4-speed integral with engine (2.57, 1.78, 1.242, 1.1).
Back axle/final drive:	Integral with gearbox (4.133:1).
Chassis/shell:	Steel 2-door, full rollcage, 5 aux. lamps (plus Q1 headlights).
Fuel tanks:	Twin steel, 4.5 imp. gals. each.
Wheels/tyres:	Front - 5x10 inch.
	Rear - 5x10 inch.
Brakes:	Front - 7 inch disc Servo assist.
	Rear - 7x1¼ inch drum.
Suspension:	Front - unequal length wishbone, rubber in compression separate damper.
	Rear - trailing arms, rubber in compression separate damper.
Weight:	1411lb.
Bhp/ton (laden):	92.
Performance:	Top speed 96mph.
Remarks:	Many crew comfort alterations — reclining seat for navigator, o/size heater, heated screen, two speed wipers, headlamp washers, internal fuseboxes, lowered steering column, extended throttle pedal.

Rally: Ford Escort (1970-1978)

The extraordinary length of competition life that the Ford Escort has enjoyed — you name it and it has probably won it in the past fifteen years — makes an intriguing contrast to the British Leyland approach, with a multiplicity of models, engines, driven wheels and so on.

Ford's economy of approach even included slipping under their brand new Mk 2 shell the same basic running gear that had already by then had eight years of development and experience lavished on it. For the fleet buyer or private customer it was a brand new car, but with virtually identical maintenance, repair and spares back-up to its forerunner. Plenty of rallymen have in fact transferred all the running gear and power train of a Mk 1 suffering from either tinworm or rolling about among Forestry Commission trees, into the newer Mk 2 with no serious snags at all.

This ability to capitalise on past knowledge was superbly supported by an engine policy that allowed a range of capacities, stronger gearboxes, and in due course technically more advanced engines with six times the power of the first 1100s, based on original or copy blocks to be deftly inserted into its wide-open engine bay with the minimum of upset.

Once all this got into its stride, the Mini in international competition terms did not know what had hit it. The problem was compounded for British Leyland by something they could hardly have foreseen or even been concerned with in 1958 with the embryo Mini — that the major rally scene would be driven off the public roads into forests, and into ever wilder unsurfaced areas of Europe and other parts of the world, where ultra low ground clearance meant trouble with a capital 'T'.

Unbothered by this, Ford also devised a very economic way of tapping the best brains outside the industry by making shells and/or parts available to various carefully chosen small tuning companies so they could prepare and compete with them.

No one has ever revealed the exact financial arrangements behind these deals, but in terms of Ford's competition budget they must have been the bargain of the decade for the factory.

From a suspension design point of view it was a relatively mundane car — solid rear axle, and Macpherson strut front with its built-in handicap of extreme difficulty in adjustment and a positive wheel angle in corners more or less directly reflecting the roll angle of the car.

Exactly like the rear end of the Stratos, the struts needed to have a permanent modification to put static negative into them or a top mounting altered so that cornering roll angles finally brought the wheel upright when it mattered.

The rear axle was dealt with in various ways from two links plus normal leaf springs, right up to four links, panhard rod and coils let into fabricated boot floor turrets.

Ford also helped balance the books with a massive and methodic approach to selling their own competition parts.

Such a hard headed business approach did not prevent the hiring of the best drivers in the world, and the toughest test area in the world too — the tank and fighting vehicle test ground at Bagshot in Surrey.

One day's rental there (and they paid for hundreds) allowed back-to-back testing, utterly vital if any worthwhile comparisons are to be made between engines, tyres or drivers.

Within hours, axle casings and wheels could be broken, gearboxes wrecked and dozens of tyres reduced to ruin, all on a time basis that permitted reliable forecasting of life under rallying conditions.

Seven years after the Escort was launched it is a staggering thought that apart from its basic pushrod power unit in various sizes, there were also 1600, 1700 and 1800 Twin Cams, BDAs giving from 130-240bhp, standard, Bullet and ZF gearboxes, half a dozen final drives, vented disc brakes, high ratio racks, a whole range of coil springs, dry sump installations, World Cup crossmembers, strengthened rear

Cutaway of a Ford Escort RS1800 rally car. (Picture Ford Motor Co.).

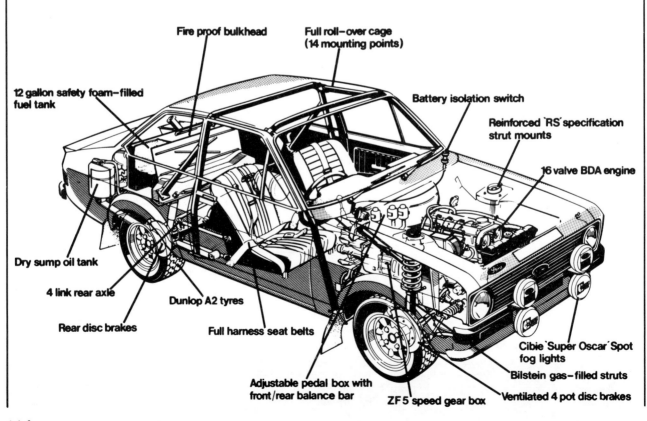

Fire proof bulkhead

Full roll–over cage (14 mounting points)

12 gallon safety foam–filled fuel tank

Battery isolation switch

Reinforced 'RS' specification strut mounts

16 valve BDA engine

Dry sump oil tank

4 link rear axle

Dunlop A2 tyres

Rear disc brakes

Full harness seat belts

Cibie 'Super Oscar' Spot fog lights

Bilstein gas–filled struts

Adjustable pedal box with front/rear balance bar

ZF 5 speed gear box

Ventilated 4 pot disc brakes

axles, better halfshafts, a variety of wheel rim widths, and a huge selection of tyres to go on them.

Add Sport, Mexico and the fabled RS versions, and the way was open to just about anybody in the world to build his own competition Escort from a simple "rollcage plus racing seat" version to a Works copy.

To make sure that anyone at all tackling the job would have the best possible chance of succeeding (and thus winning in a Ford) the factory borrowed an idea ironically conceived many years before by MG. That immortal sports car firm (until the commercial agonies of British Leyland shut it down, that is) had issued factory inspired tuning information as early as the 1930s, largely concerning the engine with a methodic approach designated Stages 1 to 5. This led you by the hand from the production power unit to a supercharged, methanol mixture-fed version that was just as powerful and sensitive as it sounds.

Ford developed this idea with a vengeance. From the works cars, together with wealthy semi-works teams and skilled privateers, came a torrent of information on every possible aspect of the cars. Rather than keep this quiet as hard-earned secrets, Ford decided to regularly pass it all on, backed by a flow of works produced parts and continually up-dated know-how.

Apart from a chain of over seventy Sport dealers, where you could actually buy most of the bits, they printed a fifteen section parts catalogue that included advice on which bits to buy and at what stage, of masterly simplicity and lack of bull, forgiving them the T-shirts and suitcases at the end.

Then they produced their master work, *Escort Rally Preparation*. It was cheap, typed and photocopied, with mediocre photographs, and simple sketches that had never seen a draughtsman's touch.

It did not matter. The contents for the would-be competitor were 156 solid gold pages. How, and why to five-link a rear axle. Wiring, coil springs, gas-filled dampers, stitching a shell in the right pieces with weld, how to pre-fade rock-hard competition disc pads, and how not to fall foul of the rule book.

It was unexpectedly honest. "Chuck away that awful pushrod system on the servo" began one bit of advice on the brand new car you had just bought. "Trying to steer with the column in your lap won't produce outstanding stage times" reinforced advice that a strip of 1 inch x $\frac{1}{8}$ inch steel was needed to help two weedy production body brackets survive. And it was blandly admitted that the cars used Mini-Cooper "S" servos until their own version was ready.

Very obviously there were a thousand further ideas and refinements not included. It was not vital. What was, was that so many tried and tested fundamentals were in it.

The results were both predictable and highly rewarding for Ford in so many race, rally, autocross, hot rod, hillclimb and grasstrack reports that they are long since beyond counting.

Probably the most sophisticated versions of all were the Broadspeed circuit racers. Ralph Broad was not only a tuner and engineer of brilliance, but a reader of the small print of international rules of equal talent. Desperate to get away from the limiting MacPherson strut, he designed fully independent front suspension all supposedly supplementary to the strut, but doing all the work and connected to it in only the most tenuous fashion.

While this was causing uproar and heart-searching among scrutineers, he also devised a way of tuning the rear of the car with a set of bolt holes.

These were drilled in the alloy plate bulkhead that took the place of the rear seat back. Employing to the full the happenstance that a coil spring effectively softens its rate as far as the road wheel is concerned when inclined to ever increasing angles, suitable calculations back in the workshop allowed very high-speed paddock changes in suspension characteristics by simply moving the top of the

---

Specification - Barry Lee's Escort "351"

Engine:	1600 pushrod, special bore/stroke, 162bhp at 7750rpm, dry sump.
Gearbox:	Bullet, using effectively two gears, bottom/second.
Rear axle:	Standard 1300 with extra oil capacity, 4.9 & LSD.
Front suspension:	1300 Bilstein struts, lowered, export coils, no anti-roll bar, compression link to rack control arm, (extra damper on left side for bumpy right-hand tracks).
Rear suspension:	4 link, coil spring with Watts linkage.
Bodywork:	No glass, fibreglass bonnet, full rollcage with door bars, steel boot, rear wing.
Brakes:	Front - 8.6 inch disc.
	Rear - 8 inch drum.
Wheels/tyres:	9x13 revolution alloys with 9.2x20x13 racing slicks or wets.
Electrics:	24 volt.

Specification - Roger Clarke's Escort "000 96M"

Engine:	1800BDA, 203bhp at 7600rpm, dry sump.
Gearbox:	ZF 5-speed, close ratio.
Rear axle:	Salisbury Atlas with LSD, six alternative ratios.
Front suspension:	Bilstein strut, negative camber and increased castor.
Rear suspension:	4 link with leaf springs. Vertical turretted dampers.
Bodywork:	All steel, seam welded, full rollcage less all trim.
Brakes:	Front - 10 inch ventilated discs with F2 four pot calipers.
	Rear - 10 inch discs.
Wheels/tyres:	7x13 (6x13 for very loose) with generally 175x13 Dunlop M&S.
Electrics:	12 volt.

suspension unit to a different position.

When combined with adjustable anti-roll bars, shock absorbers with screwed spring platforms and alternative front pickups for trailing links, there was little that could not be done to suit the handling of the car to different circuits, weather or drivers.

As an interesting contrast of just two Escorts, both at the top of the tree in their respective fields, the specifications are of, firstly, Barry Lee's hot rod with its famous "351" number and Roger Clark's equally famed '000 96M" of a year earlier.

Rally: Lancia Stratos (1971-1978)

One of the most pleasing memories of the Stratos for me has always been its appearance when all the rear bodywork fell off — a fairly frequent occurrence in its first years.

While this never seemed to slow it at all, it did reveal a remarkable likeness, with its perforated rear bulkhead, to my own Terrapin single seater, as well as a transversely mounted rear engine integral with the gearbox.

Unlike mine which was Mini, the howl of the Stratos came from one of the greatest among many great engines to emerge from Ferrari — the classic four ohc 2.4-litre V6 Dino. Sometimes it was a 12-valve, sometimes 24-valve and, on occasion, turbocharged as well; but all its life it was the Dino.

Its concept and creation gave an intriguing view of what the engineers within a huge industrial empire can do, given a reasonably free hand to tackle building a rally winner for their factory.

It drew both its name and initial inspiration from a Bertone-bodied "tart-catcher" or boulevard special designed largely to ornament the Turin Show of late 1970. There was no way anyone was likely to be building or buying a 2½ feet high confection in which you lifted up the windscreen before stepping round the steering wheel and space capsule instruments to lie down inside.

To most people in a world full of Ford Escorts, it might have seemed a totally bizarre sire for a World Rally Championship car, but the request of a far-seeing Lancia director to Bertone to turn it into a mid-engined, high-performance, practical GT car produced a prototype at the 1971 show — seven months later.

Even with ten inches added to its height, and a foot or so off the wheelbase, it was still a wickedly low, chunky, attractive device.

The concept utilised to the full rear weight bias and transverse engine reaction to achieve, by front engine/rwd standards, quite startling grip for the quality of rubber then available.

This instantly permitted a large number of the original 229 notably hairy-legged horses of its Ferrari motor to be applied usefully to the road, making it a potentially fearsome contender from the word go. One has to realise that tyres and what they will do for even a mediocre car have improved beyond all recognition since 1971 when the Stratos HF got that first go-ahead.

Power on the road as compared to wheelspin, whether on the loose in an English forest, on the tarmac of the French Alps or Isle of Man, is that for which every rally driver wishes to exchange his right arm.

An LSD and most carefully chosen gearbox ratios were augmented by transfer gears designed for rapid change allowing the gearing to be quickly tailored to special circumstances.

A monocoque centre section, given extra stength by the rollcage, made more concessions to aerodynamics than to the crew who would drive it. The low roofline was combined with a screen rake so enormous that the lower edge was well on its way to their feet.

The fall of what was left of the nose, of particular grace in daylight, hit the same headlight height rule that bedevils the aesthetics of all lowline sports cars. Putting the filaments the legal twenty four inches above the road forces some design of pop-up pivoting lights, likely to look less than beautiful in night position.

However, there will be plenty of Stratos lovers happy to argue that when the standard pair were joined by four auxiliaries to create a positive phalanx of light right across the front of the car, it became purposeful and aggressive rather than ugly.

At each end of the monocoque were, effectively, separate steel subframes to carry suspension, steering, brake master cylinders and not much else at the front, and the massive and rather high set engine at the rear.

While unequal length wishbones at the front permitted later variations in geometry to suit tyre developments as time went by, Chapman struts were chosen for the rear. While these have enormous advantages in terms of manufacture and very accurate control of castor and camber angles, they impose strict limitations on what the wheel does in bounce, droop or roll.

Experimental alterations of camber angles, are at best slow and laborious and at worst impossible. This goes for castor as well. Modification to the arc of the bottom link which controls camber change totally on hard acceleration was impossible in the short term with a cast-in lug for the outboard bearing, and space problems at the inner end.

Extra space for variations in coils was hard to come by, as was extra stroke for the suspension when the car moved from European style tarmac events to the loose and often diabolical surfaces of British forests.

The factory and Graham Warner's London-based Chequered Flag garage, running the only serious British based Stratos, made great efforts in due course to permit quite large alterations in ride height of 1⅜ inch at the spring platform and a total suspension

Lancia Stratos circuit racer at Donington. This picture reveals, in fascinating detail, the unusual structure of the Stratos — note the massive frame cradling the Dino V6 engine. (Picture: Frank Bott).

The same car in profile — still at Donington. (Picture: Frank Bott).

movement of 9 inches, major contributions to its reliability.

Perhaps the car's overriding characteristic was that it was an extremely short as well as squat car, weight all within the wheelbase, and so with a uniquely low polar moment of inertia.

That meant it was either quick and sensitive with excellent turn-in, or extremely twitchy and willing to spin at any time, depending on your viewpoint or degree of skill. It was designed and built, as might be expected, for people who had to be really able to drive if they were to get the best out of it.

Bodywork, both at the front and that somewhat ill-attached rear end was fibreglass mouldings that clothed the mechanical parts in a dramatically handsome skin that took the eye as no other rally car before, or since.

Lancia needed 500 cars to get the homologation papers for its international competition passport, and a fully documented order went very shortly to Bertone for 500 monocoques. How many were ever actually delivered is something of a mystery, but by late 1974 the Stratos was homologated and in serious competition.

Long before that the engine had,

in typical Ferrari fashion, sprouted twenty-four-valve heads bearing with them an extra 30bhp and on their heels an experimental turbo version.

Its design, rear visibility, lights, etc took so many liberties with the ever-growing forest of European and US legislation to do with motor vehicles, it was questionable where you could go out and drive it legally once you had bought one of the production versions.

That proved no handicap to winning the World Rally Championship crown almost before the ink was dry on the homologation papers, (in themselves a touch flexible in that they required a stated intention to produce 500 rather than 500 in a row outside the factory).

At the same time a 350bhp turbo version of the engine was under development, later raised to 480bhp at 12psi boost and a rather hypothetical 580bhp at 22psi. This last was more of a ten second wonder on the brake without major changes to the engine itself, but makes a stirring picture for the imagination, howling down a long, darkening avenue of pines barking orange tongues of flame at a grey sky on the overrun.

By 1975 a compact Competitions

Department of twenty-one men, plus the driving teams, had five cars and five spares on instant call. Munari won the Monte in January and well before the RAC Rally in November a second World Championship was nailed. They did not have to come to Britain that winter, if they did not want to.

Lancia's action in that circumstance should place every rally fan who could get to the course somewhere, anywhere, that year in the factory's eternal debt. It was decided to enter two works cars and the Chequered Flag car as well.

Per Inge Walfridsson in the latter had a series of problems, as did Sandro Munari in the first works car. Bjorn Waldegaard in the second broke a driveshaft and fell to 135th place.

From such an impossible position he set out on the drive that printed an unforgettable picture on the mind of anyone who saw it. A total artist at work, he put up 44 fastest stage times, balanced a thousand times on the knife

The Stratos in its true element during the 1975 Safari Rally. (Picture: Colin Taylor Productions).

edge of greatness, to take back 128 of those places.

He didn't win, but both car and man were greater in the losing.

In the future lay a third World Championship, more Monte wins, a first, second, third and fourth in the San Remo, but the Fiat 131 was waiting in the wings, and tyres were helping to make the front engine/rear wheel drive cars ever more competitive.

Just before Christmas 1978 its factory career ended officially. That did not stop Bernard Darniche, its most successful ever driver, stealing an inspired victory by seconds from the works Escorts on the 1979 Monte. It was a magnificent finale for a car that only gave of its superlative best to a driver of similar calibre.

For someone who only wished to impress the neighbours or Ferrari owners outside grand hotels, it would do that too without effort. It was not for old ladies or fat men. For the athletic and talented and girls with beautiful legs it had no equal.

Specification - Lancia Stratos.

Engine:	Rear mounted Dino V6, bore and stroke 92.5x60: 2418cc, four ohc, (2 valve and 4 valve versions), 8, 9, 9.5 & 10.5:1 compression ratios. Triple Weber IDF, Turbo/injection. Power: 190-480bhp depending on specification. Front radiator. Triple plate clutch.
Gearbox:	Integral below engine, five speed - 3.55, 2.46, 1.78, 1.32, 0.97 standard ratios. Rally & circuit CR sets available. Dog drive gears.
Back axle/FD:	3.9:1 in unit with gearbox. Variable through quick change drop gears. LSD. Alternative of 3.42:1.
Chassis/shell:	Monocoque steel centre section, steel subframes front and rear, with GRP bodywork lifting as a unit front and rear.
Fuel tanks:	Midships twin 11 imp. gal. bag tank. Twin fillers.
Wheels/tyres:	Front - 6½x15 Forest/loose up to 10.5x15 Rear - 7x15 Tarmac/circuit Pirelli P7, Michelin up to 15x15.
Brakes:	ATE, no servo. Front - 9.9in ventilated discs. Rear - 9.9in solid discs.
Suspension:	Front - unequal length wishbone, variable rate coils, anti-roll bar. Rear - Chapman strut, variable coil wishbone and brake reactive strut, anti-roll bar.
Weight:	900kg. (1980lb).
Bhp/ton (laden):	Based on 300bhp engine – 287.
Top speed:	110-150mph dependent on gearing.

Rally: Audi Quattro (1982)

Most people – drivers, designers, team managers *et al*, were well convinced that four-wheel-drive had far too many problems, whether handling or mechanical, to be worth any serious consideration when the turbo-engined Audi Quattro suddenly appeared on the scene.

Plenty more were guilty of unworthy thoughts that it was either illegal, wouldn't work, or if it did, hopefully not for long.

All these were rapidly crushed by the production of a full road version, most luxuriously equipped, soon to be found standing in various showrooms complete with brochures and a price, while the competition version immediately began to perform better than in the worst nightmares of rival team managers.

Their worries were not lightened by the fact that it was being driven by arguably the greatest rally driver of all time – Hannu Mikkola, with his long time partner Arne Hertz. As Andretti

and Petersen had taken talented advantage of the unexplored world of ground effects in F1, so Mikkola did the same with the Quattro.

Other teams were not the only ones to be upset. Perhaps unexpectedly, rally supporters and spectators were by no means all in favour either, on the twin grounds of its silence and its unspectacular arrival and departure from corners.

Nurtured and thrilled by the sideways techniques of good rally men able to put cars at impossible angles on the loose and hold them balanced there, a car from which the most dramatic happening was an occasional belch of flame from the exhaust did not offer the same visual reward for aficionados who had stood out all night and much of the following day in bitter cold and rain.

However, its handling seen from the side of the road was deceptive. It needed all Mikkola's considerable skill on occasion to get the best out of it, and one of his rare excursions off the road wrote off its chances completely in the 1981 Swedish.

Michele Mouton, the French rally girl with looks as good as her driving, coped brilliantly with its challenge to demolish every male on the San Remo.

Like F1 when Lotus venturi cars arrived it was unanimous Gloomsville among the opposition with many mutterings of "Ban it" when the rain suddenly stopped. The moment the roads dried, was the moment when everybody realised they might have been protesting too loudly and too soon. For the Quattro was vulnerable after all. The chink in its armour was that everyone who had said four-wheel-drive had a lot of inbuilt difficulties was at least partly right.

Roads slippery with mud gave the Quattro a dominating advantage, but in the dry, even with the great Mikkola's talents, it was most certainly not devastating. The battle – by Audi to improve it, and by other teams to beat it – had begun. Really it had started a long long time earlier, when an Audi won something called the TransAlpine Rally in 1913, rapidly followed twelve years, and a World War, later by a singleton NSU victory in the German

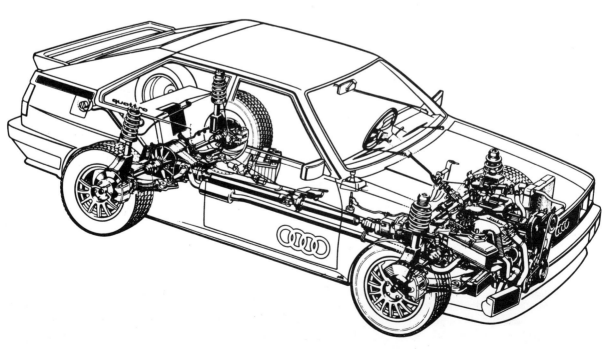

Grand Prix.

It was 1936 before the Auto-Union GP car – V16, six-litres blown to one atmosphere, rear engined, single big fuel tank amidships, driver's feet on the front axle, combined gearbox/final drive, all independent suspension (sounds familiar in the 1980s?), bore that four linked circle logo to a series of crushing world class victories. That same badge now sits on the front of the Quattro.

The Audi 80 with its oddball five cylinder engine had a solid history of winning things, when, legend has it, one of the group's development engineers began building an experimental four-wheel-drive, by the John Cooper-like expedient of hanging most of the front of an existing vehicle onto the back as well.

The prototype's off the road performance at the Audi test track was said to be so sensational, the directors gave an immediate go-ahead to get it into production.

It was unexpectedly easy for them to keep a discreet veil over the development work on the enterprise because the factory had a military four-wheel-drive device running called the Iltis. Nobody took too much notice of this hurtling about in the more exotic and distant rallies in the Sahara and West Africa. Mikkola was not driving and it was a long way from the icy roads of Keilder Forest.

But the Cooper approach of simply installing a second set of everything at the other end of the car – in this case the MacPherson struts and driven front wheels of the Audi 80 – met very few really serious difficulties.

The engineers eschewed any too-sophisticated approach to driving the rear wheels. They took a shaft out of the back of the gearbox, put a single extra differential in the drive line of a conventional propshaft to a conventional chassis-mounted

---

The Audi Quattro in full rally trim as provided for Mikkola and Hertz to contest the 1982 British Open Rally Championship. (Picture: Audi GB).

Cutaway of the Quattro showing the layout of the major mechanical components. (Picture: Audi GB).

differential at the rear.

There were no "in" and "out" levers for complex combinations of gearing, or separate drives to different axles. Just a five-speed box with all wheels permanently engaged in drive.

Even the pressings for the suspension bottom links were identical front and rear. The only thing against the car was weight – $1\frac{1}{4}$ tons. To cope with this and keep the 2.2-litre engine, it was decided to turbo-charge it.

In barely three years, a bulky, magnificently equipped and refined five-seater saloon for those with some £15,000 to spend was on view at the Geneva Motor Show. The really well kept secret behind it was that Mikkola had already driven a rally version on test months earlier and reported back with the one word the directors were waiting for – "Yes".

Its development in the next fifteen months went through two distinct stages. The factory slimmed, lightened and strengthened all they could think of, as well as raising the power from a reliable 200bhp to an equally reliable 330.

Then they handed this totally German creation to an Englishman and asked him to finish the job. David Sutton had been as near to a Ford works team as possible, without actually drawing a salary.

He and his Boreham-based organisation had an incomparable knowledge of world class rallying and how to build cars that stayed together

and they poured it all into the Quattro. To cap it all he and Hannu Mikkola were close personal friends, in accord and in tune with each other like the great partnerships in Formula 1.

With a car weighing that much, light alloy, perspex, and fibreglass all came on the scene in a fairly big way, and the NASCAR approach of making a light alloy rollcage work for its living was given a new tweak. It did not end at the screen but bored on with long extensions downwards and forwards, to the strut mountings and right on to the front bumper line.

Engine and other guards were of course in light alloy, as were the specially made door skins, bonnet, hubs, dashboard and bumpers. Windows were plastic, and a glass boot lid supported a big spoiler with two massive oil coolers slotted into it.

They were a vital part of the development, not, as normally, for the engine, but because turbos stay in one piece largely because lubricating oil is providing the heat barrier between the in-going air on one side and extremely warm out-going exhaust on the other.

Combined with a simple interior – two good seats, with full harness, fire extinguisher system and not much else – the rally car finished up almost exactly 2cwt, or 100Kg, lighter than the road version and with 65 percent more power to urge it on.

Not surprising then that eleven inch vented discs all round have still found it a sweat to stop it sometimes,

---

Specification – Audi Quattro

Engine:	Five cylinder, 2144cc, single ohc, 2 valves per cylinder, injection with KKK turbocharger and intercooler. 330bhp at 6000rpm.
Gearbox:	Five-speed, all indirect: choice of ratios.
4-WD:	Differentials available: 4.11, 4.55, 4.87.
Shell:	Steel four door. Alloy doors, bonnet. Perspex windows. Security clips on screen surround. Full alloy rollcage with forward bars.
Wheels/tyres:	6 & 7x15 alloy. Pirelli and Kleber slicks, inters wets, M & S.
Brakes:	11 inch ventilated discs all round with alloy calipers. No servo.
Suspension (front/rear):	Coils and MacPherson strut to driven alloy hubs with lower wishbone, anti-roll bars both ends.
Weight:	1190Kg. (23.37cwt)
Bhp/ton (laden):	248bhp.
Performance:	Top speed 109-158mph. 0-60: 5 seconds (average), 0-100: 13 seconds.

with Mikkola frequently left-foot braking just like the old Mini days.

The officially released specification of the car blandly referred to a "handbrake acting hydraulically on the rear wheels". Oh, tut tut! if you are a student of the British Construction and Use Act concerning legal motor vehicles on the road ....

It arrived with a formidable impact, in 1981. Three firsts, a third, and two fourths in five events for a first season, taking the Swedish, San Remo and RAC, has to be showing promise.

Mikkola, commenting after some snow and ice experience in anger, delivered the reasonably immortal observation: "No danger at all – grip the same on asphalt, ice or snow. Just a little difficult to warm up the rears".

Seen from a wider aspect, it was the times that it was beaten that probably did both the Quattro, and rallying the most good. The mere fact that it could be beaten silenced the more frantic cries of "Ban it", cutting the ground from under the feet of those who had protested, "without developing our own four-wheel-drive we haven't a chance".

On the largely dry Circuit of Ireland, tarmac to an inch, it needed all Mikkola's talents, and the skills of the Sutton mechanics, to drag it into sixth place. Broken driveshaft, broken rear suspension when a solid axle might have survived the bang, gearbox and differential failure. All got repaired. Only a slipping clutch, finally filled with flour to dry the worst of the oil out, needed more time to change than the clocks allowed.

Jimmy McRae, Russell Brookes, Henri Toivonen, John Coyne and Billy Coleman – in that order – showed the Quattro was not totally invincible. It was an important day for rallying.

Formula 750: Simplicity (1949-1953)

Just about at the same time as millionaire Tony Vandervell was pestering the Government to let him import a Ferrari as a start in trying to beat the world, Jack French was considering how anyone might race at all without the possession of real wealth.

The budget he envisaged was around £150 to include not only the car but all tyres and fuel for a full season of club racing. Before you gasp, or enquire "Jack who?" the year was 1949, racing cars were virtually non-existent and getting one was strictly a DIY job before "DIY" had ever been so called.

Much better known was the "IE" – Impecunious Enthusiast. IEs were plentiful in the small ads seeking cars for minute sums, far below even the modest going rate of £80 for a 19 year-old Austin Seven saloon or £40 for a homebuilt special.

Jack French was then, apart from crossing regular technical words with contemporaries like the young Arthur Mallock and the infant Colin Chapman, a sort of patron saint and spiritual father of all IEs.

One of the earliest members of the 750 Club, he was the man who conceived and then created "Simplicity" the basic racing car *par excellence,* one of the best examples ever of the transformation of cheap unpromising raw material into a highly successful competition vehicle.

He did more than build it. He put on record many of the trials and tribulations of the task as well as a detailed costing in successive issues of the 750 Club's magazine, all written in a style as individual as the car. He revealed the technical detail that made it what it was. Finally he lent it to almost any size and shape of driver who could be trusted to press it to the limit trying to win.

As fascinating as the advice he gave, some of it still bang up to date in the 1980s, are the glimpses of a world that had Silverstone and twin SUs, yet, in other ways, seems as distant as Queen Victoria.

"The intention" he wrote " is to demonstrate that an effective Formula racing car can be built by the enthusiast of limited means working in his garden shed". Garages beside the house were then a considerable rarity, and cars to go in them barely less so. Garden sheds were where the work was done. At that time I was not racing or even dreaming of it, but I was maintaining my first ever car, an Austin Seven special, in the street outside my parents' Birmingham home, doing every job however major, and whatever the weather, parked at the pavement edge, as were any number of my friends.

Unknown to me Jack French was at that very time "traipsing the streets of Birmingham" trying to find somebody who would shotpeen four conrods and a crank for him. Discovery of a man who could offer such a facility on a few small objects was revealed to fellow club members with the open-heartedness of the traveller in remote lands sharing food and water with another met upon the road. At that time you did not look up the adverts for somebody who could do it. Not only were there no such advertisements, there were no such really specialised magazines either, save *Motor Sport,* in which they could have appeared.

Motor Sport, even years later, still did not have a single ad offering anything more exotic than a rebore at home – and only one of those.

Birmingham was a city rich in places that might do such jobs, but you had to find them, and Jack French was having to do his research a long way from home in deepest Gloucestershire.

If knowledge of any sort about suspensions and chassis was in its amateur infancy, he had to report sadly that the only book he could trace at all on engine tuning was one on bike units of the 1930s.

As a consequence much of his saga concentrated on Simplicity's sidevalve power unit, giving originally a less than dramatic 14bhp ex-works: rebuilding, retrieving part-worn bearings and broken studs, the search for a prized Whatmough-Hewitt alloy cylinder head, filing big-end caps accurately before hand-scraping the white metal bearings back to a circle. And should they be a touch tight on assembly, how to deliver an ever-so-delicate clout with a copper hammer to settle them to perfection.

Some of it now has the air of the expertise of the mediaeval armourer, creater of the shields and swords of Kings; skills beyond price in their period but overtaken by time and technology.

Not too many engine tuners now have to machine number two and three pistons low, so that they will rise to the correct clearance and compression ratio without hitting the cylinder head as the two-bearing "bent wire" crank to which they are attached whips in an every increasing arc as its revs increase.

Nor must they selectively assemble main roller or ball bearings from secondhand, carefully washed and inspected parts to accommodate that same crank flex.

Yet among French's advice were the unchanging basics that could have been written yesterday – lightened flywheels and valve gear, cleanliness-like core plugs pushed out to syringe oilways, shaped valves with line contact seats, piston skirts filed to leave only the thrust faces, rings below the gudgeon pin consigned to the scrap bin, manifolds matched and dowelled, conrods balanced on the kitchen scales, the influence of wheels and tyres on cornering power and the value of *Exchange & Mart* in the search for needed parts.

It was *Exchange & Mart* that provided, for later development, a pair of much sought after 16 inch wheels, only made by the Austin factory for the Persian Army, an organisation which could hardly have realised that its special equipment gave perfect gearing when teamed with the correct back axle for Silverstone Club circuit at the time.

Head shapes were tuned in his case with small cutters whirled by a handbrace. There were of course electric drills in industry, but shops did not have cheap Black and Deckers stacked on the shelves for domestic use.

The qualities of all good competition cars he put into one terse sentence: "They must start, stop and go fast in between". It was a personal philosophy of great purity and practicality, and mistakes were gallently admitted if only to *"protectez les autres"* following in his wake.

The main rails of what passed for a chassis on the Seven were top hat-

section mild steel, likely to have been resisting the attack of oxygen for many years. The technique used to give them new life and stiffness, was to weld a narrow strip of steel along the bottom face thus turning them into 2 inch square tubes. Failure to tack the strips properly resulted in one such attempt bowing into a perfect, but unwanted, curve from end to end. He propped them on blocks and drove a huge borrowed lorry up to rest on each rail overnight. It made not a scrap of difference, and, suspecting that few of his readers were likely to be welders anyway, he did not even box the rails for Simplicity.

Clearly, being in love with the Seven did not protect it or its creator, Sir Herbert Austin, from criticism. There is a testy reference to the slow introduction of a decent cylinder head: "heads before 1937 were archaic – no excuse for waiting until then to improve them".

Road Sevens for almost their total lives were stopped, after a fashion, by lengths of wire linking a cross-shaft to a lever arm on each backplate. The original design meant that, in the high unlikely event of one wheel locking, no more braking could be applied to any of the other three, making an already fraught situation more so.

Simplicity, faithful to her name and concept, stayed with the wires, eschewing the new-fangled hydraulics, but with a cunning modification which balanced all four wheels automatically and permitted a chosen distribution front to rear.

His advice on building time and the money involved is ageless: "Estimate how long and how much, then triple it. You won't be far wrong".

EDD 168 never won the Goodacre Trophy, the 750 Club's Championship award for circuit racers, but it did run four years in every sort of event in its MkI form. Modifications that turned it effectively into a MkII version, included very many engine alterations, radical widening of the split axle and lowering the whole car, smaller wheels with more up-to-date rubber, and actually fitting front dampers.

What the original car did win was the gratitude of at least two dozen club

drivers other than JF, all of whom were allowed to borrow and race the car in every sort of event. Few racing cars can have had such a demanding life with, at one stage, barely more than a winter valve grind as overhaul.

Built in a remarkable five weeks of spare time, with various helpers and a lot of late nights, it did, in its first season alone, eight race meetings, often multiple-entered for other drivers, and it achieved two first places and 2000 road miles, some driving to and fro from meetings (no trailers permitted) and the rest as a "delivery van" for JF's then current job. As no photograph of Simplicity ever shows more than a single aero-screen as driver protection, one suspects he often had to wash off a Hollywood-style goggle outline in mud before entering his place of work.

All this is not to yearn for a simpler past, but to record the reality of what determination and ingenuity achieved with not much money. Engine research came from building different units, swapping them back and forth for comparison and experiment.

The best estimate of Simplicity's early top speed is 75mph, but as its creator observed drily: "It was able frequently to overtake other cars whose drivers were doing well over 80 at the time".

It did not begin to aspire to the chassis stiffness of later Formula cars, pioneered by the Worden which revolutionised the scene by superimposing spaceframes on the lowered, boxed and cranked basic chassis rails. Instead, it required the bodywork built in traditional 20g alloy sheet on wooden frames to either contribute its own quota to general rigidity or accommodate the flexing without falling to bits. At least one guard against the latter was the use, on occasion, to keep things watertight and the bonnet in place, of two of the wide elastic belts much favoured by small-waisted fashionable girls at the time.

Battery and fuel tank lived behind the rear axle, not an easy feat with no chassis as such on which to hang them. But it was an improvement from the points of view both of scrutineers and weight distribution over a one gallon oil tin standing in place of the passenger's feet. At 63mpg on the

Two pictures of Simplicity at Brands Hatch in the early 1950s. The simple structure and interesting suspension behaviour characteristics are very evident. Nevertheless this budget-priced special was a very competitive and durable car. (Pictures: John Cowley).

road, fuel resources did not have to be overlarge. Engine and gearbox were moved back as far as possible, and the driver sat roughly where the two rear seat passengers in the original four-seater saloon had perched.

When one of his engines did call it a day with oil failure and another man's foot hard on the accelerator, he used the occasion not to recriminate but to entertain. The trail of disaster began in mid-lap at Silverstone. Mr.French recalls: "The driver did not notice a big end had run. Besides he was in the act of overtaking the Binns Riley and that must have been a big moment in his first motor race.

"Anyway, the loss of white metal allowed a piston to hit the head and the piston then broke up. The con-rod, which now had nothing to guide its top end, flailed about the place clouting the inside of the crankcase here and there. The rod got tired of this eventually and broke in twain. The larger twain then motored fore an aft as well as sideways until it got jammed between the crank and the inside of the crankcase. At this stage the engine stopped with a grunt and the driver became aware that all was not well".

He built an identical replacement engine in the next six days and the car went back to winning with a selection of drivers.

Was it a cheap car? Jack French listed costings which would read too mysteriously (of 5/10d for fourteen cylinder head studs, or 8/- for a fabric coupling), for the decimal trained reader.

I have taken the liberty of translating part of it into fractions of an average week's wage at the time. Multiply it up to current wage levels and we can at least make a stab at a comparison.

Six tyres (narrow road type, of course, not racing), with steel disc or spoke wheels - 3½ weeks pay.
Power unit including all replacement parts - 3 weeks.
Rear axle, including all replacement parts - 1¾ weeks.
Gearbox - ¾ week.
Set of eight valves - 1 day.
Oil coil (THE ignition tweak of the time)

- 1½ days.
Whatmough Hewitt sidevalve head - 2 days.
Shotpeening rods/crank - 3 hours.

While all this might sound a little like history, not only is Simplicity still around, but her creator has her standing in his "garden shed" awaiting his finding time, in retirement, to rebuild her totally.

His legendary concern for, and generosity to, the beginner on the lowest of low rungs of the motor racing ladder has not altered over the yeers, any more than his astringent view of too-gilded memories of the past.

"There were never any 100mph Austin Sevens then, but I found you could sometimes read the opposition's instruments as you passed them on the straight at Silverstone.

"I've looked across into the other man's cockpit and seen his speedo reading 100mph, so I suppose that is

how it got around, but I was passing him at 75!

"None of the engines could be taken much over 6000 then and you had to peak by ⅔rds of the way down the straight or you never would. You can work it out from the gearing. After Simplicity's was lowered, she went up to about 80.

"I think the best true flywheel power would have been about 35bhp. Colin Chapman considered he was getting 30 or so compared to the best the factory ever got out of their own engines of 23-24bhp.

"Very many drivers drove Simplicity and won. Somewhere around 25 that I can remember. I used to lend her to other people when I wasn't free to drive myself. She usually did two or three races at every meeting. One of the last times she was ever out she took 1st, 2nd, 3rd and 4th in class with four different drivers, but she hasn't run since 1962. I'm going to rebuild her completely — as soon as I can find the time".

Specification - Simplicity

Engine (later version):	747cc, estimated flywheel bhp:35. Sidevalve: 1¼in inlets, 1 1/16th exhausts. Camshaft: 1929 production unit with reground base circles - 20-63-50-16 with lifts of 0.263in inlet and 0.245in exhaust. 5.8:1 comp.ratio. "Spit and hope" lubrication (two low pressure crankcase jets aimed at holes in crank webs). Shortened and flattened solid tappets. Austin 8 downdraught carb. with 19mm fixed choke.
Gearbox:	Nippy CR 4-speed (later replaced by 3-speed to save weight).
Back axle:	1931 torque tube with 5.25:1 CWP (and a legendary high mileage).
Chassis/shell:	1929 short chassis with later Ruby rear extensions. 2-seat doorless alloy sheet/body on wood frame, cycle type wings.
Wheels/tyres:	Front: 3.50x18. Rear: 400x17 fitted road cross-ply covers (later variations included 15in and 16in rears, and racing tyres).
Brakes:	7in diam. x 1¼in iron drums all round. Cable operated, fully compensating.
Suspension:	Front: Ballamy split and lowered beam axle with transverse leaf, no dampers until Mk2. Rear: solid axle on flattened quarter-elliptic leaf with friction disc damper.
Weight:	6cwt (est.).
Bhp/ton (laden):	92bhp (approx.).
Est.Coeff. of drag:	0.62.
Performance:	Top speed (Mk1): 75mph, (Mk2): 80mph. Standing ¼ mile "slightly uphill" 20 secs.

Formula 750: Forrest (1961)

A hacksaw blade used "lumber jack fashion" with a man at each end, would not immediately strike a chord as a tuning device – least of all in the field of aerodynamics.

The man at one end of the blade was so far ahead of his time in a number of ways, that he arrived in 750 racing, contributed largely through novel ideas and ingenuity, raced, and had departed again long before many of his ideas became accepted standards in every level of motor racing.

To be advocating in 1961 or 1962, that a driver might not only abandon rolled up sleeves to race but also adopt flameproof overalls, wear a face mask and gauntlet gloves of similar material overlapping his sleeves, buy a helmet capable of protecting the face as well as the skull, build a roll bar with stays strong enough to realistically resist a long slide upside down, and fit a full harness with crutch strap, was on the perilous edge of asking to be called sissy.

Mike Forrest was as unperturbed by that as by the cautious, startled reactions to his version of a 750 Formula car. He decided that as most people began with an Austin Seven saloon, and ended up having to make a new two-seater sports open body, it would save a lot of pain to keep it as a saloon. What it needed was to be a lot lower, and if one reclined gracefully within, more or less lying on the back seat it could clearly be a very great deal lower.

Though he chose never to be publicly precise about any links with the RAF, he clearly knew all about frontal area drag and the virtues of having less of it.

His first move, therefore, was to cut a three inch thick slice out of his chosen saloon above the waistline, by the use of the lumber jack hacksaw technique and a friend. Enthused by this and spare internal height still left, he took a further three and a quarter inches out below the waistline, having to cut through the engine bulkhead, rear wheel arches, door bottoms,

bonnet sides and radiator. When it still seemed a bit high a further three inches came off the top. It reduced the frontal area by three and half square feet, or some twenty per cent. It was not as haphazard as it sounds because he had already sliced up pictures of the car to see how it might finally look aesthetically and what could most happily come out of where.

Years later, Jeff Goodliffe, partner and confederate of Mini tuner Harry Ratcliffe, cut a Mini similarly and just as effectively and prettily.

In the event the Forrest 750 was not only the first Austin Seven to look like that, but the last as well – despite its success. Was nobody bold enough, did they all prefer the wind and the rain in their hair, or was the significance of several aspects of the car not fully appreciated for what it was at the time?

They are questions that cannot be answered with any degree of certainty. We can only consider what he was doing and how he was doing it with a lot of useful hindsight and later knowledge available, to help along the keen and perceptive appreciation.

His approach of never doing anything for £1 that might be done for less shines through a series of articles he wrote for the *750 Club Bulletin* at the time his car was being created and just after.

The titles both enthused other builders and lived up to every promise – "Twin SUs for £1" and "Hydraulic dampers – 2/6d [12½p] each". Even dynamic balancing of a crankshaft assembly totally for free – on the dining room table.

The car began life like most other 750 Formula cars as a road saloon that failed disastrously to live up to the wishes of the driver yearning for a fast well handling vehicle day to day. 45mph was not Mr. Forrest's idea of a speedy way from A to anywhere. Major engine work produced 60mph and the plan to race.

Once the shell had been "cut-n-shut" as our transatlantic friends term it, the engine was bolted solid to the chassis rails, its cylinder head braced rigidly to the shell bulkhead, and after the removal of the modest sound/vibration damping, (a squashed and rotting length of quarter inch felt

trapped between the floorpan and the chassis rails), these latter were also joined firmly.

The original nuts and bolts were augmented, and the floor protected in efficient and lightweight fashion from having them pull out, by loops of glass cloth bonded round the chassis and onto the underside of the floor. And in due course the passenger door was welded up, the fabric roof being retained to reassure the scrutineers he could get out in a hurry should the need arise if the car happened to be lying on its side.

While he gave details of this in a talk to club members there is no record of his labouring the point about why. But it would seem that he was avoiding both the weight and the complication of having to build any triangulated spaceframe, not even bothering with the traditional boxing-in of the top-hat-chassis rails, while discreetly achieving a high degree of stiffness, permitting his suspension plans, particularly at the front, to function well.

The forged iron solid front axle was cut in two, and converted to a low pivot swing axle. It was damped with two of his most modest purchases, Armstrong lever arm type dampers from the breaker's yard, filled with a variety of experimentally different lubricating oils (instead of the proper SAE 5 hydraulic), ranging from 10-140 SAE.

It was no surprise the manufacturers were anxious to dissociate themselves from such innovation, but Mike had already cut that ground away by writing: "this method is cheap, simple, it works and is condemned by the makers".

He cunningly employed two more similar dampers to provide the idlers for the split track rod, one having oil enough in it to damp the steering, the arms themselves linked by a short adjustable rod that made it so simple

---

Two pictures of the amazing 'cut-&-shut' Forrest 750 at Brands Hatch. An excellent example of how the resourceful home constructor can create a competitive car by radical, yet inexpensive, modifications. (Pictures: John Cowley).

to track the steering it could be done in the proverbial dinner jacket.

The "dinner-suit approach" was a phrase not infrequently used at that period when they were a common sight even at motor club dinners, as a criterion of a skilled and tricky job achieved with the minimum of dirtiness or loss of decorum.

Bill Boddy, editor of *Motor Sport*, certainly used it to define a man properly qualified to own a chain drive Frazer Nash as one capable of replacing a broken drive chain on a dark night while so dressed without becoming dishevelled.

Twelve degrees of castor, with less than one turn of wheel lock-to-lock, produced steering of such sensitivity and vicious return it had to be reduced a bit. Pictures of the car show that he also turned the track rod ends upside down at some point markedly steepening the angle of the rods.

The same free thinking extended to his engine in which the inlet ports were extensively and fundamentally altered with resin putty keyed in place with self tappers screwed into the iron at critical points.

While this latter method was employed by others, he had two other approaches to engine preparation which seem to have been original.

Unbelievable as it may sound for a racing engine, plenty of racing Austin Sevens kept the "spit and hope" lubrication system — two little jets operating at 5psi or so, pointing at the crankshaft and squirting such oil as might get into a passing hole in each of two webs every revolution to keep four big ends in good condition.

At best they were collecting oil for 25 degrees in every 360. He not only doubled the system, but devised new angles for the four jets which ensured two lubrication periods of 90 degrees each rev, a modification which not unnaturally improved his engine reliability enormously.

His other idea is as good and efficient now as it was then — avoiding the removal of the oilway core plugs in what were even then thirty-year-old blocks and cranks by inserting lengths of wire coil curtain rod. Once in place these were gripped in the chuck of a hand drill and spun while having paraffin poured in, the result being a satisfying instant torrent of years of filthy gunge.

He ground his own cam, threw away the synchro cones from the gearbox and ended up with the trouble that indicates infallibly that you have done a good job on the power output — clutch slip.

He had a phrase for his personal approach which he defined as "negative tuning — keep it simple and light". He was well qualified to add "and small". Advice just as valid now as when he offered it all those years ago.

In particular while he was no less keen to stay alive than are any of us, he was more realistic and methodic about it than most.

"In a few more years drivers will no more drive without full harnesses and roll-over bars than without a helmet", he observed, "accidents are rare but you are dead for a long time".

The car raced with its creator for barely two and a half seasons. It went in due course to other owners, one of whom cut a large hole in the roof to put his head through, but scrutineers were notably unhappy about seeing his head roll and later refused the car permission to run.

The car has now gone full circle to being rebuilt in its original form by a 750 man who was but a lad when it first ran. Not too many one-off specials achieve — or deserve — that sort of dedication from anyone.

Specification – Forrest

Engine:	747cc plus overbored by 60 thou side valve. Speedex two cam.Two inch radiused tappets. All lightened and balanced. $1\frac{1}{8}$ in inlet valves. Twin one inch SUs. Four pipe exhaust. Dante alloy head, 7.1:1 CR. Coil ignition. Morris 8 auto adv. distributor. O/size ($\frac{5}{16}$in) main bearing cap bolts. Estimated bhp: 45 at 7500 rpm.
Gearbox:	Super Accessories CR gears.
Back Axle/FD:	Solid axle, torque tube 5.25:1 CWP.
Chassis/shell:	6'3" wheelbase saloon, stressed shell/engine, welded passenger door all bolted solid to non-boxed chassis rails.
Wheels/tyres:	Front: 400x15 Alloy Speedex Rear: 520x15 Alloy Speedex Firestone road tyres
Brakes:	Balanced cables with Bowden front.
Suspension:	Front: Split swing axle and track rod with transverse leaf sliding on graphite blocks. Hydraulic lever dampers. Forward (reversed) steering arms, split track rod with damped steering. Rear: Flat $\frac{1}{4}$ in elliptic leaf, friction disc dampers.
Weight:	$7\frac{1}{4}$cwt (est.)
Bhp/ton (laden):	104 (est.)
Performance:	Top speed 90mph

Formula 750: Tristesse (1965)

For the whole of the extremely lengthy and busy life of the 750 called, enigmatically, Tristesse, a pair of kitchen scissors were never absent from creator Dick Hartle's toolbox.

Like the Forrest hacksaw blade, they sound an unlikely racing car tuning device but they were not, as it happened, unique at that time amongst 750 paddock toilers.

They were essential to the various suspensions which were utilising rubber in tension as the springing medium. The easiest and cheapest way of obtaining the raw material for such a design is to cut slices from an inner tube cast off by an appropriately sized vehicle suitably dimensioned for the planned mountings.

For those with a particularly cavalier approach to money, they would be brand new tubes, for this is speaking of the days when inner tubes were standard wear on all vehicles, reasonably priced, and, moreover were actually made of rubber that had a decent stretch and pingggg about it. Not like the later ones of butyl synthetic which might have been better at keeping air in, but were infinitely worse for the said stretch and pingggg.

Given the scissors and inner tube supply, it was a simple and speedy matter to cut new rubber bands of any required width on the spot, to be added to or subtracted from the mounting pins, so providing a very rapid change of rate, ride characteristics and height.

The Tristesse did not immediately jump in at both ends, retaining in its earlier stages the traditional rear quarter-elliptic leaf springs, suitably flattened, of the original A7 saloon. It turned out to have such a long competition life — over 10 years after

which "it just fell to bits with age and use" — that its history reflects in one car much of what was altering over the years in the Formula.

It was early on the spaceframe scene, and the second to embark on the then unexplored territory of the newly admitted Reliant engine, behind Brian Clayton with whom Dick usefully shared some garage space at that time. It allowed him easy access to Brian's hard-earned knowledge on his power unit, an excellent all-alloy 8-port-headed pushrod, just yearning to have its 23 standard ex-works bhp doubled following a Club decision that a new engine due to stay in production for some years was required. The original Austin sidevalve had shown a growing frailty and scarcity after 35 years, so who could blame them.

The choice of the Reliant unit, a move enthusiastically backed by its makers, had been the culmination of much argument and discussion within the 750 Club, but even applying that old helpful hindsight, was and is a good one.

The move was probably accelerated by a fair body of opinion holding the strong view that the A7

power unit was not only out of date but also approaching true historical rarity, and as such should not be needlessly destroyed in the process of hurtling down the Silverstone Club Circuit straight at 7000rpm before an errant con-rod tore it almost in half.

Tristesse's engine was to be united with an A7 close-ratio box, the exact count of teeth on its four cogs now lost in the mists of time, and thence rearwards to an A7 axle with 4.9:1 crownwheel and pinion. The original saloons had been fairly highly geared, and consequently the axle was an embarrassment in every way once an engine had been persuaded to revolve at a higher figure and give some more power.

Fortunately at this time, saloon car wheels were beginning to shrink a little from 15 or 16 inches, the impetus of the Mini 10 inch helping the trend on its way. But the car did not at that

Tristesse Mk I in action at Woodcote, Silverstone in May 1967. Note the SU carburettor, complete with trumpet, protruding from the bonnet. (Picture: Harold Barker).

time go immediately to Mini wheels, themselves then suspect in steel form for competition, and stood instead on 13 inch diameter wheels off the current Ford Prefect saloon.

The centres were cut out and replacements welded in with holes suitable for 3-stud hubs, the rear rims being widened, early in the cars career, by the expedient, then somewhat daring, of inserting a strip of steel into the rim by cutting and welding.

Single curvature alloy bodypanels were pop riveted into permanent place, the single long-trumpeted SU sticking so far through the bonnet top it must have dealt the coefficient of drag a bodyblow singlehanded. The front axle from the Big Seven was sawn in two and brakes front and back converted to hydraulic with cylinders from the opposition Morris Eight. Morris Motors and the Austin company were not then unhappy bedfellows as they were later but battling furiously for the small car market, and the Morris Eight was rightly famed, if for nothing else, for its brakes which were borrowed to stop a thousand vehicles other than the one for which they were originally designed.

A tasteful lowline nose around a crossflow radiator was made possible by a friend owning a borrowable fibreglass mould. The same Ford that provided the road wheels gave up its steering column too, linked to split trackrods. It also had a triangulated roll-over bar, as pioneering at that time as Nomex or a fullface helmet.

But the real step towards biting off more than might be chewable, as opposed to duffing up the opposition via a tried and tested route, was the front, and later rear suspension, medium. This was in the general term to be rubber in tension, and in the particular, after some research, Michelin rubber inner tubes from the Mini. These were the stretchiest material and provided the right length of loop when sliced very carefully across every $1\frac{1}{4}$ inch or so with the aforementioned scissors.

Because of the uncertainties of rubber compared with the steel coil, about which you can ascertain the necessary technical data very quickly, any design to employ rubber has to be capable of accepting rapid and easy alteration in the field. The method used for the Tristesse may be clearer in the

sketch than words. Essentially it had two substantial steel pegs on the chassis and two more on a small tower welded on top of the swing axle at each side. Each pair of pegs would accept a number of inner tube loops, however many might prove with experiment to be necessary. A jack to remove the tension was the sole tool needed to do such a job.

Only later was the rear axle modified from the standard quarter elliptic leaf to Michelin bands to match the front. In this case, a welded steel bridge over the top of the axle casing held the tops of the bands which were anchored to the low-line tubes of the chassis below, by similar pins to those at the front.

Once again alterations were simple. All that had to be ascertained was the correct number of bands for the right time and place. Once the basics had been sorted, tuning became a highly sensitive affair, sometimes of a

---

These two illustrations show the construction of the 'rubber-band' suspension used in Tristesse. (Drawings: Dale Kitching).

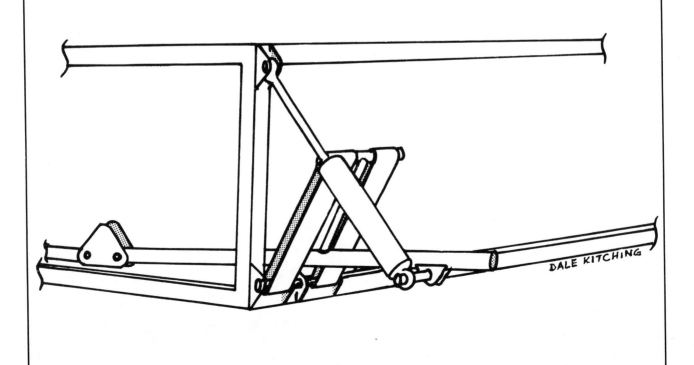

DALE KITCHING

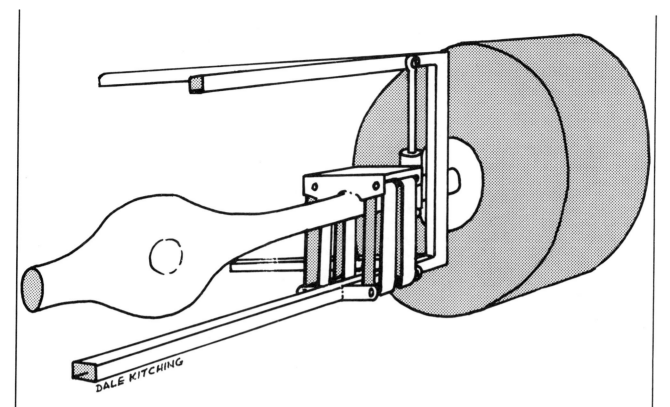

DALE KITCHING

single loop alteration to enhance grip and balance at one corner of a particular circuit. Conventional dampers complemented each end of the car.

From the very beginning really radical design changes rarely waited for the winter rebuild. Halfway through the first season, the rear wheels had widened, the Ford 100E steering column and box had given way to a Mini rack and pinion, the engine was further modified, and Mini 10 inch wheels were fitted to the front. Then more revs meant overall gearing problems and a move to Mini wheels on the rear as well, to permit the engine to employ to the full its new better breathing at the top end.

Mysterious front dampers of totally unknown parentage lost their place to a pair of Konis, and the axle itself was exchanged for a Ford version similarly split in the middle but providing a jump in brake drum diameter from 7 to 10 inches. These Ford brakes were incidentally, bearing in mind rod rather than hydraulic operation, some of the best brakes ever fitted to a road saloon and when employed on something half the weight of the original gave truly

impressive stopping.

A BMC axle not only pushed up the reliability but also the supply and variety of final drive ratios. The Mini rack and pinion in turn gave way to an Imp version, specifically designed for the split trackrod used on this saloon thus permitting an offset of the steering column without pushing the geometry into an area of nightmare.

The Mini wheels were widened to take improved racing tyres, and a Minnow Fish carburetter replaced a trio of various sized and angled SUs. This and other steps had raised the power at the rear wheels from 31bhp to 39.

With all this development behind it, the car took second place in the Championship three years after first

Specification – Tristesse Mk I (1965)

Engine:	Reliant all alloy, 598cc pushrod ohv. $1\frac{1}{4}$in downdraught SU (later $1\frac{1}{4}$in semi-DD, later still $1\frac{1}{2}$in horizontal). Exhaust 4-2-1. Est. bhp: 38
Gearbox:	A7 close-ratio (gearing forgotten).
Back axle/final drive:	A7 solid axle, 4.9:1.
Chassis/shell:	Boxed A7 side chassis rails, with spaceframe welded on and around.
Wheels/tyres:	Front: $3\frac{1}{2}$x13in steel, various road tyres. Rear: Same
Brakes:	Front: Big 7, 7in x$1\frac{1}{4}$, converted to hydraulic. Rear: A7 7in x$1\frac{1}{4}$, converted to hydraulic.
Suspension:	Front: Double rubber bands in tension. "Unknown" dampers ($1\frac{1}{2}$ inch wide, 5-6 in fitted length).
Rear:	Quarter-elliptic steel leaf (later double rubber bands, $1\frac{3}{4}$in in tension). Dampers ex-$1\frac{1}{2}$ ton GPO van.
Weight:	$6\frac{1}{4}$cwt (est.)
Bhp/Ton (laden):	98
Performance:	80-85mph.

conception, thus adhering to the mysterious rule that seems very often to ordain that it takes three years to achieve real success in a chosen branch of the sport with a new vehicle. A few take less, more longer still.

In this form the car went on racing – and racing – until it finally gave up of old age, a nice way to go considering how much pleasure and experience it had brought its drivers over those ten years.

Formula 750: Warren/Reliant (1973)

Nobody will ever know what further ideas and achievements the talented partnership of designer Jerry Evershed and driver Robin Smyth might have gone on to after their Championship win in 1973. All too soon they were gone from motor racing, both dying of cancer within months of each other, and before either of them was forty.

Their deaths were not only an extraordinary double tragedy, but lost motorsport in general, and the 750 Formula in particular, that successful duo of driver/designer still all too rare.

The car they created had a number of touches entirely in keeping with the average 750 clubman's low cost approach including a set of platinum tipped Lodge plugs previously owned, used and then passed on by at least two other Formula racers. No brain power was wasted on a trendy name. Warren came from the road in which Evershed happened to live.

Like most "overnight successes" whom everybody notices when they win, they had a very long apprenticeship behind them, a mutual special building interest and friendship since their school days going back 21 years and including 750 racing. Both had built cars before.

The one that made such a mark had two particularly distinguishing points to the casual eye – possibly the longest front radius rods from the top wishbones ever seen, and four exhaust stubs sticking up behind the driver. This in a Formula tied apparently tightly not only to the conventional front engine/gearbox unit but also a conventional live rear axle, banning anything faintly resembling a Hewland. A rear engined 750 appeared theoretically impossible to most people.

Not content with the idea of going rear engined they also decided to supercharge the car on top of the certain snags of an engine brand new to racing. For the 1972 season, the 750 club, seeing only too correctly that supplies of power units from Lord Austin's original Seven, long since out of production, would not last for ever,

The Warren/Reliant illustrates the very high standards that can be achieved by the home constructor with good design and attention to detail. (Picture: Richard Towndrow).

had cast around for a replacement.

The decision was to admit the all alloy engine, of considerably more modern concept normally found under the fibreglass skin of the Reliant three wheeler.

It came in both 600cc ohv and 750cc sv form, and the club decided to admit both, to be used by anyone who could no longer find, or keep together, an original 747 sidevalve.

Messrs. Smyth and Evershed who had long, and often troublesome, experience, of that original engine, decided the new sv unit with a blower might be the recipe for real success. They first secretly sounded out with club officials the admissibility of forced induction, and having got a friendly reply, began work.

Apart from highly individual touches like fabricating their own front uprights, deciding they could make a better cylinder head than the producers of the original engine, and realigning the ports in the block while employing Isopon bodyfiller to get the internal contours they wanted, the engine installation was their master stroke.

First they turned the engine round back to front so they could take a chain drive from the gearbox. This ran perilously near to the driver's left elbow across to a jackshaft set in self adjusting ball bearings mounted in the chassis.

The engine, already lying over at a 25 degree angle was also offset to the left to help balance the driver in a two seater. This worked beautifully and economically to also provide the space for the jackshaft and thence a short but conventional propshaft to the differential. The axle came off a "jelly mould" type Morris Minor, which thanks to the demands of the Post Office and other commercial users offered a number of low priced alternative components given a little knackers yard research time.

Alert engineers will have perceived that without some precaution the car would end up going backwards in four gears and forward only in one, because turning the engine back to front had reversed its rotation relative to the car.

Turning the axle upside down cured this, but Jerry and Robin were never averse to telling the tale that on the first assembly they did indeed have four reverse gears. Looking at the quality of the thinking that went into the rest of the car, I have serious reservations whether this ever happened, but who am I to dispute such a claim?

As if there was not enough pioneering thought going in to the rest of the car, Evershed also designed and produced his own cylinder head. While the engine was, admittedly, a side valve, it was still an ambitious move to get cast a bathtub bottom half, bolt a top plate on to keep the water in and mill out and finally shape the combustion chambers with tools amounting to little more than a home woodworker's stand drill.

It necessitated handmade head gaskets carved from Lionite (well known to ship's engineers involved with steam piping) and later laboriously faced with 0.006 copper sheet.

While he was about it, Evershed also did patterns for casting a new alloy baffled sump to suit the highly non-standard angle of the engine.

They toyed with the idea of horizontal coil spring/damper units worked through bellcranks, but it was never used in the finished car.

For supercharging they had already acquired some years earlier (for £4), a Godfrey-made, Roots (interlocking lobe) type blower intended to modestly pressurise aircraft. Contemporary records give it as a 600cc swept volume unit, but having used one myself — and bearing in mind Robin Smyth's figure of 12psi on the gauge when flat out — I think it more likely it was actually 760cc. Running at 1.08 engine speed via a one inch toothed-belt it appears to have given no trouble.

In keeping with the size of car and power available, it sat on Mini racing tyres on six inch front rims, seven and a half inch rear, but with a

Specification – Warren/Reliant

Engine:	Rear mounted 747cc all alloy Reliant s/valve. 62.5 bore x 60.96 stroke. Comp. ratio 7.4:1. Newman camshaft (37-76-79-35). Single 1¾ins SU carb on Godfrey supercharger driven at 1.08 engine speed. 1¹³⁄₁₆in inlets, 1¹⁄₁₆in exh. Exhaust 4 x 16in separate pipes.
	Fixed advance of 24 degs. Lodge HLNP plugs. Bhp (est.) 44.
Gearbox:	Reliant with Newman close ratios (2.67:1, 1.54:1, 1.18:1, 1:1).
Back axle/final drive:	BMC solid axle, FD including 1.19:1 step up on chain transfer to jackshaft (3.54:1, 3.82:1, 4.1:1, 4.31:1).
Chassis/shell:	Twin 2in square chassis rails, fully triangulated with ⅝in and ¾in 18g round tube; three fabricated bulkheads, 20g alloy body panels. Angled side radiators in ducts.
Fuel tank:	Welded alloy, nose mounted, 2½ imp gals.
Wheels/tyres:	Front: alloy 6x10in, 450/700/10 Dunlop CR81 D34/350.
	Rear: alloy 7½x10in, same tyres as front at first, later modified to 8x13in rim with Goodyear low profile, possibly G50.
Brakes:	Front & rear: ex-Morris Minor 7in all round with alloy drums.
Suspension:	Front: Unequal wishbones, coil spring/damper units, 130lb/in coils. Ultra-long top radius arms, anti-roll bar.
	Rear: Solid axle, quarter elliptic u/slung leaf springs with top radius arms and Panhard rod.
Weight:	5¼cwt (est.)
Bhp/Ton (laden):	130.
Performance:	Top speed: 105-108mph (est.)

handicap of the hard compounds of the time designed to cope with heat generated by Minis doing their traditional balancing act on the outer front wheel rather than a flat handling proper racing car.

For a vehicle with so many unknowns built in, it was incredibly successful within a year of first running. In its second season it took a maximum possible score of eight firsts with seven fastest laps and five outright lap records.

Because there were actually twenty rounds with a ''best eight'' scoring system this was not quite as overwhelming as it sounds, the car being soundly beaten by unblown cars on half a dozen occasions.

Despite that, ''blower-phobia'' rapidly reared its head and by the following year regulations had banned the future use of any form of supercharging. Alas for innovators.

Formula 750: Omag 2/Reliant

Nobody normally loves winners or innovators. If it should happen it has to be for their transcendentally lovable characters rather than their victories or pioneering creations.

My own most successful season ever with a Mini which took a row of wins and class records ended with an anonymous suggestion to the stewards of the year's final meeting that I was running an oversize engine. As I did not utilise a trailer — it was also my road and business transport — it meant that after the final runs, I had to strip a very hot head off to permit the bore and stroke to be measured (at some 60ccs less than the class limit for reasons I will not waste time with here). It all then had to be put together again before loading my somewhat irritated wife and small son aboard for the drive back home.

Omag 2's creater, Ray Wilson, slots into the second category — that of the innovator. Like Colin Chapman, he fell foul of the interpretation of the rule book with the inevitable result that if you are treading new ground one man's rule rapidly becomes another man's supposed fiddle. It depends on your point of view.

Certainly Ray Wilson's vision was long enough and clear enough to perceive that his concept might bring him trouble as well as delight before he ever cut metal. He had already built and raced a monocoque-stiffened 750 formula car, moved to karting and absorbed with new emphasis the lesson that small is beautiful. It also means less weight and reduced frontal area, the absolutely certain recipe for better performance.

In the same way that the mid-sixties saw a revolution in the 750 Formula — as it moved from modified Austin Sevens to spaceframe and then monocoque-stiffened cars utilising little more than the required power unit and rear axle — Ray's plan was no less than to revolutionise it again.

The car he was to christen ''Omag 2'' was not only going to be tiny, but what was to be an ultra-small ground clearance meant he needed minimal movement of the suspension required by the definition of an acceptable vehicle in the RAC's all-powerful *Blue Book*. This stated that the cars of this formula should ''be fitted with a sprung suspension between the wheels and chassis''.

He could not have known it at the time, but he was embarking on an

The radical Omag 2/Reliant — a Formula 750 Kart? These pictures (below and above right) of the car's CanAm-like body show a high standard of design and construction. (Pictures: Tony Walton).

approach (for different reasons) that would be quite acceptable in F1 four years later: suspension so hard that any movement would be restrained by the springing medium to tiny fractions of an inch. Whilst, when the time came, F1 took the route of 6000lbs/in steel coils, Ray felt that rubber bushes would suit his purpose. The ones he had in mind normally dwelt in the engine stabiliser rod of the Mini. These had the traditional virtues for the amateur of instant availability from the local goodie shop or BL dealer, and low

The Omag 2/Reliant's engine/transaxle. Also evident are the axle locating arms complete with eyes for the rubber bushes which constituted the suspension. (Picture: Tony Walton)

price: even though eight sets would be needed.

To be certain he would not be wasting his time, he wrote to the powers-that-be at the RAC outlining his plan and got a cheering reply that they were "not opposed to the concept", the only reservation being that if a bumpy circuit should bring it to the fringes of controllability, its acceptance might then be in question.

In fact the design walked a delicate tightrope between two-seater sports racer and kart; virtually the latter to its critics, but a CanAm car seen through reversed field glasses, in exquisite miniature, to its admirers.

Everything one might expect to see in a racing car was to be there. Mandatory square tube side members, rollover bar, room to stretch the driver's legs to conventional pedals and hydraulics, rear axle with offset differential dry sumped motor lying on its side, discs all round and a single carb rising vertically into a bodywork snorkel-style air intake.

With these would go water cooling by an ex-oil cooler, front mounted car-type battery, full circle steering wheel and instrument array. The radiator sat (at first) intriguingly behind the driver (invisibly recessed below his seat was a NACA duct, shaped into the undertray, to feed it with cooling air).

Finally it would be clothed in a superbly simple, pretty and well finished one-piece fibreglass moulded body, hinging at the rear so that lifting it would reveal everything to mechanic, scrutineer or casual observer alike.

Ray explains about the concept and execution: "Above all it was a low-cost motorcar, a fundamental aspect of the 750 Formula. The design of the rubber suspension saved at least £200 at current prices straight off in suspension units, coil springs and Rose joints. In plan it was just a bit bigger than a double bed. The inspiration came from getting involved in schoolboy karting as my lads were growing up. I looked at karts, how they were built, how small they were, and felt that with appropriate alterations I might get away with the application of such ideas to a 750.

"But I didn't want to waste a lot of time so I wrote to the RAC first,

outlining the design concept and was told they agreed in principle so I got started".

As a one-time De Havilland apprentice and BUA flight engineer his constructional standards were high, though the problems were just as numerous. Not the least was how to fit a full-sized conventional four-cylinder watercooled Reliant engine and gearbox somewhere under the driver's right elbow in a space that barely existed. It turned out to be so tight the gearbox flange was bolted directly to that of the axle's final drive, thus making the power unit do duty as locator and torque reactor as well.

Finally, a fuel tank and the space in which to put a passenger of carefully specified size, had also to be squeezed into the outline. In the manner of many sparetime projects, it proceeded erratically over the next $3\frac{1}{2}$ years. As it progressed, Ray kept a note of the sources of many of the parts used. It made a strange directory of motorsport: F1, F2, F3, FF, Reliant, Morris Minor, Mini, VW, Imp, commercial tanker, combine harvester, redundant coffee table, and a cup from a dolly's tea set.

So far so good. We now come to the heart of the concept, the seed that was to grow to future frustration, fury, attack, retreat, and finally a somewhat qualified victory: the suspension.

Rubber bushes are not now and were not then a novel medium of suspension, but how he proposed to use them — simply compressed through their wall thickness — was. Rather than twisting the bushes, they were to be used exactly as on the Mini engine bracing link. They would be mounted at the rear of the car at the bottom of short pillars welded underneath the rear axle casing and bolted through their centres direct into the chassis tubes. At the front there would be a pair of bushes on each side this time chassis-mounted, so that the front axle beam sat between them with a long bolt running through the whole assembly.

As the rubber bushes had big end washers to trap and squeeze them as well as the tapered steel internal bushes used to help dissuade the Mini engine from jumping about, the two axles on Omag 2 were similarly tightly

restrained. They could not move much, but without any doubt they could move.

Whether that movement was two inches, half an inch, or 10 thou was irrelevant, Ray reasoned. There was no dimension for such movement specified in the regulations, only that the suspension had to be capable of it. The whole aspect of miniaturisation permitted the same approach to wheels and tyres. Like any other high power/weight ratio competition car it had big rears (Mini alloys) and smaller fronts (6 inch diameter kart alloys).

However, long before this novel rubberware partnership ran at all, F1 was far embarked on the "solid" suspension needed to cope with the continual disintegration or jamming of sliding skirts and moving centres of pressure. But the sight of wishbones and coilsprings, even if of a strength that would have given a doubledecker corporation bus a hard ride, left scrutineers' minds free to concentrate on ground clearances, brake watercooling tanks, fire extinguishers or the size of the advertising lettering, depending on their special fields of interest.

Not so for Mr. Wilson and Omag 2 when the great day came on a warm May Saturday at Snetterton. Brand new car, clean overalls, fullface helmet, and ready to go. But he never went anywhere except back to the trailer and towcar and home again, without even a chance to see if his pride and joy approached that fringe of controllability that had been the RAC's only initial worry.

He still has the rejection ticket, No.16568, with the reason for the car's being forbidden to run stated as: "Not a *sprung* suspension". The parallel with Colin Chapman and the Lotus 88 was extraordinary. To say its creator was much upset has to be the understatement of that, or most other, years. Like Chapman, though without his resources, Ray Wilson took up the fight instantly.

Although Ray himself still keeps the substantial file of letters, phone calls, notes, data and arguments that he marshalled in defence of Omag 2, suffice it to say May became November without result. Even letters to the magazines, and the Oxford

English Dictionary definition of the word "spring" seemed equally impotent. His season had gone. Omag 2 stood in the garage beside his house, pristine and unused.

On November 14th he got the letter he had been hoping and fighting for. It confirmed after all that his car had been legal all along, that the scrutineer had been wrong to turn it down, and enclosed a free copy of the new regulations concerning the definition of a spring suspension that would come in force for the following season, The sting was certainly in the tail.

One paragraph had become eight, and the inference was inescapable: Omag 2 might well be legal for the next six non-racing weeks, but it would be most certainly illegal by the time racing recommenced. Specifically banned were bolts through flexible bushes.

Lesser men might have been crushed. RW sat down to consider the wording at length. "Bolts" appeared to be the key forbidden item. Without them rubber bushes appeared admissible. There was still no dimensional requirement for suspension movement. He decided to substitute a pin for the bolts, locked by collar and cotter which would do the same job.

More drawings, letter writing, phone calls, and in due course a further top-level technical consideration of the car as modified. In the following February it came: "Your car complies for 1981 – but this does not imply that it will comply with any future regulations ...".

It would be nice to say that Omag went out, devastated the opposition from its first race, and Ray was offered a job by Chapman, if not to drive the 88, at least to oversee its acceptance by the FIA. The real life version was that Omag 2 hit all the snags and problems of most new and untried projects. It was fast in a straight line, suffered serious cooling troubles, would not drift or slide though it stayed glued to the road most of the time, while needing a brave man to cope with some bumps and corners. On one dramatic occasion when the engine died with mysterious suddenness in mid lap, it was found that flex in the one-piece bodywork had been sufficient to knock the ignition switch off. That plastic dolly's tea cup came into its own as a safety cowl to prevent any recurrence.

He did a series of meetings, curing a series of snags at each one. The underfloor NACA duct proved reluctant to feed the slightest draught to the rear radiator which had to be moved to the front. But the brakes were always superb, and the handling light and sensitive. There was nothing that could not be dealt with by steady development, but the battle had taken more out of one of the protagonists than perhaps he wanted to admit.

Said Ray later, "Even after the car was finally accepted, they always seemed to keep dreaming up some snag or other. Extra springs to hold the body on in case the front lock pins came out and the body flipped up. What would happen if the car went under the Armco if I went off? Moving the fuel tank. Extra side bracing against T-boning the car. Take the cover off the passenger space. Some of them were quite reasonable really, but it seemed one long argument.

"The irony is that even when they re-wrote the suspension rules they still got it wrong. If they'd put in a requirement for a certain suspension movement at the wheel they would have shot me down. But then every F1 car would have been illegal as well in a paddock check, so maybe they didn't want a lot of problems there. I'll never know.

Specifications – Omag 2/Reliant

Engine:	Reliant 700cc to full race spec. Weber 32IMPE downdraught carb with fabricated 4-2-1 exhaust. Est. 60bhp.
Gearbox:	Close ratio with Edmonton Eng. uprated 2nd and 3rd gears.
Back axle/final drive:	4.9:1 CW&P in BMC solid axle.
Chassis/shell:	2x2in square underslung main tubes, dashboard tube frame braced to front bulkhead. Centre seat. One-piece fibreglass all-enveloping bodywork hinged at rear to allow complete front lift.
Fuel tank:	Alloy 3 Imp gal, rear mounted
Wheels/tyres:	Front: 4in rims x 6in diameter kart pattern alloy with 12x6.00 - 6 slicks. Rear: 6in rim x 10in diameter Mamba alloys: CR65 160x490 10 Dunlops.
Brakes:	Front: 6in modified Kart disc/caliper Rear: 7in Mini disc/caliper.
Suspension:	Front: beam axle with Imp stub axles, alloy hubs, twin rubber bushes in compression, rearward brake torque stay. Rear: BMC solid axle with offset differential, twin pairs of rubber bushes in compression.
Weight:	5½ cwt.
Bhp/ton (laden):	171
Performance	"100 plus on Snetterton back straight".

"I felt suddenly too old, too fed up – and I'd rather see my two boys race and help them. So I decided to do just that; sell Omag 2 complete with the letter saying it was legal at least for a season, start on building a roadgoing GT special and help my sons".

He went on to do precisely that. Only his fat file of letters and a handful of coloured snaps now remain in his possession, but there is a *PS* to it all.

Omag 2 did not disappear. it went to another 750 member, but one who had never before raced a car in his life. It was to give him an eye-opening introduction and training course all in one. Garage owner Tony Walton began his racing career in it, and rapidly discovered that most club racers are,

perforce, development engineers for many more hours than they are racing drivers. Some of his first notes read:

"Mallory Park; first time out, retired after all oil pumped into catch tank. Later discovered blocked filter in one line.

"Donington; retired after water pipe dropped out of cylinder head and emptied cooling system.

"Silverstone; retired, fuel pouring out of too-low breather once car got into a fast corner, compounded by electrical trouble in heavy rain.

"Testing on local farm track; retired after undertray ripped off by grounding on bumps and developed a chassis crack.

"Cadwell Park; retired after

gearlever came off in driver's hand.

"Silverstone; (last meeting of year) finished successfully and in good order.

In no way put off, Tony talks of the season and the car: "It has been very enjoyable. It goes well, although we could do with more power now. Being able to run it at all depends on the RAC agreeing year-by-year, but as long as they accept it as legal I shall carry on racing. It's always a centre of interest in the paddock, and I'm never without the RAC letter at scrutineering. I've just stripped it down for the winter and have a lot of modifications in mind, including a new and much lighter body. Oh, and more power of course".

Omag 2 lives.

Formula Ford – "Entrance to the arena"

Whatever Formula Ford is, it is not a place for the faint-hearted or the man unwilling, or unable, to go to endless laborious pains with every tiny detail of his racing car.

Anyone competing seriously has got to be quite remarkably conscientious as well as talented if he is to finish anywhere near the front. Non-finishers, however brilliant, do not score points or get their names in the results and team managers' notebooks.

Perhaps more than in any formula, the cars look superficially similar, but vary infinitely in detail. That detail, bodywork and tiny but vital differences in suspension geometry are just about all the leeway permitted by a rule book laid down in 1966 that was so well done and so watertight it would make an F1 designer wince.

For the benefit of anybody who has been living on Mars or Venus since that day when Ford decided to back a Ford-engined single-seater formula, a brief résumé of its original form will illuminate the guidelines – "strait-jacket" might be a better word – within which designers involved have had to work:

Engine: Cortina GT pushrod ohv. All parts within maker's tolerances. Fixed compression ratio at 9.5:1. Standard

dynamo, starter and flywheel. Polish and balance if you wish, and please yourself about aircleaner, plugs, carburettor jets and exhaust system. No messing with cam, valves, timing.
Chassis: Steel tube, no stressed panels (except undertray).
Wheels: Steel, 5½ inch limit on rim width, and road tyres from the RAC Group 1 list.
Brakes: Drum or disc from a homologated production car.
Gearbox: Four speed and no LSD.

Design your own suspension but no exotic metals, although you could cast or fabricate rear uprights while watching out for the minimum weight of 400Kg.

A free hand in the radiator, bodywork, clutch, steering, fuel tanks, fuel pump and dampers. No wings. Cars not to exceed £1000 retail cost complete and in running order.

Not unexpectedly, this last rule was the one that got changed first, and unfortunately went on having to be modified.

The going rate now would be nearer £7000 plus the dreaded VAT or an increase of a steady 15% a year compound. Racing cars once carried no tax, believe it or not, in deference to their relatively small production and value in helping along Britain's ability to export its gear and talent to the rest of the world.

If you are planning to start in FF yourself, you should instantly acquire a copy of the RAC Motorsport Year

Book, which gives the exact current dimensions of the strait-jacket such as every stage of cam lift to closer than one ten thousandth of an inch, and woe betide you if your valves are more than two thou too long or short.

What has changed in the passing sixteen years or so?

Well, you cannot polish engine internals any more, or alter the clutch. Endless ingenuity by professional engine tuners, has meant two columns of small print to define exactly what shape and size everything should be from valve seat angles to the radius on the end of the carburettor chokes.

You can have a non-standard rocker cover with your name on it as long as it does not improve the performance in any way.

Non-standard fuel pumps are out. Electronic ignition is in. Please yourself on the dynamo. No alloy brake calipers or dampers. And you must have a silencer, not any old silencer, but Ford Part No. 9054 270 or 9054 277.

Tyres are now chosen: hard rubber, narrow racer, currently Dunlop. No slicks please, we're British, but OK in the United States.

Mandatory rollover bars, full harness, rubber tanks for long races, fire extinguisher system for cockpit and engine, red rear warning light, electric circuit breaker, fire-resistant overalls, and head restraint to stop your official 37.4lb head going backwards at 5G, have all arrived for safety reasons, and not in FF alone.

Just so designers and builders did not start cheeseparing on vital bits to keep the weight down, the minimum weight was increased by 20Kg to 420 (924lb) to take account of those extras that had crept in through new general rules over the years.

All this has produced a form of racing that is just about all things to all men.

A springboard for drivers, engine builders and car producers. A source of endless close-fought wheel-to-wheel dices that have become closer rather than wider over the years. Superb training in the twin problems of getting the very best out of a car, and driving skill in heavy traffic at the closest of close quarters. A lot of fun for many not intent on the professional big-time. Good value for spectators in Britain, all over Europe, across America plus half a dozen other countries.

Perhaps the framework has proved just too tight for real innovation, as opposed to a thousand refinements. The problem has more usually been how to build the cars cheaply enough while still remaining strong, simple and easy to repair. Winning at any cost is not usually the thing most FF drivers want to know about.

High speed repairs, even for the front runners, are often vital to Championship points, perhaps between practice and the race. Wishbones and other suspension links are the expendables while hopefully chassis survive. A reversible wishbone that fits either side of the car may be as useful in selling a new model as revised geometry on all eight.

With aerodynamics totally barred the grip of an FF car on the road is not high, but they can be retrieved from tail-out situations far beyond hope in other formulae. And, unlike in F1, or nearly every other area of motor sport come to that, you may not have to shatter all the lap records, or even equal them to make a major impact.

Really? Can that be true with McLaren, Brabham, Ferrari, etc taking a totally impossible three to six seconds off lap records from one year to the next? A little research shows it certainly is. Allowing that the weather can influence some of the figures – even the best driver is going to be hard put to set a new lap record in pouring

rain against a figure set in blazing sun – only three of the sixteen standing UK circuit records were touched, for example, in the 1981 season.

Ingliston had a tiny 0.1 second shaved off. Cadwell Park, a swooping, diving, climbing driver's circuit if ever there was one, was cut by 0.4 and its antithesis, flat-out streamliner's Silverstone, lost 0.32.

And the only mention in the whole list of that year's Champion, brilliant Brazilian Ayrton da Silva, was his equalling of a three year old mark at Snetterton set by Kenny Acheson in a relatively vintage Royale RP24.

Can Formula Ford lap speeds have actually done the impossible and reached a plateau on the mountain normally considered to have no peak? Different tyres are almost certainly going to answer that question. Dunlop, with a monopoly supply to every car, effectively control whether there should be a major step-up in speed, and while the car makers are all working to a price, Dunlop are also working to some sort of tyre life a good deal longer than the four laps of an F1 qualifier. Quick runners are already having to budget for five or six sets a year. They cannot go much softer.

This extreme closeness has two great advantages for the hopefuls entering the fray. The first is the extraordinary difficulty of winning, which in its turn enhances the value of victory in terms of the driver himself.

Although it is said, quite truthfully that F/Ford never taught anyone to handle power, there is still an appreciable list of men who began in its ranks and then climbed high.

Formula Ford is also relatively cheap and easy to enter, though a lot more expensive and difficult to stay in once you have bought your second-hand racing outfit.

In terms of F3 or F2, it is incredibly low-priced – but how cheap is cheap? Without cheating by forgetting hotel bills, or some of the tow-car petrol, or tyres bought secondhand instead of new, three sets of figures will give an approximation.

Neither success and prize money, nor failure and expensive accidents normally enter the first, which is a full pay-drive contract with a works supplied and maintained car.

The second is a serious, well financed endeavour, buying new engine, car and gearbox, proper spares and engine rebuilds, staying in a hotel instead of a tent, and combining a European round or two with your summer holiday.

The third is running in the pre-1974 Championship (cars not drivers of course) on a relatively tight budget, but certainly not shoestring. You could get under this last figure, but you are unlikely to be at the front. In the second and third cases, the car and equipment is sold at the end of the season, so all three drivers end up with nothing in hand.

Right, take a deep breath. Category One: £650 per race. Category Two: £375 per race and Category Three: £130. If you are feeling a bit faint, remember that F1 is currently around £67,000 per race for a fully professional outfit, and they still have to qualify to get a run.

For the historically, as well as technically, inclined I will condense what properly needs a full book of its own into a few of the major happenings since it all began.

1966: First concept by Geoff Clarke, of Motor Racing Stables, looking for a cheap racer for his pupils. "Ford pushrod in secondhand F3 car". Put to Ford themselves by John Webb of MCD, and Ford jump in with both feet.

1967: Over-the-winter deal with Lotus ensures production of a dozen simple Lotus 51s, (hardly a Rose joint, and built right down to a price), fitted with the old Cortina GT engine and fixed ratio Renault boxes. Jim Russell of driving school fame enters the arena with the Alexis, and so does Arthur Mallock with a U2. Front radiators.

1968: Merlyn, already established constructors come in with Mk II. Big expansion of races, and beginning to get going on the Continent.

1969: Lotus have a rethink and come back with boxy, wedge-car 61M. Names of Emerson Fittipaldi and James Hunt creep into entry lists. Ford's new Kent X-flow engine becomes standard fitting. New car builders still coming, including Elden, Hawke and Royale, who build 40 cars and sell 37 to the United States.

Early 1970s: Still more makers, Crossle, Ray, Dulon, Image. Much experiment with tyres, beginning to polarise on Firestone "Wide Ovals".

1973: Van Diemen start up and start winning. Jody Scheckter on way to World Championship. Adrian Reynard builds his first car. Firestone Torino "Wide Oval" three-quarter worn softies become essential wear.

1975: Tiga founded. Geoff Lees wins just about everything in a Royale. Radiators going back and sideways. First generation of "stiff chassis" cars emerging.

1976/77: Change-over to controlled racing tyres.

1977: Royale takes front suspension inboard.

Late 1970s: New car builders including Lola, PRS, Pacer, Sparton, Sark Nomad, Delta, Martlet, Quest and Zeus, to name but a few, come in but find it a tough life against Royale and Van Diemen.

1979: Pre-1974 "sub-formula" founded – an instant success.

1980 on: Detail refinements begin to include builder's own front uprights (instead of faithful Triumph) full inboard suspension, up and over exhausts, unstressed engines, needle noses and very carefully smoothed and shaped bodywork panels. Better and faster turn-in on corners and better transfer of power to road in tight corners. Cockpit controlled rollbars and brakes admissible.

1982: Dunlop change carcase, and compound specifications, and sizes of their mandatory tyres amid complaint and arguments. Pre-1974 men buy up all the new "oldies".

In constant parallel, the engine builders were hard at work, but as fast as they thought up a brilliant new way round the Regs. these were more closely defined to make life tougher. It is forbidden any longer to make an exact copy of any part or grind a Ford cam from a blank. Original, or nothing, is the rule. If things get too hot please leave the kitchen. Among those still in are Auriga, Minister Nelson, Rowland and Scholar.

Selective assembly, fanatical attention to detail in blue-printing every single part, has gradually pushed power up from the standard 87 at 6000 to around 105 at 6200, and willingness to rev to 7000 on standard

valve springs (but shimmed to an identical thou in length). Differences between them are now more akin to several cooks given the identical ingredients. They all make a slightly different cake – and the customers swear by their chosen favourite for quality.

Given a car and that essential determination, there is no lack of things to try and win. At the last count there were fifteen different National Championships plus those of Belgium, Denmark, Switzerland and Austria, two in Germany and two major ones in America.

One of the more forthcoming as well as talented designers in the Formula is ex-Marcos, ex-Cooper, ex-Lola man, Bob Marston, of Royale cars. His observations could hardly be better informed. "Things simply do not change dramatically in Formula Ford. Generally there are just tendencies or slow trends. Radiators have gone from front to back to sides and back to the front again. You tend to keep finding you have turned full circle. Sorting the geometry for a particular tyre is not too difficult. You may make small refinements after that, but not major ones.

"It is hard to spot any particular trend, but it is really streamlining now – or getting the car as slim and clean on the outside as possible. This has shown positive gains, but in other areas you devise some tweak that works for that day and that circuit and then does not work again. Setting the car up properly is possibly the most important thing.

"Invariably things get more complicated and you sort it out and simplify it again. We went inboard five years ago with the suspension units after complaints about straight line speed, then outboard again, and now we are inboard at the front, with rear units outboard but tucked as near to the wheel as possible with an alloy crossbeam allowing them to be nearly vertical. It makes for a very slim clean line beside the engine bay. I think bodywork has been overlooked a bit recently.

"New developments produce complications with the regulations. Both Reynard and Lola have crossbeams like ourselves but with rear

bodywork fairing them in. They could form small wing sections on each side of the car at the back. If they are symmetrically shaped top and bottom that seems to me to be OK, but if they are aerofoil shaped, do they break the regs?

"It needs to be clarified with the RAC. Even if they are symmetrical and you set them parallel to the ground with no angle of incidence, they might still exert an aerodynamic force as soon as you alter attitude of the car through the front or rear ground clearances.

"The rules say no part of the car may augment the downforce on it. But that is ambiguous. Any sloping surface, particularly for example the front bodywork, exerts an aerodynamic effect. You would need a car shaped like a brick to stick to the letter of that law – and then nobody would buy it.

"It needs sorting out because it is very expensive to change bodywork. I want to avoid arguing later.

"People in Formula Ford are very faddy. If anyone does something different you usually have to follow. People will not buy a car if it does not look right to them. People are easily led, because most of them are just starting in motor racing and they do not know. If somebody fitted square wheels and won, everyone would want square wheels."

On those new tyres: "The change in tyres is causing problems because of variations in different sets. I do not know if it is the stiffness of the sidewall, the stability of the tread rubber or the compound. The tyre has been widened across the walls and the tread and, in my opinion, is now really too wide for the fixed $5\frac{1}{2}$ inch rim. If you run it on last year's pressures, 16-18psi, it is a bit unstable. The car feels all squashy and we have gone up to 22-24psi, but this makes it dome more in the centre and the end result is less rubber on the road not more. It is self defeating.

"We have yet to find any advantage in the new tyres. You can tune some problems out, then they come back again as under or oversteer, depending on the tyres at each end as they wear".

Engines – to stress or not to stress? "Ours are unstressed, bouncing about in rubber mountings. Lola, my

old firm, build them in as a stressed part of the structure. I think this is wrong. I avoid it totally, and all our suspension loads go into the chassis not the gearbox. The Hewland is very marginal on the endplates used fully stressed. You put a very strong twisting force into the power unit, which in my view is a bad state of affairs. Vibration and stress make things crack and break and you tend to distort the block. Formula Ford is a cheap formula and you do not want that".

On aerodynamics. "Bodywork has slimmed down and smoothed. I would like to do wind tunnel work, but it is too expensive to be realistic in FF. It can save a lot of time, but costs too much money. Open wheels make aerodynamics very difficult.

"While the body in a sports car may be ninety per cent and the wheels ten per cent of your drag total, in an open wheel car the wheels can be up to 45 per cent. That was the figure on some MIRA tests I did with the Cooper F1 car when tyres were much, much narrower, about the same proportions as FF2000 now, and wheels constituted about 45 per cent of our drag total then".

Top Speeds? "Obviously this depends on gearing, but an honest best, with no following gale or downhill, is currently about 115mph".

Costs and prices – "Costs are absolutely paramount. It is a cheap formula and you do not want anything

that will cause costs to escalate, killing FF if we are not careful. This is shown by the huge success of the pre-74 racing. They are all over subscribed. A lot of guys are just racing for pleasure or to gain a bit of experience. They do not plan to be World Champion. You have to remember that about FF".

As an indication not only of the state of the art, but also the state of the market at the present time, this is an

The Royale RP31M Formula Ford 1600 is typical state-of-the-art for this Formula in the early 80s. (Picture: Royale)

outline of what you get for your money from one of the current front runners. But look around that market before you sign any cheques.

Specification – Royale RP31M

Engine:	1600cc Ford Kent engine to blueprinted spec. Pushrod 2 valve. Mounted vertically standard carb/inlet manifold. 95-105bhp at 6000rpm.
Gearbox:	Hewland Mk 9, 4 speed, variable ratios.
Back axle/FD:	Transaxle, variable, no LSD.
Chassis/shell:	Round/square mild steel tube with light alloy stressed undertray and bulkheads. GRP bodywork in six pieces with integral cooling ducts and colour. No aerodynamic downforce component permitted.
Fuel tank:	Alloy with glassfibre outer skin, $4\frac{1}{2}$ imp gals.
Wheels/tyres:	$5\frac{1}{2}$x13 steel bolt on: variable offset. Statutory Dunlop treaded race covers.
Brakes:	$9\frac{3}{4}$in diameter discs front and rear with iron calipers. Non-remote setting balance bar.
Suspension:	Front: wide based lower wishbone on nylon bushes. Rocking top arm with inboard coil/Bilstein gas filled dampers. Steel fabricated upright/hub. Rear: Mag-alloy wide base upright. Single adjustable top link and radius rod. Wide base adjustable lower wishbone. Top beam pickup for coil/Bilstein damper unit set near wheel.
Weight:	420Kg minimum (924lb).
Bhp/ton (laden):	182.
Performance:	Top speed, 115/120mph.

Formula 1: Vanwall (1958)

Contemporary photographs of the Vanwall team – Gaffer Tony Vandervell, mechanics, supporters, even the drivers – have an odd look twenty five years or so later. Hair was short. Mechanics worked in collar and tie.

City suits, felt hats, and raincoats in the pits are forgotten in the 1980s world of multi-zipped nylon jackets, team coloured overalls, the shouting badges and the sponsor decals.

That old-world look only proves that clothes never made the man. The styles have gone, as have, in the sad nature of things, many of the men in those photographs as well.

But what they achieved will never be erased as long as anyone is interested in the history of the racing motor car. They put a total and magnificent stop to an almost unbroken record of defeat for Britain at the highest levels of racing that had gone on, and on, for the worst part of forty years. In terms of Rome's amphitheatres, they started naked to try and beat the best equipped, hardest, most experienced gladiators in the world.

To do it required not only the equipment, but the architect.

Tony Vandervell, millionaire, martinet, one man band, an organiser of brilliance, who managed to conceal from the world much sign of a soft heart until racing tragedy finally pulled that veil aside, was exactly the right man at the right time. He tried first in harness with others as a powerful member of the ill-fated BRM project. The endless complications of what was really a committee car, one of the great heroic failures in racing history, drove him finally to take the only route for the man he was – his own.

Think of Cosworth. Vandervell had no engine. Think of Hewland. He had no gearbox. Think of monocoques and wind tunnels. He didn't have a chassis. Or an aerodynamicist, a chief mechanic, or any sort of racing department.

In fact, due to the ironclad restrictions on how Britain used its money and resources shortly after World War II he didn't have a racing car of any sort.

What Tony Vandervell did have was the massive factory he had built up to produce and market the Thinwall shell bearing – the ubiquitous big ends and mains now taken totally for granted. It gave him an excellent economic argument that at least one avenue of development in the years ahead had to be in high revving, high performance power units.

Happily for Britain, he was able to explain to the relevant Government Departments that there was a man in Italy who would be able to supply a suitable unit and testbed, subject only to the granting of a formality or two like an import licence and permission to send out the required British pound notes. The man in question happened to be Enzo Ferrari and the test bed a Tipo 125 GP car with a supercharged 1.5-litre engine.

The deal was by no means hampered by the fact that Vandervell had already supplied not only vast numbers of bearings for bombers, fighters, tanks and lorries but also those Ferrari was using in his engine.

All that meant that in due course one of those cars arrived in Britain, complete with modest spares kit that included two wheels, two pistons and a bag of tools. All taxes paid – £5430.

It was May, 1949, and the beginning of a nine year long hard road to total and overwhelming domination of the Grand Prix scene. The job was done, finally, with a dramatically beautiful car, a strange amalgam of the work of new young lions for bodywork, chassis and aerodynamics, and motorcycle engine knowhow going back a quarter of a century that fundamentally strung together four British bike units onto a common crankcase.

Tall, and bicycle wheeled to the modern eye, it was also front engined, and so the last and greatest of its breed. To those who enquired who was the designer, Tony Vandervell always had the same answer – "There isn't one. We've all worked together on it".

Strictly speaking he was probably right, but nothing like the Vanwall could have just happened by accident. How Tony Vandervell did it is worthy of study, not only because it is a fascinating contrast with how other people tackled it in the following years, but because it may never ever be done in the same way again.

To begin with he was not in a qualified sense an engineer, yet he knew not only what he wanted, but how to find the men who could give it to him. He used the first four years as an apprenticeship on Ferraris, bought, modified, broken, repaired, and often bitterly criticised in long acrimonious, technically detailed letters to Ferrari. That alone made him one of a very small band.

The next two years were his first tentative, own-car experiments. It was an odd mixture: a John Cooper tubular chassis, gearbox internals designed by Porsche and made half in Germany and half in the Vandervell toolroom, Rolls-Royce crankcase with four of the rightly fabled Norton "double knocker" (or twin cam) motorcycle engines converted to water cooling bolted on top, Ferrari suspension parts, homemade disc brakes to an American patent, Italian wheels, and the body by an English panelbasher. For all that it was individual and instantly recognizable by one feature it was to keep throughout its life – a four into one exhaust elegantly and completely recessed into the bodywork.

A modest fifteen events in two years gave the development and racing miles the team and its car needed, while the engine grew rapidly from 2-litres to 2.3 and then to the full permitted 2.5 of the then current Formula 1 limit. It was unblown, but ran on a methanol mixture fuel. Four promising British short race wins were overlaid by a growing list of problems: crashed, retired with oil leak, broken throttle pedal, injection pump failure, sheared driveshaft bolts.

Vandervell knew well what design and development was all about. Failures rarely if ever happened a second time. The materials, or brains, or design modifications to make sure were always found whether in America or another part of London.

By the final stages he had 89 different firms all making parts, developing ideas and suggestions, lending experts and delivering the goods on time. This alone could be

considered a major part of his achievement.

1956 was the turning point, though not immediately obvious during a season filled to heartbreak by retirements for every possible reason. It was particularly depressing that they followed a first-time-out win and lap record with Stirling Moss driving at Silverstone – a promise continually unfulfilled month-after-month thereafter. But early that year Vandervell had met Colin Chapman through the unlikely verbal recommendation of a mutual acquaintance – the man driving the race transporter that year. Close behind Chapman was airflow expert Frank Costin.

Youthful as they both then were, Vandervell rapidly recognized they were the people he needed to tie together rigidly, correctly suspend, and clothe in low drag form his unique engine and drivetrain. The car that ran and won within four months of that meeting was essentially the one that was to make history, and it needed the best to drive it. He chose a considerable number ranging from good to brilliant, in the next two seasons, but for that classic year of 1958, he made contracts with just

three.

His choice of gladiators, to use the equipment produced with so much work and dedication, made an unusual trio. Stirling Moss, first and arguably still the greatest of the true professionals. CAS 'Tony' Brooks, capable of equalling Moss's record of wins in that year, yet due soon to retire, transferring his skills back to dentistry. Stuart Lewis-Evans, a frail looking utterly relaxed ex-500cc car driver who could hold Moss at his best, but was to die before the year was out.

There were two cars for each driver and they did the old man proud. Between them they trounced Ferrari, Maserati, Cooper, BRM and Connaught, winning the great classics in Holland, Belgium, Germany, Portugal, Italy and Monaco. With the scoring system as it then worked, Moss still lost the World Championship by one point despite a final race win and lap record. Vanwall took the Constructor's Championship.

In what turned out to be the car's last ever successful appearance Lewis-Evans crashed in the North African Morocco GP and was terribly burned. Nobody really knows if Tony Vandervell, in the very moments of achieving all he had worked, planned

A tribute to Tony Vandervell's determination and vision, the Vanwalls of the late 1950s were formidable competitors. While not truly innovative, they combined many avant-garde ideas into a single well-balanced package. (Picture: National Motor Museum).

and striven for for nine years, guessed his young driver might be dying. Certainly he knew he was desperately injured.

He organised a private aircraft, nursing on the journey, with the most skilled hospital burns treatment and surgeons waiting in England for when the plane landed. It was not enough. Six days later Lewis-Evans died. The tragedy seemed to extinguish Tony Vandervell's inner driving force to go motor racing virtually on the spot. Within four months, broken in health, he said his farewells and was gone from the scene.

So what had made his car such a triumph in the end? It was not really pioneering or hugely innovative. De Dion had had the idea for its backend in the late 19th century. Other builders had gearboxes in unit with the final drive. And twin overhead camshafts. And fuel-injection. It had an excellent low drag bodywork (a co-efficient of drag of around 0.38), genuine power and good handling.

The magic ingredient has to be Tony Vandervell himself. While no man is, they say, indispensable, CAV gave an excellent impression of disproving the rule. Without him, the cars appeared only four times in the next three years. They retired twice and won nothing, but those three seasons were an irrelevance.

The factory that held the racing department has since been demolished and CAV died in 1967. He was 68. But his real monument can still be seen in all its artistry. Vanwall VW9 still stands, sleek and immaculate, in the front hall of Vandervell Products Ltd. A monument, in my view, infinitely preferable to engraved bronze or carved marble.

Specification – Vanwall VW4/5

Engine:	Front mounted 4 cyl, twin ohc, 2 valve with hairpin springs, 2490cc, 96x86mm, 270/285bhp at 7500rpm, Bosch port fuel injection, 5 bearing crank, twin magneto ignition. Multiplate clutch.
Gearbox:	5-speed (in unit with final drive): 2.8, 1.96, 1.4, 1.12, 1.0.
Back axle/FD:	De-Dion tube, chassis mounted differential. Choice of drives from 3.27:1 to 6.06:1.
Chassis/shell:	Multiplate spaceframe, alloy panelled bodywork. Front ducted radiator.
Fuel tank:	Riveted alloy mounted in tail, 35 imp. gals.
Wheels/tyres:	Front: knock-on 16 inch spoked: Dunlop 5.50. Rear: knock-on 16 inch cast magnesium: Dunlop 7.00.
Brakes:	Front: 12 inch ventilated discs/swinging caliper. Rear: 11.75 inch discs, chassis mounted calipers, inboard.
Suspension:	Front: unequal length wishbones, coil springs, anti-roll bar. Rear: De-Dion tube axle on coil springs/radius rods.
Weight:	Approx: 640Kg (1408lb).
Bhp/ton (laden):	358/378.
Performance:	Top speed 175/180mph.

Formula 1: Cooper T51 (1959)

With the glow and glory of Vanwall's demolition job in taking the World Championship still warm, John Cooper and his father Charles were far along a road that would turn even the superb Vanwall into a museum piece.

They were not the first to build successful rear-engined, all independent racing cars. Germany had done it before the war with huge power, huge money, and drivers of the huge talent required to deal with swing axles, fearsome road-holding and 600bhp.

As has been oft and truthfully told, John and Charles got themselves mobile in a car-parched post-World War II world by constructing a racer from two halves of Fiat saloons (the little 500cc Topolino) dying from terminal tinworm attack.

This provided all independent four-wheel suspension, by means of a transverse leaf spring above a robust road going lower wishbone at each end. Nearly a quarter of a century later, a rather larger firm used the identical approach with MacPherson struts,

coils and bottom link to create the Audi Quattro.

The Fiat halves were connected together by what could be most kindly called a simple metal structure sufficient to stop the driver falling on the road and to support a single-cylinder motorcycle engine driving the rear wheels by chain. If it sounds an unlikely way for a revolution to begin, that is indeed true, but nonetheless it did.

The car was one of the founder members of Formula 500 – half a litre was the permitted engine capacity limit – and it laid the base for Cooper knowledge, fame and modest fortune when they began to build further versions commercially.

Although the Coopers' path was to cross that of Tony Vandervell in the years ahead, first as chassis builders and then not so much as vanquisher but as worthy successors to the throne left vacant, they finally found themselves in F1 as much by accident as design.

Unlike Tony Vandervell, a man driven by formidable personal determination about a very serious business, to which a personal fortune and the resources of a large business empire were harnessed, racing was

much more a laugh-a-minute way of enjoying life, while actually earning a living for John Cooper.

Like so many men who started with more or less bare hands, he was a better than competent racing driver himself and could not get in the cockpit of what he and his father had built fast enough.

They went straight to Prescott Hillclimb in Gloucestershire, still going strong as one of the most beautiful motorsport venues in the world, where John hurled their creation up the winding road, not merely without a crash helmet but without goggles too. As he was shortly to be in the habit of testing all his racing cars quite illegally on his local main road, a demand from officials that he protect either his skull or his eyes would probably have been regarded as a gross intrusion on his personal freedom.

He was most certainly the right man in the right place at the right time. Unlike so many of us, who only recognise such a moment too late, he took it with both hands.

Progress was almost bewilderingly fast. Half a season to gain several wins with that incredibly simple prototype, followed by a winter to build two new, and improved, cars:

one a rear-engined sports car and the other a replica of the first single-seater for friend and fellow driver Eric Brandon.

What they did with them in the second season, 1947, which was to win a majority of the events they entered, brought the hopefuls to the door of the Surbiton garage of Cooper senior looking for more replicas.

If John had any doubts about becoming a racing car constructor the fact that many of the visitors had cash for a deposit in their hands rapidly allayed them. Cooper racing cars were on their way.

It proved no handicap for the infant enterprise, that one of the hopefuls at the door happened to be a 16-year old schoolboy, keen to be a racing driver, called Stirling Moss. When a works "factory group" photograph of the first seven brand new production 500s was taken eight months later, his was one of that seven. Curiously enough, he also chose to race under the number 7 every time it was possible during the whole of his career.

His mount had all the basic virtues. Simple, light, good power from what Britain then did best – tuned single-cylinder motorcycle engines – combined with excellent handling and brakes. What Moss proved able to do with that combination is as much a part of motor racing history as are the Coopers and their cars.

From that moment on, if John Cooper was not thinking of something to build, somebody else was doing the suggesting and offering him money to do it.

Not unnaturally the supply of decrepit secondhand Fiat Topolinos ran out almost as soon as things got started, forcing the young company to start making, or persuading somebody else to make, new parts from scratch. They took the opportunity to improve from the very beginning. Cast alloy wheels with integral and bigger iron drums, with twin leading shoe hydraulics, gave superb braking, and stayed a part of the design for the whole of its life. Leaf springs, uprights, a steadily improving tube chassis and well finished alloy bodywork, the beauty of which depended a little on the eye of the beholder, meant it

looked good and went better.

Obviously that did not keep this popular and growing section of the sport as the Coopers' sole preserve. Others of very varying talents and business acumen began to build 500s. They may well have been under the impression that beating Cooper might be easy meat, nurtured by the impression John Cooper was not averse to claiming, with a pint firmly held in one hand, that his racing establishment's research, development and design was not carried out in chalk on the floor and walls of the workshop but was done in licensed premises on the backs of old envelopes.

It was a picture that would have got him into trouble under the Trades Descriptions Act had it then existed, for a succession of refined and improved 500s went on appearing, and winning alongside a series of parallel developments, inspired sometimes by customer request and sometimes by John Cooper himself lying, according to his own account, in the bath, thinking.

They included the 1000 and the 1100cc versions of the 500, which annexed the British Hillclimb Championship seven times in ten years, a baby streamliner for record breaking, 1100, 1220 and 1500 Climax rear-engined, all enveloping sports/racers, 1500 MG front-engined sports cars of great beauty, and the front-engined single-seater 2-litre Cooper-Bristol which future World Champion, Mike Hawthorn, used so brilliantly as his lever to wrench open the door into F1.

Throughout all this the design stayed extraordinarily faithful to transverse leaf springs, a tube chassis with a lot of curved tubes in it, light weight and simplicity. Its weakness, not yet revealed, was that in a world of front-engined, rear wheel drive cars about the only larger gearbox/transaxle (other than Volkswagen, of course) pinchable for a racing car was the one in the French Citroen Light 15 *Traction Avant*, which, while it behaved impeccably for a million French gendarmes, Sureté officers, taxi drivers and family men, got steadily more unhappy with the power being fed through it once John Cooper got hold of one and began its steady adaptation.

Nonetheless when the 1500cc F2 Formula turned up in the middle fifties, Cooper was poised perfectly, with Climax engine, rear gearbox, and a two-seater that was instantly slimmed into an open wheel single-seater.

As the tiny firm embarked on building what would become sixty of the F2s, friend and customer Rob Walker's racing plans affected Cooper radically. Walker's very substantial personal wealth was backed by superb judgement and ability at running his own team, extensive personal F1 driving experience and tenacity.

He had at one time fought a long battle with the Customs and Excise after they confiscated a couple of near priceless cars he had lent to a friend for a continental meeting. Returning to England the friend had chosen to bring in a little modest contraband and found himself minus both cars.

Walker argued that as the Customs men did not confiscate the Queen Mary Atlantic liner every time one of its crew was caught bringing in an illicit packet of cigarettes or bottle of Scotch, they had no right to take his cars thus. It was one of his rare failures, but a magnificent one, marred only by having to buy the cars back at auction later on.

By 1958 he was running a Cooper for Stirling Moss, with the ever growing Climax engines creeping towards the utmost practical maximum of 2.2-litre in a 2.5-litre Formula. Moss worked a miracle by using it to win the Argentinian GP, inspiring Cooper to inspire Coventry Climax within a matter of days to embark on a full 2.5-litre, a unit that was to have a sadly short life due to a change in F1 regulations decreeing 1.5-litres as a maximum.

The car in which the 2.5 engine was installed, the T51, began something achieved by very few people – the production and commercial sale of a series of over 100 full F1 cars – right through to the T86 in 1968.

Cooper had always had a propensity for supporting his curved body panels on matching curved chassis tubes, and even his F1 car did not forsake this liberty for total rigidity.

Similarly he did not quibble over hanging some of the rear suspension on brackets out in thin air on unsupported tubes. This risked

nullifying to some degree the excellent double top and bottom linkage to the rear uprights. A massive radiator was shaped to the front body, and the faithful Triumph saloon front upright, support of 10,000 racing front suspensions, was on duty as usual while the coils, though outboard, were set partially within the bodywork.

The rear transverse leaf spring had its roll stiffness and consequent weight transfer vastly reduced because of the way in which it was mounted. Geometry verged on parallel equal length links with wheels staying vertical in bump and droop, but leaning with the car in corners, something not fatal with the narrowness of existing tyres.

The irrepressible Cooper was not, as usual, above some gross psyching of the opposition, talking gaily at the time of the car scaling nine cwt, a figure which got helpfully quoted in stories at the time. It must have made opposition designers' knees tremble, but it was later clear it was actually around ten cwt dry; quite a difference, but still an excellent figure.

The new 2.5-litre Climax was dropped a massive 2½ inches by use of transfer gears from the front of the adapted Citroen box. In the event these were perilously near to being an Achilles' heel in the chase for the World Championship – but not quite.

in these and the box did not stop Jack Brabham winning the Championship, in the car and engine's first season, by three points. Although the tubes were straightened, and the leaf gave way to rear coils in a new car for 1960 (and a second World Championship for Jack Brabham), it was the 1959 car that not only made history, but put writing on the wall that is still clearly legible today.

The Cooper-Climax T51 put the engine in the back, a revolutionary step forward in post-war F1 design. Despite the lack of a really suitable gearbox/final drive, the rear engine installation changed the whole concept of racing cars everywhere. (Picture: Geoffrey Goddard).

Specification - Cooper T51

Engine:	Coventry Climax FPF 2495cc, four cylinder, eight valve twin ohc. Bore and stroke 94x90. Twin double choke Weber 38 carbs. 240bhp at 6750rpm. 12.1:1 CR, dry sump.
Gearbox/Final Drive:	Citroen/ERSA/Cooper, four-speed in unit with transaxle. All ratios variable. Early splash lubrication, later pump fed and five-speeds.
Chassis:	Round tube spaceframe using 1½in, 1¼in, ¾in, ½in, 18g and 16g stressed alloy undertray sections.
Wheels/tyres:	Front: Alloy Cooper bolt-on Dunlop 4.50x15, later 5.00x15.
	Rear: Alloy Cooper bolt-on Dunlop 5.50x15, later 6.50x15.
Brakes:	Discs, Girling calipers, front: 10.25in dia., Rear: 9.75 inches.
Suspension:	Front: Wishbone with coils and anti-roll bar.
	Rear: Double top and bottom wishbone with transverse leaf.
Weight:	1118lb dry (44% front/56% rear).
Bhp/ton (laden):	384 Est. Cd: 0.43.
Performance:	Top speed: 170-180mph.
Fuel:	31/33 imp gallons (pump petrol), pannier alloy tanks.

Formula 1: Lotus 25 (1962-1963)

Failures in these and the box did not stop Jack Brabham winning the Championship, in the car and engine's first season, by three points. Although the tubes were straightened, and the leaf gave way to rear coils in a new car for 1960 (and a second World Championship for Jack Brabham), it was the 1959 car that not only made history, but put writing on the wall that is still clearly legible today.

It was the "18" destined for a triple life with a variety of engines. One was the 2.5-litre, four-cylinder, Climax engine. When that was consigned to the dustbin by an international ruling that imposed, amid British uproar and general frenzy, a 1.5-litre limit in F1, the 18 got the four-cylinder Climax FPF. Chapman had hoped for a new V8 that was in the pipeline but not ready. The business success of the "18" was by no means hindered by selling it as a highly successful 1100cc formula junior car too.

The 18 achieved a sort of immortality with Stirling Moss's classic Monaco Grand Prix win, not only because it beat everyone from Ferrari down, an experience Britain had only just begun to savour, but because of Moss's decision to run for the sake of coolness with side panels removed: memorably revealing his legs, or the tubes of the classical spaceframe, depending on your sphere of interest.

Refined, lowered, smoothed and wider-tyred the 18 became the still spaceframed 20, then 21 and 24. Along the way, the Triumph Herald front upright — surely the most successful production car component ever pinched for racing — finally said one of its numerous farewells so that Chapman could not only choose his own suspension pick-ups, having gone inboard with the damper coil units but also move the rack and pinion steering up into perfect line with the top wishbone.

Climax's V8 had arrived and built up a reasonable, if erratic, record of wins in full GPs within two years. Reasonable that is for some teams. It was not a level of achievement that

recommended itself to ACBC whose intertwined initials sat on the front of the cars, win or lose.

1962 brought an extraordinary mixture of events. The still potent 21 enabled Trevor Taylor and Jim Clark to take a quick first, second and fastest lap for openers in South Africa. A load of happy customers paid up for their brand new 24 spaceframe cars (not least being Jack Brabham and the Rob Walker Racing Team who were fielding Stirling Moss).

Then from the Team Lotus transporter at Zandvoort, in May, they saw the then un-buyable 25 monocoque emerge. There were only ever to be seven of them. Within sixteen months the perfectly integrated partnership of Jim Clark and Colin Chapman with the 25, created by one to be used with dominating perfection by the other, gave both car and driver their respective Championships of the World.

In fact it had been so good out of the box, that starting halfway through 1962, Clark only missed the Championship in its first season when a much publicised $\frac{1}{4}$ inch bolt fell out of the distributor mounting, near the end of the final and key race, to be rapidly followed by all the engine's oil.

Everyone knows how it is done — *afterwards*. The boldness is in the workshop and drawing office, the thinking and the risk taking. The world is quite full of people with ideas, some of which are potentially excellent. Carrying them through is a different story.

Hollywood would have been proud of the 25's faintly novel-like beginnings, sketched in rough outline on a restaurant napkin. But Chapman had his misgivings, as he was later willing to publicly admit in Doug Nye's book, *Theme Lotus:* "Why not space the sides of a backbone far enough apart for the driver to sit between them. Made as box sections we could carry fuel inside in rubber bags. It was the first monocoque racing car, so far as I was concerned". (He was not unreasonably ignorant of the 1912 French version of this idea in laminated wood veneer).

"I'd never seen one before and we didn't know if it would work. We sold the spaceframe to our customers.

We could not sell them a revolutionary car which might not work at all and might need a long and expensive development programme. At that time it was really an unknown animal".

As it turned out, it must have had one of the shortest development programmes ever for a totally successful car, but who is counting the days? Certainly it was still being cut and riveted, its bulkheads fabricated, and suspension borrowed from the 24 a long time after Christmas 1961.

Twenty years later it was only just giving way to what the 25 itself was often called but was not — the "bathtub" car. This latter came about with the neat, tall, narrow hipbath-shaped structure of the glued honeycomb, true venturi, cars in the very late seventies.

Until this was both forced and made possible by side pods and new materials, it is instructive to see how much of the 25 conception was so right from the word go that it became the pattern for every F1 to follow. While the Brabham BT26 was determinedly soldiering on — very successfully — with tubes seven years later, it was the farewell flourish of a bravely dying man.

Imagine if you will, in a world totally dominated by and dedicated to the tubular spaceframe, a cardboard tube a couple of inches in diameter and eight or nine inches long. Bending or twisting it with your bare hands verges on the impossible. Lay another parallel to it three inches away.

The difficulty is not to make them stiff, but to join them in such a way they are held rigidly parallel to each other, no easy matter. The methods conceived for the 25 were virtually those of everyone since. Two vital bulkheads, one behind the driver and one beyond his feet, link the two tubes, together with a marginally less rigid one at instrument panel level. Our two side tubes have become flattened into D sections, to permit economic insertion of the driver between them while keeping everything as narrow as possible.

Those flat inner surfaces, together with the floor linking the two are now tied together with panels that begin behind the driver's neck, support his reclining back, then posterior and

The Lotus 25 as the first
monocoque F1 machine was a
'milestone' car. Here Chris Amon pilots
R3 to fifth place in the Daily Mirror
Trophy race held at Snetterton on
March 14, 1964. This car had a BRM
V8 engine. (Picture: Colin Taylor
Productions)

Another Lotus 25 but this time
it's Jim Clark at the wheel of R5 during
the Aintree 200 of April 27, 1963 – he
finished third. This car had a Climax V8
engine. (Picture: Colin Taylor
Productions).

rising thighs, to his knees, falling again towards his heels. These zig-zagging surfaces, provide on their way triangular boxes into which can be usefully inserted another fuel tank, fire extinguisher bottle, battery or other electrics.

The two sections of pontoon left projecting rearwards into thin air beyond the bulkhead separating driver and engine are then tied together by a power unit, bolted in solid, making it all one integrated structure. The final small bonus is that beyond the driver's feet a totally rigid subframe can be made, not only carrying the front suspension but giving a portion of its own strength to keeping those original two tubes accurately and rigidly alongside each other.

Really the only major change in the monocoque's history since then was that the Cosworth DFV when it arrived had been conceived from the very beginning as half the car, 4-bolted to the engine bulkhead at its front, and carrying suspension links damper/coil units, rollbars, wings, gearchange and assorted other bric-a-brac all by itself at the rear end.

Chapman had always been a man inclined to controlling, as closely as possible, exactly what the wheels and tyres of his racing cars were doing by carefully planned suspension geometry allied to soft springs with stiff dampers adjustable in both bump and rebound. The success of such an approach is founded on the pickup points for the suspension staying where they are supposed to be, dependent in their turn totally on the torsional stiffness of the chassis.

The monocoque rocketed the torsional stiffness figures by some 200 per cent, and saved ten or fifteen pounds of weight into the bargain.

As this happened to be the twilight of the fifteen inch diameter "bicycle wheels" and narrow tyres, control of wheel angles through the suspension was shortly to become ever more important.

The internal dimensions of the car were so closely controlled it would have been practically impossible to get taller or fatter drivers than the modestly proportioned Clark and Taylor into the cockpits at all.

Beside their lie-down seats the gearchange, travelling through tubes let into the monocoque sides, had a lever operable by hardly more than rotating the right arm to allow a couple of fingers to move it in a tiny gate. Space was so limited Jim Clark once said he had to allow himself time somewhere in every lap to drive with one hand while he flexed his gearchange arm to avoid cramp.

Astonishingly there were still quite a number of rubber bushes in the suspension but these did not last long and were gone by the Championship year of 1963 – as were carburettors in favour of fuel-injection.

Other development thinned the L72 alloy sheet of which the car was largely built by a couple of gauges, improved the cooling and altered the geometry. Further, the victorious year of 1963 was used – apart from winning the Belgian, Dutch, French, British, Italian, Mexican and South African Grands Prix – for a succession of experiments on thirteen inch wheels, totally different tyres and suspension geometry and location – all for the coming 33.

Though nearly all the 25s created were either wrecked or ended in the hands of private collectors you can still go and study R7, the last one, and ponder its technicalities, in Tom Wheatcroft's incomparable museum at Donington.

There could be few better ways to spend a quiet hour.

Specification - Lotus 25
(Data by courtesy of Autocourse)

Engine:	Coventry Climax V8 FWMV, 1500cc. 63mm bore x 60 mm stroke. Weber carburettors with Lucas electronic ignition. 174 BHP at 8600 rpm. Also fitted with BRM 1500cc V8.
Gearbox:	ZF 5-speed with full range of ratios.
Back axle/final drive:	ZF in unit with transaxle.
Chassis/shell:	Monocoque of steel and alloy sheet.
Fuel/tanks:	Alloy welded and rivetted. Later rubberised fabric. Two main tanks interconnected. Approx 27 gals.
Wheels/tyres:	Front: 5.5in rim x 15in diam. Dunlop 500-15. Rear: 8in rim x 15in diam. Dunlop 700-15.
Brakes:	Outboard 10.5in discs with 4-pot calipers all round.
Suspension:	Front: Unequal length wishbones, top rocking arm operating inboard mounted coil spring/damper unit. Rear: Unequal length links with bottom "A" brackets, radius rods, outboard coil spring/damper units.
Weight:	478kg. (1052lb).
BHP/ton laden:	268.
Top speed:	Approx 173mph.
Remarks:	The first of the monocoques. Front radiator tailored to precise body shape.

Formula 1: Brabham BT26 (1968)

Not too many designers of anything stay at the top of their field for a lifetime, least of all in the world of car racing.

They finally cannot – or do not wish to – cope with the endless pressure to win, the need to continually progress technically and the regular arrival of the next wave of young brains set on proving the old world has had its day and should decently take its grey hair somewhere quiet with a book and a deckchair.

This, Ron Tauranac continually and embarrassingly refuses to do. He compounds the insult of having built motorbike-engined specials in Australia that could win before much of his opposition was born, by still designing and building cars that can, and do, win anywhere in the rest of the civilised world. Add to this that he does it as a business, staying solvent, while selling to the most fickle market in the world, young up and coming racing drivers desperate to win, and you have someone well out of the ordinary.

He views what he is doing, and how it should be done, with total clarity. Designing and building racing cars commercially is a different philosophy from running a team. "The aim is to be slightly better than the opposition", says the lucid Mr. T. "Not a scrap more than is needed. Just enough. Do not describe any ideas you do not have to.

"I aim at the best engineered car that is easy to drive, not the most technically advanced. Particularly I do not want the risk of anything causing somebody's death. Constant pioneering is the way to commercial suicide. A great deal of design is evolution and there is little time to be innovative".

The cars are filled with proofs of this philosophy. The monocoques end at the driver's rollbar, but pontoon box extensions attached with six small bolts can be altered to accept a variety of engines, Toyota, Alfa and VW being current favourites.

Brakes, hubs, wheelstuds and driveshafts that cope with F2 give a bonus of reliability and life in his best selling F3 car.

Aerodynamics are kept similar or identical on both. Two or three aerofoil sections including NACA 4412 and 4415 have given years of faithful and useful service. He regards rear wings as air straighteners, and goes to the trouble of fairings on the rollover bar that turn them into perfect teardrop outlines.

Two things dominate his designs, and have done for a long time – rigidity in the chassis and in the location and control of the rear wheels.
"Any rear wheel steering, even a few thou, and boy have you got problems! A driver can correct to some degree for movements – flex, bump steer – at the front, but at the rear it makes it extremely difficult for him.

"Rigidity is far more important that being clever with the geometry of the suspension. Whatever you hope to achieve with that it is ridiculous to then

have the pick-ups moving about. It cannot work.

"If there is rear toe-in and out, there is no way a driver can collect it up properly. I was using a top toe control link in 1964, about the first time it was done I think."

Perhaps Ron Tauranac could have been World Champion instead of what he now is. He was regularly beating J. Brabham back home in Australian hillclimbs and circuit racing with a homebuilt special. But the partnership that finally made the real mark, bearing the code prefix of BT for the car type numbers, was strictly Brabham doing the driving while Tauranac did design and construction. Jack Brabham decided to go it alone after Cooper, and the two went into partnership.

"The car was stiff and light, and as tyres began going wider and wider, we went to longer and longer swing axle lengths. Control of the wheel contact patch became more vital and I think we had an advantage in this over most of the opposition until about 1970, sometimes by accident, sometimes by design.

"Nowadays, of course, geometry is far less important as suspension movement is becoming so small.

"At the time I did not really want to do F1. We were already doing sports cars, F2 and F3. F1 is enormously time consuming, but Jack got me interested and our first car was very hurried.

"I found the brightest ideas may have no future if they are not in the current mainstream. You have to design within the limiting factors of available equipment.

"We were involved in a Colotti box which gave a lot of trouble and our F1 box was originally based on VW, with a lot of help from Hewland who did not then make a proper F1 box.

"After the end of the 1.5-litre Formula, Jack's links with Repco, a big firm in Australia, meant we embarked on a single cam V8 from them with 310bhp. It was excellent.

"The constructors had got together and it was felt that with 3-litre motors, fifteen inch wheels and tyres would be needed to take the brakes necessary for the extra power, but four pot calipers and vented discs weren't

around.

"Looking back I think it was a wrong decision, but the tyre people then concentrated their development on fifteen inch tyres so you had to go with it.

"We were still using a spaceframe – we did until 1970, and into 1972 in F3, because every car was logically carried on from the previous one. We had built a monocoque for Indy because they required bag tanks, and the monocoque was the perfect way of doing this, but in Europe they were not required, and we felt the spaceframe would still do the job.

"It carried alloy tanks down each side which I think at the time was safer. Early bag tanks had a lot of trouble with leaks, but tanks made from soft aluminium would stand a lot of damage and distortion without leaking. Certainly we never had a fire.

"I stiffened the chassis a lot further with riveted panels, particularly the undertray, down the sides inside the tanks, the rear bulkhead and around the dash area.

"We built both front and back wings that stood up on long legs, with Bowden cable adjustment of the angles.

"I cannot remember now whether you were allowed to do this or not The wings had polystyrene cores with very thin Swedish veneer outer skin and sometimes glassfibre as well. The first time we didn't put them both on until the last practice. It was the first time anybody had done it. The opposition were all rushing round trying to make copies in time for the race.

"The front one certainly worked, although it was mounted on the chassis rather than the uprights where it needed to be. On the chassis of course it compressed the suspension. I remember Jack coming in after trying it and saying, 'Christ, it doesn't half stick the front down. Now the back is all over the place'."

That history-making front wing – Lotus copied it immediately – was combined with another brilliant concept. The rear wing was split, pivoting each half on the centre line to permit mounting it on the rear uprights for the most effective downforce but keeping it strong and stable with a

pyramid of thin tubes to its centre.

While the dihedral angle altered as the wheels bounced up and down, the vital angle of attack controlling the downforce and thus the car's rear stability stayed constant.

Two years after Jack the Giant-killer had taken the World Championship with a "low-powered" 310bhp single cam Repco, the engine had developed into a four cam four valve device with nearly 400bhp – and built-in trouble. "It made 1968 disaster year, and 1969 was not much better even when we got our first Cosworth. At its best it was suspect. Rindt on pole in Canada was its very best. But that Repco would not finish a race". The engine suffered chronic boiling, displaced valve seats and thrown rods. With its new sophisticated multi-valved and cammed top end, it needed urgent and continual development by its builders, and they were 10,000 miles away from the circuits of Europe. It was a hurdle that was never surmounted.

It was not only the last F1 spaceframe car. It was virtually the end of the road for Jack and Ron's partnership and their participation in F1. Jack Brabham went home to Australia, Tauranac had a brief association with Bernie Ecclestone, but then sold out.

He was not yet fifty and being at home all day appealed even less, it turned out, to his wife then it did to him. The happy answer for them both was Ralt Cars, but away from F1.

The success of his F3 and F2 cars since then is continual proof of their inbuilt qualities, but if anyone has counted the victories, it is not Ron Tauranac. His bare office has no trophies, no photographs and a vague air of having been left empty by someone who got the bullet six months ago. Tauranac's place is in a tiny drawing office, a large machine shop, or the long bay in which the cars are built.

The worst difficulty in building successful cars commercially he soon found is that everyone wants them in three months. "Soon after the end of the season the drivers with money place their orders. We take all we can cope with. Then, in January, the quick men make up their minds, and you can't refuse their orders. Two months after that one or two of the others ask you as well. It's all a bit tricky. You end up with everyone working all hours – including some of the drivers and their mechanics as well if they want the cars badly enough.'

He views the relative novices who come and go in F3 with a fatherly eye, issuing sheets of instructions with

The Brabham BT26 featured great attention to suspension design coupled to the downforce produced by these fledgeling wings – the shape of things to come. (Picture: Colin Taylor Productions).

his cars on engine temperatures, running-in discs and pads, changing brake fluid, and looking after the clutch. It might sound simple – but he found it was needed.

Tauranac's advice is so good I pass it along. After all, it really works. The current F3 and F2 cars are faster by a long way than that F1 that had such promise for a grand finale in 1969, but never made it in the record books.

The Ralt guide to your new racer

Discs: Bed in new ones gently, using soft pads or old ones faced off in a lathe or grinder. Five laps without violent braking can prevent subsequent cracking. Do not use new discs to fade new pads.

Pads: Ferodo DS11 (marked on the edge of pad material) need to be faded. Get them really hot with a series of applications to soak heat fully into the whole brake, then fade them with a really hard application. Follow this with a gently cooling down lap. DS11 minimum efficient working temperatures 500°C up to 650°C.

Use thermal paint to check, and blank brake air scoops if not getting warm enough. Running too cold glazes pads and discs. cs.

For anywhere not so demanding on brakes, use Ferodo 2430. Temperature 300°C to 600°C with 400°C ideal. Do not fade these. Faded soft pads give wheel locking because of inconsistent coefficient of friction.

Bleed brakes and refill with new racing fluid after fading new pads or other excessive temperatures. Refill and bleed for each race. Keep tops of cans and master cylinders free from dirt or moisture.

Clutch: 20-30 minutes between full racing starts is needed for heat dissipation, so don't do one on the warm-up lap.

Oil Temperature: Keep it up around 110°C.

Water Temperature: Keep it down to 70°C -80°C to fight detonation and improve power.

And he suggests that warmth will always help the car — engine, gearbox, tyres, hubs and wheels. A big cover over the car with a hot air supply at the rear, or laying everything out in the sun when it's shining. In this way optimum tyre pressures and other temperatures can then be achieved quickly.

Specification — Brabham BT26 *(Data by courtesy of Autocourse/Ron Tauranac)*

Engine:	Repco 3-litre V8. 4 valves per cyl. 88.9mm bore x 60mm stroke. Lucas injection. Bosch coil/distributor. 375/BHP at 8700rpm.
Gearbox:	Hewland DG 300 with full range interchangeable ratios.
Back axle/final drive:	ZF crownwheel/pinion built into Hewland transaxle.
Chassis/shell:	Steel tube spaceframe with stressed panels rivetted and welded.
Fuel/tanks:	Aluminium welded. 35 gals. in three tanks with interconnected feeds.
Wheels/tyres:	Front: 11in rim x 15in diam. Rear: 14in rim x 15in diam. Goodyear, various sizes and compounds.
Brakes:	Girling outboard discs and calipers all round.
Suspension:	Front: Unequal length wishbone with outboard coilspring/damper units. Rear: Unequal length links with radius rods; outboard coil spring/damper units.
Weight:	527kg (1159lb).
BHP/ton laden:	525.
Top speed:	174mph (Est.)
Remarks:	First F1 car with full wings. Contemporary reports give gearbox as Hewland FG 400, Tauranac's personal records read DG 300. Wing downforce figures: 140lb front, 420lb rear.

Formula 1: Tyrrell P34 — 6-wheeler (1976)

When designer Derek Gardner put his reputation on the line with a totally novel approach to a set of difficulties that faced every other designer in F1, he was living dangerously.

He later told an engineering audience: "There is a time to take bold and imaginative steps, but they also bring the risk of failure. I felt the time was right for changes in the concept of design".

A casual view of the results achieved by the Tyrrell P34 with its double paired front wheels might label it just that. But would it be right? Did Gardner indeed have the secret of another world beater in his hands — he had already conceived the regular four-wheeler that carried Jackie Stewart to the World Championship — but then discover too late that the design lost

him control of some aspects that were vital to its development?

Or did his ingenious and beautifully executed conception injure itself fatally on the edge of Occam's Razor?

Certainly Gardner did not take the simplest solution when he considered the primary things he had to deal with and improve for 1976 during the closing months of 1975. These were: reduce drag, improve cornering power and increase braking grip.

Four much smaller wheels at the front not only seemed a logical solution to all three problems, but a path to a major edge over the opposition; precisely what a designer is expected to provide for his salary.

His first calculations showed just about everything going for it. A drop in height of the wheel and tyre of four inches, a forty per cent increase in the area of contact patch "footprint" on the road, 34 per cent more brake pad pressing on 26.5 per cent more disc swept area; smaller, lighter discs, wheels, tyres, dampers and coils to set

against having twice as many of everything.

A tyre spinning in free air, with its upper surface moving towards the air ahead creates lift. The downforce needed to counteract lift on any car creates drag. Reducing drag in any way, given the more or less common engine power for nearly all entrants at the time of 465bhp from the Cosworth DFV would mean a higher straight line speed.

The new tiny wheels and tyres would be more than two inches narrower each side. The car's frontal area would be slimmed down. More calculations suggested they were going to be worth 10-15bhp "for free", possibly quite a bit more.

Highly secret discussions were begun with Goodyear about production of the unique tyres that were going to be required. Barely a dozen men knew what was afoot until it finally became public knowledge. Goodyear agreed to make the tyres in at least two compounds and constructions, both wets and dry slicks. It needed not only new machinery, and brand new thinking on a carcase to deal with conditions that were still theoretical, but included at least one unpalatable fact of life, an RPM step up of 25 per cent to 3750 at 180mph.

At the same time, Gardner sat down to pen not only his new car, but a complex front end in conventional terms. All four wheels had to have steering linkages of course, be damped and sprung, with adjustable connections to anti-roll bar or bars. With a ten inch diameter wheel, the brakes were limited to an eight inch disc needing in turn a tiny caliper which was developed from that of the famed Mini-Cooper saloons, built into a miniature magnesium upright.

He also took the opportunity to narrow the rear track by three inches to match the smaller front, but already there was a tiny hint of future trouble.

The need for such unusual dimensions cut the car off from some of the semi "off-the-shelf" parts and services obtainable at high speed and short notice within Britain's racing car industry.

Nonetheless, these were but imperceptible pinpricks at this point, although it was decided it should run when complete in harness with the previous season's 007 series car.

The shock when Tyrrell took the wraps off their new six-wheeler at its formal presentation to the outside world was so great that some people at the unveiling thought for a moment that if the champagne was not making them see double, at least someone was pulling their legs. There were audible gasps from motoring writers who had not been surprised for years.

What nobody suspected at the time (or I can find no contemporary mention of it) was that the six-wheeler revealed that day was essentially a fake. It was the previous year's monocoque with a cobbled up front end that gave no secrets away about the car other than the obvious, but was to be a mobile test bed to investigate if the idea would really work.

Ken Tyrrell had cannily and accurately perceived there was no way such a car could stay a secret the moment it appeared on test anywhere in the motor racing world, so it had been decided to reveal it first and

create it later. When tests at Paul Ricard showed instant promise, work went ahead immediately on the totally new version. Sheer pressure of work meant that testing time available would be short, but it rapidly proved faster than the previous car with loads rising to a formidable 1.88G as the driver turned into a corner.

Braking was better and those three main objectives on which the original concept had been based had initially at least, been achieved. Whether the new margins would prove to be enough to cope with the inevitable development work of rival teams over the winter could only be answered at one place – a racing circuit.

There were plenty of unknowns. Paradoxically, a higher top speed is not necessarily a total blessing in a racing car. The driver arrives at a higher speed than previously experienced at every corner. How much has got to be given away in harder or earlier braking, extra heat, tyre wear, a slightly different line of approach or attitude in the corner itself?

Bigger brake and tyre contact areas were theoretically going to deal with two aspects, but the laws of thermo-dynamics were not going to permit the evasion of more heat, none of it wanted, as well as more weight however miniaturised the multiple front end.

None of this worried the team unduly, if at all. They had top class everything – drivers, designer, development, team mechanics and an organisation that had been best in the world before under Ken Tyrrell, a man with one of the longest and most talented records in running a team in the business.

There would be no rushing off at half cock, which meant the car missed the first couple of races of the season. Until it was ready it would not run, and it wasn't ready until the Swedish GP at Anderstorp in June.

It won. First and second with a commanding 9 second lead. It was enough to strike instant terror into the hearts of the opposition, and temporarily it did just that. Yet from then on, it seemed to be all downhill – or was it? Nine second places and nine other places over the full season gave

Scheckter and Depailler third and fourth places in the Drivers' World Championship – and that behind McLaren with Hunt and Ferrari with Lauda in their great years. The cars also brought Tyrrell third place in the Constructors' Championship with 71 points. Compare that with Ferrari's winning 83 and Lotus's fourth place score of 29.

For a brand new, pioneering car it was a superb and solid achievement. So what went amiss? There cannot be a single clearcut answer, but even an outsider utilising hindsight and the knowledge that has since emerged, can perceive some of the hurdles that ended as insurmountable in the time available. Time indeed played a large part, probably at the root of everything, with tyres not far behind.

A Formula 1 car is a difficult, delicate, hard to balance creature at best. Two extra wheels emphasised this. And tyre developments were taking continual leaps forward.

All other teams were then using similarly-sized front tyres on 13 inch wheels, so any new experiment in carcase, tread rubber or combination of the two could be produced in relatively high numbers. They went to half a dozen teams, different cars, different drivers. The feedback was considerable with easy crosschecks to filter out really way-out compliments, or criticisms.

Tyres are a curious product with variable parameters and performance depending a great deal on temperature. Making 16 inch copies of a 20 inch tyre by no means meant they would work identically. And they didn't. For one thing, the small tyres went against all the calculations by refusing to heat up properly on the first compounds. Tyrrell had no crosschecks, however informal, with the opposition, simply because there was no common ground for comparison. Other designers had forged ahead to utilise altered front suspensions with newer front tyres, and were a long way on to their own improved high G turn-in success. With every race they nibbled away at the P34 advantage.

Drivers and other heavy objects were edging forward in the chassis, increasing the front weight distribution. And somewhat ironically for the Tyrrell,

The Tyrrell P34 6-wheeler was a bold experiment in the reduction of frontal area combined with an enhanced tyre contact area. With the car's front bodywork removed the design of the linked front suspension can be seen. (Pictures: Colin Taylor Productions).

the much greater tyre contact area of four patches meant correspondingly less weight pressing on them.

The grip of a tyre on the road is an extremely complex affair, but one undisputed component is the actual weight on the contact patch. Tyrrell were very much on their own, and Goodyear was having to produce the special tiny tyres in tiny numbers. One of the Goodyear staff involved with the P34 project remembers: "It was our best kept secret ever. Only about 12 people knew about those tyres. Nobody in the UK had ever made such tyres or suitable wheels to carry them at those speeds and revs.

"Obviously there were surprises. One was that they wouldn't come up to temperature. They weren't being worked hard enough, and needed special compounds developed for that.

"Another thing was that it was a single team using them. With several you not only have feedback all the time, but also crosschecks that allow you to weed out odd results that might otherwise put you down a *cul de sac* With the Tyrrell fronts that was not possible. Given time, I think we could have solved all that – but time is what you've never got enough of in racing."

For the opposition, better turn-in grip was also improving their braking – and they had the elbow room to experiment with larger, multi-pot calipers, double installations and bigger, thicker discs. Such alternatives on the Tyrrell, where the caliper was actually an integral part of the upright, verged on the impossible. Bit by bit the weight load crept up as well.

Finally the reduced drag was not so much improving on the opposition as getting rid of a self-imposed Tyrrell handicap. Excellent handling, exploited to its ultimate by what Gardner called "the uncanny ability of Jackie Stewart" had balanced out any slight lack of

straight line speed in previous seasons but this was four years on from the heady days of World Championship laurels in 1972. The still massive rear, together with the wing, largely governed frontal area of a grossly un-aerodynamic shape for all cars. Smaller fronts could not exert decisive effects.

Curiously the car's greatest triumph came on the long sweeping curves of the same circuit on which uproar was to explode two years later around the Brabham Fan Car – Anderstorp in Sweden.

The heady heights were never scaled again. After six fast and furious years in F1 and the disappointments of the P34 project, Derek Gardner's thoughts were turning back to industry. His avowed intention to try and turn the whole business from an art into a science was a long way away from achievement. He told Ken Tyrrell of his feelings, and before the year was out he had departed, transferring his skills (with some considerable foresight) to work on the future of small four-wheel-drive automatic transmission technology.

Looking back, or attempting to, Ken Tyrrell is so much a man of the present or future he's not exactly sure what happened to the six P34 cars he and his team created and where they have all gone.

"One in France, two, I think, in Japan, certainly one in the Montagu Museum – I'm not really sure", he offers. "It was always quicker than the

previous car in a straight line. It achieved that objective. But having reduced the width of the car at the front, we had to recover the cornering force. Its weakness was its cornering capabilities, partly due to heaviness.

"Probably it was weight that killed it. We weren't using exotic materials to get the weight down. That first year the car was quite successful. We only started using it a third of the way through the season and ended up third and fourth in the World Championship for Scheckter and Depailler, and third in the Constructors' Cup, although we also raced the previous year's 007 in parallel part of the time.

"Its win in Sweden was a good decisive one by nine seconds. There was certainly a lack of tyre development. Goodyear efforts are obviously applied towards a car that might be winning the Championship, rather than some other car. And we couldn't do any development work on it anywhere until it had been shown to the Press. If we had it would never have stayed a secret. It never saw a race track before it was shown to them.

"The actual car shown was our existing monocoque modified to take a 4-wheeler front end. We had to test at Paul Ricard to see if it was worth going ahead, and then design the car finally.

"Depailler was always very enthusiastic about the car. He was a very good test driver, able to give us

Specification – Tyrrell P34 (6-wheeler)

Engine:	Ford Cosworth DFV, 3-litre, 465bhp.
Gearbox:	Hewland FG400.
Back Axle/final drive:	In unit with transaxle. Full range of ratios.
Chassis/shell:	Alloy monocoque, riveted tub.
Fuel/tanks:	42 imp gals in Marston flexi-bag tank.
Wheels/tyres:	Front: Twin wheels. 10 in diameter 9 in wide. Rear: 13 in diameter x 18 in rim width. Goodyear (Special fronts with 16 in OD).
Brakes:	Outboard disc all round. Front calipers integral with uprights.
Suspension:	Front: Twin double wishbones with outboard coils. Steered by single rack with slave link to each axle. Rear: Parallel lower links, single top link, twin radius rods, outboard coils.
Weight:	575 kg.
Bhp/ton (laden):	618
Top speed:	175mph.

information all the time. Scheckter was not so sure about it, and was never a good test driver."

Gardner was replaced by Maurice Phillipe, rightly famed for his contributions to the Lotus 72, to name but one of many. The 6-wheeler did run in 1977, but even the incomparable

Ronnie Peterson could not get what he wanted out of it. Phillipe was hard at work on the 008 destined to have just four wheels like the rest of the world, and he is by no means unqualified to have the last word.

He was later to say: "I think it was brilliant, but it gradually failed

because while constant development was going into rear tyres which all teams were using, the same work could not go into the little fronts so it gradually fell behind everyone else. I decided to build a four wheeler from the word go ..."

Formula 1: Lotus 78 (1977)

With the Lotus 78, Colin Chapman finally opened Pandora's box – with a vengeance.

It truly contained all the promise, success and honest difficulties of the venturi cars that were to push lap speeds up by margins that had previously been wild dreams. But the devils and demons poured out as well. Within three years the sport had been almost torn apart by rows ostensibly over speeds, wings, downforce, skirts, hydro-pneumatic ride level controls, ground clearance, iron-hard suspensions.

Really these were too often excuses or triggers for battles in the long war between a newly muscle-flexing FISA (*Federation International Sportive Automobile*) and the hard and far-seeing business heads in FOCA (Formula One Constructors' Association).

The most extraordinary demon of all to emerge was one that in due course turned Lotus' whole magnificent conception into near disaster for the team that lifted the lid. But that is to jump ahead.

The 78 had a more complex birth than the 25 – from the legendary, or apocryphal serviette, things had moved on to twenty seven pages of foolscap, outlining for a bigger and highly technically accomplished team, Chapman's view of what his car of the future was to be. Formula One had been wearing wings, high and low, front, back and both for six or more years. Chapman's vision in essence was to turn the whole car, or as much of it as might prove practicable, into a wing.

Given that downforce was proportional to the area over which it might be exerted, a very small

reduction indeed below atmosphere would be operating over several thousand square inches. The step up in tyre grip was potentially mind-boggling.

This was summer 1975, and it promised to be a long hard slog that needed secrecy just as much as technical achievement, if it was to really succeed. Lotus were in the middle of an appallingly bad patch, the once all conquering 72s though vastly modified over the years, were still pale non-race-winning shadows of their former kingly selves.

It was typical of Chapman 'the great innovator' that he had always been reluctant to take a small step any time a big one seemed possible. This philosophy had the chequered and hazardous result that when the step was the right one, Team Lotus was overwhelming. When it was not, they were in a deep morass of problems, race following race, endless and often major changes being made non-stop, sometimes within days, while the opposition, confining itself to the minimum of methodical and meticulous change, were in there winning.

It was not the first time – and was not to be the last – that Lotus would find itself in that depressing position of 1975, but phoenix-like, the ashes were alive and stirring.

A full year was spent on, amongst other things, several hundred hours experiment in a university wind tunnel with a succession of exquisitely detailed body models. They incorporated the coming Lotus 'secret weapon' – a wing-shaped pod that would be attached to each side of the body. The depression created below the familar rear banana wings, was to be transferred to the area beneath the car's body. More, that precious depression was going to be protected by something to make it very difficult

for air outside the car to rush underneath and destroy it – skirts. These skirts were, in the first instance, lengths of dense bristled draught excluder that would skim along the road surface.

As the new car took shape it was apparent that the whole design had an incidental but most useful advantage. It was going to be extremely difficult for the opposition to peer underneath or otherwise investigate exactly what was going on.

The skirts, later changed to thick plastic lips, and later still to vertically sliding metal plates with ultra hard ceramic wear-resistant edges, blocked any casual inspection from underneath. And matt black paint on all internal surfaces, particularly the air intakes, made it difficult to see, and worse to photograph, in any attempt to discover exactly what was going on within that mysterious side bodywork.

Anyone with long enough technical memories of the World War II fighter/bombers might have recognised the radiator approach – buried in leading edge slots with ducted exits for the hot air – that had helped the performance of one of the greatest propeller driven aircraft of all time, the wooden De Havilland Mosquito.

Some of the more exotic and troublesome aspects of earlier cars – rising rate torsion bars, four-wheel-drive, inboard front brakes, multi-section wings, Lotus's own gearbox, dozens of adjustables – all were eliminated before they could cause any difficulties. At least three 'novelties' earned their place in the 78 – a rear anti-roll bar that could be adjusted by the pilot while driving, honeycomb sheet with its two thin outer skins glued to a centre sandwich filling of ultra-thin webbed alloy foil, and a fuel tank system that allowed the driver a choice of which tanks he preferred to empty first.

Inboard coils with top rocking arms had finally come into their own. The car had a distinctively wide front track with the double advantage of the minimum possible restriction to air passing through towards those mysterious side pods, and excellent turn-in to corners. This was so good there was to be much later talk of a 'solid rear axle' when it proved possible to wind up the LSD almost to maximum, while still keeping that superb turn-in.

Much of its non-aerodynamic development had been carried out as Lotus had often done before, by being bolted on the current racers, the 77s, for test and assessment.

The wheelbase came down three inches combining a modest contribution to weight saving, with a lower polar moment aiding that turn-in and 'quickness' in handling.

Radiators, which had tended to drift further and further rearwards and more and more parallel to the centre line of the car as the power of a low pressure area around the engine became more clearly understood, suddenly shot the other way, leaning sharply forward to get the required length into the limited depth of side pod available. With them, to some degree, went the driver as well. All of this was beginning to radically alter the weight distribution of the rear-engined single-seater from what had been two thirds on the back wheels to much nearer an even split.

By now extremely well established, with internal foam baffling against surge or rapid leak, three rubber tanks sat across the car not far from its centre line.

Andretti's long experience in American racing had taught him how to employ with rare skill certain arts of adjusting the balance of a racing car, and its subsequent handling, both before leaving the pits, and while in mid-race if the means was available.

Built into the 78 design was a fuel tap system that gave the driver control over his fuel load, and therefore where its reducing weight was distributed, as well as a lever that allowed him to stiffen or slacken off the rear anti-roll bar.

To the casual observer, the advent of the 78 – formally the John Player Special Mk. 3 in that beautiful black, gold lined livery – was strangely mixed. Five Grand Prix wins, but it kept breaking down.

For the more perceptive, or closely involved, five engine blow-ups and three other mechanical failures did nothing to obscure the fact that the new Lotus had led every single race of the year at some time or another, and sat on pole position more often than any other car on the grid.

The disasters did not prevent Andretti coming third in the World Championship and Lotus second to Ferrari in the Constructors' Championship. There was an air of King Canute in the other teams. They desperately wanted to stop the tide coming in but nobody knew how to do it. Worse still, it was clear that the tide, in the shape of Chapman and his team, was going to spend the winter improving its skills.

Not the least remarkable thing is that none of the opposition teams had a good enough idea of exactly what was going on under the 78 to gamble on trying to create their own version during the coming winter. Even if they had, Lotus were already building a priceless and seemingly uncatchable lead in any number of the new mysteries the system was beginning to hint at.

For example movements in the centre of pressure – the point through which the downforce of an aerofoil exerts itself is not fixed, but this factor had not been significant enough within the limited chord of a fixed rear wing to upset a car in a major way. However, really hefty downforce moving forwards and backwards not far behind the front wheels and varying its position with speed, was clearly going to give a driver real problems balancing his car. It was to become the violent pitch change porpoising of the not too distant future.

Chapman had already realised that the 78 rear suspension with its outboard damper/coilspring, fat uprights coming several inches inboard from the tyre walls, rollbar links and exhaust pipes, was presenting an almost solid wall to air trying to find its way out of the side pods, but could do nothing about it in the existing car.

The exiting airstream from under

Specification – Lotus 78
(Data by courtesy of Autocourse)

Engine:	Ford-Cosworth DFV 3-litre; 485BHP.
Gearbox:	Hewland FG 400. 5-speed with full range of ratios.
Backaxle/final drive:	ZF limited slip in unit with transaxle.
Chassis/shell:	Alloy monocoque, with inverted aircraft wing section and radiators mounted within side pods.
Fuel/tanks:	Marston rubberised foam filled bag; 39 gal capacity.
Wheels/tyres:	Front: 10in rim x 13in diam. alloy centrelock. Rear: 18.5in rim x 13in diam. alloy centrelock. Fitted Goodyears in range of sizes and compounds.
Brakes:	Lockheed vented disc/calipers all round.
Suspension:	Front: Unequal length wishbone with top rocking arm pivoting on outriggers to inboard coilspring/damper units. Rear: Twin top link bottom wishbone with twin radius rods, outboard mounted coil spring/damper units.
Weight:	594kg (1307lb).
Bhp/ton laden:	610.
Top speed:	180mph, plus.
Remarks:	Very unusually for Lotus, the car was over 40lb outside the minimum formula weight regulation of 575kg.

In 1977, the Lotus 78s of Andretti and Peterson were quite simply in a different league from all the other F1 cars – Colin Chapman had discovered 'ground effect'. A new technology which changed the face of Grand Prix racing. (Pictures: Colin Taylor Productions).

the side pods also had join up with air flowing over the tops, and this was altering the required angle of the rear wing and, consequently, its effect.

Further, the 78's wing sections were to all intents and purposes fixed and unalterable, governed both by the required radiator area, and the need to slither under the side fuel tanks made mandatory by a 'maximum size' rule then in force.

These might have been shortcomings if your viewpoint was inside Ketteringham Hall, Lotus' country house H.Q., but even with these problems the 78 was fast demolishing lap times, if not in a straight line.

Rather fortuitously, the fuel tank rule was changed in good time for the following year's all conquering 79 to be given a single big central fuel cell no wider than the driver, a design feature not as new as it looked. The V16 rear-engined Auto Unions of the later 1930s had one exactly the same.

It was late autumn before the 78's successor began taking shape. The first thing to disappear was much of that rear suspension barrier, thanks to different uprights, inboard rocking arm suspensions and much lowered and streamlined bottom links permitting the side pods to alter radically.

First they were much lengthened, giving a major increase in their area, and they also moved a long way towards becoming venturi tubes rather than a wing section on each side of the car.

Downforce, previously inferior to theory, improved by leaps and bounds. Once Andretti and Peterson climbed aboard, that threatening tide started coming in for opposing teams with an awful inevitability. By the end of the year the undisputed king of F1 was a chunky figure in that well known corduroy peaked cap – Colin Chapman.

Anyone who had then chosen to forecast that the Team Lotus would be fighting to gain even a slot in the middle of the grid within a few months would have been considered a total clown, due for a long rest in his local funny farm. Yet he would have been absolutely correct ....

Formula 1: Brabham BT46/B 'Fan Car'

The code name was "Automatic Clutch" – on drawings, for parts, in conversation – successfully shielding one of the best kept secrets ever, in the security colander that envelopes most of Formula One.

Twenty one weeks from the first tentative thoughts to a car that won first time out in commanding fashion. It had stayed a secret for twenty of those weeks. By the twenty second week it was past history, for loan in silent display, defeated not by another car, but by a war of words. The war raged without a break throughout its brief life, until the team that created it killed it voluntarily – the Brabham BT46/B, the Fan Car.

It never ran again after Niki Lauda ran rings round everyone, generally on the outside of corners, in Sweden in July 1978. Yet astonishingly, it had not only been accepted as legal by officials at the race, but also in later inspection by a French aerodynamicist and airflow expert commissioned by the then CSI to cross check its designers' claims.

It promised to alter the whole technical approach and construction of cars in F1, so good it threatened to make everyone else a non-runner overnight. Nobody in the then up and coming FOCA wanted to rock the boat that badly. Bernie Ecclestone, architect and chief of the Association was also head of Brabham. It was his car, his hope for victories and Championships. But the whole future of F1 was moving into a new era. The future was full of uncertainties and threat. A united front was judged by everyone as the most important thing at the time – and the Fan Car was finished. It no longer needed sponsor Parmalat's inscribed dustbid lid that covered most of the secrets so briefly from paddock prowlers.

But the work and ingenuity that had gone into putting it on the grid at all was staggering even by the inventive, high speed standards of F1.

It began in February 1978 beneath the almost visible cloud of depression then covering everybody not connected with the Lotus 78 at Kyalami, in South Africa. With two wins in three Grands Prix, and the Lotus 79 a ghastly apparition peeping over the horizon, the opposition were not happy men, not happy at all.

Brabham's designer Gordon Murray, and his right-hand man David North had only a few weeks earlier been viewing the coming season with reasonable good cheer. They had three hard years of development on the Alfa Romeo flat-12 behind them, a highly promising degree of reliability and hopefully a useful power advantage over anyone else.

Whatever else they needed it was not the Lotus 78. Said Gordon Murray looking back "You could watch it pulling itself into the ground.

"Everybody was looking at it, trying to figure out exactly how Chapman was doing it. It was so hard to visualise what was hidden under those pods at the time.

"Our 46 was a brand new car. We'd done three years getting the engine good and reliable, but with a flat-12 there was no way, no way at all, we could build a wing car.

"Bernie (Ecclestone, Brabham boss) asked me how Lotus would do in the rest of the season. I said that with that sort of downforce it must have a lot of drag. Once we got on the fast circuits we would not have to worry.

"But it was just about as fast. It was definitely despair time. Lotus appeared to be getting about double the downforce of our ordinary wings with only the same drag. A conventional wing was not enough any more to keep up in the corners. Our problem was what to do having a flat-12. It was 32 per cent wider than the Cosworth.

"We did consider trying to build a true mid-engine car – flat-12 in the middle with two monocoques one ahead and one behind, but it would have been too heavy.

"David and I sat down and had a very hard look at the rules concerning aerodynamic devices. They had been written to stop adjustable wings and flaps. The wording was to the effect that anything with a primarily aerodynamic function had to be rigidly fixed to the fully sprung parts of the car. The word 'primarily' was presumably to avoid a lot of arguments about wing cross-sections on wishbone tubes – something like that.

"We had already been working along the lines of keeping air from getting under the car, lowering the separation point so that as much as possible went over the top. That was part of the thinking behind the triangular section monocoque, and we had a Vee-shaped barrier under the car as well.

"We didn't have a sudden revelation looking at the office vacuum cleaner ...! We knew Chaparral had used two small Snowmobile engines to pull air out from under one of their sports cars. All these things were in the back of our minds as we kept on passing ideas backwards and forwards.

"We gradually began to wonder what size of fan you needed to pull air out, how much air, how much power and what would it do? We decided we had five primary problems to solve: 1) could it be fitted on the existing car, 2) a skirt system that would have to seal round all the suspension, driveshafts and exhausts, 3) size and position of a radiator, 4) how to drive a fan and 5) size and material of the fan.

"We felt that if the primary job of the fan was to cool the engine, any suction effect was an extra and stayed within the rules.

"The thing was we didn't know anything about fans at all, but after asking around a bit we were told of a plastic fan about 18" diameter, developed for the Chieftain tank radiators, that might be a start.

"Once we had that a whole new series of difficulties appeared. Would its inertia affect the clutch feel for the driver, could we declutch it in some way, could our gearbox be made to drive it, what speed would a plastic fan designed for 2000rpm go to, what did it need to go to anyway, and what happened if the blade tips went supersonic?

"There were only three months to Monaco. We made that our target and called the project 'Automatic Clutch' to try and keep total secrecy."

Work began. Initial airflow calculations indicated that around 7000rpm would be needed for the fan. Fortunately the gearbox had a reverse shaft with a spline in a usable position. An extra sub-box was designed to replace the endplate, and containing a reduction gear, a sprag clutch that disengaged on the overrun and an idler that not only reversed rotation but could be knocked out of gear by mechanics when it came into the pits. (Only the reduction gear survived to the end, the rest were eliminated).

The first tests soon showed that the fan exploded long before 7000rpm! There were experiments with 3, 4, 5 and 6 blade versions. The manufacturers offered sixteen weeks delivery of blades reinforced with fibreglass, but did it in a week after some enthusiastic suggestions that they might do it by the next afternoon. A friction clutch was fitted externally to give the fan a chance to accelerate a bit more gently – only to later join the sprag clutch in the scrap bin.

It needed 100 drawings for the patterns, parts and gears – and there were still the total unknowns of cooling, radiator size, shape and position, not to mention the sealing system.

Murray continues: "We had theoretical figures of airflow through the fan, but we were going to trap all the exhaust, block and gearbox heat under a sealed box. We needed all new rear bodywork, a radiator lying flat on top of the engine, but by far our biggest task was devising, making and sealing a set of skirts.

"They were plastic with flexible plastic lips curved inwards and the edges in turn had little stainless steel springs pressing them onto the road. The uprights had to have panels cut to match their shape exactly, and these in turn needed to slide up and down in the side plates.

"The rear wing would no longer go on the gearbox and had to be carried on vertical endplates. The exhaust pipes needed a heatproof and leakproof seal round them. If the side and back skirts were bad the one across the car was terrible.

"The little springs that held the side and rear down in contact with the road were successfully blown-up by the force of air under the car long before the top speed of 170 or so, and just destroyed the suction. If we strengthened the springs to hold it down at speed, the lip wore itself away in no time when the car slowed down.

"We had modified an aircraft airspeed indicator, with pitot tube on the front bodywork, and the other feed into the suction area, so the driver could see it was all working. I think the reading was 70 knots. He just had to watch the dial to see it didn't fall below that.

"We nearly gave up on the front skirt. Finally David got a brilliant idea to back the lip of the seal with little sewn-up sailcloth bags fed with higher pressure air by pipes from the forward side which then pressurised the bags according to how fast the car was going, and pushed the lip down harder onto the road. The bags also had a series of inter-connecting holes, and finally they blew up exactly right.

"At this stage we took it to Alfa's test track near Milan and tried it out. The fan immediately disintegrated. We put in our second generation blades and they were torn in two. Before they went we found it wouldn't cool either. We had to keep making different radiators, altering both area and thickness of the matrix.

"But the most memorable thing about those tests, when it did work briefly, was John Watson doing standing starts. I have never seen anything that went like it. He was

Secret series of pictures taken for Gordon Murray during testing and development of the fan car. These particular photographs were taken at Brands Hatch to analyse skirt behaviour and show: 1) braking for Paddock bend; 2) apex of Paddock bend; 3 & 4) exit of Druids bend. (Pictures: Gordon Murray/Brabham)

dropping the clutch straight in at 11,000rpm and getting virtually 2G acceleration. Then our third generation blades started holding together – at any rate for an hour though not for the full length of a race and we had a smaller area, but very thick radiator matrix that could just about cope. We never ran it that long.

"We then made two decisions – not to go to Monaco, making Sweden the first outing, and to start building two more cars. It was all or nothing. When we were less than two weeks away from Sweden, we decided to go to Brands Hatch for two days, try to keep it private, testing and taking pictures on all the corners to see what was happening to the skirt sealing at speed.

"It was the first time anybody got any hint of what we were doing and not much then. We got fuel vaporisation with all that heat locked inside, but that was dealt with. We had small removable panels in the bodywork to get at the rollbars, shock absorbers and metering unit to avoid having to take any bodywork off. Everything looked good – and then the fan exploded again.

"But this time it was the hub, and it was a very very complicated plastic moulding that held the blades in such a way that their angles were adjustable. There was no way we could get it strengthened like the blades.

"We decided to try and make one ourselves in magnesium from the solid. They were so difficult that one of our best blokes working on the lathe full time only got four halves done in the week available. On top of that we had found one of the blades cracked. So in that week we also drew new blades, had them cast in magnesium, machined them and fitted them in the new hubs, but we got to Anderstorp."

When the cars rolled down out of the Brabham transporter, the acrimony really hit the fan. The sporting scene was instantly rent by criticism, envy, cries of "Illegal!", "Unfair!", "Dangerous!" and a series of paddock motorhome meetings began pulsating as the opposition sought any way of dealing with this threat that didn't involve having to actually race against it on the track.

Heads down against the hullabaloo, the team got on with trying to qualify their brainchild. The scrutineers cleared it. Practice began disastrously. Every time the car went out it came back with the front transverse skirt, which lay across the car somewhere under the driver's knees, either ripped off or badly damaged. When it went the suction went with it. Replaced or repaired it was promptly pulled off again.

Murray takes up the tale again: "Finally, talking to both drivers after the front skirt was pulled bodily right out of the monocoque we realised at long last what was happening. There was one bit on the course that had been resurfaced and there was a tiny ramp – perhaps $\frac{3}{8}$ of an inch at the most that the car had to go up and over. The skirt was catching on it.

"We made some long narrow tapered wedge ramps from plastic strip and fixed them underneath ahead of the skirt to lift the car up over the bump, and they worked".

With that cured, the cars were in with a serious chance. Both Lauda and Watson were discreetly advised to take it a bit easy, and they practised with the weight of full tanks. Extra wing drag and power loss driving the fan meant the cars were relatively slow on the straight – an estimated 20mph down – but in long sweeping corners they were effortlessly faster.

For the first time the drivers were able to really stretch them. It was instantly obvious the downforce was enough to squash the rear suspension straight down onto the bump stops, upset the balance of the car and make it seriously nose light.

It needed much harder coils and the team did not have them. They had to be content with setting the car rear high statically while the big front wings had maximum flap wound on. It didn't help the straight line speed one bit, but in the corners it had so much grip the opposition had extremely good reason to be worried. Then in the middle of all the paddock aggro one of the spare plastic fans exploded in practice. Murray: "We were going to meetings, arguing, pleading the case for the car and at the same time trying to cure all the last minute snags.

"The embarrassing thing, as the fan ran all the time, was that the car really sat down on the rear springs and then jumped up again every time the mechanics blipped the throttle working on the engine. Everyone could see it worked."

Despite "discretion" Watson found himself on the front row – and the paddock arguments exploded into formal protest. The fan was said to be a "moving aerodynamic aid".

"No" said the team "Not so. Nearly 70 per cent of its work is as a cooling fan for the engine. That is its primary function. Only 30 per cent of its work is providing downforce".

Pocket calculators positively steamed in the hands of rival team managers and designers anxious to disprove it on the spot. They lacked almost any of the pertinent data, but it didn't stop them both trying and announcing that the car was certainly illegal.

Other drivers proclaimed it dangerous to follow because of the blast of stones and gravel it would be hurling at them out of the fan housing.

A huge row within FOCA itself before the race resulted in a decision that the car could run once but would have to be withdrawn after that. It started and with Niki Lauda driving took its unique first place – just.

"I don't think it would have done more than another couple of laps or so. The fan was loose on its shaft. The cooling only just coped. It ran at over boiling point for the whole race. And the course suited it with long loop type corners. On a really fast course with long straights the top speed handicap would have been too much to pull back.

"The really interesting thing is that the CSI Technical Committee sent a French aerodynamics and airflow expert to England immediately after the race, to measure the fan, its airflow and everything to do with it. His figures agreed very closely with ours – just over 60 percent of airflow was doing the cooling and the rest being utilised for downforce. They agreed it was within the rules. But we had already started on the 47 – the day we got back from Sweden.

"In retrospect perhaps it was right to stop using it because I think the logical result was that teams would have needed two types of vehicle at once – venturi cars on fast circuits and fan cars on the slow ones. Think of the cost of that!"

Technical data on fan:

Axial Flow Fan with static vanes – 6 blade, 17.8 inch diameter.
Maximum Speed – 7000rpm.
Blade angle – 26 degrees.
Tip clearances – 0.040 in.
Tip speed at maximum rpm – 371mph.
Flow – 14,000cfm free air.
Maximum exit speed – 50mph.
Power required – 25bhp.
Estimated extra drag (transverse skirts and front wing angle) – 15bhp.
Extra weight of installation – 70lbs.
Maximum depression with perfect seal – 0.25psi.
Area – 31.8 square feet.
Total maximum downforce – 1145lbs.

Specification – Brabham BT46/B 'Fan Car'

Engine:	Rear-mounted 3-litre Alfa-Romeo flat-12, 4-cam. Fuel injected. Marelli ignition. 520bhp.
Final drive:	Brabham/Alfa 5 or 6-speed transaxle unit. Full range of interchangeable gear ratios, with alternative final drives.
Chassis/shell:	Aluminium alloy monocoque, rear outriggers to semi-stressed engine block. GRP body panelling.
Fuel tank:	Five interconnected foam-filled tanks with balance system. Maximum capacity of 46 gal.
Wheels/tyres:	Front: Centrelock alloy: 11in rim x 13 in diam. Rear: Centrelock alloy: 18in rim x 13in diam.
Brakes:	Front and rear: 10.5in diam. x 1 in thick ventilated iron discs with 4-pot calipers.
Suspension:	Front: Unequal length double wishbone; tubular pullrod links to inboard coil spring/damper units. Anti-roll bar. Rear: Transverse links with radius rods; outboard coil spring/damper units mounted outboard on base of upright. Anti-rollbar.
Weight:	640kg (1408lb).
Bhp/ton (laden):	600/735 (dependant on fuel load).
Top speed:	170mph plus.
Remarks:	Gearbox specially modified to provide external drive to fan through 2-stage gears and torque-limiting clutch.

⑥ A Case History ~ the conception, development and building of the Gould~Terrapin.

After more years than I care to be exact about, messing with cars of every possible type from filthy rusting road hacks to my latest Terrapin single-seater, on any part of which I could invite a friend to eat his lunch, I made a decision ....

It was the decision never, ever again to embark on building another car. The only way I would become involved was to the extent of offering advice to someone who would supply all the money, all the energy and be an enjoyable personality with it.

David Gould had entered my life at a southern hillclimb one summer day, towing two small boys, diffidently mentioning he had been building a Terrapin for some years but was about to give up. When he explained he had no garage, worked sixty miles from where he lived, had four youngsters, often had to cycle three miles to reach the chassis taking slow shape in a relative's smithy before he could do anything with it, I was suitably impressed. Who wouldn't have been!

When, much later that night, I staggered and tripped my way over a sea of metallic bric-a-brac in the

aforementioned smithy, the quality of his workmanship left me open-mouthed. Only the fact that I lived 200 miles away stopped an immediate promise to share the completion work as long as he would please keep going.

However, somewhat surprisingly, just the knowledge that other cars and builders existed relit his enthusiasm. The car that emerged in due course finally held every 1100cc hillclimb record in Britain but one (Prescott), though it took seven years of painfully dedicated development to achieve.

While reaching the top of that particular mountain, David's business life progressed too, which meant that when thoughts of a 1600cc arose, the use of a first class engine and other components didn't have to be a pipe-dream. Also he now had the Standard British Garage near the back door of his home and it had been possible long since to relegate the faithful bicycle first to his sons, and thence to the big bicycle shed in the sky.

If you have to sit around a lot discussing a plan to attack the very best of opposition in any sphere, a good place is the edge of a Majorcan

swimming pool. Our families shared a villa holiday, whilst we drank and sketched and talked and drank.

His existing Terrapin already had an 1100 BDA Ford grafted onto a Mini gearbox, sitting in exactly the same place as a normal Mini engine but delivering some 136bhp instead of 100.

Could a 1600cc be persuaded into the same car? The short answer was yes — but at the cost of an unreliable gearbox, already showing serious signs of unhappiness with those 136 Cosworth horses, let alone 220. Not to mention the outrigged flywheel on a taper and ratio change limitations.

Such power would require better-than-Mini driveshafts, plunging joints, different hubs to accept them, different wheels to fit new hubs, discs instead of the faithful alloy drums and, probably, totally new geometry. Different front and rear pickups for wishbones alone dictated a new chassis.

The long answer had got to be a new car from the ground up. Could it be built as light and small as the 1100 without entering the exotic worlds of titanium and aircraft light alloys? If so that had to be a flying start to tackling one of the hardest fought classes in British motorsport. So far as we could ascertain the opposition weight hovered between 9-10cwt and our aim was 7cwt.

Really good transverse engines with gearbox in unit underneath rather than stuck on the end are thin on the ground. When you have said "Ferrari Dino" and moved yourself up into the unlimited class the list is nearly finished.

The result of many hours agonising was that a transverse rear engine with its superlative ability to put every ounce of available power on the road was no longer possible. It had to be a 1600BDA with Hewland box. One advantage of such a box, we estimated, was that only 18 or 19 gearchanges would be needed during the 43 seconds it takes to go up Prescott Hill instead of 25 with a Mini box.

It is not easy now to visualise how difficult it was as recently as the summer of 1978 to understand what Colin Chapman was doing underneath his revolutionary Lotus 78 wing car. However long we talked and drank, we could not conceive such results coming simply off a shaped bit of side bodywork, yet, crudely speaking that was exactly what *was* happening. Strangely enough I had been so near and yet so far from part of the answer on two occasions without being aware of it.

The first time was failing to understand what was happening to my first Terrapin at 140mph when it took various British and International speed records some ten years earlier.

I had some excellent pictures of the car in profile at speed in which the whole car had tilted nose down to the extent that the special alloy "droop snout" covering the front radiator intake scraped the concrete surface of the runway at Elvington airfield in Yorkshire where the attempts were being timed.

I now realise that the underside of the car – for reasons entirely to do with getting suspension pickups in the right place – actually formed an excellent venturi shape. Although of course it was not skirted, it seems now that the only possible reason for

downforce strong enough to crush the soft front down over two inches, to the bump stops, and hold it there, had to be a degree of ground effect.

The second time was in an article for the Monoposto Racing Club magazine in which I had argued that a slice off a wing section, even if narrow, could still give worthwhile downforce if it was long enough to produce a useful working area. But the argument happened to be aimed at using large chord rear wings, not side pods.

Being able to see the precise shape of the furniture that can be made from the wood in the forest is one of a number of differences that existed between Mr Chapman and the rest of the world.

We were to blunder about in the semi-dark over ground effects for another six months before finalising the design, but it was integrated in such a way that this did not delay the car. Only its builder having to go on working for a living between stints in the garage did that.

Decision one was whether the structure was to be a tube chassis or monocoque? Our friend and fellow designer Keith Gowers had not then constructed his cunningly simple Monopin (already described) or offered the immortal advice: "I'll never build a tube chassis again as long as I live".

Largely because the experience of both of us was founded in space frame cars and some private reservations about stressing a monocoque in "life and death" areas, it was decided to stay with tubes, but narrowing and lowering the concept to cut frontal area and weight. This was assisted materially by the fact that D.G. is not only fairly small but has sufficient iron self-control, when desperately required, to diet his weight down to a minimum at the beginning of the season.

Other aims we planned to try and stick with through thick and thin were, in order of priority:

1)   Maximum possible stiffness.
2)   No stressing of engine or gearbox casing.
3)   Suspension geometry founded on long swing axle lengths to keep camber alteration in braking and acceleration to a minimum.

4)   The best aerodynamics we could devise without having access to a wind tunnel.
5)   Lightest and best brakes available.

The primary hurdles these put before us to support were:-

1)   How to get the engine/box out if it was caged within a properly rigid structure.
2)   How to feed the enormous loads reacted by a 226bhp motor into the chassis safely and reliably without putting the crankshaft main bearings even a potential 0.001 in out of line.
3)   What angles would available tyres tolerate and how large could suspension movements be if it became a wing car?
4)   How did one approach designing a car with ground effect? Having worked out at least the skirts these were promptly banned by the FIA and a lot of re-thinking became necessary. As it happened, need we have bothered?
5)   How to persuade racing discs skimmed down by 60% thickness to $\frac{1}{4}$ inch at most, to function in available calipers.

At this point, living as we did 220 miles apart, we decided to set up a design centre at which to meet regularly.

It was on the large table nearest to the coffee machines at Leicester Forest East Service Centre on the M1.

It proved practical to transport drawings, models, pencils and copious notes from Newbury in Berkshire and Pateley Bridge in Yorkshire to the table by 8.30pm on any chosen evening. We would then work together until normally about 2.0am, to the polite fascination of staff, lorry drivers, returning holiday-makers and all the other mysterious post-midnight eaters on the M1.

There is, seriously, absolutely no substitute for the endless kicking back and forth of ideas as the car takes shape if it is a combined operation of design, and it was during those late winter nights, and early mornings, that a large part of the design was worked out.

It was probably helpful that the environment was a totally non-alcoholic one, together with the constant pressure to get as much done

This joint between two identical bulkhead cum rollover bars allows the Gould-Terrapin tube chassis to be separated into two halves to allow engine removal. The eyes in the vertical bar are to allow alterations in anti-squat geometry. (Picture: David Gould).

He solved it by proposing to make the car in two parts joined in the middle. This would be achieved by having identical twin rollover bars, one on the front half, the other on the rear, joined by a ring of small bolts passing through bushes that aligned themselves automatically by taper seating ends (see photograph).

I suggested that if some of these bushes had suitable gaps between them they would accept the ears of a large alloy plate welded on the front of the engine. This dual approach solved engine/gearbox removal, the front engine mountings, and all torque reaction into the frame at one fell swoop. For good measure the engine plate triangulated the centre bulkhead, thus permitting the engine to stay totally unstressed — all with a piece of NS4 alloy plate weighing $2\frac{1}{2}$lb.

At the power unit's opposite end, the gearbox would be suspended from the massive "ears" already cast in it from the now perfectly triangulated rear bulkhead.

The inboard rear brakes, were going to give the rear suspension links a slightly happier life, although loadings are anyway much less than those fed in under acceleration, thanks to the rearward weight transfer, ultra soft sticky rears and a lot of everybody else's rubber plastered on the average start line.

More effort, clandestine and open measurement of other cars, plus thinking and drinking went into the wheel frequencies to be used and the coils that would be required to do the job. As the car did not at that time of course, even exist, our figures of sprung/unsprung weight and front/rear distribution had to be calculated — well, calculated guesses if you wish.

It is possible to execute a diagram which will provide such information, but to do one you have to know exactly what is going into the car

in the time available, before having not only to complete the 260 mile round trip home but to get up next morning to give of one's best earning the daily bread.

Four months after the first discussions we had most of the decisions made, a balsa wood model including Hewland with inboard discs, plus a BDA exactly down to scale length of the longest injection trumpets expected to be used.

DG had the most ingenious idea

in the whole concept — but which also turned out to be nearly as much trouble to actually construct as the rest of the car put together. Roll bar struts, both forwards and backwards to construct a pyramid over three quarters of the chassis length, were all to be welded in permanently.

It meant the engine, once installed, could not be removed again without hacksaw, welding torch, or both, clearly not the best idea in the world.

and weights of all individual items involved.

These are precisely what you usually do not have at the time you need them. Better to guesstimate the total weight, having read all you can about the opposition, split it 50 front/50 rear for a front engined two seater and 35 front/65 rear for a rear engined car as a basis for planning your coil spring spaces. Equip yourself with a list of off-the-shelf coils, for instance those supplied by David Faulkner (see Appendix), so you don't end up needing some technically or otherwise impossible article at a desperately late stage of the construction.

As we were aiming at a 7cwt, or so, vehicle, it was decided to stay near to previously highly successful wheel frequencies of about 100 CPM in the fronts and 115 CPM in the rears.

Later refinements would have to follow a visit to a weighbridge with the driver in the car. Despite a tendency of people to think a driver's head is large and heavy, the legs from the hip joints down are a lot heavier — about half your total body weight. As they will lie almost completely ahead of the vehicle's centre of gravity, whereas the trunk, head and arms rest more or less vertically near the same point, the driver affects the front sprung weight of the car more than he does the rear in the average single-seater and even more so in a rally or circuit racing saloon.

Actual figures on the DG car were later found to be 54% of his bodyweight onto the front wheels and 46% on the rears, this in an ultra-short-wheelbase car where the engine front pulley was almost in the driver's kidneys.

Among the data we did have were the figures for a March 763 — well before the advent of ground effect and perhaps an indicator we hoped might still have some relevance. These were a front frequency of 104 CPM and rear of 125 and, while we chose to ignore them at the time, it is curious that after one half season of endless experiment the DG car — running on infinitely poorer surfaces in terms of grip and endless camber variations — arrived at wheel frequencies of 126.5 CPM front and 129.4 rear, on a physically appreciably lighter vehicle,

but with ground effect making it heavier to some degree, possibly 96 CPM front and 111 CPM rear.

However, before one draws too concrete a set of conclusions from this you have to remember there were several other parts of the equation, including total weight distribution and the unsprung/sprung weight ratios differing quite substantially from the March.

By the second season things were beginning to get so sensitive that a frequency alteration at the front of only 7 CPM from 126 to 133, could make an appreciable difference in feel — for the worse.

The biggest unknown of all in those four years had to be tyres, and we had no base line founded in mechanics, like a spring rate, on which to attempt comparisons, let alone any detailed technical information on how tyres had altered or in what direction or manner.

There were also to be quite strong anti-roll bars front and rear. Despite all our calculations and theorising, they turned out to be far too soft and were more than doubled in stiffness by changes of size within the first season.

There remained the exact suspension geometry wheel rates and the aerodynamics.

DG was strongly inclined to get away from wheels going more than a very small amount negative or positive in bounce and droop — a major departure from the thinking in the original Terrapin.

He also had to obtain whatever uprights were going into the car to give us at least an idea of where the outboard pivots would be. Under the usual technological guidelines of "What can you get?" and "How much?", they ended up as ex-Ralt F3 fronts and FF Titan rears.

Once measured, they were modelled into two String Computers — my original "old faithful" and a very superior Rolls-Royce version in white melamine (the stuff they make bathroom and white bedroom furniture from) which DG constructed full size.

While this certainly halves errors straight away, the average designer's arm is ill-suited to instantaneous roll centres some ten or fifteen feet away

when locating the intersection point of long swing axle layouts.

A helper is essential and David's son, Sean, spent many restless hours on this vital but unglamorous part of the job. Hopefully he was suitably rewarded when in due course he was let loose on Donington's test track to try out the result some 15 months later. Exchanging results of endless experiments by post, the geometry was finalised so that exact dimensions of the frame could be fixed.

At least we had been confident working in this area, but then the train plunged well and truly into the blackness of the tunnel as we started on the aerodynamics.

It did seem to us not sensible to simply sketch some wing shaped outline into our design when accurate patterns of known airfoil sections and their aerodynamic properties are available (see bibliography in appendices).

We chose three final possibles that seemed appropriate to the speeds involved in a hillclimb car, NACA 4415, 4418 and 4421. Scale drawings of the chassis side view soon eliminated 4421 because when made to the length available — right to the end of the gearbox, its curvature at an 8 degree angle of attack had it scraping along the ground.

We also could not easily then decide the clearance between the deepest point of the curve and the ground, which would govern the cross section of the venturi into which we hoped the air would be flowing. Cutting short the dozens of hours of discussion, we chose 4415 at 9 degree angle of attack with a two inch gap to the bottom edge of the chassis plus the ground clearance of the car.

It was planned that the vertical side panels of bodywork on the pods would in due course be as low as we would get away with — skirted to the ground with plastic or draught excluder brush if possible, but clear of it by some unknown dimension if not.

Talking of draught excluder brush, this is so resistant to airflow at about quarter inch thick that you cannot blow through it. As the lungs develop about 2psi with your eyes out like chapel hat pegs and you are talking only of ounces in the most successful of ground effect cars, it has often mystified me a little why it went out in favour of the tungsten and diamond edged skirts that began all the trouble.

While undoubtedly impervious to air trying to blow through them, the contact of solid skirts with the road has to be more erratic and less perfect than a correctly riding edge of several hundred thousand flexible bristles.

In the end a fullsize copy of NACA 4415 cut from hardboard was used as a master to tailor left and right hand pods individually to each side of the car.

Support brackets were governed absolutely by its outline, with radiators, dry sump tank, tiny fuel tank, pumps and piping being subordinated to the space that resulted.

The only major point on which we disagreed, but didn't fall out, was the top bodywork. I wanted the whole top deck to flow to the rear of the car and beyond, ending in a small slotted flap with considerable adjustment.

DG preferred to go for a full wing on a Hewland mounted single centre pole — and as he happened to be doing the work as well as paying for it, a

separate wing it was and is.

A full front wing was also used so that the car could be trimmed front and rear if our theories on the side pods gave some unexpectedly horrific results.

About this time DG revealed an unsuspected talent, in that he could actually do proper engineering drawings of what had hitherto been only sketches and a model. These were so successful that he was even able to perceive that part of the clutch lever and slave cylinder would be in the centre of a chassis tube, unless moved. I was deeply impressed, as reading an engineering drawing is one of a considerable number of talents I do not possess.

As soon as building begins it is best, if at all possible, to have the engine and box you are going to use (or at least a borrowed block and empty gearbox casing) on the spot. These, together with that other major item of unalterable size and proportions to be installed, the driver, make it a great deal easier to check and locate brackets, clearances and so on as construction proceeds.

I am well aware that factory professionals do it a little more scientifically, but they also have drawing offices and need to instruct third parties in exactly what they want made to the last thou. Interestingly enough, Hewland subscribe so strongly to the "build round it" approach they will make a dummy box available if you ask nicely.

So work began ....
Despite hopes of being quicker, it took nine months in a wooden garage of such modest size that it was difficult to move one's elbow to raise a tea mug once the car began to take shape. Constant weight checking of everything that went into it was always considered vital. Unsprung weight

The completed multi-tube spaceframe (below and overleaf) of the Gould-Terrapin, a structure which provided almost perfect rigidity. Note the triangulated rollover bar cum bulkhead and the outline of the underbody venturi sections built into the sides of the structure. (Pictures: David Gould).

(wheel, tyre, upright, half coil spring, damper units etc.) almost exactly 50 pounds a corner, power unit and box 310 pounds (less than the Mini which gave barely half the power in previous years), chassis totally complete: 120 pounds.

On the Oulton weighbridge, in late autumn, it missed the target from the previous 1100 car by only 26 pounds at $7\frac{1}{2}$cwt.

But two months earlier, in August, it was still some way off completion.

My previous resolution never to have anything to do with constructing another car weakened to the extent of taking a few days holiday, residing on Dave's front room settee and helping with the mountain of small tasks that still needed doing. To spur and inspire us both, I suggested he enter the car for the two last sprints of the year – both at Oulton Park in mid-October.

One modification forced originally by lack of space but which saves a very useful pound of weight can be applied to any car with a self-starter. The Bendix drive and coil spring that accepts the shock of the starter dog being hurled out of mesh when an engine fires, wanted to go through a chassis tube. The starter as it happened had never been on any drawing. The solution employed was to cut almost two inches off the end of the shaft, slinging the redundant bits into the scrap bin, and leaving only space to hold a slice of old rubber doorstop, the end being rethreaded to take the retaining nut and big washer. It has given no trouble and worked perfectly – even after the doorstop disintegrated and fell out.

Not at the time having a clear understanding of what the air might be doing under the car we had come down finally in favour of staying with outboard suspension. This was on the twin grounds that at the rear there would be quite a generous clearance between foil surface and any links and driveshaft, while at the front inboard units would need not only a top rocking arm with all its complications of construction and pivoting, but also space that would effectively force us to lengthen the car three or four inches. That would not only increase the weight but also alter the track/wheelbase ratio, which was being kept as low as possible.

Both, in retrospect, were errors, and highlight at least one of the reasons why F1 teams build new cars every year – difficulties and mistakes can so often only be eliminated by starting all over again if a design is totally compact and perfectly integrated. The alternative can only be to cut and bodge.

Two aspects of the car's construction are directly applicable to much wider fields. One is bodywork, always a thorny situation, though much eased latterly by fibreglass mouldings, but still far from easy either practically or aesthetically.

Side panels and the flat top deck leading to a rear wing have made things simpler, as have needle noses, but there remains the need for some sort of surround for the driver, not to mention the engine.

Research into photographs of Formula Ford produced a possible top panel that would not only do the job for the front half, but suitably shortened and turned about face would produce a graceful and usable rear panel covering the engine and helping airflow towards the leading edge of the rear wing.

As beauty is in the eye of the beholder, you will have to judge the degree of success from the car itself, but we were very happy with it, at much less cost and vastly less work than having to produce a full size model, mould and frame and finally moulding fibreglass.

The second decision that was helpful was to almost totally standardise the size and pattern of the spherical joints to be used at $\frac{3}{8}$ inch UNF shank taking a $\frac{5}{16}$ inch ball bolt. Any future constructor would probably be well advised to use 10mm/8mm, its rough metric equivalent.

It means you can often get handsome discounts by being able to buy more at a time and nearly every situation of making threads for adjustable links can be dealt with by the purchase of only two sets of taps – one left hand and one normal right, in a single size. Higher load factors are often better dealt with by simply buying a better quality joint in the same size rather than going up in physical dimensions.

We aso devised a micro-adjuster that saves a lot of time and trouble in any link, particularly when it is advantageous or essential to bolt in one end solid with maximum possible strength, which normally permits only a half turn adjustment at a time.

This is shown in the illustration. There is a most ingenious approach pioneered so far as I know by March, for a joint on the outboard ends of the wishbones, essentially for camber adjustment.

Much easier to sketch than explain, this is also shown in the illustration. It avoids having to remove the joint from its ballpin to rotate it, and has certainly been "borrowed" by many constructors.

Building had begun on January 31st. On October 6th, DG towed the almost complete work of art into my driveway *en route* to Oulton, having never run, unpainted, and with only the suspension angles set.

It was tried there and then, a road silencer only managing to take the worst off the howl of a truly formidable 1600BDA. The clutch worked, the gears appeared to select and the throttle showed reasonable delicacy and no sign of a reluctance to close. Both of us had, in the past, had a stuck throttle. (Mine hurled an early Mini into a concrete lamp post, protected only by a single straw bale, and broke it clean off at the base), so we were very wary of such a possibility with a power weight ration of some 520bhp/ton.

The next morning it faced the scrutineer, fired up on the button and rolled onto the start line. Working with some of the first Michelins outside works teams, there were plenty of unknowns and one of them was grip.

The engine only came properly on cam at about 6500rpm with some 140bhp climbing to a maximum of 226BHP at just over 10,000. First time off it had so much grip it tried to die on the line at 6000rpm. This had to be good news.

As everyone knows, all new cars work perfectly "straight out of the box" – but mysteriously go downhill thereafter. Before the day was out there was oil getting out of the clutch and a marked reluctance to go into gear. It was grossly undergeared, running out of revs everywhere, and so

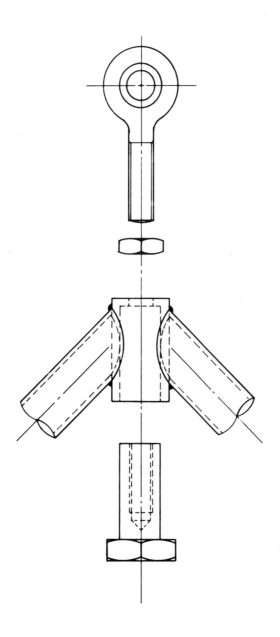

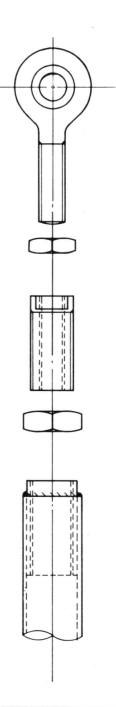

far as its owner was concerned, something was badly amiss with the handling at the front end.

I was sharing the driving, and in somebody else's car with more power than I had ever handled available before it even came on cam, I was suitably cautious. It seemed OK to me, running some five seconds slower than the owner.

Despite all this we got a first and third in a modestly supported class. A cheering start. DG brought the car back a week later for the final meeting of the year to take another first and third FTD. third FTD.

The new clutch oilseal was still leaking, it still crunched horribly going into bottom, and it was a long time before it was discovered that a Hewland gearbox spigot does not necessarily match the bearing in the centre of a Cosworth crankshaft, leaving it to float about and wreck a series of oilseals. The correct Ford Escort bearing cured the problem instantly. Flow into the sidepods and over the converted central heating

Two methods of achieving fine rod end adjustment – see text. (Drawing: Darell Staniforth).

The Gould-Terrapin's first appearance at Oulton Park – where a number of teething problems were to be experienced ... (Picture: Mark Harbord).

...The author, having been entrusted with a go, is shown on the startline ... (Picture: Mark Harbord).

...Off and running. A 'research' picture taken to study suspension behaviour from a standing start ... (Picture: Mark Harbord).

... Still at Oulton Park, the car at speed for the first time. Despite several problems the car achieved a 1st and a 3rd at this first outing — albeit in a modestly supported class. (Pictures: Mark Harbord).

elements that made up the radiator was insufficient, even for a sprint course and it boiled its head off. Then, a plug disintegrated producing the faintest hint of a miss in subsequent runs at high speed.

But we at least took into the winter two cheering clues to hopes that our ground effects, even minus skirts, were working — a generous amount of the bottom edge of each side panel had been filed off by the tarmac.

It could have been various things including roll or bottoming somewhere due to too soft springing, but a hastily snatched photograph later showed the whole car was running visibly nearer the ground at speed than at standstill in the pits.

Doing those two events at all costs had been eminently worthwhile. By the following March, it was magnificent in new white and green paintwork, a dozen small details tidied, valve seat damage caused by that failed plug expensively repaired, bushes made to accept various diameters of rollbar, a front wing designed and mounted.

This last was filled with solid foam, made by mixing two chemicals and then hastily pouring the boiling swelling result into whatever it has to fill. Strongly recommended, as long as the internal access routes and vent points are generous.

DG had to watch helplessly as his first wing bulged and distorted into useless wreckage as the foam mixture expanded all too violently inside it, but the second attempt was successful. It imparts quite extraordinary strength and rigidity to a featherlight 24g or 26g construction.

You can also use it to make an integral seat that will fit you at least as well as your skin. Graham Hill once demonstrated the process in a TV programme, sitting in a plastic bag to protect him from becoming a permanent part of the moulding. His situation allowed him to deftly insert into the script a crafty and typical witticism referring to the necessity of protecting any vulnerable orifice from permanent blockage by first covering it with a patch of tank tape. Nor was it "bleeped" out on a later repeat!

Unlike the earlier car, he (DG not Graham Hill) had chosen to design the cockpit to the smallest possible dimensions with minimal elbow room for either steering or gearchanges, but it did not seem cramped as the really vital clearances for elbows, knuckles and toes were all there. Possibly the only long term handicap of such tailor-making is seriously narrowing the market of buyers the day you want to sell by eliminating anyone over about 5'8" tall or 11 stone — probably 50% of the possible population.

Anyway, nobody, least of all DG was thinking about a buyer just then. All that mattered was the arrival of the early spring test days at Wiscombe and Loton. When they did come it took no time at all for disaster to strike. Wiscombe has a 100mph bumpy straight leading to a left hand hairpin tight enough to have a qualified nanny in trouble with a well handling pram.

The outer bank took the offside front wheel and most of the suspension straight off as the car finally understeered into trouble instead of going round.

Surely not the dreaded slow corner understeer again? It had been in the forefront of our thinking, but having been eliminated from the previous car had not seemed too serious a threat. DG had felt there could be something not right at the front during those all too short Oulton runs, but had been unable to pinpoint it. It certainly had to be pinpointed now.

Several things were hastily altered during repairs, by far the most important an increase in effective travel of the front dampers to try and remove any chance whatever of their getting onto the bump stops. This was augmented by two moves which might at first seem quite wrong — stiffer front coils and anti-roll bar.

Both these latter are conventional answers to oversteer, not understeer. But slow tight corners are places that induce extremes of "skewed roll" — either diving onto an outer front in braking and turn-in or squatting unevenly at the back accelerating out again.

In both situations you need to avoid at all costs the suspension's going down to a bump stop, and the resultant instant rise of the wheelrate either to infinity or well on the way.

Extra roll-resistance not only helps prevent this, but also keeps the wheel at a better angle to the road.

Then there was the new front wing, with its adjustable flap which combined with the other modifications to produce another ten million or so variations to try. Not to mention the back ....

Perhaps the most difficult thing with which to come to terms — as had been observed by many men entering faster formulae — was how late it was possible to use the better brakes, despite the much higher speeds.

Just talking, it had seemed reasonable that because the car would be travelling so much faster, lift-off and braking points would be similar to those engraved on the driver's mind in the 1100 car.

That turned out to be rubbish. With big discs and calipers, downforce and a bigger tyre footprint area, the car was taken further and further past the previous year's braking points, and still stopped.

This meant the driver had to learn to override all the semi-automatic reactions built up during the seven previous seasons to go repeatedly into areas where every instinct was screaming: "too fast — you're going off"

While a circuit man may get time and practice to ease himself into this situation (a Lotus F1 test for instance will give perhaps 70 or 80 laps in which to settle), neither the hillclimber nor a rallydriver is permitted such luxury. The first gets only a couple of practice runs, or tries at each corner before he's having to win or lose for real, while the second doesn't even get one.

The result of an error in either case, while not as devastating as in F1, is usually that you might as well not have entered.

Given all this, the target from the very beginning had been to win the 1600 class at every possible opportunity and set new records at the same time. This was not so much bigheaded as a cold look at the minimum requirements to make the car successful, such are the constant improvements year on year virtually without pause.

As it turned out DG did break almost every record that could be broken, excepting only Doune and Harewood, and would have ended that first season covered in total glory and fame, but for one snag. Somebody else broke them all as well – and by a slightly greater margin than he did. He had come up against the worst situation anyone can ever bite off – a superb car, with matching back-up, the very best of equipment and preparation, driven by a man combining exceptional talent with real, gritty determination.

Anyone following that branch of the sport will know the name Martin Bolsover. His results in a 1600cc humbled men with 2.2 and 2.5-litre Harts or 3-litre DFVs on embarrassingly frequent occasions, as well as gaining him several slots in the Top Ten.

To diabolically mix a metaphor, he was a double edged thorn in the side all year, an enormous spur to do even better, but we could have done without him at that stage of the game.

Back to the nitty gritty of what went well, or not so well.

Lengthy design-stage discussions on anti-squat (and rather less on anti-dive) had tended to result in suspicion of their virtues, but insertion of a number of alternative points for rear radius links which would allow easy experiment with it once the car was functioning well in other directions.

You have to overcome one thing at a time, even though as in the understeer debacle you may be forced by time to do several things at once attempting a cure, and thus never be quite sure precisely what succeeded or what proportions of the answers they contributed.

An almost immediate discovery was that anti-squat could soon destroy rear grip if overdone. While in theory 100% anti-squat should allow the maximum possible traction by the rear tyres, it simply did not work in this car in practice. 35% virtually destroyed rear grip and it was finally settled at about 12%.

In due course experiments setting the rear dampers harder and harder in bounce, in general terms a totally unorthodox and wrong approach, was not only much more successful, but appeared to bring with it little penalty in handling at speed on poor surfaces.

The Michelins had been discarded as too much of an unknown quantity in favour of the 1100 car layout well proven by competition: M&H fronts and Goodyear rears.

The front change to, perhaps, the best tailor-made hillclimb tyre then available – M&H with their 21 ultra-soft compound tread rubber – gave a very considerable increase in front grip and turn-in.

Yet again we return to the unknown "X" in the equation, the exact part tyres were playing in all this. Even had we been complete experts on the British made tyres available, which we weren't, Goodyear executives had decided to move race design and manufacturing back to America lock stock and barrel.

Future tyres were going to come from the States, with their thinking, their compounds and worst of all their new codings. And it is a good deal harder and more expensive to get informal friendly advice from Akron in distant Ohio, 4000 miles away, than from the British headquarters in Wolverhampton.

The effect of this was the secretive and mysterious arrival of a new breed of demon tyre, "Blue Streak" and "Eagle" covers with strange numbers, unknown qualities – all fitted to other cars.

After watching some of the first deliveries perform, it was very obvious that American dragster standing-start knowhow was mixed into them somewhere, but a new limitation immediately crept in.

The rear suspension had been designed around tyres with a nominal diameter of 20 inches. Ground clearance, hub centres, wishbones, were all tailored into this dimension. To take advantage of the widest F1 fronts, we had planned to use between 10.2 and 10.6 inch rear tread width.

It proved a miscalculation that caused serious trouble, as to get what proved necessary, a massive increase in the size of the contact patch demanded a 23.5 inch diameter cover as the only way of getting the necessary width.

Practising what has already been loudly preached in the suspension chapter, it forced a re-design and re-location of the rear suspension pickup points, rather than just bolting the new wheels and tyres on and lowering the spring platforms.

Very fortunately, the new pivots did not want to go in the middle of the second gear cluster or any other horribly impossible spot, but it was still a great deal of work to cut out the original mountings and re-locate them properly.

It also required wider wheels to accept the new covers. While there was a modest economy in the fact that Mamba alloy wheels are made in three pieces held together with a multitude of Allen screws permitting one or other of the rims to be bought separately in a bigger dimension and reassembled, it made it an expensive exercise.

The successive steps at the rear of the car were:

Original design: 20x10 Michelins on 11 inch rims.
First Mod: 20x10 Michelins on 12 inch rims.
Second Mod: 20x10.6 British Goodyear G55 on 12 inch rims.
Third Mod: 20x10.6 British Goodyear G55 on 13 inch rims.
Fourth Mod: 23x12 M&H 21 compound on 14 inch rims, plus suspension alterations.
Fifth Mod: 23.5x13 US Goodyears on 15 inch rims.

The car was still only at the second stage of the foregoing just in time for the Shelsley Walsh 75th anniversary, but was easily inside 31 seconds, more than quick enough to take the most coveted award, available to anyone who has ever built his own car, for some half a century.

Or so it seemed until scrutineers reported on the car to the officials of the meeting. Unbelievably it was at

Shelsley — the spiritual home of all one-off cars as enshrined in the Midland Automobile Club's "Shelsley Specials Award" — where the standards of the car's construction and its double-barrelled "Gould-Terrapin" name caused it to be rejected on the grounds that it was a professionally-built, production car!

To say DG and I were outraged was to put it mildly, and we challenged the club's decision with a barrage of letters, photographs, drawings, etc, to prove that it was what it was — a one-off vehicle built by one man in his spare time in a suburban home garage.

The infinitely diplomatic reaction of the club was to admit no past error on the information then available to them, so there could be no alteration in past awards, but as we had proved

---

Gurston Down, August 1980, and the much refined and developed Gould-Terrapin has become more seriously competitive, managing a steady stream of 3rds and 4ths. (Picture: Robert Cooper).

---

satisfactorily that it was a one-off we were eligible to compete in that category in future. It was now completely acceptable.

While these arguments were going on the rear suspension was having the major modification already described to fit the new wheels and tyres. "Stage four" was on in time for the August meeting when DG went back to put up a shattering performance.

He reduced the Shelsley Special record to wreckage with the hill's first ever sub-thirty seconds time for a home-built car, cutting it from 30.45 to 29.00 dead. It gave an extra pleasure later to be presented with the exquisite handmade model that is the trophy, adding his name to an illustrious list already engraved on the base.

The new bigger diameter covers were not only a major step forward in acceleration off the line, but permitted still harder suspensions to work on irregular surfaces.

The extraordinary thing out of all this was that they made massive improvements in times possible

without demanding miracles from the driver who felt he was trying no harder than before. A long thirty seconds became 29.00, a simply enormous improvement however you looked at it, with the identical weight and power of two months earlier. And the front still stuck down, leaving the handling very little altered.

There was a period of nasty instability until the rims were finally widened to 14 inches and then 15 inches to stretch the walls of the new and, for dry tyres, unexpectedly flexible covers. After that it was down to a few small adjustments to brake balance, wing settings, flap angles, rollbars, tyre pressures, cleaning and polishing the bodywork — just the normal activities of an everyday sparetime racing driver, working out a specification for when it rained.

Halfway through the first season, the car was only still managing a steady third or fourth position but, by the time the season had finished, was into an all too regular second behind MB, except the hillclimb at Wiscombe, a record still standing.

But winter and re-build time had arrived. What was to be done?

The decision was based on two aims – increasing effectiveness in steering and turn-in of the front end and lowering centre of gravity.

The winter vanished all too rapidly when it was required for a list of modifications that included widening the front track, new top and bottom wishbones, new front bodywork and wing, together with brackets to carry it, and almost total re-location of the fuel system – pumps, filters and pipework.

We were already well aware of the impact that professional designer Mike Pilbeam was having on cars and speeds. His success in persuading hillclimb cars (among other things) to both turn-in well, and put their power on the road, had already made him THE designer on the scene.

In consequence he had a constant stream of development information coming from several cars and teams using his know-how in the Top Ten. Very obviously it would be applied to the Bolsover Pilbeam in the coming year. Whatever it did for Mr. Bolsover, it wasn't going to make life any easier for Mr. Gould.

As has already been observed, cars that look the same to a casual, or even a very careful, glance meeting-after-meeting may be very different. To give an idea of the behind-the-scenes work that produces a successful, but by no means board-sweeping car, the following are notes and results, many inconclusive or at strange variance with what might have been expected, during the car's second full season (1981):

March 14/15: Wiscombe practice day: "Loads of grip with new front but seems impossible to generate sufficient rear traction. Front steadily stiffened on rollbar and shocks. Better. Front wing off, better still. Generally insensitive to even major anti-roll bar changes. Car seemed almost entirely controlled by its front end"

March 22: Loton practice: "Careful checks on front end during previous week discovered and eliminated $\frac{1}{16}$ toe-in bumpsteer at bump. Slightly stiff rack and pinion eased. Car bit easier to drive, but still an alarming ride over bumpy or undulating surface with driver feeling more like a passenger"

March 28/29: Loton: "First time out properly. So much weather variation any alterations inconclusive. Second in class".

April 4/5: Prescott: "Appalling lack of rear traction. Excellent turn-in with violent oversteer out of corners. No response to series of rear anti-roll bar and damper changes. Everyone else got better, and finished in fourth place. Big depression. Why, why, why?"

Very unusually for the hillclimb world, people had become suddenly tight-lipped about exactly how you could get hold of those latest American-made Goodyears, and if you thought you could, what to ask for.

The situation was much complicated by contracts between the various tyre companies at that time agreeing not to poach on each other's areas for F2 supplies. And the tyres in which we were interested were, by and large, F2 sizes.

A very elaborate co-operative plan to get some bought at trade price in the US and flown to Britain ended with their arriving successfully at Heathrow – but embossed with a totally strange set of codes. No information came with them. Were they right or wrong – or perhaps even better than the ones ordered? No one knew – or if they did, weren't saying anything.

By lengthy detective work, DG finally traced a man in Germany who could tell some of what he needed to know, including the fact that they were already in stock in Britain – despite previous emphatic denials.

The man in Germany must have provided the right password in some way, as they suddenly became available "for hillclimbs only – not F2 under any circumstances".

April 12: Wiscombe: "New rear tyres. Immediate vast increase in traction. Feeling really good in damp practice. Fastest 1600. Road dried out and unnerving oversteer suddenly appeared in quick bits. Most unsettling, but second to MB".

April 19/20: Loton: "New Goodyear fronts to match rears. Front tyre grip yet further improved to point that the fronts can only be locked with extreme pedal pressure. Some instability controlled with stiffened front dampers and bar. Driver feels safer. Sudden oversteer still causing problems. Successful corrections to this seem to be wrong way round, ie oversteer reduced by stiffening bar?"

May 2/3: Prescott: 'Massive increase in rear coil stiffness (up from 250 to 325, or 30%) yet still felt good over bumps. Slight reduction in sudden oversteer. Rear anti-roll bar wound up to maximum stiffness, combined with very stiff settings both bump and rebound on rear dampers. Effortless second but nowhere near MB"

May 10: Wiscombe: "Appalling practice weather. (MB considered it too bad and went home). Dried out a lot and qualified eighth in Top Ten. Broke drive joint on line. Repaired in time to get fifth in Top Ten and commanding 1600 victory".

May 16: Barbon: "Late night and early start meant driver shagged out. Plus rain for practice, *but* quicker than MB. Dried in afternoon, brakes appalling and sudden oversteer in flat-out left-hander. Third".

May 30/31: Shelsley: "Ultra thin discs had warped bowl shaped and had to be replaced with thicker ones. Four pot calipers to go with them. Plus balance bar alterations to retrieve rear brakes. All sadly to no avail. Rear hub driveshaft flange sheared in practice (designed for FF so difficult to complain under guarantee) and no option but to go home".

June 6/7: Prescott: "Even bigger anti-roll bar against my better judgement. Brakes feeling superb. Stiffer and stiffer rear roll bar settings made car better and better! Second to MB".

June 21: Gurston: "No MB. Won class easily. Track partly resurfaced and very slippery so comparisons with past times not relevant".

June 27/28: Prescott: "Did personal best ever time on the hill – but second to MB. Best handling yet".

July 4: Valence: "Bit of a shambles, finishing almost in dark, but able to see well enough to get first (No MB)".

July 5: Shelsley: "Car OK but driver ill. Reactions definitely slow, and showed in slow time, but managed a third".

July 11/12: Harewood: "Severe oversteer in 180 degree left-hander cured by stiffer rear dampers in rebound. Personal best ever time, taking second by miles – behind MB''.

July 23: Bouley Bay: ''Road course with kerbs, drains, etc and a lot to learn in a short time as it was first visit. Dry/damp/dry day ended with second (while MB set new outright record against everyone)''.

July 25: Val de Terres: ''Another road course and first visit. Broke bottom gear in practice and broke replacement spare on first run. Left with no choice of gears suitable, so reduced to low second for the steep uphill start. Scraped a third place''.

August 2: Great Farthingloe: ''Night before check disgorged a crownwheel tooth from gearbox, but went anyway. Loony risk to whole box but worth it with new outright record for hill. Three more teeth fell off crownwheel but rest of box unharmed, and all still worked''.

August 8/9: Shelsley: ''Extraordinary weather and track changes from cloudburst to almost dry, so impossible to learn anything or make useful comparisons. Time trap speeds were 102mph in blind narrow Crossing Bend, and 105mph on steep finish straight. Nailed Shelsley Special award again, and second to MB''.

August 15/16: Loton: ''Broke MB's record on first run with personal best ever. Bottom gear failed again on second run while MB set yet another record, so second again''.

August 23: Harewood: ''MB on holiday, so won class by miles. No gearbox problems and another personal best ever''.

August 29/30: Gurston: ''Second to MB by 0.07 of a second, although both of us slower than previous year. Could it be poor grip off slippery start line affecting smaller engined cars more than big classes who were generally quicker?''

September 5/6: Prescott: ''Took full second off own personal best to break MB's record. A best ever 1.81 seconds for first 64 feet, handsomely better than 1G acceleration off the line. Car handling immaculately, although more teeth fell off new crownwheel. MB re-broke my minutes old record. Second''.

September 13: Wiscombe: ''Dry, wet, dry, wet, and handling suddenly became indifferent without any alterations to car. Track surface? MB's Pilbeam seems better balanced in adverse conditions. Second yet again''.

September 19/20: Doune: ''Annual pilgrimage to distant north spoiled by dry, wet, dry, soaking conditions. Driver error on only dry run consigned me to third – but still good enough for fifth in Top Ten''.

September 26/27: Harewood: ''Cloudbursts in practice turned road into river and left a lot of mud on it. Bitterly cold, so tyres the same. Car difficult to balance. Severe understeer suddenly appeared and off the road at

---

Three photographs showing the Gould-Terrapin in its final (spaceframe) form. At this stage of development the car was achieving regular 2nds, some 1sts and one FTD (and new record). The quality of design and construction evident throughout this car serves to illustrate the standards that can be achieved by the diy constructor. (Pictures: Bob Light/Allan Staniforth).

the first corner while fighting for sixth in Top Ten. Second to guess who?''.

The final tally from twenty five meetings read: FTD (and new record): 1, firsts: 4, seconds: 13, thirds: 4, fourths: 1, non-start: 1.

We couldn't bear to think how good it would have looked but for the opposition of the relentless Bolsover — responsible single-handed for putting DG into umpteen second places.

Certainly not any excuse, but how talented an opponent David had been facing all year was shown the following season when Martin B. moved into the unlimited class up against a row of past British Hillclimb Champions.

Virtually every one of them was long experienced in employing 350-500BHP on narrow, bumpy wet roads. The move from a 1600BDA to a 2.5-litre ''stretched'' Hart engine is far from easy. Using it to its full value from the word go is even less so. By his third event he headed the Top Ten — and at his first ever try demolished the lot and took the crown of British Hillclimb Champion by the end of the year. And he proved it was neither luck nor a flash-in-pan by repeating it 12 months later.

For the DG car it was different. A month after being towed back south, filthy and mud-layered from that final torrential Harewood meeting in Yorkshire, it had been washed, totally stripped down, future plans clarified and the formidable decision taken.

It would never be put together again. David would instead build a new car with an alloy sandwich honeycomb monocoque. Christmas was coming and spring would not be far behind ... but all that is another story.

7 The Anatomy of a Racing Team ~ Williams.

The distinctive green barred "W" is painted on the end of the building, and appears on the transporters and letter heads, but it is unobtrusive by most industrial standards.

A miniature avenue of recently planted six feet high, bushy trees shroud visitors for the last ten feet or so of their approach to the office door on a notably unlovely industrial estate.

Inside and up one flight of stairs is the office of the man who holds a secret thousands of people, a large number of them in motor racing, would give a very great deal to know. The question everybody asks is "How do you get to the very top, raising several million pounds on the way, reduce established giants like Lotus, Ferrari, Renault, March and Brabham to second place, or worse, in three years or so from scratch?"

Frank Williams is normally willing to answer the question in quite considerable detail — if you can catch him in that office at all. Dates, numbers of employees, costs, decisions, victories, disasters, all flow from him without reference to files or notes.

Stop questioning him and he will fill the empty seconds with a quick request for action on something or other through the buttons on his office intercom. Renew the inquisition and he is instantly at your disposal again. He never appears to hedge. If he does not want to tell you he says so. From the point of view of copying his blueprint for success the major outline is soon complete.

Where the cash comes from. How he spends it. What his sponsors get for their money. Immediate plans. What motivates him, and how he motivates others.

It is all there. The mystery, of course, is why it all works for him, but not for so many others desperate to occupy the position on which he so precariously perches.

Certainly he has had a single-minded dedication to racing the four-wheeled vehicle for some twenty years. He was racing an Austin A35 heavily modified saloon when Graham Hill was a mechanic, before moving to single-seaters.

Three years in F3, then a hoard of 1-litre screamers that destroyed themselves all too comprehensively when things went wrong and drained his finances beyond continuing. Modest wheeling and dealing, not in the motor trade ("I'm not a motor trader. That is incorrect. I've only sold perhaps half a dozen cars in my life."), brought him back as an entrant in 1967 with Piers Courage, and putting a first toe into the F1 pool in 1969. "It was an endless struggle with nondescript cars and not enough money."

The witty cocktail bar remark of the time was "Frank's hardly got two IOUs to rub together" — but he had enough know-how and status when the moment came to be approached to lead Canadian multi-millionaire Walter Wolf's venture into F1 in 1976. When they parted it was on good terms with Frank Williams selling out his interest, engineering facilities, the lot.

He had a fresh start as well as some money — though not nearly enough.

He'd also met a 22 stone Saudi Airlines advertising manager who had never seen a motor race, and certainly didn't know a Ralt from an Osella.

Unpromising? Presumably quite a number of people *could* have persuaded the Saudis it was worthwhile to gamble a modest £40,000 to organise and back Patrick Neve with a March. His sponsorship money plus Williams' own savings convinced a small number of others to invest cash with no visible return. The total was £210,000. A lot by anybody's standard, but capable of vanishing like a spring frost in the Formula One furnace given a wrong decision or two.

But Williams already had the design structure of the team firmly outlined. It had five points:

1) A designer able to produce an extremely good car.

Keke Rosberg and Williams at the 1982 Brazilian Grand Prix where they finished 2nd only to be disqualified because the car was underweight. (Picture: Colin Taylor Productions).

---

2) A driver who could not only drive, but if at all possible could understand what the car was doing and help with its development.
3) A team of really good mechanics.
4) A factory back-up, able to provide parts that would not break.
5) Money to make it all possible.

He picked with what he, but few other people, calls "a lot of luck", Patrick Head, now unquestionably one of the best car creators in the world; Alan Jones, once and almost twice World Champion; plus men with a range of other skills, who have nearly all stayed with him from the beginning.

From the very start he used part of the available money to set up a base with ever-growing manufacturing facilities aimed at doing everything themselves.

"1977 was finding our way. Staff started at six people. By December the new FWO 6 was designed, we had a very small factory, and I came to an arrangement with Alan Jones. I also met two young Saudi Princes, through a friend, who were in London buying a

new Ferrari each. I had a lot of breaks at the same time, and I had never smelled real success before.

"It was a case of first surviving and then doing something with my life. I am fundamentally a salesman. I'm no good at maths, chemistry, physics, anything like that, but I sell motor racing to people. I can convince people that they will get value for money in worldwide TV exposure, from being associated with and involved in F1, the prestige, even the atmosphere of it all.

"The sponsorship deal with the Saudis is a written contract. We are talking about very large sums of money. But some of the lesser backers are simply a handshake arrangement.

"The office staff records of employees show – 1977 six, 1978 eighteen, 1979 thirty-five, 1980 fifty-five, 1981 seventy-five, 1982 ninety – and turbos will mean half a dozen more".

The facilities include numerical control machine tools and the only moving floor wind tunnel in Britain outside a university. "The results from it now are rarely wrong. It allows us to

do the initial balancing-up of a new car at the very outset of the design without going anywhere near a track."

By 1980 that elusive smell of success was all pervading for Frank Williams and his team. Constructors' Championship and World Drivers Championship. What more? "The first three Constructors' Championships on the trot. That's never been done before. And then five in a row.

"I believe I shall be racing for many more years yet, but if motor racing was banned tonight, we could stay in business. We have quite a bit to sell in experience and expertise. We are already doing research for a major manufacturer – a trade secret – that they cannot do themselves."

He documents his every flying minute, and nights away from home – "151 last year", gives talks on the team out of season, organised an unashamedly flag-waving film on the team for British Leyland when they backed him despite public criticism.

Two million pounds sounds a whole lot of money – until you take almost half of it away for his wage bill, and the key to next year's money is almost certainly winning.

That, he claims, is also his criterion in picking his drivers, "I look at the results in *Autosport*. They're not a bad guide. Winners win. I can't afford to try out the up-and-coming in my team. I'd rather they had their accidents with other people's cars." The look is humorous, but the words have a steely edge.

The same edge reappears when asked about the exact cause of an intermittent misfire which appeared in a fuel system that had worked perfectly for two and a half years – and certainly lost Jones his second World Championship. "It gave me my worst ever day in motor racing. It came down finally to three separate things all of which had to occur together, but only did so erratically. I don't propose to say what they were. It cost us a very great deal of time and money to eradicate. It might happen to one of the opposition sometime."

The missing bit of the blueprint, the sixth item in the list of five for a successful team is clear. It needs somebody to conceive and plan it, to put it together, and hold it together thereafter. It is the bit not available to copiers. It is Frank Williams.

Appendices

1 Tools and Useful Materials.

Essential and basic tools

Set AF or Metric open-ended spanners.
Set AF or Metric sockets $\frac{1}{2}$in or $\frac{3}{8}$in
square drive, 6'' or 9'' extension and
ratchet (other accessories to taste).
Pliers – 8in
Pliers – Snipe nosed.
Pliers, circlip – internal/external.
Files – 12in flat in coarse, medium and
fine.
    – 6in flat in medium and fine.
    – half-round: 10in medium.
    – round in $\frac{5}{8}$in, $\frac{3}{8}$in and $\frac{1}{4}$in dia.
Hacksaw – 10in or 12in frame and fine
cut blades (about 22 teeth/inch, high-
speed, nor carbon steel).
Hacksaw – miniature and blades.
Tinsnips – 12in.
Medium hammer (1lb).
Screwdrivers – slot end in large,
medium and electrical sizes.
Screwdrivers – crosshead in medium
and small.
Electric drill and vertical stand.
Bench and vice.
Use or loan of welding gear (torch,
gauges, pipes and nozzles – Nos. 2, 3,
5 and 7, at least).
Some ring spanners AF or Metric.
Pop rivet pliers and good quality rivets
($\frac{1}{8}$in & $\frac{5}{32}$in).

Hole-saw(s).
Set of feeler gauges.
Set of high-speed steel twist drills.
Set of Allen keys (for socket screws)
American and Metric.
Adjustable pipe wrench – 15in.

Important tools

Electrical crimping pliers
Mole grips – plain end and hollow jaw.
'G' clamps – 6in, 9in and 12in.
Roller wheel cutter for sheet up to 16g.
Monodex-type sheet cutter (nibbler).
U-magnets (tube joint holding).
Large copper or lead hammer.
Torque wrench(es).

One-job or special tools

Flexi driveshaft (drill attachment).
Rotary cutters (Picador-type).
Rubber disc and abrasive discs (drill
attachment).
Valve seat cutters 45° and 30°.
Stud extractor (knurled wheel type).
Large sockets (fan pulley, flywheel,
etc).
Access to tube bending gear.
Access to lathe.
Access to sheet metal folder.

Useful materials

Alloy sheet (L72 or N24) 18g & 20g.
Mild steel sheet in 16g, 18g and 20g.
Round and square tube in $\frac{3}{4}$in, $\frac{7}{8}$in and
1 in.
HT steel bolts, set screws and nuts
(standardise thread on UNF or metric)
– $\frac{3}{16}$in (2BA), $\frac{1}{4}$in, $\frac{5}{16}$in and $\frac{3}{8}$in diam 4, 6,
8 and 10 mm. All 'S' quality.
Nyloc or Cleveloc nuts to similar sizes
as above. Light alloy nuts, bolts and
washers for use where strength not
vital: mainly $\frac{1}{4}$in and $\frac{5}{16}$in diam.
Rubber water hose – 1in I.D.; straight
and various curves.
Rubber and plastic tubing (for bushes,
sleeves, grommets).
Flat and spring washers (rust-proofed if
possible).
Self-adhesive rubber/plastic strip.
Rivets: Monel or similar high strength,
non-rust material.
Welding rod and nozzles – 9% Nickel
Bronze rods ($\frac{1}{8}$in or $\frac{3}{32}$in dia.) and
suitable flux. Mild steel rods ($\frac{3}{32}$ in or $\frac{1}{16}$in
dia.).
Nozzles Nos. 2, 3, 5, 7 minimum.
Recommended material for brazing up
chassis shell, links, braces etc is British
Oxygen 9% Nickel Bronze rod or
equivalent.

2 General Data and Conversions.

Comparative material weights

	lb/cu ft
Lead	710
Brass	505
Steel	490
Cast iron	449
Dural	178
Aluminium	161
Safety glass	159
Magnesium	114
Glass fibre moulding	105
Carbon fibre moulding	95
Kevlar moulding	90
Perspex	74
Water	62.5
Oil	56
Petrol	44
Honeycomb filler:	
0.0015 x $\frac{1}{4}$ ins cell	3.4
0.001 x $\frac{1}{8}$ ins cell	4.5
Rigid foam	2

Metal comparison in sheet form (lb/wt per sq ft)
Thickness

SWG	Magnes.	Alum.	Dural	Steel
10	1.46	2.05	2.28	6.27
16	0.73	1.02	1.14	3.13
18	0.54	0.76	0.85	2.33
20	0.41	0.57	0.64	1.75
22	0.32	0.45	0.50	1.36
24	0.25	0.35	0.39	1.07

Selection of typical steels and their uses

Description and usage	Ref No	Tensile strength tons/sq in
Ordinary carbon mild steel – tube, bolts, nuts, studs for general use	EN1A	up to 32
Improved carbon steel, widely used for similar products	EN 8	35-45
Alloy steel for HT bolts, cyl head studs, cranks	EN 16	45-50
Extra high quality alloy steel for socket screws, special studs, bolts, etc	EN 24	Up to 100
Still higher duty alloy steel for special applications	EN 34,39A	85
Valve springs	EN 42, 45, 48	90-110
Nitrided cranks	EN 40B	60

All may be affected or altered by heat treatment. EN codes are now being superseded by European metric classifications. See also Torque Settings table.

Imperial Standard Wire Gauge equivalents (sheet)

swg	in(approx)	in	mm
24	1/64	0.022	0.558
22	–	0.028	0.711
20	$\frac{1}{32}$	0.036	0.914
18	3/64	0.048	1.219
16	$\frac{1}{16}$	0.064	1.626
14	5/64	0.080	2.032
13	$\frac{3}{32}$	0.092	2.337
12	7/64	0.104	2.641
10	$\frac{1}{8}$	0.128	3.251
8	$\frac{5}{32}$	0.160	4.064
6	$\frac{3}{16}$	0.192	4.877
3	$\frac{1}{4}$	0.252	6.400

Cubic capacity

1 gallon = 277.274 cu in = 10lb pure water.
1 cu in = 16.387cc.
1728 cu in = 1 cu ft = 28.317 litres.
1 cu ft of distilled water at 62°F and barometer 30 in weighs 1000oz (avoir 62.5 lbs) and contains 6.23 gallons.
Weight of one gallon of petrol approximately 7lb.
Weight of one gallon of oil approximately 9lb.

General conversion table

Multiply by	To convert	To	
6.24	cubic feet	gallons	0.1602
0.4536	pounds (Avoir)	kilogrammes	2.2046
28.35	ounces (Avoir)	grammes	0.0353
50.8	cwt	kilogrammes	0.01968
4.546	gallons	litres	0.22
10	gallons of water	pounds	0.1
0.454	pounds of water	litres	0.2202
70.3	lb per sq in	gm/sq cm	0.0142
0.068	lb per sq in	atmospheres	14.7

Multiply by	To convert	To	
1.575	tons per sq in	kg/sq mm	0.635
4.883	lb per sq ft	kg/sq metre	0.205
16.02	lb per cu ft	kg/cu metre	0.0624
0.138	ft-lb	k'grammetres	7.23
1.014	horsepower	force de cheval	0.9861
746	horsepower	watts	0.00134
33,000	horsepower	ft-lb/min	–
0.252	heat units	calories	3.97
14.7	atmospheres	lb/sq inch	0.068
88	miles/hour	ft/min	0.01134
197	metres/sec	ft/min	0.00508
1.8	CHU	BThU	0.5555
0.01639	cu in	litres	61.02
2.54	inches	centimetres	0.3937
30.48	feet	centimetres	0.0328
0.914	yards	metres	1.094
1609.3	miles	metres	0.000621
6.45	square ins	sq cm	0.155
0.093	square feet	sq metres	10.864
16.39	cubic inches	cu cm	0.061
28.3	cubic feet	litres	0.0353
	To convert	**From**	**Multiply by above**

Some comparisons in typical tube

Dia or section sq/(in)	Sq/ Rnd/	Wall thickness (gauge) SWG	Weight lb per ft	Welded/ cold drawn	Relative strength metal area in cross-section (sq in) similar tensile	Notes
½	Rnd	20	0.178	Both	0.0525	
½	Rnd	16	0.298	Both	0.0877	
½	Sq	20	0.226	Welded	0.0664	
⅝	Rnd	16	0.383	Both	0.1128	
⅝	Sq	20	0.286	Welded	0.0842	
¾	Rnd	16	0.469	Both	0.1379	CD for wishbones
¾	Sq	18	0.468	Welded	0.1375	
⅞	Rnd	16	0.554	Both	0.1631	
⅞	Sq	18	0.552	Welded	0.161	
1	Rnd	18	0.488	Both	0.1436	
1	Sq	18	0.643	Welded	0.189	
1¼	Rnd	18	0.616	Both	0.1812	
1¼	Sq	18	0.800	Welded	0.235	
1½	Rnd	18/16	0.75/0.98	Welded	⎧ Welded exhaust	
1¾	Rnd	18/16	0.90/1.15	Welded	⎨ tube; thickness	
2	Rnd	18/16	1.00/1.32	Welded	⎩ only approximate ⎭	

Notes: Welded seam is normally BS 980 ERW.1 (approx 20 tons tensile) mild steel, or ERW.2 (approx 25 tons tensile). Cold drawn can be anything, but is often BS 980 CDS.1 (approx 20 tons tensile) or CDS.2 approx 28 tons tensile). Other cold drawn specs include T1-35 tons, T45-45 tons, T50-50 tons chrome nickel.

A guide to torque wrench settings for common sizes/material/applications

C = Unified National Coarse and Whitworth
F = Unified National Fine and British Standard Fine

Bolt Diam.		'A' Qual. 28 tons tensile min	'R' Qual 45-55 ton tensile	'S' Qual 55-66 ton tensile	'X' Qual 75-85 ton tensile
3/16in	C	–	–	–	–
2BA	F	2.4	3.0	4.6	6.4
1/4in	C	5.4	8.5	10.8	14.2
	F	6.0	9.5	11.9	15.8
5/16in	C	10.9	17.5	21.0	27.8
	F	11.7	19.0	23.4	30.9
3/8in	C	19.3	31.0	39.5	51.9
	F	21.0	33.8	42.5	56.0
7/16in	C	31.0	49.6	62.6	82.5
	F	33.7	54.7	68.5	90.2
1/2in	C	45.8	73.2	93.5	123.0
	F	50.6	81.2	103.0	136.0
5/8in	C	68.2	107.6	140.0	183.0
	F	74.2	119.0	151.0	198.0
3/4in	C	94.8	131.9	193.0	252.0
	F	101.0	163.0	205.0	270.0

All figures in ft/lb for un-lubricated bolts.
All calculated to stress bolt to 2/3rds ultimate braking strength.
As they are calculated on Tensile Strength, the figures are a reasonable reflection of comparative strengths in actual use.

Formulae for calculating mph per 1000rpm for any overall gear ratio:

Speed in mph =
$$\frac{rpm \times 60}{\text{overall gear ratio} \times \text{revs per mile of tyre}}$$

or

Speed in mph =
$$\frac{\text{tyre circumference (in)} \times rpm}{1056 \times \text{overall gear ratio}}$$

③ Guide to Spherical Joints (Rose and Ampep).

Racing and other competition cars are full of spherical joints, often called 'Rose' or 'Ampeps' for short (from the manufacturers names).

Catalogues can be very confusing, especially if you have no detailed knowledge with which to start.

Joints with a $\frac{3}{8}$in, or 10mm shank are widely used in varying qualities, and some are compared in the table below.

The listing is based simply on radial load figures (lbs) in order of strength. It is likely, but not certain, that the stronger the joints are, the more expensive. When buying it is worth checking not only different suppliers and manufacturers, but also a "strength/cost" ratio which may show that it is worthwhile to buy a smaller (but better material and stronger) joint

rather than a larger but apparently cheaper one.

All figures given and codes relate to $\frac{3}{8}$in x $\frac{3}{8}$in male joints. Female strength figures normally slightly better than male. Axial strength figures (trying to push ball out sideways) may be as low as 10% of radial figure, so use a big safety washer if the situation warrants it.

Comparison guide to Spherical Joints

Code	Outer housing and finish	Ball and finish	Interliner	Radial load (lb)	Remarks
RMR 6	Stainless	Stainless hardened thru	PTFE/fibre	9850	Best of the best
RMX 6	Chrome moly cad. plated	1% chrome, chrome plated	Aluminium/ bronze	9589	Will insert squeeze out at all?
RCA 06	Stainless	Stainless hardened thru	PTFE/fibre "Type R"	7150	Racing catalogue "best wide angle". No females
RMC 6NU	Carbon steel phosphated	1% carb. chrome chrome plated	PTFE/fibre	7070	Heim "aircraft quality"

Code	Outer housing and finish	Ball and finish	Interliner	Radial load (lb)	Remarks
RBJ 73	Nickel chrome moly phosphated	1% carb. chrome chrome plated	None	6300	Original Terrapin. Rusts and wears.
AMPEP 2185P	Med.carbon, low alloy. Phosphated	Med.chrome,low alloy,chromed	"Fibreglide" PTFE/fibre	5242	No females in this size
RC6H	Carbon steel phosphated	Stainless thru, hardened	PTFE/fibre "Type R"	4420	Racing catalogue "ordinary" no females
RM6	Carbon steel Cad. plated	1% carb. chrome plated	Naval bronze/ sintered copper	2450	Standard Heim – insert squeezes out
RMP 6U	Carbon steel phosphated	1% carb. chrome plated	Acetyl Copolymer	2100	Latest Rose "cheapie" but seems well up to the job

Note: *These codes will have variations or additions to indicate thread (Metric, left hand etc).*

4 Tyres

Further to the general discourse on tyres earlier in this book, this is a more specific guide to identifying the secondhand and out of date professional tyres available – precisely the tyres that very many competitors will be concerned with for some, or all,

of their career on four wheels.

Rule one will always be to write for a current size and type list. Surprisingly quite a number of the compounds, many constructions and almost all the basic sizes stay unaltered for considerable periods of time,

presumably for very good commercial reasons.

You can then compare and fit current information with that listed here. The examples in the table illustrate variations in sizes and markings:

Comparisons in three basic sizes of tyre (manufacturers' data)

Maker	Size Code	Tread width	Max dia.	Standard rim width	Alt. rims	Revs per mile circumference
Dunlop	180/500/13	177mm/7in	520mm/20.5in	7in	7-9in	985
Avon	7.0/20/13	183mm/7.2in	510mm/20.1in	8in	–	–
Michelin	18/53/13 (260/13)	195mm/7.7in	526mm/20.7in	9.5in	9-10.5in	–

Maker	Size Code	Tread Width	Max dia.	Standard rim width	Alt. rims	Revs per mile circumference
Goodyear	7.5/20/13	7.3in	20.3in	8in	–	–
M & H	7.0/20/13	7.0in	20.0in	–	6-8in	62.8 in Circ.
Dunlop	225/500/13	217mm/8.5in	520mm/20.5in	10in	8.5-11in	981
Avon	9.0/20/13	233mm/9.2in	515mm/20.3in	10in	–	–
Michelin	21/50/13 (240/13)	210mm/8.3in	500mm/19.7in	8in	8-9.5in	–
Goodyear	9.0/20/13	8.6in	20.3in	10in	–	–
M & H	9.0/20/13	9.0in	20.0in	–	8-10in	62.8in Circ.
Dunlop	305/550/13	315mm/12.4in	564mm/22.2in	14in	10-15in	908
Avon	120.0/23/13	307mm/12.1in	589mm/23.2in	14in	–	–
Michelin	No comparable sized tyre on 13 inch rim listed					
Goodyear	13/23/13	12.5in	23.3in	15in	–	–
M & H	13.0/23/13	13.0in	23.0in	–	12-16in	72.0 in Circ.

Other possible markings:

Dunlop	Carcase (*eg:* D15). Compound (*eg:* 622).
Avon	Compound (*eg:* A6).
Michelin	Type *(eg:* S = sec = dry). Carcase (*eg:* B = radial). Compound (*eg:* 9).
Goodyear	Compound – can be 'G' and two figures, four figures or seven figures. Sometimes 'W' (wet) following tread width figure. Also US made: A, R, M, D & G + 1 or 2 figures for US compounds, D with four figures, and reversed order of tyre size figures (*ie:* 20/7.5/13).
M & H	Compound – (*eg:* 21). Multi-figure for works identification.

Code guide: rubber compounds (Dunlop)

Green Spot – Prehistoric wet.
Yellow Spot – Less prehistoric wet.
White Spot – Softest till the numbers started.
184 – Early classic wet – end of hard rubber era.
194 – Hard circuit.
204 – Hard, vintage tyres. Still Mini Clubmans.
232 – Less hard, early Minis.
236 – Hard, early Minis.
240 – 18/19 inch tyres only: very hard.
342 – Medium F3 slick 1970/1.
350 – Old, hard by current standards.
356 – Very old wet.
370 – Soft, F3 dry slick.
376 – Recent Gp 1 saloon dry slick.
380 – Similar 376.
384 – Tarmac slick, hardish.
418 – Current hard dry wear.
442 – Soft, damp or sprint slick.
450 – Hardish circuit tyre.
458 – Medium when warm.
462 – Hard one time FF1600.

472 – Hardish dry.
482 – Hardish, intermediate.
484 – Touch softer than 462.
512 – F.S./Vee dry, hardish.
534 – Soft on big cars as wellcut wet.
550 – Hard/medium.
566 – Softish, but only in Gp 2/5 terms.
578 – Tougher than 566, intermediate.
592 – General saloon Gp. 1. Hardish until fully hot.
614 – Softer version of 566 for small single seater, clubmans, circuits.
622 – Very soft wet. Good sprint slick.
680 – "Intermediate" wet for radials.
970 – Very old wet. Hard now, but was first of the softs.
752 – FF2000 dries. Fairly soft circuit with good wear.
756 – Bit softer than 752.
764 – Fairly hard endurance.
768 – Medium, s/seaters, Gp5, S-Vee.
780 – Softish slick.
792 – Later wet than 622.
800 – Soft, special Rallycross version of 622.
Plus heaven knows how many more – Good hunting.

Code guide: carcase construction (Dunlop)

D15 – Stiff for narrow rims.
D22A – Standard medium flexy walls.
D27 – Very flexy walls.
D40 – Heavy tread version of D27 to permit wet cut.
D30 – No longer produced. Tarmac, medium stiff wall.
D38 – Very stiff sidewall for Gp.1.
D42 – Heavy tread version of D15.
D49 – Lightweight version of D27 with more flexy sidewall.
D52 – Very stiff and thick sidewalls, heavy tread (rally loose).
D53 – Modified D38 with lighter construction and cooler running.
D54 – Rally racer (replaced D30). Puncture resistant. Heavy case.

Code guide: rubber compounds (Avon)

A1 – Medium single-seater, club racing, motorcycle sidecars.
A2 – Soft single/seater, hotrod, rallycross, durable wet.
A3 – Soft wet. Good spring slick, motorcycle sidecar wet.
A4 – Very hard durable. FF1600. Narrow saloon circuit.
A5 – Hard saloon slick.
A6 – Hard durable single-seater, small saloon circuit.
A7 – Hard durable single-seater and sports car circuit.
A8 – Cool running medium compound for thick tread tyres.
A9 – Very soft, single seater, hillclimb etc.

Code guides: rubber compounds (Goodyear), wear rates in brackets

G31 – 1972, very tough needs lot of warming-up. (Good).
G32 – 1972 Very soft for the year. (Fair).
G34 – Hard, although softer than G31. (Good).
G35 – 1975 quick warm-up version of G37. (Good).
G37 – Softish F1 inters and F2 dries. (Good).
G40 – First of "demon soft" wets, but chunks in less than rain. (Poor).
G42 – Fast compound for cold conditions. (Fair).

G43 – Tough, hot running. (Good).
G44 – Tough, replaced by G57 later. (Good).
G45 – THE classic wet. Excellent slick on stiff carcase for sprint/hillclimb. (Good).
G46 – Even softer. Heavy rain only. Superb rain tyre. (Poor).
G47 – Very soft in circuit terms. Similar G53. (Fair).
G49 – Tough hot running. Similar but faster than G44, particularly for abrasive tracks. 1975/medium hard. (Good).
G50 – Softish, fast. 1975 soft slick. (Average).
G51 – Tougher than 50, but similar. (Good).
G52 – Slightly harder than 51, but quicker warm-up. (Good).
G53 – Softer and faster than 50. 1978 very soft slick. (Poor).
G54 – Good all round. Better than 49/52. 1978 medium slick. (Good).
G55 – Soft and fast. Hillclimb compound (for big cars). (Poor).
G56 – Fast wet compound, but withdrawn after short life. (Good).
G57 – Tough and hard. Replaced G44. 1978 hard slick. (Good).
G58 – Very tough, hard, heavy saloons only. (Good).
G60 – Harder still! (Good).
G61 – Tough wet, for big circuit saloons. (Good).
G62 – Softish, and quicker than G50. (Average).
G65 – Medium soft. 1978 slick "1½ sets per meeting". (Good).
G67 – Improved alternative to G65. (Good).

Note that American produced Goodyears employ a different identification system. For details write to: Goodyear Competition Tyre East, 133 Riverfront Drive, P.O. Box 301, Reading, Pennsylvania 19603.

Code guide: carcase (Michelin)

S – Sec: dry, slicks.
T – Tous: all, or intermediate, wet or dry.
P – Pluie: rain, full wet for heavy rain.
B – Type of radial casing.
Nora and Cocotte – Two speed rally carcases with different tread patterns.

Code guide: compounds (Michelin)

1   – Very durable (rally).
5   – All weather medium compound, tough (race and rally).
9   – Strong, hardwearing, last a clubman all season (race).
10 – Soft, high wear at high temperatures (Hot rod and single-seater).
11 – Standard dry, good grip in hot weather (race).
12 – Soft, high performance (rally).
14 – Medium (rally).
15 – Similar to 10, very good in damp (race).
20 – Ultra soft wet, do not use in dry (race).

Note a number of other compounds (including 18, 21 and 22, at least) not normally available in UK.

Code guide: general (M & H)

Very complex marking methods (you may find it quicker to 'phone them), but an outline is possible for various crosschecks. Tyres will normally carry, apart from size markings, three numbers from brand new, one of which is on the tread itself and will vanish as soon as it is run.

A) 4-figure code, sometimes called "indent width" beginning with 10, 20 or 30. 20 numbers by far the most common and they denote the exact works specification for the tyre builder covering mould, construction, carcase, different rubbers, etc.
B) 2-figure numbers. "Sales Code No", indicating both tread compound and type of car for which they are intended.
C) 3-figure code (rare). A factory tread number as opposed to the Sales Code No. normally used.

Code guide: compound/vehicle type (M & H)

Twenties: F3. Thirties: Rallycross. Forties: F-Vee. Fifties: Saloons. Sixties: F2. The following is a partial selection:

20 – Hard slick.
21 – Ultra soft (as 61).
22 – Medium.
50 – Medium.
51 – Soft.
52 – Medium.
53 – Medium.
56 – Soft saloon, wet.
57 – Medium soft saloon, wet.
58 – Softest saloon, wet.
60 – Hard.
65 – Medium.
62 – Soft.
61 – Ultra soft (as 21).
91, 95 – Rally compounds.
868 – Medium circuit slick (code now obsolete).
92, 94, 866, 830, 803 – Factory numbers for compounds (usually rubbed off by initial wear).

5 Bibliography

Title	Author
All but my life	Ken Purdy on Stirling Moss.
Austin 7 Competition Cars 1922 to 82	Martin Eyre (750 Motor Club).
Auto-Electrics	Dave Westgate/Speed Sport Pubs. Ltd.
Automobile Suspensions	Colin Campbell.
Automotive Fuel-Injection Systems	Jan Norbye/Haynes.
BMC Minis Maintenance Overhaul & Tuning	Marshall & Fraser.
Building and Racing my 750	P. J. Stephens.
Carburettor/pump list: AUC 9631A (including springs & pistons)	SU Carburettor Co. Ltd.
Carburettor needle list: AUC 9618	SU Carburettor Co. Ltd.
Competition Driving	Paul Frere.
Design & Behaviour of a Racing Car	Moss & Pomeroy.
Design for Competition	750 Motor Club.
Design of Racing Sports Cars	Colin Campbell.
F1 Car (Anatomy & Development)	Sal Incandela/Haynes.
Fibreglass Composites Design Data	Fibreglass Ltd.
Ford Escort Rally Preparation	FoMoCo.
Ford Rallye Sport Parts List	FoMoCo.
GP Team — Elf-Tyrrell	Barrie Gill.
Handbook for Oxy-Acetylene Welders	British Oxygen Publication.
High Speed Internal Combustion Engine	Sir Harry Ricardo.
How to Modify your Mini	David Vizard.
How to make your car handle	Fred Puhn.
Mechanical World Year Book	Martin Simons.
Model Aircraft Aerodynamics	Martin Simons.
Modern Petrol Engines	A. W. Judge.
Motor Racing Directory	Mike Kettlewell.
Motor Racing in Safety	Dr. Michael Henderson.
Motor Vehicles Calculations & Science	R. Champion & E. Arnold.
NACA Submerged Air Intakes	Royal Aeronautical Society Paper 66029.
New Soaring Pilot	Welch & Irving.
Performance Tuning in Theory & Practice (4-stroke)	A. Graham Bell/Haynes.
Practical Automobile Engineering	Odhams.
Prepare to Win	Carroll Smith.
Racing Car Design & Development	Len Terry & Alan Baker.
Racing Drivers Manual	Frank Gardner.
Racing Mechanic	Alf Francis told to Peter Lewis.
Racing & Sports Car Chassis Design	Costin & Phipps.
Racing Porsches	Paul Frere.
Reliant Tuning	750 Club.
Sports Car: Design & Performance	Colin Campbell.
Sports Car Engine	Colin Campbell.

SU Carburettors	Haynes.
Supercharging Cars & Motorcycles	Maurice Brierley.
The Anatomy & Development of the Formula One Racing Car from 1975	Sal Incandela/Haynes.
Theme Lotus	Doug Nye.
Theory and Practice of Cylinder Head Tuning	David Vizard.
Theory of Wing Sections	Ira Abbott & Albert Doenhoff.
The Internal Combustion Engine	Fritz A. Schmidt.
The Racing Driver	Denis Jenkinson.
The Unfair Advantage	Mark Donahue.
Tune to Win	Carroll Smith.
Tuning SU Carbs	Cars & Car Conversions.
Turbocharging & Supercharging	L. J. K. Setright/Haynes.
Vanwall	Jenkinson & Posthumus.
Weber Carburettors	Havnes.
Weber Carburettors – Parts I & II	John Passini.
Weber Carburettors – Complete Tuning Manual	Weber Factory.
Zenith/Stromberg carburettors	Haynes.

Note: *Not all the above books are still in print but nevertheless it should be possible and well worthwhile to seek out secondhand or library copies.*

⑥ Effects of inclining coil spring suspension units.

Any suspension design that already has (or requires for unavoidable reasons) a coilspring/damper unit inclined beyond a few degrees will mean that the Effective Coil Rate will be altered.

Normally (except in certain arrangements of inboard units or complex linkages aimed at providing a rising rate) the ECR will fall and the spring becomes effectively weaker, or softer, as far as the car is concerned.

This is bad news, particularly in terms of nosedive under braking and squat in acceleration. Only fundamental changes to the geometry can remove it, so it is important for the designer or developer to know two things:

A. By how much at any given inclination the suspension will soften and at what point it becomes really serious.

B. How to work out the rate of a new or replacement spring which will in reality provide at least the coil rate planned for the design or modification.

The fall of rate in the coil can be found quite accurately by a scale drawing, or very accurately and more speedily by trigonometric calculation. The drawing should make clear how the rate of a vertical coil stays constant, how a 10 degree inclination alters the rate quite modestly, and how a 40 degree inclination produces dramatic effects for the worse.

Increasing inclination requires ever harder coils both to reduce movement to a minimum and to try and achieve the actual coil rate required. Without this, as the ECR goes on falling, the vehicle will finally collapse onto the bumpstops – or even the ground when bump loads are fed in.

There are two simplifications in the drawing, one of which introduces a small but barely significant error.

Firstly the chassis is considered to drop vertically, whereas in an actual vehicle the wheel and bottom mounting eye of the damper rise in an arc dictated by the length and mounting of the bottom wishbone.

Secondly the calculations, for the sake of clarity, are only for the positions of static ride height and one dimension of full bump. Working out a

series of smaller increments will show a curve for the reducing ECR if plotted as a graph of ECR against angle of inclination. Neither of these liberties should cause any problem when you insert your own figures and dimensions to determine what is happening.

Inclining the coil gives a situation not dissimilar geometrically to that of the leverage variations resulting from an inboard unit, or one mounted partway along the bottom suspension link (see page 63).

The load (100lb) has not altered, nor has the rate of the coil (100lb/in) BUT because the chassis is moving downwards vertically while the coil swings about an arc, the chassis has to travel further than one inch to compress the coil one inch and thus reach equilibrium. When a further 150lb of load is fed in (the bump force necessary to compress the coil a further 1.5 inches) the chassis must travel down further than a total of 2.5 inches to again reach equilibrium.

In our 40 degree example, the chassis moves down 1.376in (a) for a static load of 100lb, with a further 2.42in (a_1) making 3.796in for a total load of 250lb (100lb static plus 150lb bump).

Effective Coil Rate (static)= $\frac{100}{1.376}$ = 72.67lb/in.

Effective Coil Rate (full bump) = $\frac{250}{3.796}$ = 65.86lb/in.

Clearly if our design aim is a 100lb/in coil rate we cannot get this as a constant. We can only take a rate of, say, halfway between static and full bump (ie 69lb/in) and work it backwards to find a coil that will give this compromise figure.

We can obtain this with the formula:

$\frac{\text{Required rate}^2}{\text{ECR}}$ or $\frac{100 \times 100}{69}$ = 144.9lb/in.

This coil will in fact now be harder in the static position (105.4lb/in) and softer in full bounce (95.49lb/in), but still a vast improvement over doing nothing and wondering why the rivet heads or exhaust system are being filed off the bottom of the car every time you put the brakes on.

How to discover the amount of vertical fall of the chassis (1.376in and 3.796in in our example) mathematically?

Use the Sine Rule formula:

$\frac{\text{Side a}}{\text{Sin angle A}} = \frac{\text{Side b}}{\text{Sin angle B}} = \frac{\text{Side c}}{\text{Sin angle C}}$

Note that when solving this particular problem, angle C will always be obtuse and obtuse angles do not appear in the SIN tables. What you will get will be an angle somewhere between nil and 90 degrees. This angle must then be subtracted from 180 to obtain the actual angle C.

Sequence:

$\frac{\text{Side b}}{\text{Sin B}}$ = Fitted coil length = Constant K.
Sin unit angle

If $\frac{\text{Side c}}{\text{Sin C}}$ = constant K,

then Sin C = $\frac{\text{Free coil length}}{\text{Constant K}}$

Obtain angle C as noted above.
Angle A = 180 - (B + C)
If $\frac{\text{Side a}}{\text{Sin A}}$ = constant K, then a = K x Sin A.

Graphical illustration showing the effects of inclining coil spring suspension units (see text for full explanation).

Three final points before you embark:

1. To get any rising rate into a design, the static angle between unit and operating arm compressing it must be less than 90 degrees and *increasing,* or more than 90 degrees and *decreasing,* as the wheel rises in bump. Far from easy, and one of the reasons for inboard units and push or pull suspension linkages.

2. The drawing is based on the dimensions and actions of the coil itself, but the length of damper above and below the support collars to the mounting eyes of standard units will not affect the calculations significantly.

3. Finally, and most importantly, you will have to do all this *before* any work can begin on wheel frequencies, because it will be necessary to use the Effective Coil Rate obtained from the above calculations as the actual Coil Rate in the table on page 65.

Maths consultants: R. Blackmore, K. Gowers, R. Lane, A. Newton, F. Smith, D. Staniforth, J. Swift, B. Whitehead, and others.

EFFECTS of INCLINING COIL SPRING SUSPENSION UNITS

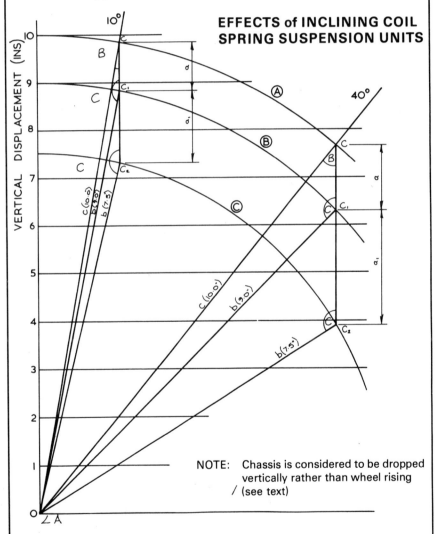

NOTE: Chassis is considered to be dropped vertically rather than wheel rising (see text)

BASE DATA:
100lb/in Coilspring.
100lb Vertical load.
10in Coil Free length.
ARC A: Free length (10in).

ARC B: Coil under 100lb load (9in).
ARC C: Coil under 250lb load/(100 lb static plus 150lb bump) 7.5in.

Index

Note: Capitals indicate whole section dealing with subject.